THE BEST OF THE BEST OF BROCHURE *Design*

THE BEST OF THE BEST OF BROCHURE *Design*

BEVERLY MASSACHUSETTS

ROCKPORT PUBLISHERS

First published in the United States of America by
Rockport Publishers, a member of
Quayside Publishing Group
100 Cummings Center
Suite 406-L
Beverly, Massachusetts 01915-6101
Telephone: (978) 282-9590
Fax: (978) 283-2742
www.rockpub.com

ISBN: 978-1-59253-792-1

10 9 8 7 6 5 4 3 2 1

Edited by: Rachel Hewes and Allison Hodges

Printed in China

contents

CORPORATE
AND ANNUAL
REPORTS

Simultaneously we sought to provide real alternative thinking and options, whether it was through covering holistic health, visionary human-potential-movement leaders, or solutions to social conditions proffered by local grassroots activists.

On the cultural front, first off we wanted to be a real writer's paper. Also, we had a vision of creating a home base for the unheard smart voices, the new visions, and the artistic creativity exploding in the community — for instance, we opened the pages to the power of the punk and new wave music movements and put together a remarkable team of movie reviewers.

A big part of the vision was to help forge a real citywide community out of what we found to be a collection of adjacent neighborhoods that scarcely knew about each other. We sought to show readers the richness of who they were, the wealth of remarkable places and people all around the L.A. basin, and the creative and intellectual juices actually surging here outside the entertainment industry. Our vision was extremely democratic — we wanted to be the people's hip paper that celebrated the rebel in everyone. We very much wanted to be a paper that people took personally because it had heart and soul as well as good information.

—Jay Levin, Founding Editor

2

OF *LA WEEKLY*

It's hard to imagine life in Los Angeles without the *LA Weekly*. Since the first edition appeared 20 years and over 1,000 issues ago, there have been millions of words, photos, ads, cartoons and illustrations; thousands of bands, movies, plays and books reviewed; popular and unpopular positions taken, readers moved and offended, lives and a city transformed. For a whole generation, it's always been there, letting people know what's happening, helping to define L.A., telling stories, offering opinions. And, like that first issue, it's still free.

3

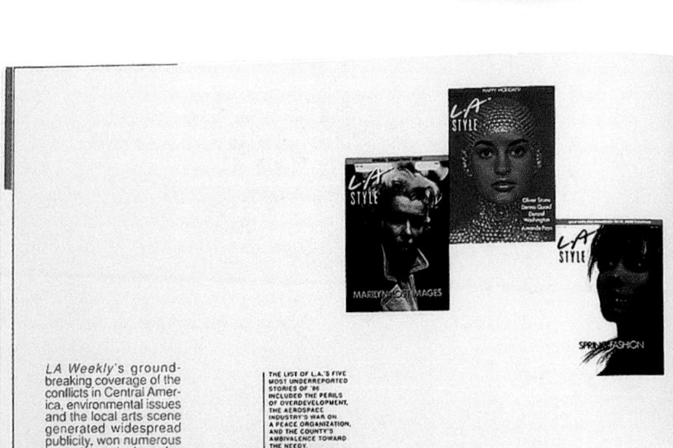

LA Weekly's groundbreaking coverage of the conflicts in Central America, environmental issues and the local arts scene generated widespread publicity, won numerous awards and played a significant role in shaping the life of the city.

THE LIST OF L.A.'S FIVE MOST UNDERREPORTED STORIES OF '86 INCLUDED THE PERILS OF OVERDEVELOPMENT, THE AEROSPACE INDUSTRY'S WAR ON A PEACE ORGANIZATION, AND THE COUNTY'S AMBIVALENCE TOWARD THE NEEDY.

10

magazine called *L.A. Style*, edited by Joie Davidow. The magazine, the result of the fashion boom of the mid-'80s, catered to advertisers and readers who were already familiar with the *Weekly*'s format but wanted a glossy vehicle. During the mid-'80s, *L.A. Style* was one of the fastest-growing magazines in the country and winner of many design awards. In 1988, *L.A. Style* was sold to American Express Publishing.

Throughout the 1980s, *LA Weekly* continued to cover the city — and the nation and the world — from an alternative point of view. Its groundbreaking coverage of the conflicts in Central America, environmental issues and the local arts scene generated widespread publicity, won numerous awards and played a significant role in shaping the life of the city. In-depth articles on politics, on poverty and race, on culture, which could not be found in any other publication, caused elected officials to respond and citizens to become active.

In 1988, as Jay Levin became involved in other

11

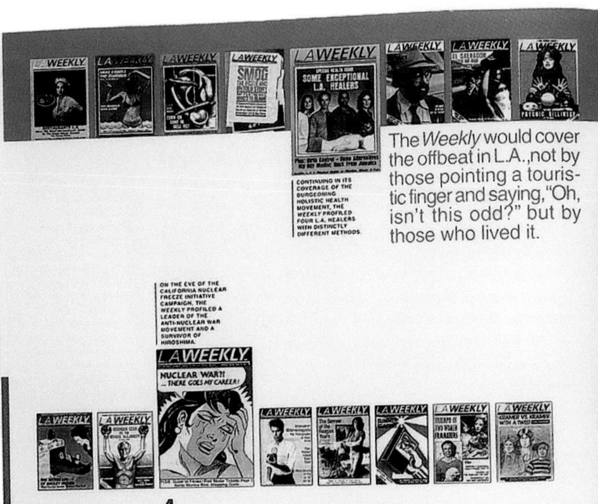

CONTINUING IN ITS COVERAGE OF THE BURGEONING HOLISTIC HEALTH MOVEMENT, THE WEEKLY PROFILED FOUR L.A. HEALERS WITH DISTINCTLY DIFFERENT METHODS.

The *Weekly* would cover the offbeat in L.A., not by those pointing a touristic finger and saying, "Oh, isn't this odd?" but by those who lived it.

ON THE EVE OF THE CALIFORNIA NUCLEAR FREEZE INITIATIVE CAMPAIGN, THE WEEKLY PROFILED A LEADER OF THE ANTI-NUCLEAR WAR MOVEMENT AND A SURVIVOR OF HIROSHIMA.

4

Jay Levin, a journalist who was editor of Flynt Publications' *L.A. Free Press* when it folded in 1978, had a vision of Los Angeles as a disparate group of towns that could be linked together and galvanized by a newspaper like the *Weekly* — one that would inform readers all over the city about what was going on in the arts, politics, movies and music. The *Weekly* would cover the offbeat in L.A., not by those pointing a touristic finger and saying, "Oh, isn't this odd?" but by those who lived it. It would create a sense of community among the myriad local neighborhoods.

After the demise of the *Free Press*, Levin approached local businesses and entertainment figures for their support of a new weekly paper in L.A. Actor-producer Michael Douglas and entrepreneur Pete Kameron were among the original investors in the project and remained on its board of directors for many years.

In November of 1978, with Jay Levin as editor, Joie Davidow as Calendar editor

5

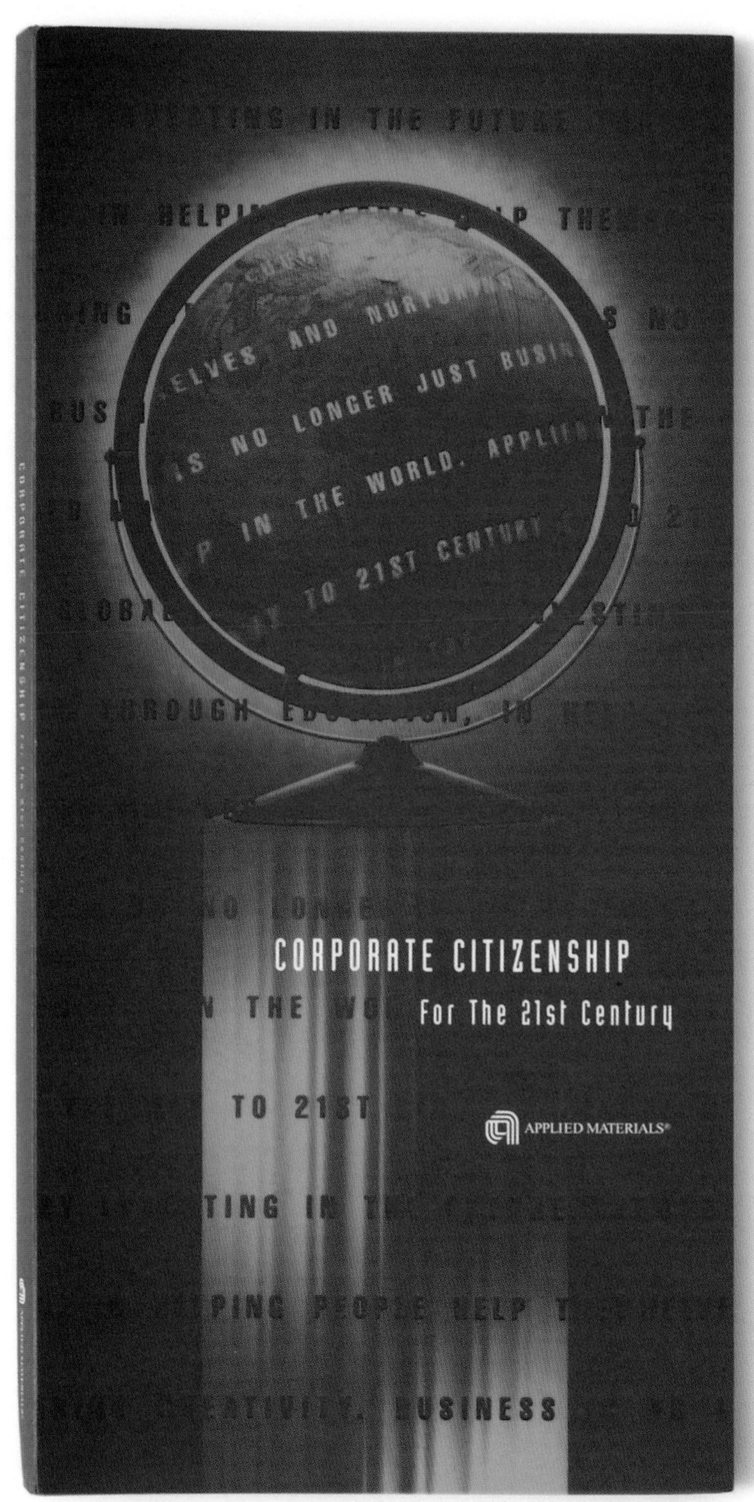

DESIGN FIRM › Melissa Passehl Design
ART DIRECTOR › Melissa Passehl
DESIGNER › Melissa Passehl
PHOTOGRAPHER › Robert Cardin
COPYWRITER › Susan Sharpe
CLIENT › Applied Materials
TOOLS (SOFTWARE/PLATFORM) › Macintosh, QuarkXPress
PAPER STOCK › Starwhite Vicksburg
PRINTING PROCESS › Four-color PMS

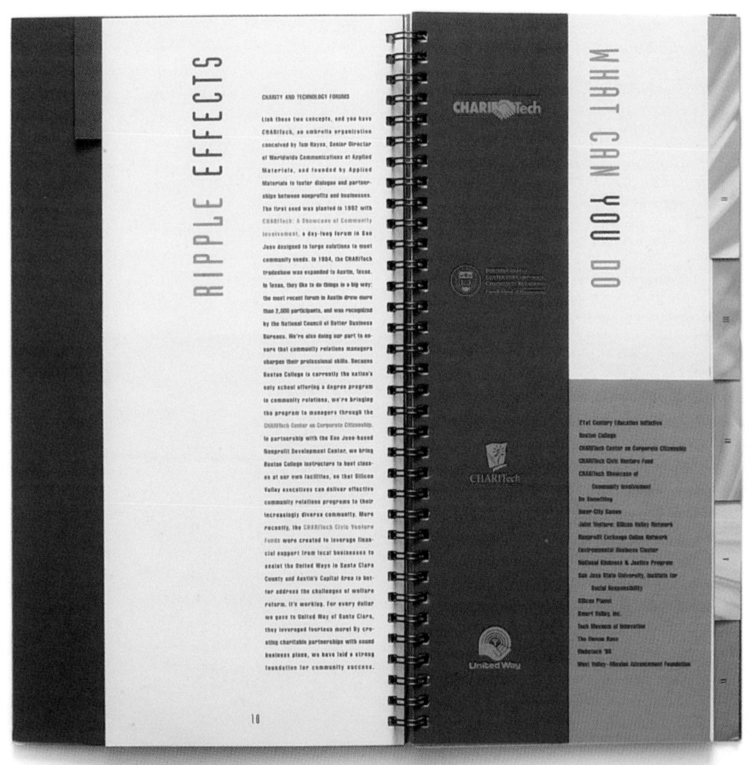
RIPPLE EFFECTS
CHARITY AND TECHNOLOGY FORUMS
10
CHARITech
WHAT CAN YOU DO
CHARITech
United Way

CORPORATE CITIZENSHIP
For The 21st Century
James C. Morgan
CHAIRMAN AND CEO
Dan Maydan
PRESIDENT
II. INVESTING IN THE FUTURE
III. PRACTICING GLOBAL CITIZENSHIP

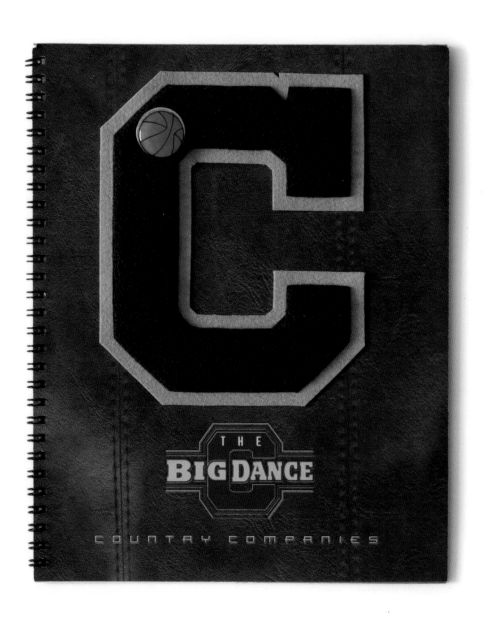

DESIGN FIRM › Country Companies Design Services
ART DIRECTOR › Tracy Griffin Sleeter
DESIGNER › Tracy Griffin Sleeter
PHOTOGRAPHER › Stock Photography
COPYWRITER › Greg Martin
CLIENT › Agency
TOOLS (SOFTWARE/PLATFORM) › Macintosh
PAPER STOCK › Frasier
PRINTING PROCESS › Offset by original Smith printing

THE BIG DANCE

HYATT REGENCY SAN DIEGO

SAN DIEGO, CALIFORNIA

JUNE 30 - JULY 5, 2001

What better way to reward your efforts than a trip the entire family will enjoy - to beautiful San Diego, California? If you've never been there, or haven't been there for awhile, you'll be amazed how much there is to do and see.

San Diego is an excellent place the whole family can enjoy. If you're looking for a wild time, you'll find three of the wildest just minutes away - Sea World, Wild Animal Park and the world-famous San Diego Zoo. Looking to enjoy the weather? Rent some bikes, skates or kayaks and soak up the sunshine on Mission Bay or along any of the city's 70 miles of beach.

If golf is your game, you'll like what San Diego County has to offer - 50 public courses to challenge all levels of golfer. From desert landscapes to country hillsides to views of the Pacific, San Diego has it all, including Torrey Pines Golf Course - home of the Buick Invitational.

Want something a little more relaxing? Enjoy lunch at one of San Diego's ocean-view restaurants. Go antique shopping, stroll the boutiques or take a quiet walk along the beach at sunset. Finish off the day in Gaslamp Quarter, where you'll find one of the city's liveliest nighttime street scenes.

Of course, what would July 4th be without a picnic and fireworks? Following a picnic with all our Big Dance qualifiers and their families, enjoy a front row seat to fireworks right from the grounds of your hotel - the Hyatt Regency San Diego, located on San Diego Bay.

Fun for everyone – that's what San Diego has to offer. And it's a fitting reward for making it to The Big Dance.

Here's how you do it:

QUALIFICATION CRITERIA

Contest Period:
December 1, 1999 - November 30, 2000

Requirements

Agents: Must be ranked in Top 640, based on Contest Credits
Must have produced at least 48 Contest Units

Agencies: Must be ranked in Top 64, based on Contest Credits Percent Base.
Must have met at least 90 percent of Contest Unit Base

Experience Factors
Contest Credits vary, based on the length of time a person has served as a Country Companies agent, as shown below. These factors will also impact the agency's Contest Credit totals.

Agent Experience (As of 12-1-1999)
Contest Credits Received

Basic Needs Agents
125% of Contest Credits Earned
0-12 months
120% of Contest Credits Earned
13-24 months
115% of Contest Credits Earned
25-36 months
110% of Contest Credits Earned
37-48 months
105% of Contest Credits Earned
More than 48 months
100% of Contest Credits Earned

THE BIG DANCE.

That's what fans call the NCAA Division I tournament. And whether they say so or not, everyone who loves college basketball wants to make it there. Little else matters. Because regardless of the success a player, coach or team enjoys, they all dream of making it to *"the dance."*

It's a reward for a year's worth of focus and effort. It's about talent and heart and making sacrifices others did not. It's about doing what it takes to rise above the rest. It's about fulfilling a dream and earning the *National Champion's ring.*

This year, we're introducing our own version of **"THE BIG DANCE."** It, too, will reward focus, heart and sacrifice. It, too, will be about fulfilling dreams.

Are You Ready to Play?

At the end of each NCAA season, 64 teams are invited to "the dance." Once the tourney begins, the field quickly narrows. *From 64 to 32, from 32 to the "Sweet Sixteen," "Elite Eight" and "Final Four."* The battles end only after the *National Champion* has been crowned.

In our dance, agents and agencies will compete during a yearlong contest. At the conclusion, we will rank all agents and agencies based on their performance. The **TOP 640 AGENTS AND 64 AGENCIES** meeting our contest requirements will earn their invitation to **THE BIG DANCE** and participate in our **NATIONAL TOURNAMENT.** We'll host two very special **ALL STAR TRIPS** for all agents and managers meeting our midyear qualification requirements, too.

Here's Your Letter

We've attached your letter to this book, to help serve as a reminder of your goals during this contest. Each step of the way, from **ALL STAR** to **THE BIG DANCE** and beyond, we'll award a special pin to all that qualify. It's a mark of distinction shared by a select few...those who pay the price to be among the best.

Here's Your Playbook

This book contains everything you need to know about **THE BIG DANCE.** How the contest works. How to earn your invitation. And most importantly, all the great prizes you can win along the way if you've got what it takes to make it to the dance. *Interested?* Take a look inside to learn more.

DESIGN FIRM › Michael Courtney Design
ART DIRECTORS › Mike Courtney, Scott Souchok
DESIGNERS › Mike Courtney, Scott Souchok
PHOTOGRAPHER › Stock, Kevin Latona
COPYWRITER › The Frause Group
CLIENT › Vulcan Northwest
TOOLS (SOFTWARE/PLATFORM) › Freehand, Photoshop
PAPER STOCK › Potlatch McCoy
PRINTING PROCESS › Four-color offset

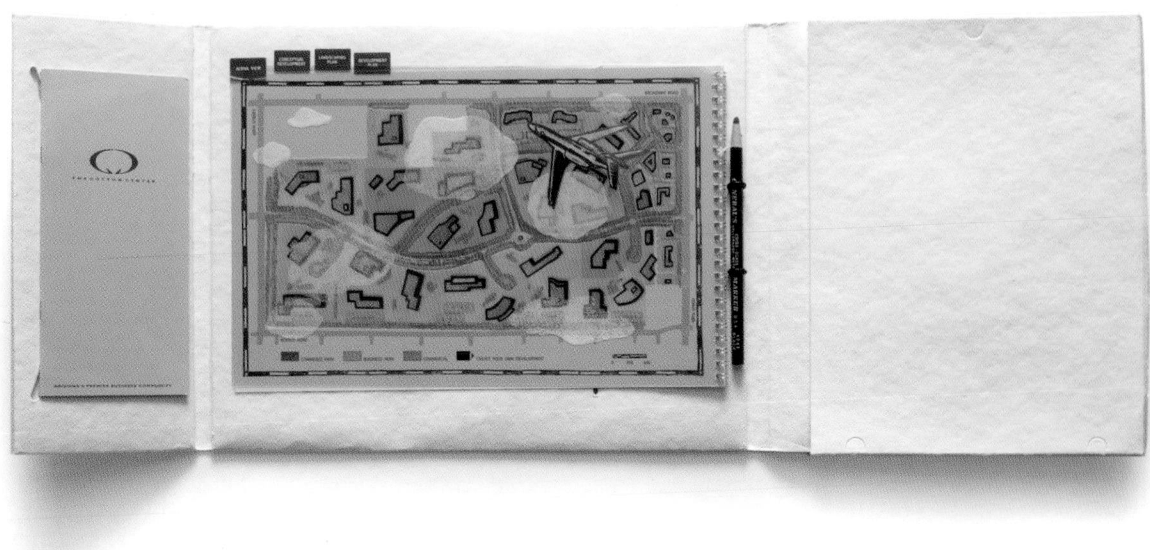

The Cotton Center is 280 acres of extraordinary business opportunity.

Strategically located less than five minutes from Phoenix Sky Harbor International Airport, The Cotton Center provides incomparable access to the entire Phoenix metropolitan area.

Because The Cotton Center is in the center of the region's freeway system, more than 95% of the population of America's sixth largest city lives within 40 minutes of the heart of The Cotton Center.

The affluent and fast-growing communities of Scottsdale, Tempe, Ahwatukee, Chandler, Gilbert and Mesa are within 20 minutes of The Cotton Center.

Arizona State University, with its renowned undergraduate and graduate schools, research facilities, business incubator programs and think-tanks is only 25 blocks away. 19 additional institutions of higher learning are within 20 minutes.

This is not your typical commercial real estate. This is the very definition of a premier business community.

DESIGN FIRM > After Hours Creative
ART DIRECTOR > After Hours Creative
DESIGNER > After Hours Creative
ILLUSTRATOR > Rick Allen
COPYWRITER > After Hours Creative
CLIENT > Cotton Center
TOOLS (SOFTWARE/PLATFORM) > Macintosh G4, Adobe Illustrator

BOEING
737 — 800
BASIC AIRCRAFT SPECIFICATION
Maximum Take-Off Weight
Seating Capacity
Galleys
Engines
Thrust
27,300 lbs.

POWER
AIRCRAFT

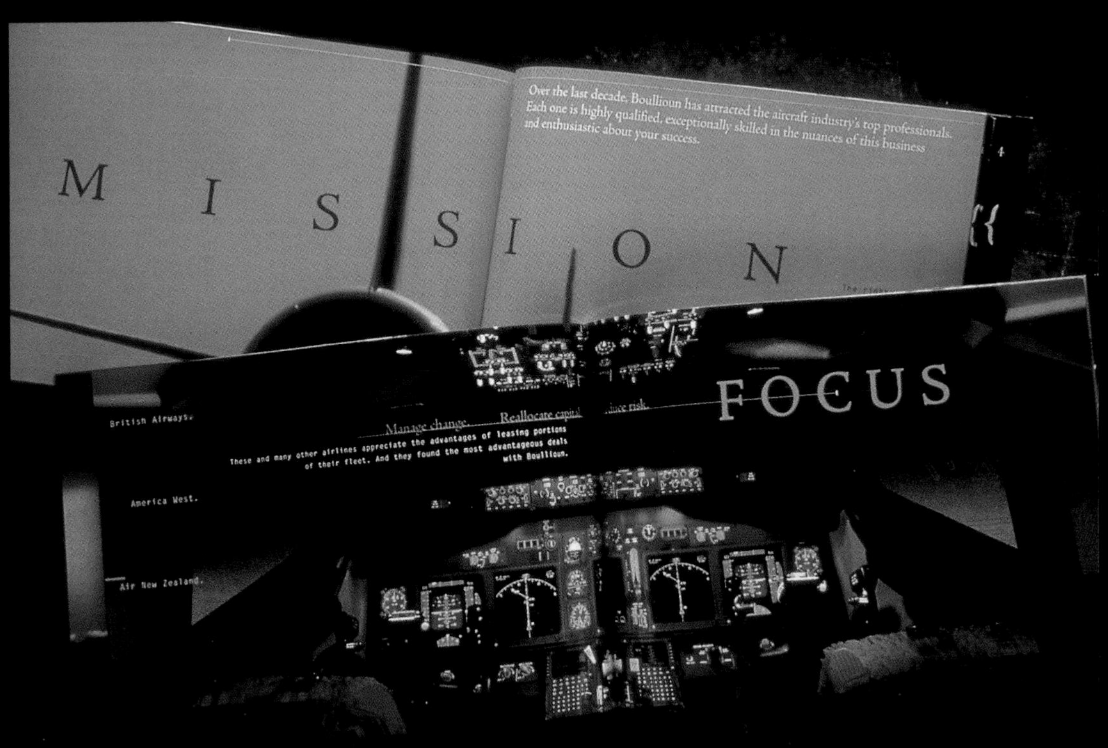

DESIGN FIRM › Hornall Anderson Design Works, Inc.
ART DIRECTORS › Jack Anderson, Katha Dalton
DESIGNERS › Katha Dalton, Ryan Wilderson, Belinda Bowling
PHOTOGRAPHERS › Boeing, West Stock, Tony Stone, Alan Abramowitz
COPYWRITER › John Koval
CLIENT › Boullioun Aviation Services
TOOLS (SOFTWARE/PLATFORM) › QuarkXPress
PAPER STOCK › McCoy, Strathmore

DESIGN FIRM › Cox Design
ART DIRECTOR › Randy Cox
DESIGNER › Randy Cox
COPYWRITER › Mike Furnary
CLIENT › San Jose Mercury News
TOOLS (SOFTWARE/PLATFORM) › Photoshop, QuarkXPress, Macintosh
PAPER STOCK › French
PRINTING PROCESS › Offset

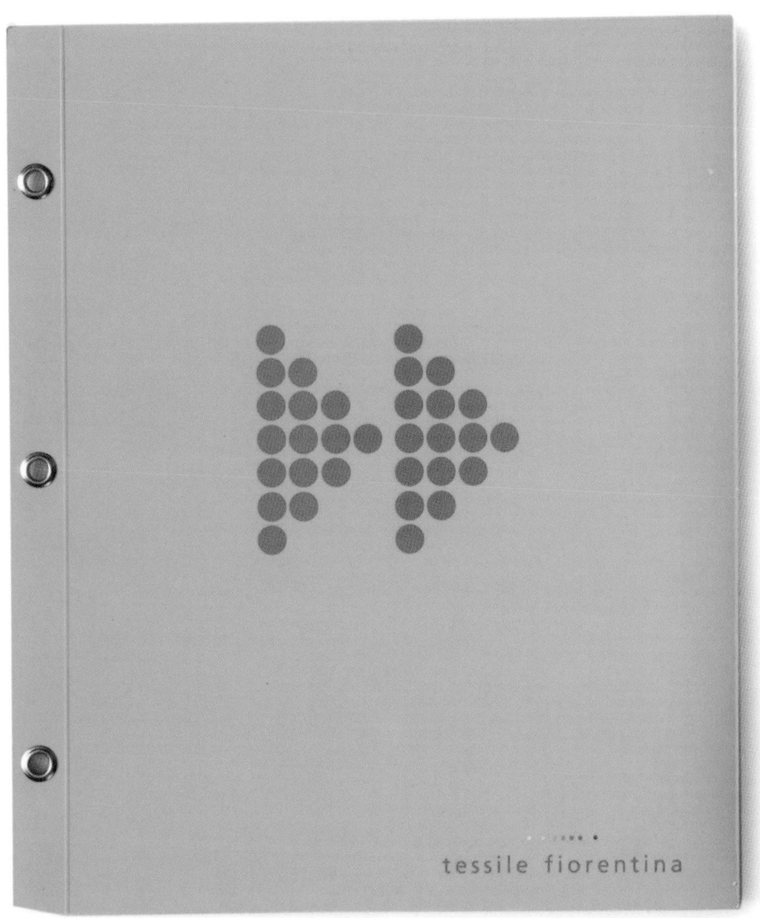

DESIGN FIRM › Hand Made Group
ART DIRECTORS › Alessandro Esteri, Giona Maisrelli
DESIGNERS › Alessandro Esteri, Giona Maisrelli
ILLUSTRATOR/PHOTOGRAPHER › Alessandro Esteri
COPYWRITER › Verdiana Maggiorelli
CLIENT › Tessile Fiorentina
TOOLS (SOFTWARE/PLATFORM) › QuarkXpress, Photoshop
PAPER STOCK › Zanders
PRINTING PROCESS › Printed in Pantone

DESIGN FIRM > Gee + Chung Design
ART DIRECTOR > Earl Gee
DESIGNERS > Earl Gee, Qui Tong
PHOTOGRAPHER > Stock
COPYWRITERS > Tracy Harvey, Susan Berman
CLIENT > Netigy Corporation
TOOLS (SOFTWARE/PLATFORM) > QuarkXPress, Adobe Illustrator, Photoshop
PAPER STOCK > Springhill SBS C25 24 pt., Appleton Utopia, 65 lb. cover
PRINTING PROCESS > Offset lithography, die-cut cover

DESIGN FIRM › The Bonsey Design Partnership
ART DIRECTOR › Chris Lee
DESIGNER › Damien Thomasz
PHOTOGRAPHERS › Andrew Hun, Alex Ow
COPYWRITER › Jane Cotter
CLIENT › Transtel Engineering
TOOLS (SOFTWARE/PLATFORM) › Macintosh, Freehand, Photoshop
PAPER STOCK › Matt art card
PRINTING PROCESS › Five-color plus one special

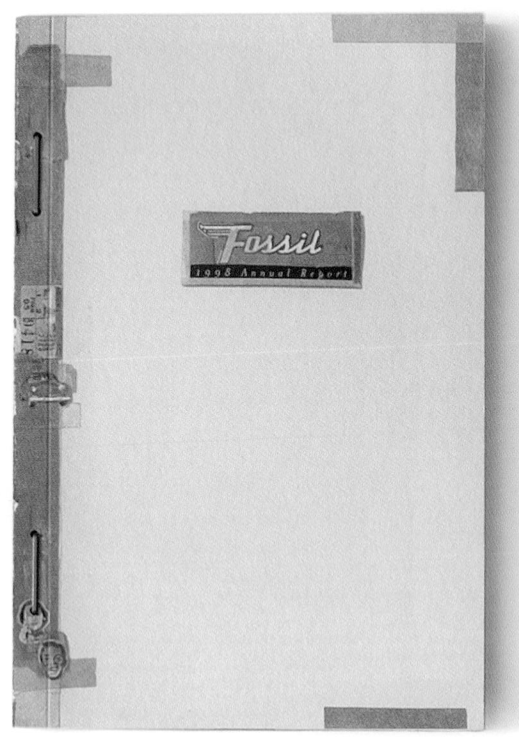

DESIGN FIRM › Fossil
ART DIRECTORS › Tim Hale, Stephen Zhang
DESIGNER › Stephen Zhang
ILLUSTRATORS › Ellen Tanner, Paula Wallace, John Vineyard, Jennifer Burk, Andrea Haynes
PHOTOGRAPHER › Dave McCormack
CLIENT › Fossil
TOOLS (SOFTWARE/PLATFORM) › QuarkXPress, Photoshop, Illustrator, Macintosh G3, Power PC
PAPER STOCK › Fox River Protera
PRINTING PROCESS › Four-color offset

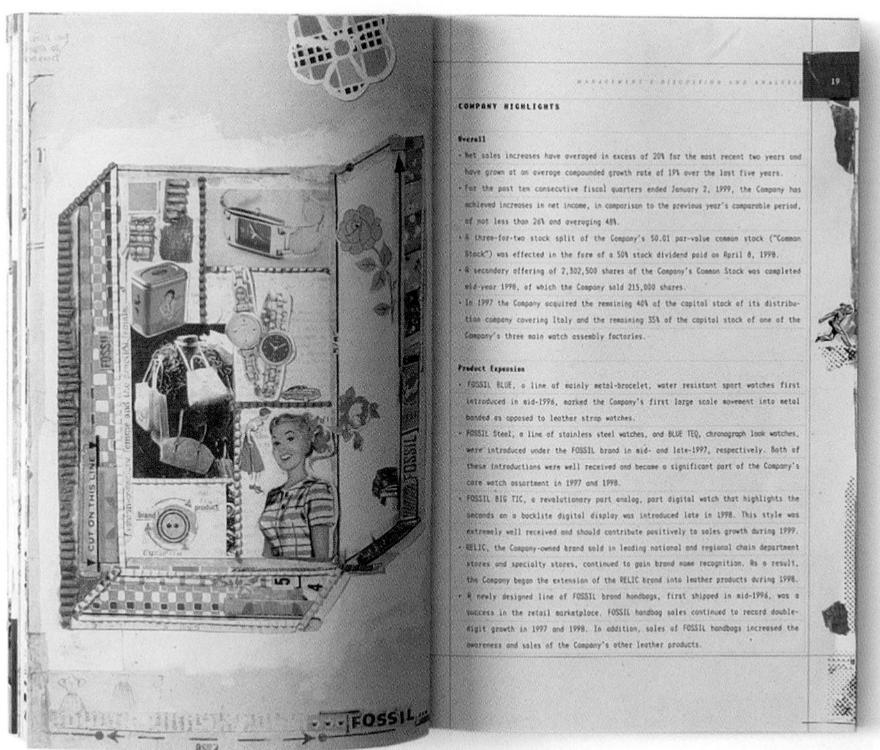

COMPANY HIGHLIGHTS

Overall

- Net sales increases have averaged in excess of 20% for the most recent two years and have grown at an average compounded growth rate of 19% over the last five years.
- For the past ten consecutive fiscal quarters ended January 2, 1999, the Company has achieved increases in net income, in comparison to the previous year's comparable period, of not less than 26% and averaging 48%.
- A three-for-two stock split of the Company's $0.01 par-value common stock ("Common Stock") was effected in the form of a 50% stock dividend paid on April 8, 1998.
- A secondary offering of 2,302,500 shares of the Company's Common Stock was completed mid-year 1998, of which the Company sold 215,000 shares.
- In 1997 the Company acquired the remaining 40% of the capital stock of its distribution company covering Italy and the remaining 55% of the capital stock of one of the Company's three main watch assembly factories.

Product Expansion

- FOSSIL BLUE, a line of mainly metal-bracelet, water resistant sport watches first introduced in mid-1996, marked the Company's first large scale movement into metal banded as opposed to leather strap watches.
- FOSSIL Steel, a line of stainless steel watches, and BLUE TEQ, chronograph look watches, were introduced under the FOSSIL brand in mid- and late-1997, respectively. Both of these introductions were well received and became a significant part of the Company's core watch assortment in 1997 and 1998.
- FOSSIL BIG TIC, a revolutionary part analog, part digital watch that highlights the seconds on a backlite digital display was introduced late in 1998. This style was extremely well received and should contribute positively to sales growth during 1999.
- RELIC, the Company-owned brand sold in leading national and regional chain department stores and specialty stores, continued to gain brand name recognition. As a result, the Company began the extension of the RELIC brand into leather products during 1998.
- A newly designed line of FOSSIL brand handbags, first shipped in mid-1996, was a success in the retail marketplace. FOSSIL handbag sales continued to record double-digit growth in 1997 and 1998. In addition, sales of FOSSIL handbags increased the awareness and sales of the Company's other leather products.

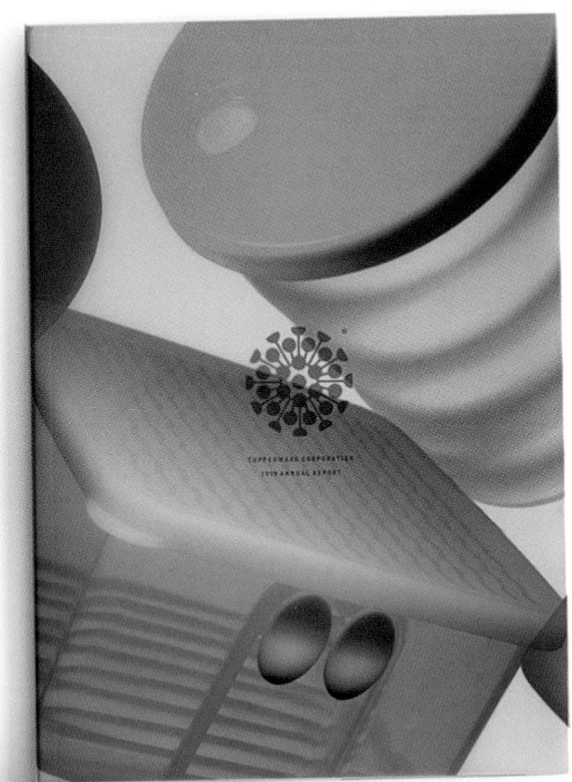

DESIGN FIRM › SamataMason, Inc.
ART DIRECTOR › Greg Samata
DESIGNER › Steve Kull
PHOTOGRAPHERS › Sandro, Marc Norberg, Mark Craig
COPYWRITER › Laurence Pearson
CLIENT › Tupperware Corporation
TOOLS (SSOFTWARE/PLATFORM) › QuarkXPress, Macintosh
PAPER STOCK › Fox River, Coronado Vellum, Fox River Sundance, Canson satin
PRINTING PROCESS › Offset, sheet fed

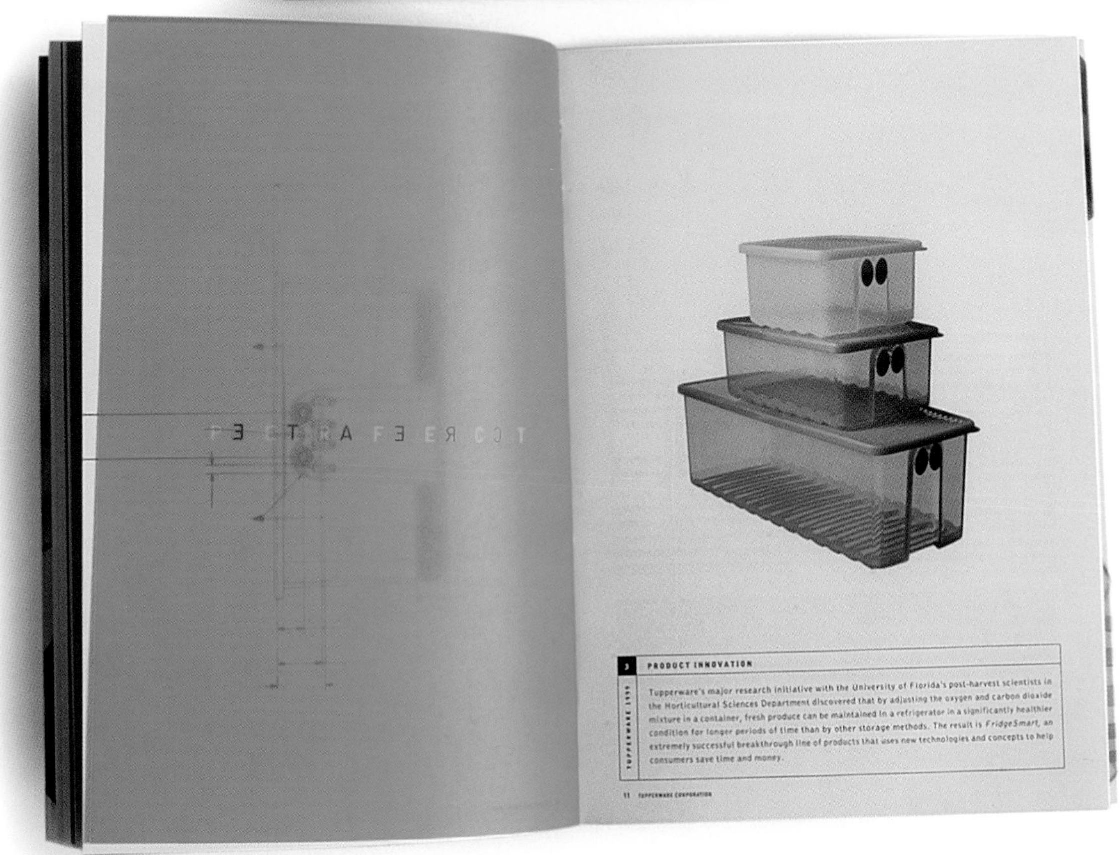

3
PRODUCT INNOVATION
Tupperware's major research initiative with the University of Florida's post-harvest scientists in the Horticultural Sciences Department discovered that by adjusting the oxygen and carbon dioxide mixture in a container, fresh produce can be maintained in a refrigerator in a significantly healthier condition for longer periods of time than by other storage methods. The result is FridgeSmart, an extremely successful breakthrough line of products that uses new technologies and concepts to help consumers save time and money.
11 TUPPERWARE CORPORATION

DESIGN FIRM › Bloch + Coulter Design Group
ART DIRECTORS › Hollie Hory, Thomas Bloch, Ellie Young Sutt
DESIGNERS › Hollie Hory, Thomas Bloch, Ellie Young Sutt
PHOTOGRAPHER › Jerry Garns
COPYWRITER › Paul Losie
CLIENT › Amwest Insurance Group, Inc.
TOOLS (SOFTWARE/PLATFORM) › Macintosh, QuarkXPress, Photoshop, Illustrator
PAPER STOCK › Editorial: Potlatch Karma 100 lb. text; Flysheet: French Parchtone cream 60 lb. text, Financial: Beckett embossed enhanced silk 80 lb., text
PRINTING PROCESS › All but cover sheet fed, hand bound with Acco fastener

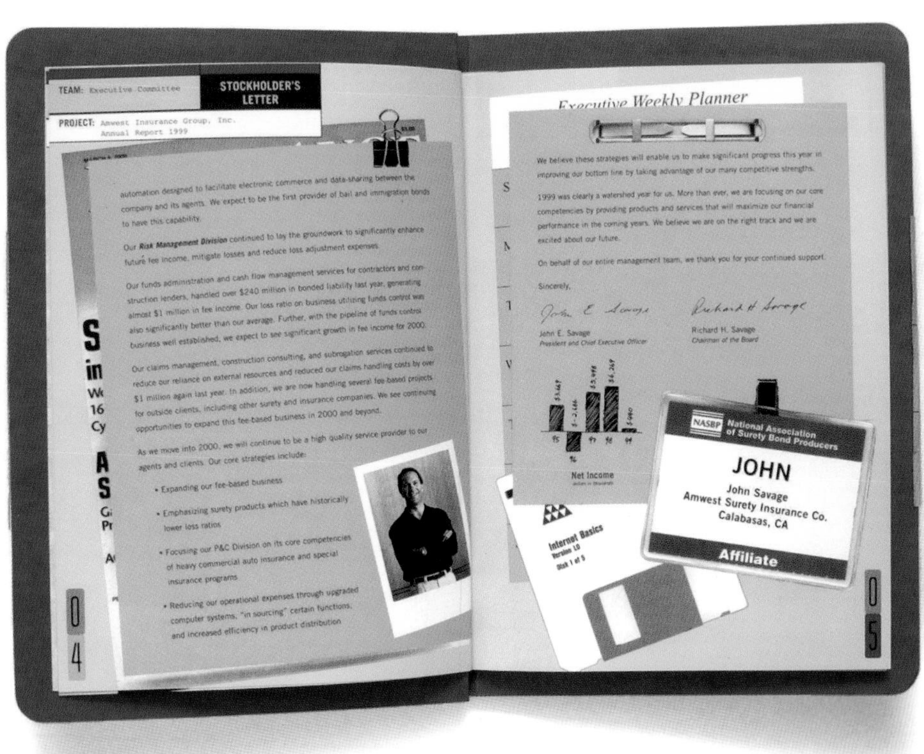
TEAM: Executive Committee
STOCKHOLDER'S LETTER
PROJECT: Amwest Insurance Group, Inc. Annual Report 1999
automation designed to facilitate electronic commerce and data-sharing between the company and its agents. We expect to be the first provider of bail and immigration bonds to have this capability.
Our Risk Management Division continued to lay the groundwork to significantly enhance future fee income, mitigate losses and reduce loss adjustment expenses.
Our funds administration and cash flow management services for contractors and construction lenders, handled over $240 million in bonded liability last year, generating almost $1 million in fee income. Our loss ratio on business utilizing funds control was also significantly better than our average. Further, with the pipeline of funds control business well established, we expect to see significant growth in fee income for 2000.
Our claims management, construction consulting, and subrogation services continued to reduce our reliance on external resources and reduced our claims handling costs by over $1 million again last year. In addition, we are now handling several fee-based projects for outside clients, including other surety and insurance companies. We see continuing opportunities to expand this fee-based business in 2000 and beyond.
As we move into 2000, we will continue to be a high quality service provider to our agents and clients. Our core strategies include:
• Expanding our fee-based business
• Emphasizing surety products which have historically lower loss ratios
• Focusing our P&C Division on its core competencies of heavy commercial auto insurance and special insurance programs
• Reducing our operational expenses through upgraded computer systems, "in sourcing" certain functions, and increased efficiency in product distribution
04
Executive Weekly Planner
We believe these strategies will enable us to make significant progress this year in improving our bottom line by taking advantage of our many competitive strengths.
1999 was clearly a watershed year for us. More than ever, we are focusing on our core competencies by providing products and services that will maximize our financial performance in the coming years. We believe we are on the right track and we are excited about our future.
On behalf of our entire management team, we thank you for your continued support.
Sincerely,
John E. Savage
President and Chief Executive Officer
Richard H. Savage
Chairman of the Board
Net Income
NASBP National Association of Surety Bond Producers
JOHN
John Savage
Amwest Surety Insurance Co.
Calabasas, CA
Affiliate
Internet Basics
05

TEAM: Surety Management Committee
SURETY DIVISION
PROJECT: Contract Surety operation review for Annual Report 1999
Surety is our largest product and represents about 79 percent of our total written premium.
Over the past few years we have evolved from a specialty market, writing small contract and License & Permit bonds using collateral, to a standard market, writing contract and commercial surety bonds up to $25 million or more with no collateral.
With over $108 million in written premium last year, we are the eighth largest surety writer in the country and the leading surety for middle market accounts.
Contract Surety
Contract surety is our largest surety product line and represents 57 percent of our total surety premium. We offer a full line of contract bonds, including Bid, Performance & Payment, Supply, Maintenance and Subdivision bonds.
Last year, we wrote $61.9 million in contract surety premium, which was about $0.4 million less (0.6%) than the year before. This small decrease in written premium was intentional. In this current soft market, we do not believe we can profitably expand this product. Further, given the contract accounts recently eliminated in certain geographic areas to help improve our loss experience, we do not anticipate growth during 2000 for this product.
We are continually refining our underwriting process in order to reduce our risk. In this soft market, it is very important that we employ every risk mitigating technique available to us, including:
Steve Ray
CFO
06
• Greater emphasis on risk-based underwriting
• More extensive analysis of loss experience by class of business and producer
• Reducing underwriting authority on certain classes of business
• Taking a more proactive role in assessing territories with higher loss ratios
While these techniques will not completely eliminate our underwriting risk, we believe they greatly enhance our ability to produce profitable business.
Product Mix
07

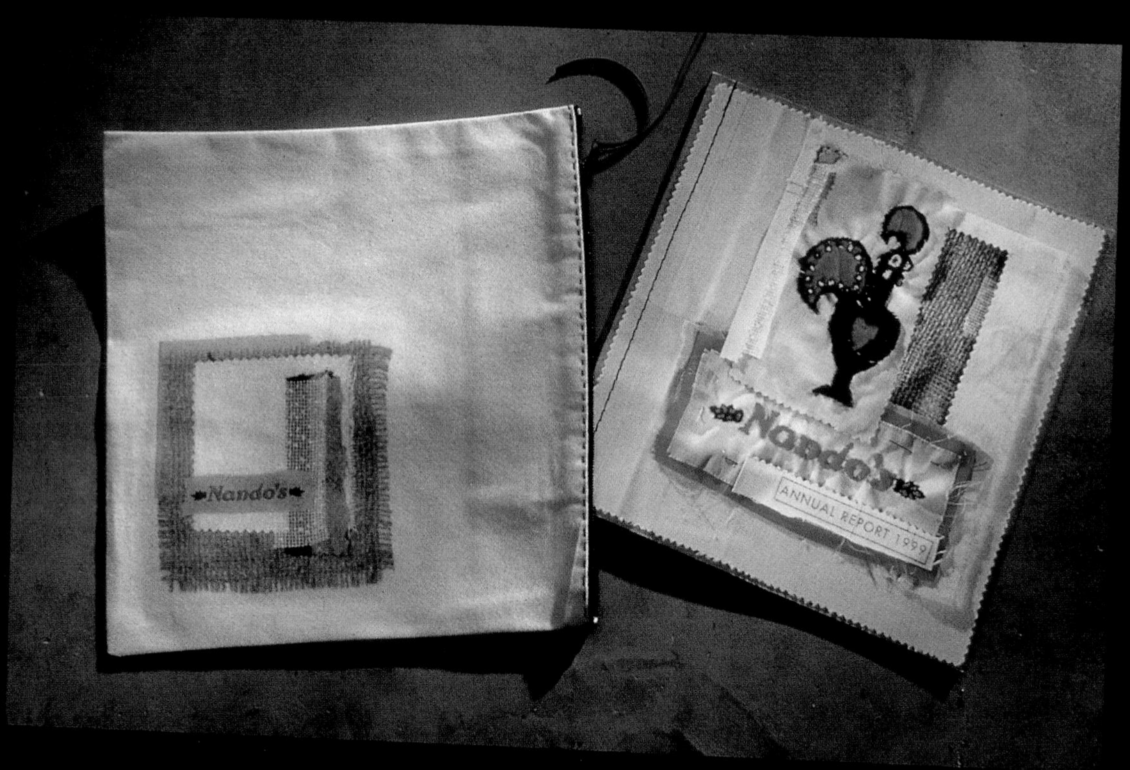

DESIGN FIRM › Cross Colours Ink
ART DIRECTOR › Janice Beddington
DESIGNER › Janice Beddington
ILLUSTRATOR/PHOTOGRAPHER › David Pastoll
CLIENT › Nando's Chickenland
TOOLS (SOFTWARE/PLATFORM) › Macintosh, Freehand, Photoshop
PRINTING PROCESS › Lithography

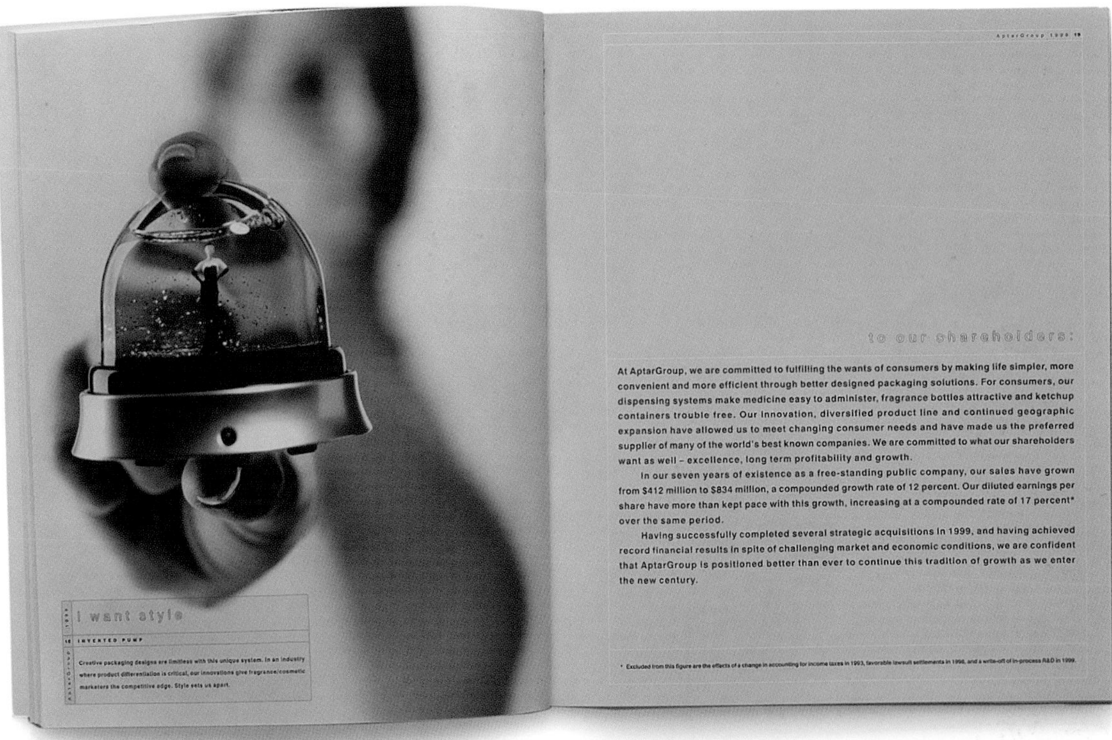

i want style
INVENTED PUMP
Creative packaging designs are limitless with this unique system. In an industry where product differentiation is critical, our innovations give fragrance/cosmetic marketers the competitive edge. Style sets us apart.
to our shareholders:
At AptarGroup, we are committed to fulfilling the wants of consumers by making life simpler, more convenient and more efficient through better designed packaging solutions. For consumers, our dispensing systems make medicine easy to administer, fragrance bottles attractive and ketchup containers trouble free. Our innovation, diversified product line and continued geographic expansion have allowed us to meet changing consumer needs and have made us the preferred supplier of many of the world's best known companies. We are committed to what our shareholders want as well – excellence, long term profitability and growth.
In our seven years of existence as a free-standing public company, our sales have grown from $412 million to $834 million, a compounded growth rate of 12 percent. Our diluted earnings per share have more than kept pace with this growth, increasing at a compounded rate of 17 percent* over the same period.
Having successfully completed several strategic acquisitions in 1999, and having achieved record financial results in spite of challenging market and economic conditions, we are confident that AptarGroup is positioned better than ever to continue this tradition of growth as we enter the new century.
* Excluded from this figure are the effects of a change in accounting for income taxes in 1993, favorable lawsuit settlements in 1998, and a write-off of in-process R&D in 1999.

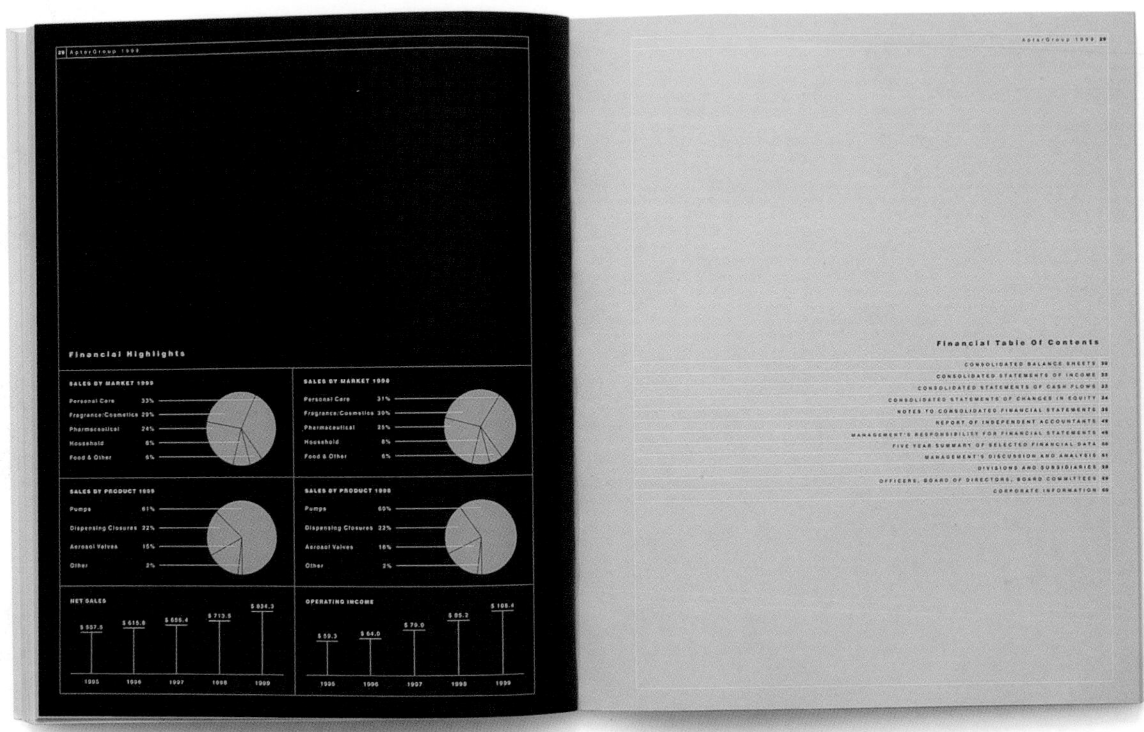

DESIGN FIRM > SamataMason, Inc.
ART DIRECTORS > Pat & Greg Samata
DESIGNER > Kevin Krueger
PHOTOGRAPHER > Sandro
CLIENT > Aptar Group
TOOLS (SOFTWARE/PLATFORM) > QuarkXPress, Macintosh
PAPER STOCK > Appleton–coated Utopia one, dull; Monadnock Aastrolite vellum
PRINTING PROCESS > Offset, sheet fed

DESIGN FIRM › Edelman Public Relations Worldwide
ART DIRECTOR › Mary Ackerly
DESIGNERS › Rosanne Kang, Lana Le
PHOTOGRAPHERS › Josef Astor, Whitney Cox, Doug Levere, Peter Loppacher, William Vasquez
COPYWRITER › Various
CLIENT › Barnes and Noble
TOOLS (SOFTWARE/PLATFORM) › QuarkXpress, Adobe Illustrator, Macintosh
PAPER STOCK › Mohawk 50/10
PRINTING PROCESS › Offset lithography

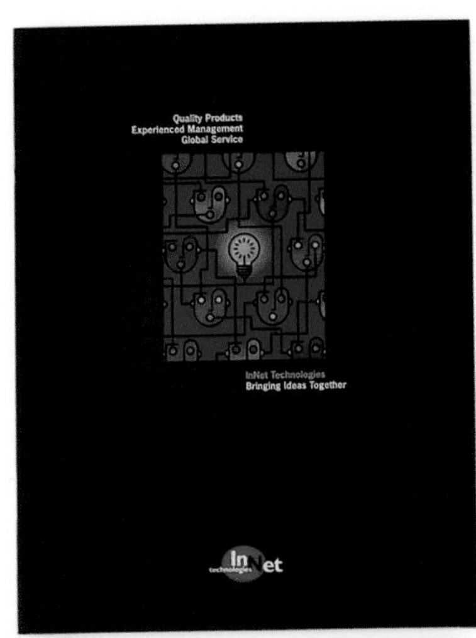

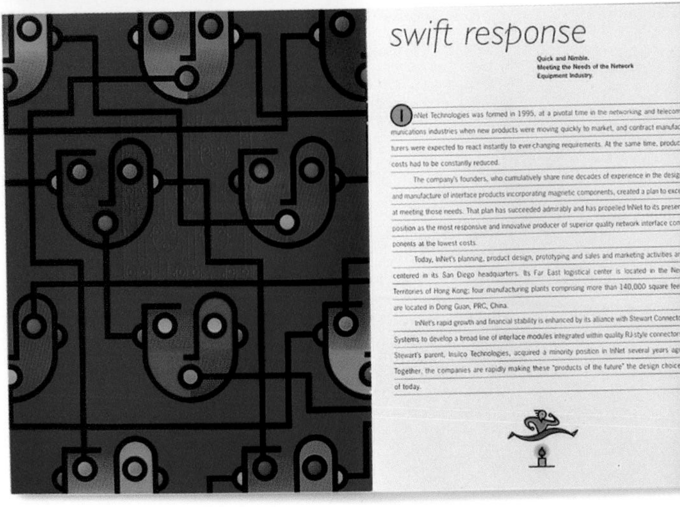

swift response

**Quick and Nimble.
Meeting the Needs of the Network
Equipment Industry.**

InNet Technologies was formed in 1995, at a pivotal time in the networking and telecommunications industries when new products were moving quickly to market, and contract manufacturers were expected to react instantly to ever-changing requirements. At the same time, product costs had to be constantly reduced.

The company's founders, who cumulatively share nine decades of experience in the design and manufacture of interface products incorporating magnetic components, created a plan to excel at meeting those needs. That plan has succeeded admirably and has propelled InNet to its present position as the most responsive and innovative producer of superior quality network interface components at the lowest costs.

Today, InNet's planning, product design, prototyping and sales and marketing activities are centered in its San Diego headquarters. Its Far East logistical center is located in the New Territories of Hong Kong; four manufacturing plants comprising more than 140,000 square feet, are located in Dong Guan, PRC, China.

InNet's rapid growth and financial stability is enhanced by its alliance with Stewart Connector Systems to develop a broad line of interface modules integrated within quality RJ-style connectors. Stewart's parent, Insilco Technologies, acquired a minority position in InNet several years ago. Together, the companies are rapidly making these "products of the future" the design choices of today.

DESIGN FIRM › Lorenz Advertising
ART DIRECTOR › Arne Ratermanis
DESIGNER › Arne Ratermanis
ILLUSTRATORS/PHOTOGRAPHERS › Arne Ratermanis, Michael Balderas
COPYWRITER › Carm Greco
CLIENT › InNet Technologies
TOOLS (SOFTWARE/PLATFORM) › QuarkXPress, Illustrator, Macintosh
PAPER STOCK › Potlatch McCoy Gloss
PRINTING PROCESS › Four-color litho with dull and gloss varnish; embossed cover

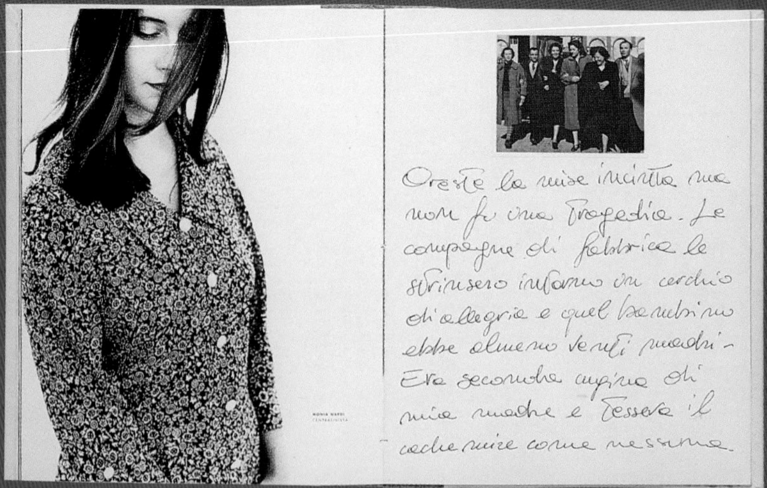

ART DIRECTOR:
ALESSANDRO ESTERI

DESIGNER:
GIONA MAIARELLI

PHOTOGRAPHER:
ALESSANDRO ESTERI

CLIENT:
LANIFICIO DEL CASENTINO

SOFTWARE AND HARDWARE:
QUARK
MAC

MATERIALS:
FEDRIGONI

PRINTING:
OFFSET

HAND MADE GROUP

LANIFICIO DEL CASENTINO
CORPORATE PROFILE

ITALY

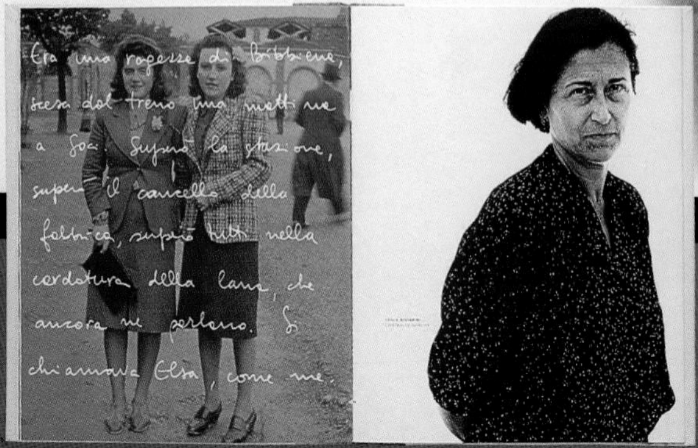

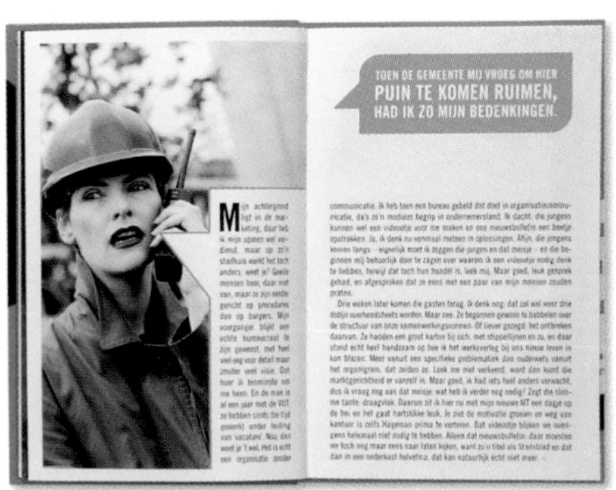

LAVA GRAPHIC DESIGNERS
WERKELIJKHEID (REALITY)

THE NETHERLANDS

ART DIRECTOR:
YKE BARTELS

DESIGNERS:
YKE BARTELS
DAAN JANSSENS

PHOTOGRAPHER:
ROYALTY-FREE
STOCK PHOTOS

CLIENT:
SIGNUM

SOFTWARE AND
HARDWARE:
ILLUSTRATOR
QUARKXPRESS
MAC G4

MATERIALS:
CHRONOLUX

PRINTING:
RIJSER

TENDENZE PRIMAVERA-ESTATE 1999/SPRING-SUMMER 1999 TRENDS

Una stagione dedicata alle seduzioni tattili
A season dedicated to tactil seductions

By Angelo Uslenghi

filtrate **PREZIOSITA'**

Visione attraverso una grata di un interno esotico-coloniale. Penombre e sfumature, luci soffuse, luminosità discreta, riflessi dorati. Aspetti setosi, mescolanze di lucido e opaco, fluidità e leggerezza. Minuscoli armaturati ed intrecci a canestro.

FILTERED PRECIOUSNESS. *View of an exotic-colonial interior through a grid. Semi-darkness and shades, soft lights, discrete brightness, golden hues. Silky appearance, mixture of bright and mat, fluidity and lightness. Tiny weaves and basket weaves.*

perfette

colori **MATERICI**

Le gamme colore si rifanno ai cromatismi presi da sostanze e materie alquanto inedite.
Gessosi. Colori impuri che richiamano i colori della calce, gesso, stucco, sabbie, pietre.
Cosmetici. Colori delle polveri e creme da make-up. Tonalità epidermiche e tocco metallico polverizzato.
Preziosi. Colori scuri, filtrati, ombreggiati. L'oriente nei toni delle penombre: i violacei, i blu, i beige dorati.
Bucolici. Colori olfattivi. Un bouquet di fiori, erbe, piante presi da orti e giardini.
Energetici. Colori forti ispirati dal mondo pubblicitario, dal dinamismo moderno e da folklori latini.

MATERIAL COLOURS. *Colour shades with chromatisms of substances and materials that border on the unusual.*
Chalky. *The impure colours of lime, chalk, putty, sand, stone.*
Cosmetics. *Powder and make-up colours. Skin-deep hues and a powder metal touch.*
Precious. *Dark, filtered, shadowy colours. Oriental semi-dark hues: purples, blues, golden beiges.*
Bucolic. *Olfactory colours. A bouquet of flowers, herbs, vegetable and flower gardens.*
Energetic. *Bright colours inspired by the world of advertising, modern verve and Latin folklore.*

CLASS

seduzione **TATTILE**

E' sicuramente una stagione all'insegna dei piaceri sensoriali dove il tatto acquista sempre più importanza. Le sensazioni più innovative provengono da mischie plurime di fibre: lana/seta/mohair, cotone/lino/lana e dall'uso di prodotti ausiliari inediti come il lattice, il silicone, il Teflon. Inoltre i finissaggi completano il risultato tattile con l'utilizzo di enzimi, sabbiature, lavaggi "stone".

SEDUCTIVE TOUCH. *This is certainly a season under the banner of sensory pleasures where touch becomes increasingly important. The most innovative sensations come from multi-fibre blends such as wool/silk/mohair, cotton/linen/wool and from unexpected auxiliary products such as latex, silicon, Teflon. Enzyme and sandblast finishes, "stone" washing give the final touch.*

armonie **BOTANICHE**

Natura vegetale in mostra. Aspetto delavato, tinture organiche. Raffinata semplicità. Freschezza e cromatismi presi da giardini in fiore. Armature semplici come tela, canvas e panama. Disegnature con leggeri riquadri da fazzoletti d'epoca.

BOTANIC HARMONIES. *Natural plant life on display. Washed-out appearance, organic dyes. Refined simplicity. Freshness and shades from blossomed gardens. Simple weaves such as in cloth, canvas and panama. Old-handkerchief patterns with light window panes.*

aspetti **ARTIGIANALI**

Imperfezioni volute, superfici irregolari, aspetti granulosi. Rilievi e rugosità con uso di filati grossi alternati a filati sottili. Una nuova rusticità contenuta e raffinata con fondi leggermente crêpe.

HANDICRAFT APPEARANCE. *Hand-made imperfections, uneven surfaces, grainy effect. Reliefs or roughness obtained with alternating coarse and fine yarns. A new restrained and refined rustic look with slightly crepe backgrounds.*

ITALY

ART DIRECTOR: ALESSANDRO ESTERI
DESIGNER: GIONA MAIARELLI
CLIENT: LANIFICIO DEL CASENTINO
SOFTWARE AND HARDWARE: QUARKXPRESS MAC
MATERIALS: FEDRIGONI
PRINTING: OFFSET

della bellezza e
Tessile
' Tesauti che si
o, seducono.
cie e levigate, grana
fine e compatta
idratata. Aspetti
, porcellanati,
di filati sottilissimi.

SMOOTHENSS.
beauty and well-
netic" textiles.
seductive textiles.
f polished surfaces,
mpact fabric grains
drated skin. Silky,
, pearlescent
: Use of extra-thin

CI

rivisitati

Basic modernizzato.
Ritorno a tipologie tradizionali
re-interpretate. Disegnature
spesso in bianco e nero ma
con interventi tecnologici.

CLASSICS REVISITED.
Modern basics. Traditional
reinterpretations return. Frequent
black and white motifs with
technological additions.

Intervista/Interview

Alfio Aldrovandi

Direttore generale del Lanificio del Casentino
General manager of Lanificio del Casentino

ORE 8 DEL MATTINO:

il Lanificio si sveglia con il rumore incessante delle sue macchine e già risuonano i passi di Alfio Aldrovandi, che incontriamo davanti al suo primo caffè nero bollente. 47 anni, trent'anni di lavoro nel settore tessile e nove al Lanificio del Casentino, da due anni dirige questa azienda con quella abilità imprenditoriale che deriva dalla lunga esperienza maturata sul campo.

A che punto siamo con la produzione, direttore?

Ormai il Lanificio del Casentino si è stabilizzato sulla fascia media e medio-alta di mercato con 2,5 milioni di metri venduti annui. Lei capisce che a questo livello non possiamo permetterci il minimo errore. Quindi lo sforzo maggiore in questo momento è quello di "affinare", in tutti i sensi. Ogni persona che lavora qui dentro deve essere sensibilizzata alla nuova realtà e quindi esercitare la massima attenzione ed il massimo controllo. Ogni reparto deve essere messo a punto, dalla tessitura, all'orditura, alla rifinizione... Inoltre stiamo potenziando il servizio e ampliando la ricerca.

La tipologia di prodotti è cambiata in questa nuova realtà?

No, e questa è la scelta più importante che abbiamo fatto quest'anno.
La nostra attenzione è sempre puntata sul cachemire, ed in questo senso siamo stati premiati da richieste importanti da parte di grossi compratori come Armani, Aquascutum, Escada. Ma in genere curiamo molto le fibre pregiate, camel, alpaca, angora... senza dimenticare i tessuti in pura lana di cui abbiamo un campionario ricchissimo.

Che collezione presenta il Lanificio del Casentino per la primavera-estate?

A rischio di essere monotoni, abbiamo riconfermato le nostre specializzazioni arricchendole di qualità e di performance. Non a caso le nostre collezioni si chiamano "Lana" e "Lana e...". Cioè da una parte un campionario tutto 100% lana e dall'altra le mischie nobili: abbiamo fatto dei lana-seta, lana-seta-mohair, lana-lino, lana-viscosa, ma sempre lana, e della migliore. In questo campo stiamo facendo una grossa ricerca e a Prato Expo presentiamo una lana "effetto vegetale" dove il classico sposa le ultime tecnologie, con un effetto molto interessante.

Come vanno gli affari all'estero?

A Colonia è andata molto bene, incominciamo a ricevere ora le prime telefonate, le prime proposte... anche se quest'anno i tedeschi hanno rischiato ben poco, a differenza degli altri anni. Non male l'America, che con il Giappone e la Cina fa ormai parte del nostro quotidiano. Stiamo approfondendo il discorso con i Paesi dell'Est... Li ci sono solo 4-5 grandi confezionisti che stanno piano piano mettendo a punto le loro collezioni per la Germania. Abbiamo grossi contatti con Polonia e Cecoslovacchia, ma i risultati si vedranno a fine stagione. La Turchia invece sta andando molto bene: confeziona per Germania e Bielorussia, richiede tessuti pregiati...
Per quanto sia un anno difficile, questo, per tutta la produzione tessile, posso dirmi abbastanza soddisfatto.

It is 8 o'clock in the morning. The Lanificio awakes to the incessant noise of its machines and to the footsteps of Alfio Aldrovandi whom we meet whilst he is savouring his first hot black coffee. Now aged 47, with 30 years experience in the textile industry - nine of them with the Lanificio del Casentino - he now manages this business with the ability of an entrepreneur, a maturity which derives from a long commitment to this field.

At what point are we with production, Mr. Aldrovandi?

The Lanificio del Casentino now concentrates on the medium, medium-high range, with 2,5 million metres sold. You will understand that at this level we cannot afford the slightest error. Our greatest effort at the present time is, therefore, to improve, in every sense. All those who work here must be very aware of this new reality; they must pay the greatest attention and exert the maximum control. Every department must be "on alert" from the weaving to the warping and on to the finishing touches. Besides this, we are strengthening our service and widening our research.

Has the type of product changed in this new reality?

No. And this is the most important choice that we have made this year. Our attention is always on cashmere and in this regard we have been rewarded by very important requests on the part of large buyers like Armani, Aquascutum, Escada. We generally deal in high quality fibres, camel, alpaca, angora, without forgetting our vast selection of fabrics in pure wool.

What is the Lanificio del Casentino presenting for their SpringSummer Collection?

At the risk of being monotonous, we have reaffirmed our specializations, enriching their quality and performance. It is not by chance that we have entitled our Collections: 'Wool' and 'Wool and ...' This means that some of our samples are 100% wool and others a rich mixture. We have produced wool-silk; wool-silk-mohair; wool-linen; wool-viscose, but always wool and of the best quality.
We are conducting wide research in this sector and at Prato Expo we are presenting a 'vegetable effect' wool where the classic blends with the latest technology offering very interesting results.

How is business abroad?

In Cologne everything went very well. We are just beginning to receive our first telephone calls - the first proposals. Even if the German clients have risked very little this year compared to others. We can classified America as 'not bad' as they together with Japan and China, make up part of our daily contacts. We are deepening our relationships with Eastern European countries. There are only about 4 or 5 large garment makers there who are, little by little, putting together collections for Germany. We have frequent contact with Poland and Czecoslovakia but any results here will be seen at the end of the season. Turkey is going well: they make garments for Germany and Bielorussia; richer materials are in demand here. Even though it is a difficult year for all textile production, I consider myself satisfied."

PRONTO
SIGNORA
WILSON,
MI SENTE
SIGNORA
WILSON?

HAND MADE GROUP
LANIFICIO DEL CASENTINO NEWS

Lanificio del Casentino
News

Our second issue One hundred and fifty years Anniversary The market at the millenium's end Trends for Spring Summer '99 The new collection at Prato Expo Vogue Tessuti on Lanificio del Casentino Oliviero Toscani on Utopia and other projects Interviews. And more...

C150

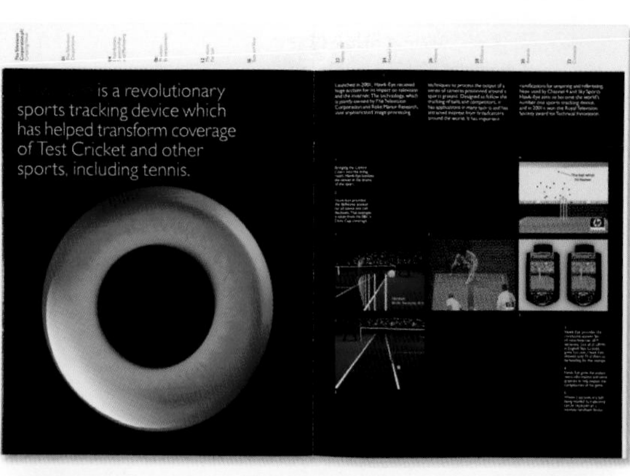

is a revolutionary sports tracking device which has helped transform coverage of Test Cricket and other sports, including tennis.

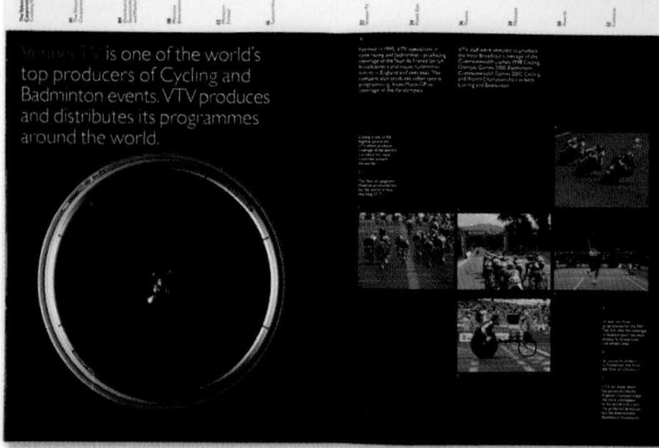

is one of the world's top producers of Cycling and Badminton events. VTV produces and distributes its programmes around the world.

ROSE DESIGN ASSOCIATES

TELEVISION CORPORATION
CORPORATE BROCHURE

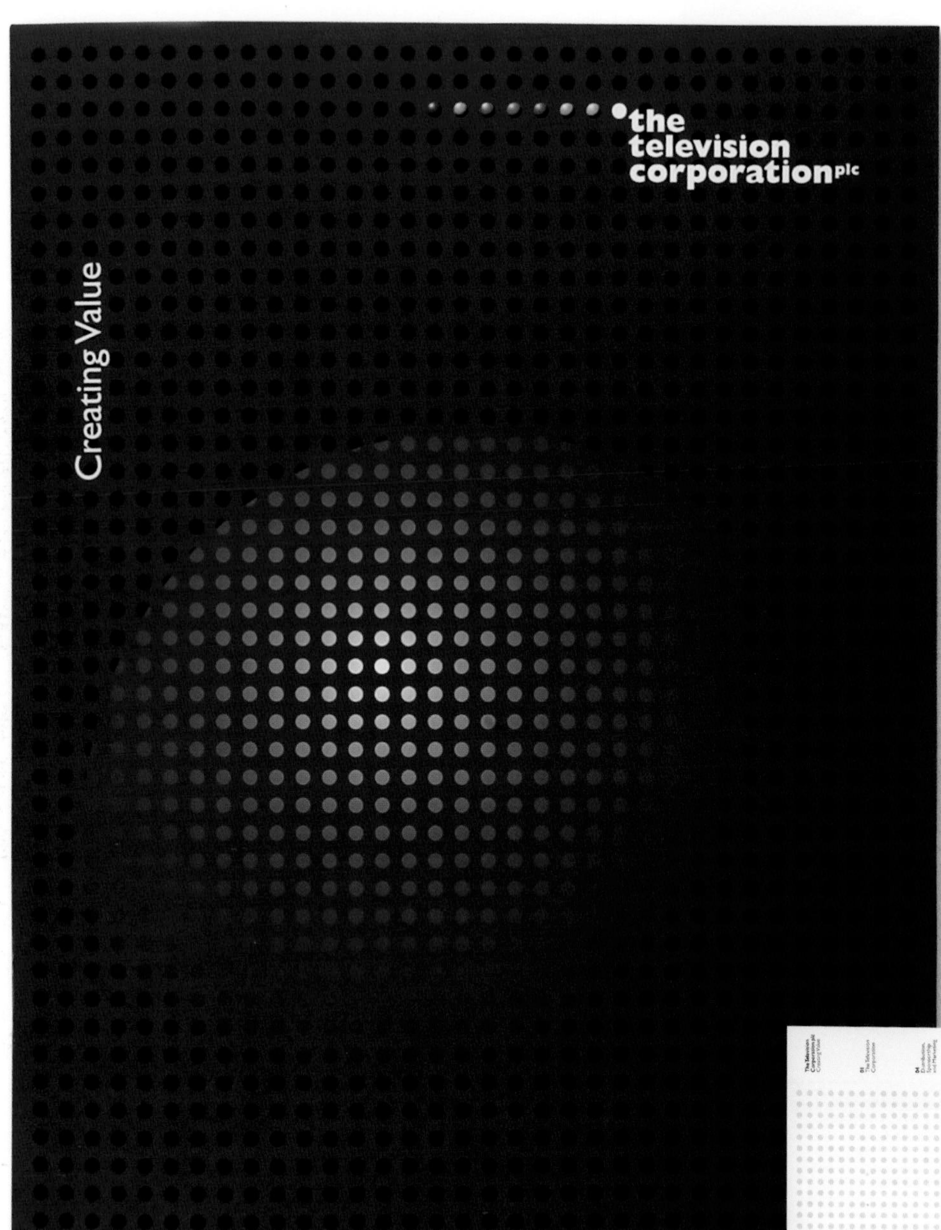

The Television Corporation is the UK's leading independent supplier of programmes to broadcasters worldwide. Combining two of Britain's largest production companies, Mentorn and Sunset+Vine, with one of the UK's most respected production facilities operations, The Television Corporation is a fast-growing media business. The Group produces over 3000 hours of television each year for all the UK's major television channels, distributing them to around 200 countries . . . . . .

ART DIRECTOR: SIMON ELLIOTT

DESIGNER: SIMON ELLIOTT

PHOTOGRAPHERS: PAUL ZAK, LOL KEEGAN

CLIENT: TELEVISION CORPORATION PLC

SOFTWARE: ILLUSTRATOR, PHOTOSHOP, QUARKXPRESS

MATERIALS: VALLIANT GLOSS ART

PRINTING: OFFSET LITHO

UK

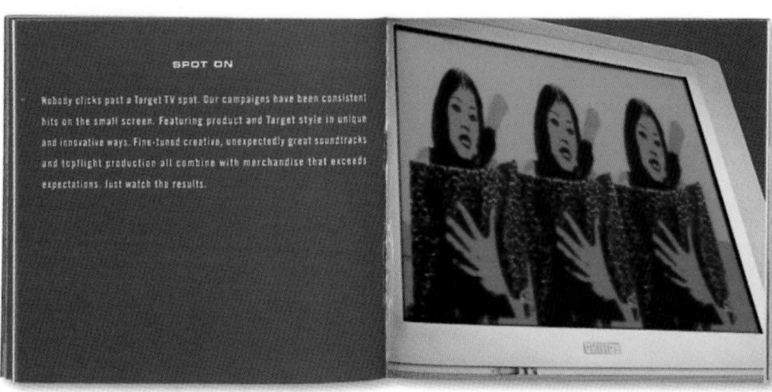

ART DIRECTOR:
CHERYL WATSON

DESIGNERS:
CHERYL WATSON
SHARON McKENDRY

CLIENT:
TARGET

GRAPHICULTURE
TARGET BRAND BOOK & DVD

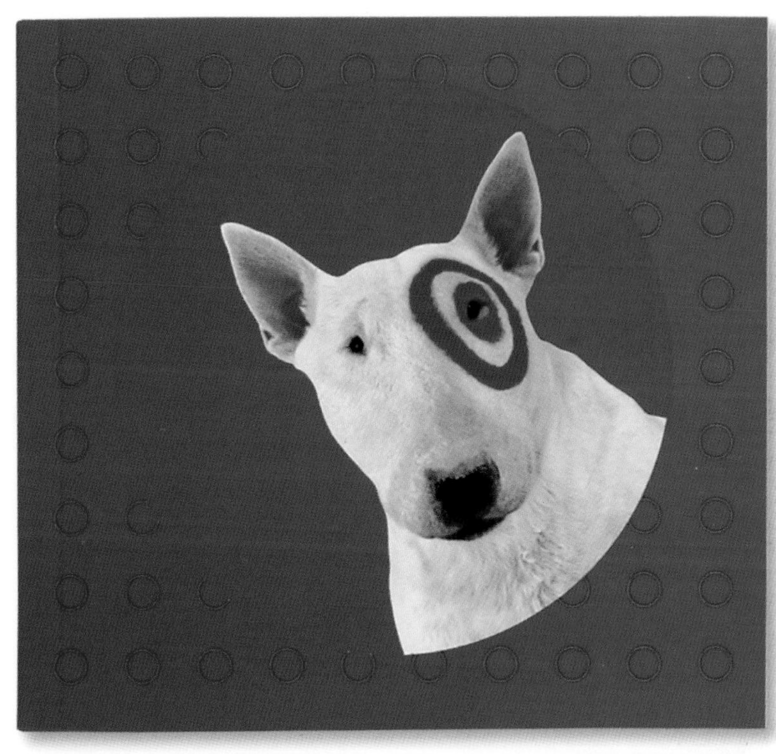

USA

TARGET.COM HITS THE DOT

Target is a bona fide power in e-commerce. Nielsen NetRatings consistently rank target.com among the top twenty retail sites for total monthly unique visitors.* And we consistently rank in the top five among unique visitors at home and at work, outpacing our competitors' shopping sites.

*Unique visitors are calculated monthly. One unique visitor is defined as one individual who visits a Web site during the month, regardless of the number of visits.

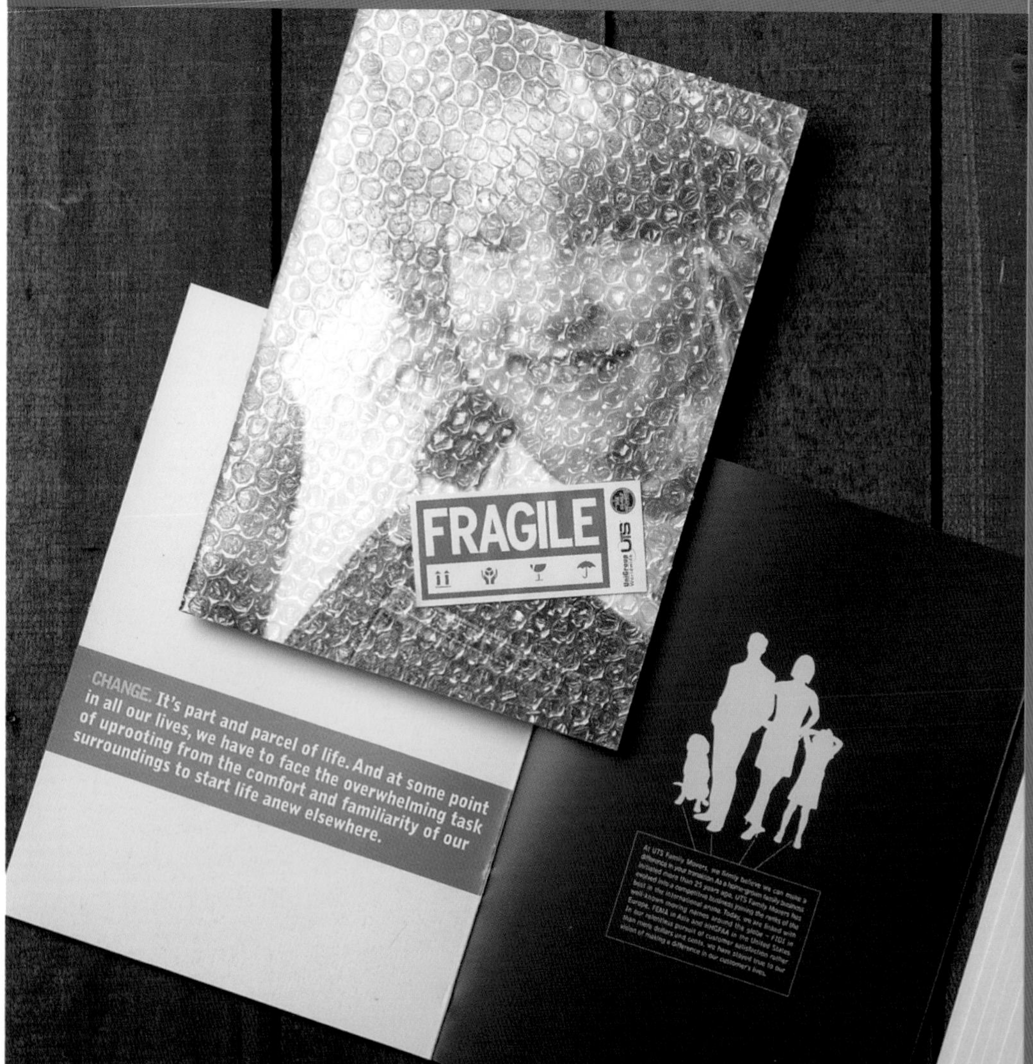

FRAGILE
CHANGE. It's part and parcel of life. And at some point in all our lives, we have to face the overwhelming task of uprooting from the comfort and familiarity of our surroundings to start life anew elsewhere.

DESIGN ASYLUM PTE LTD
FAMILY MOVERS CORPORATE BROCHURE

ART DIRECTOR:	DESIGNER:	CLIENT:	SOFTWARE:	MATERIALS:	PRINTING:
CHRISTOPHER LEE	KAI	UTS FAMILY MOVERS	FREEHAND PHOTOSHOP	MATT ARTPAPER	4C X 4C

SINGAPORE

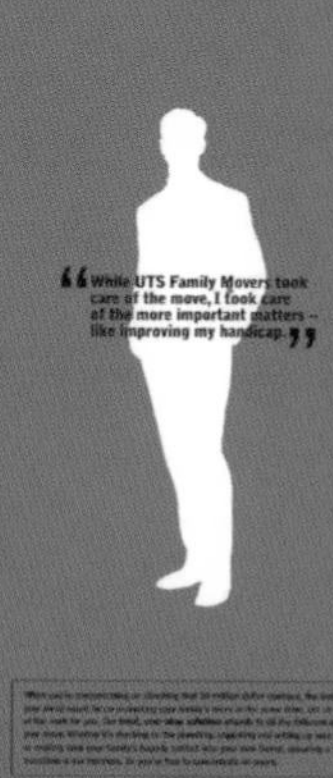

While UTS Family Movers took care of the move, I took care of the more important matters – like improving my handicap.

FABIO ONGARATO DESIGN
ARNOLD BLOCK LEIBLER
2002 YEAR IN REVIEW

WHAT REALLY MATTERS IN A LAW FIRM?

INAUGURAL AUSTRALIAN LAW AWARDS WINNER

CLIENTS' RIGHTS: MAINTAINED, DEFENDED & ENFORCED

AUSTRALIA

DESIGNER:
RYAN GUPPY

CLIENT:
ARNOLD BLOCK LEIBLER

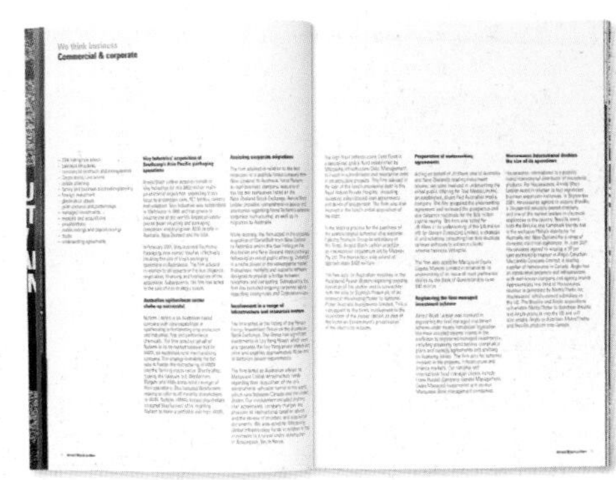

UK

ART DIRECTOR:
ANDREW GORMAN

DESIGNER:
ROB RICHE

PHOTOGRAPHERS:
PAUL DIXON
ROB RICHE
JOHN EDWARDS

CLIENT:
GALLAHER GROUP PLC

SOFTWARE AND HARDWARE:
PHOTOSHOP
QUARKXPRESS
MAC

MATERIALS:
MANNO ART MATT

PRINTING:
6-COLOR LITHO
CTD CAPITA

RADLEY YELDAR
GALLAHER ANNUAL REPORT 2000

SQUIRES & COMPANY
BELLWETHER 99 ANNUAL REPORT

USA

DESIGNER: BRANDON MURPHY

PHOTOGRAPHER: VARIOUS

CLIENT: BELLWETHER EXPLORATION

SOFTWARE AND HARDWARE: QUARKXPRESS MAC G4

MATERIALS: DULCET/FRENCH

PRINTING: WILLIAMSON PRINTING

SOUND
PRACTICE
Environment & Community Summary Report 2001
The EMI Group

SALTERBAXTER
SOUND PRACTICE

Eco-efficiency
Using fewer resources, and wasting less of those we do use, makes economic as well as environmental sense.
COMPARED TO 1995, WE NOW USE 63 PERCENT FEWER SOLVENTS AND GENERATE 45 PERCENT LESS HAZARDOUS WASTE AND 32 PERCENT LESS POLYCARBONATE SCRAP FOR EVERY UNIT OF PRODUCT THAT WE MANUFACTURE.
SOUND PRACTICE
The Christian Music Group (CMG) in the US has reduced by two-thirds the standard number of samples it orders for every new release. It has also changed its procedures to ensure that any samples that still remain surplus to requirements can be booked back into stock. This will significantly reduce product waste in the CMG offices.
Our impact
All aspects of our business use resources and create waste. Manufacturing is an area where we have undertaken formal reviews of the impacts resulting from this, and closely monitored our performance against some key indicators.
Our manufacturing sites use raw materials including polycarbonate, aluminium, solvents and inks. We continually strive to improve the efficiency of the process and minimise the quantity of material which is wasted, at the same time reducing the environmental impact caused by the wastes.
Some waste is inevitable. A proportion of the solvents used are emitted as vapours; these can present a health hazard in the working environment and contribute to smog formation when released to the atmosphere. Water-based effluents are treated on site and then discharged to sewer for further treatment. Any waste that can't be recycled, including hazardous waste, is sent for external disposal at landfill sites or incinerators.
We also use ozone depleting substances across our businesses, in air-conditioning and some fire protection systems. If released, these substances will damage the ozone layer.
Our performance
Solvents
We made good progress in solvent reduction, achieving a 31% drop in the quantity used and a 24% reduction per million units output (pmuo). This was significantly better than our target reduction of 5% pmuo.
The improvements were mainly due to a change of solvent specification at Uden (Netherlands) and improved controls at Jacksonville (US).
Hazardous waste
We reduced hazardous waste by 7%. This was equivalent to a 3% increase pmuo and fell short of our target 10% reduction pmuo. The main reason for this was the deferral of a new waste water treatment plant at Uden (now installed).
Polycarbonate efficiency
Procedural improvements at Toshiba-EMI (Japan) and Jacksonville contributed to a 16% reduction in polycarbonate scrap, equivalent to 10% pmuo. This was better than our 5% reduction target.
Ozone depleters
We record purchases of ozone depleting substances. No CFCs or halons were purchased. Purchases of HCFCs, used to maintain existing units or install new ones, increased by 5%. We also purchased 170kgs of HFCs as replacements for HCFCs. These gases are ozone friendly but have a high global warming potential.

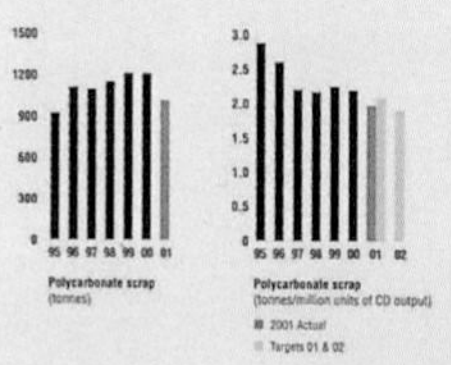

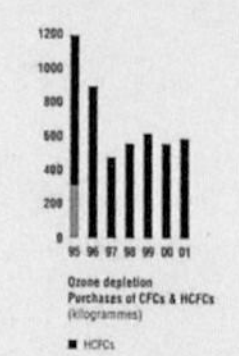

4

UK

ART DIRECTOR:
PENNY BAXTER

DESIGNER:
IVAN ANGELL

ILLUSTRATOR:
IVAN ANGELL

CLIENT:
THE EMI GROUP

SOFTWARE AND HARDWARE:
QUARKXPRESS
MAC

MATERIALS:
CYCLUS OFFSET

PRINTING:
LITHO +
LETTERPRESS

From 1993 to 2001:
In the charts and behind the scenes
93 94 95 96 97 98 99 00 01
02 03 04 05
SOUND PRACTICE

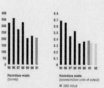

Sociaal Jaarverslag 2001 > Sociale Verzekeringsbank (SVB)
SVB Sociale Verzekeringsbank

THE NETHERLANDS

ART DIRECTORS:	DESIGNERS:	PHOTOGRAPHER:	CLIENT:	SOFTWARE AND HARDWARE:	MATERIALS:	PRINTING:
TIEMEN HARDER YEW-KEE CHUNG	TIEMEN HARDER YEW-KEE CHUNG	STAFF OF SOCIALE VERZEKERINGSBANK	SOCIALE VERZEKERINGSBANK	PHOTOSHOP QUARKXPRESS MAC	INVERCOTE ALBATO 250GSM + OXFORD 120GSM	OFFSET, 4-PROCESS COLORS

otaal
foto's
Sociaal Jaarverslag 2001 > Sociale Verzekeringsbank (SVB)
537 Reacties

2D3D
INTERNAL ANNUAL REPORT: SOCIALE VERZEKERINGSBANK

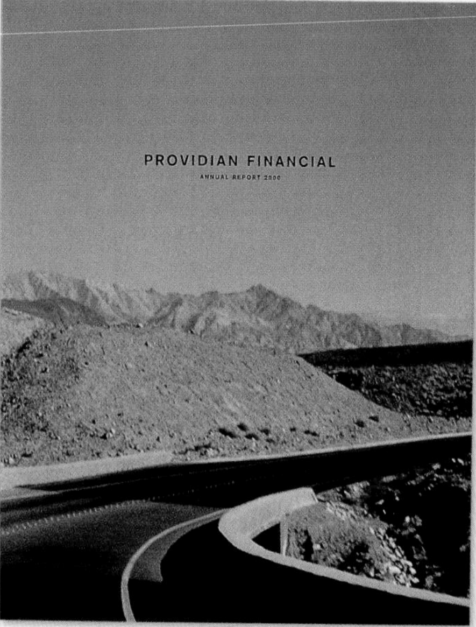

ART DIRECTOR: BILL CAHAN

DESIGNER: BOB DINETZ

CLIENT: PROVIDIAN FINANCIAL

SOFTWARE: ILLUSTRATOR, PHOTOSHOP, QUARKXPRESS

MATERIALS: UTOPIA 2 DULL

PRINTING: LITHOGRAPHIX

CAHAN & ASSOCIATES

PROVIDIAN 2000 ANNUAL REPORT

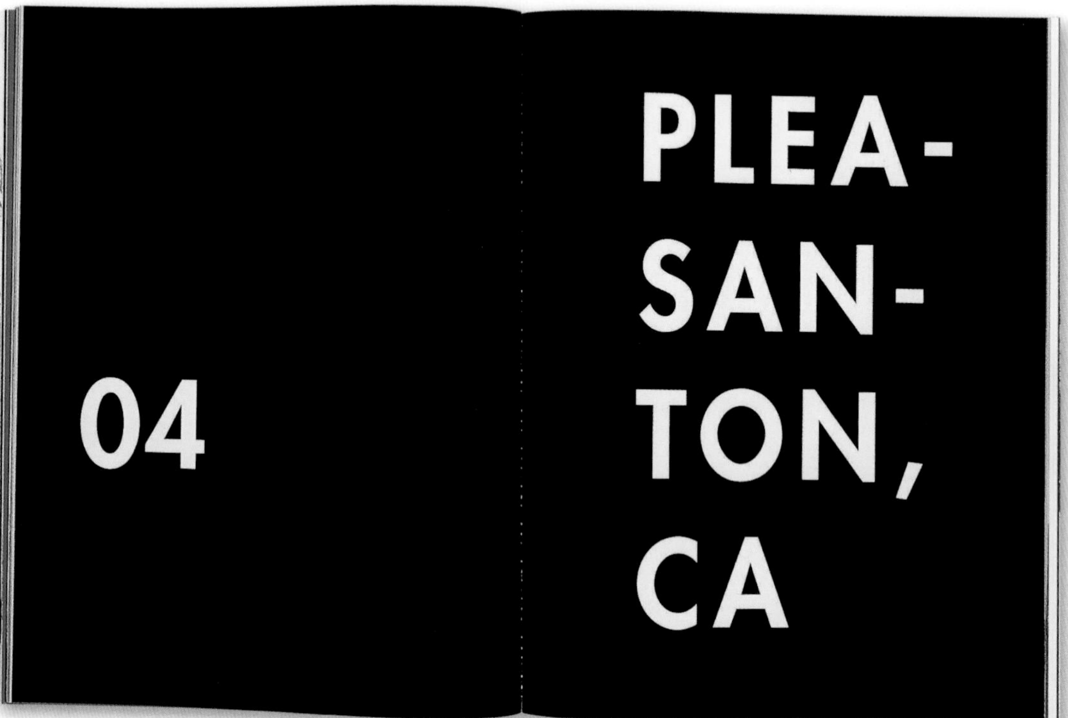

USA

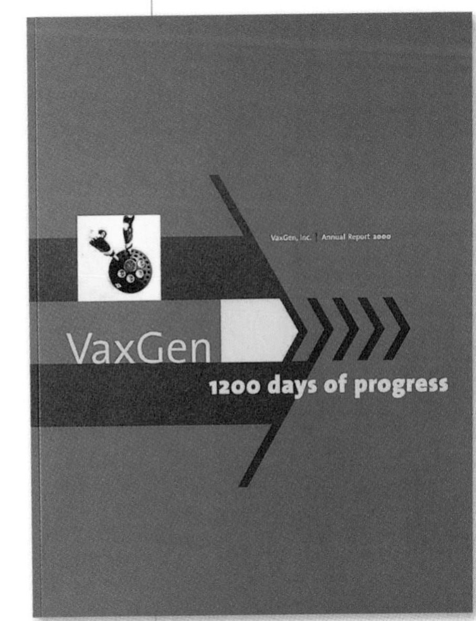

VaxGen, Inc. | Annual Report 2000
VaxGen
1200 days of progress

ART DIRECTOR: ANDREAS KELLER

DESIGNER: ANDREAS KELLER

PHOTOGRAPHER: JAMES CHIANG

CLIENT: VAXGEN, INC

SOFTWARE AND HARDWARE: QUARKXPRESS MAC

MATERIALS: FRENCH PAPER SMART WHITE

PRINTING: ANDERSON LITHOGRAPH

USA

"After years of working on preclinical studies with animal models, I came to VaxGen because the company is applying all the years of animal research to human testing. That is the only way to determine if a vaccine is effective in preventing infection in people, and the only way we will ever develop a vaccine."

Riri Shibata, D.V.M., Ph.D.
Scientist

"Helping to take VaxGen public in 1999 was a once-in-a-lifetime opportunity. But I am equally gratified by the work we have accomplished in developing the infrastructure for a public company and ensuring that our development projects continue on time and on budget."

Carter Lee, M.B.A.
Senior Vice President
Finance & Administration

"As founder of the International Vaccine Institute, I have seen how important proactive international development campaigns are for vaccines. That's why we're putting so much effort here on working with international agencies such as UNAIDS, the World Health Organization and the World Bank, as well as and private foundations, to plan for the introduction and distribution of AIDSVAX if it proves effective."

Seung-il Shin, Ph.D.
Senior Advisor
International Development

"The success so far of our trials has established us as a leader in AIDS vaccine clinical development. As the first company to conduct Phase III trials for an AIDS vaccine, we realized we had a special responsibility, especially to the volunteers. That's why we designed safety protocols and ethical practices that we believe set a new standard for clinical trials. I think it's a big reason why the trials have progressed so well."

Karin Orelind
Clinical Program Manager

"VaxGen has proved the skeptics wrong at every step. They said you couldn't protect chimps against HIV. We did. They said we'd fail in Phase I and II trials. We didn't. Then they said we'd never be able to enroll the Phase III trials and even if we did we'd have trouble keeping volunteers. Wrong again. But I guess they don't call it conventional wisdom for nothing."

William Heyward, M.D., M.P.H.
Vice President
International Clinical Research

12

13

VINJE DESIGN INC

VAXGEN ANNUAL REPORT 2000

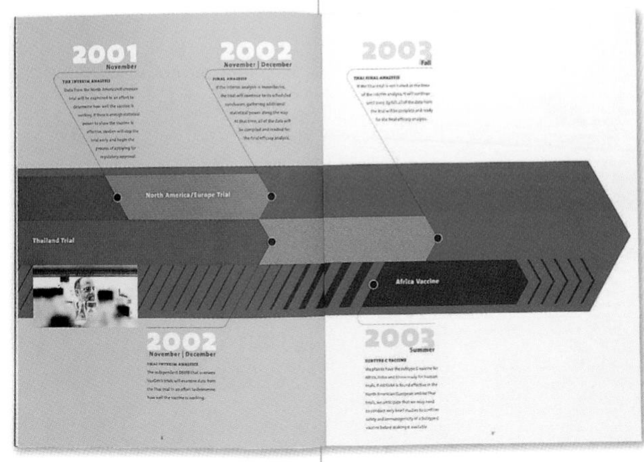

Ascend
amara holdings limited annual report 2001 Ascend

SINGAPORE

ART DIRECTORS:
LENG SOH
PANN LIM
ROY POH

DESIGNERS:
LENG SOH
PANN LIM
ROY POH

ILLUSTRATORS:
LENG SOH
PANN LIM
ROY POH

CLIENT:
AMARA SINGAPORE

SOFTWARE AND HARDWARE:
FREEHAND
PHOTOSHOP
MAC

MATERIALS:
ART PAPER + MAN-MADE GRASS PATCH

PRINTING:
5CX5C + GLOSS VARNISH

KINETIC SINGAPORE
ASCEND

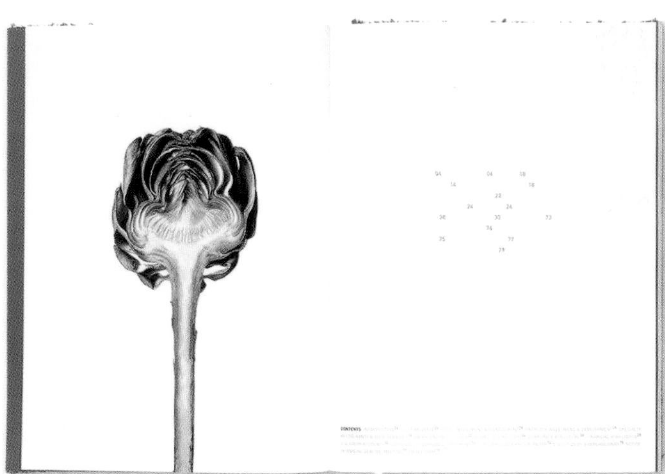

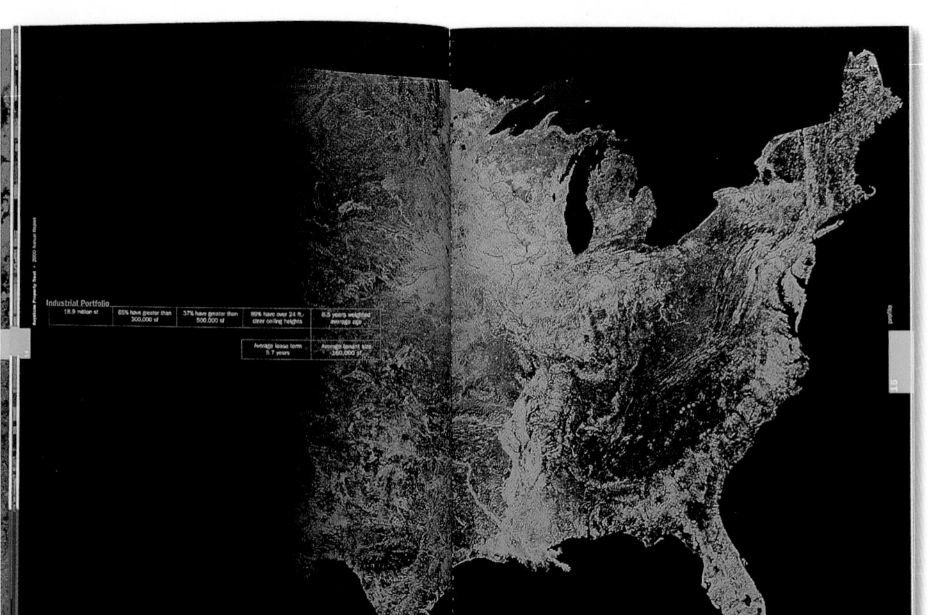

USA

ALLEMANN ALMQUIST & JONES

KEYSTONE PROPERTY TRUST
ANNUAL REPORT 2000

ART DIRECTOR:
JAN ALMQUIST

DESIGNER:
ANNE WREN

PHOTOGRAPHER:
CAMERON DAVIDSON

CLIENT:
KEYSTONE PROPERTY TRUST

SOFTWARE AND HARDWARE:
ILLUSTRATOR
PHOTOSHOP
QUARKXPRESS
MAC G4

MATERIALS:
POTLATCH McCOY GLOSS

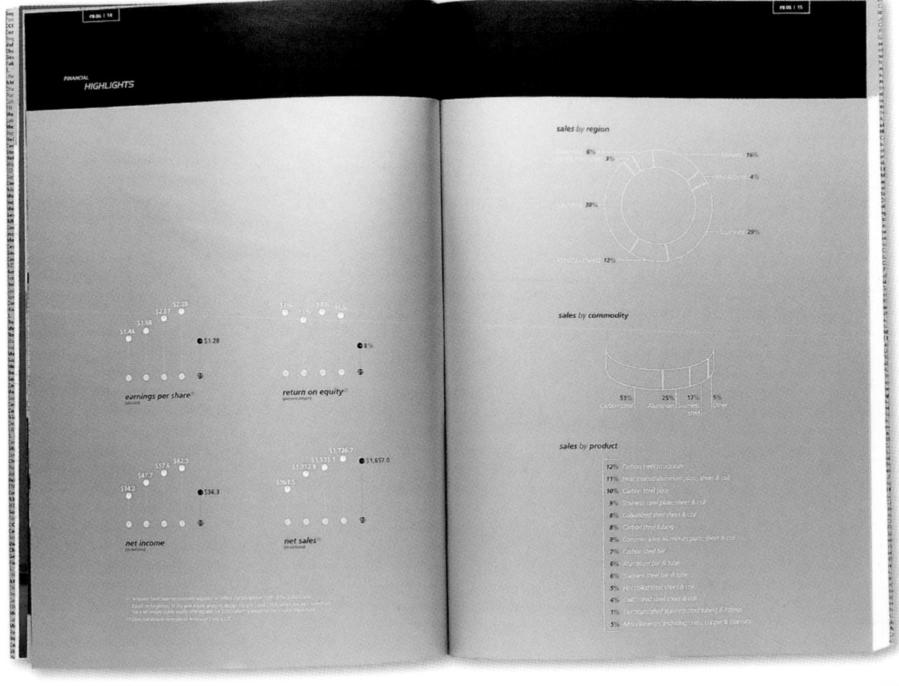

METAL
RS01

USA

ART DIRECTOR:
PEAT JARIYA

DESIGNERS:
PEAT JARIYA
GABE SCHREIBER

CLIENT:
RELIANCE STEEL
& ALU

SOFTWARE AND
HARDWARE:
ILLUSTRATOR
PAGEMAKER
PHOTOSHOP
MAC G4

MATERIALS:
POTLATCH M[C]COY

PRINTING:
AW

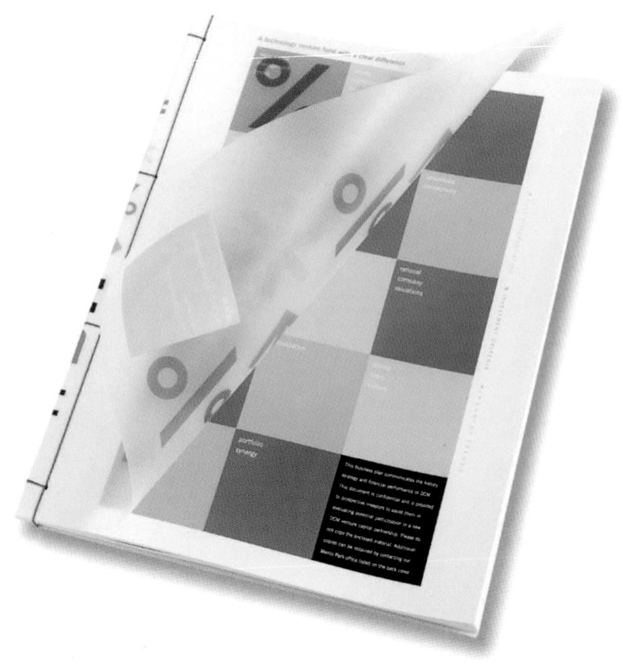

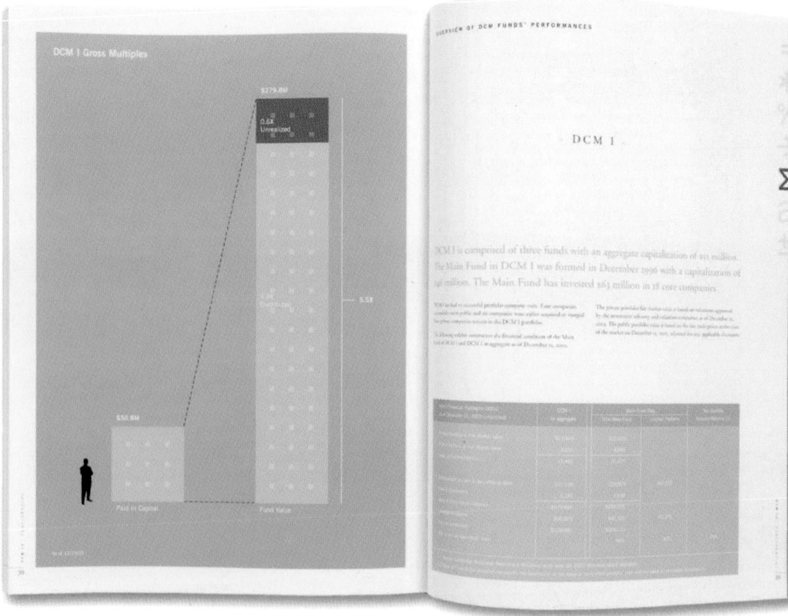

GEE + CHUNG DESIGN

DCM IV Offering Memorandum

ART DIRECTOR:	DESIGNERS:	CLIENT:	TOOLS:	MATERIALS:
Earl Gee	Earl Gee Fani Chung	DCM—Doll Capital Management	Adobe Photoshop Adobe InDesign	Stora Enso Centura Dull 100 lb (text)

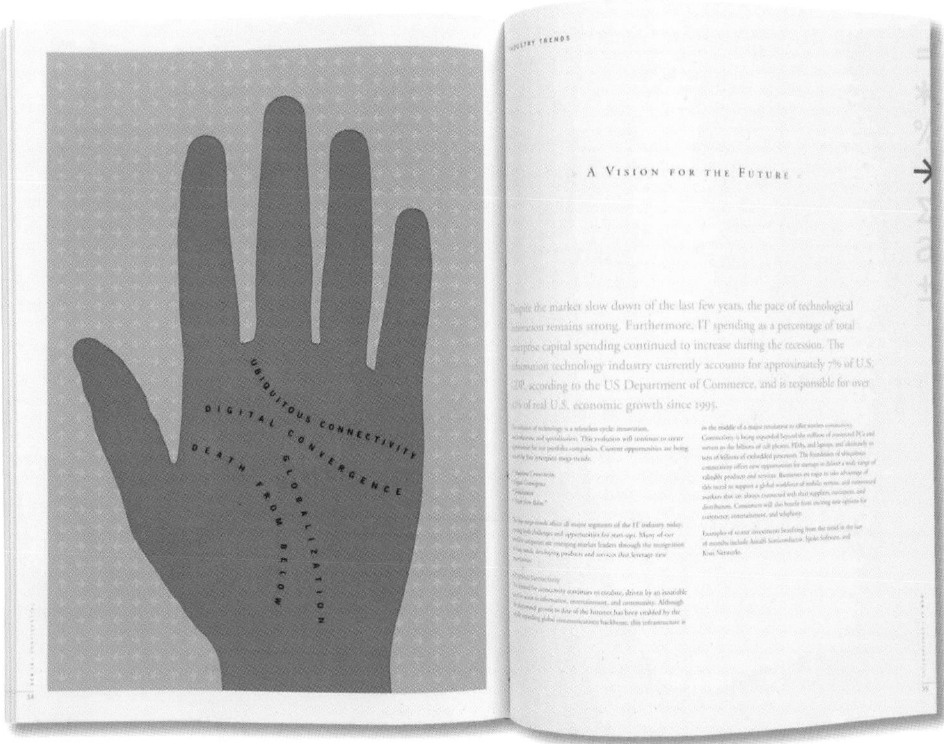
UBIQUITOUS CONNECTIVITY
DIGITAL CONVERGENCE
GLOBALIZATION
DEATH FROM BELOW
A Vision for the Future

輪
廻
転
生
CASE STUDY
A Cycle of Collaborations

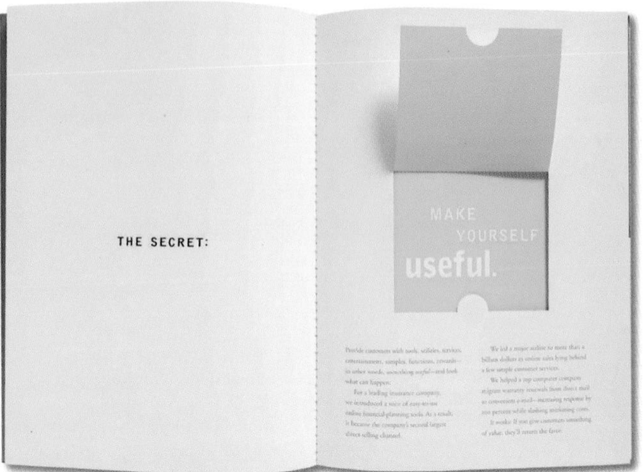

THE DAVE AND ALEX SHOW

Modem Media View Book

ART DIRECTORS:
Alexander Isley
Dave Goldenber

DESIGNER:
Tracie Rosenkopf-Lissauer

CLIENT:
Modem Media

TOOLS:
QuarkXPress

MATERIALS:
Monadnock

WE'RE GOING TO DO IT

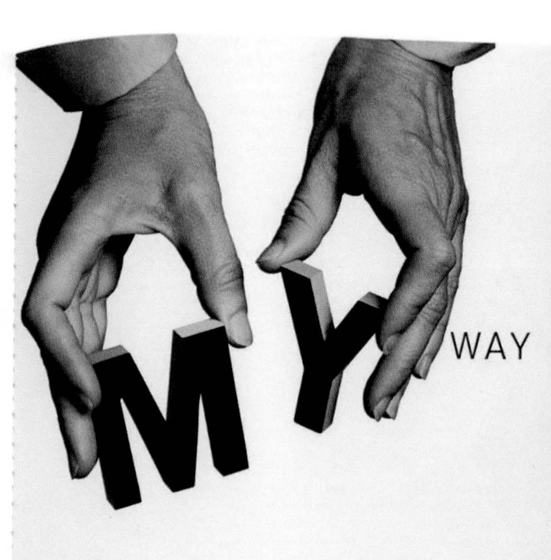

SALTERBAXTER

Boodle Hatfield Corporate Brochure

ART DIRECTOR:	**DESIGNER:**	**CLIENT:**	**TOOLS:**	**MATERIALS:**
Alan Delgado	Alan Delgado	Boodle Hatfield	QuarkXPress	Rives Reflections (cover) Robert Horne Natural (text)

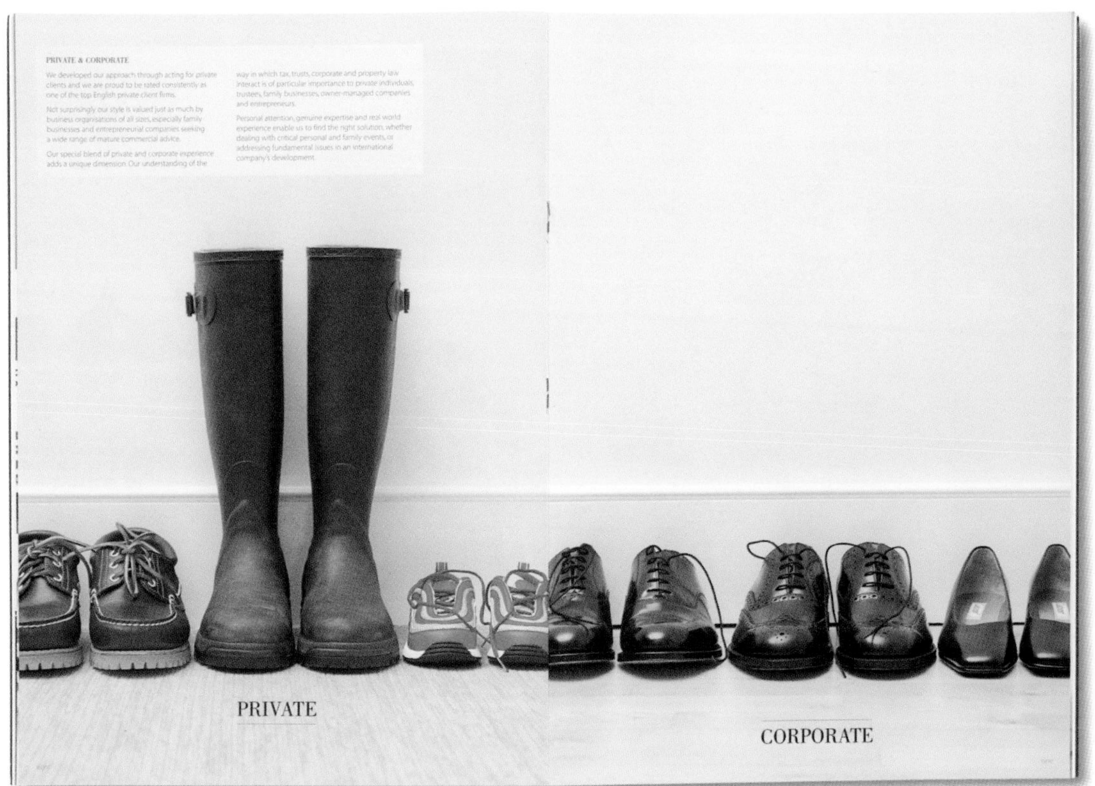

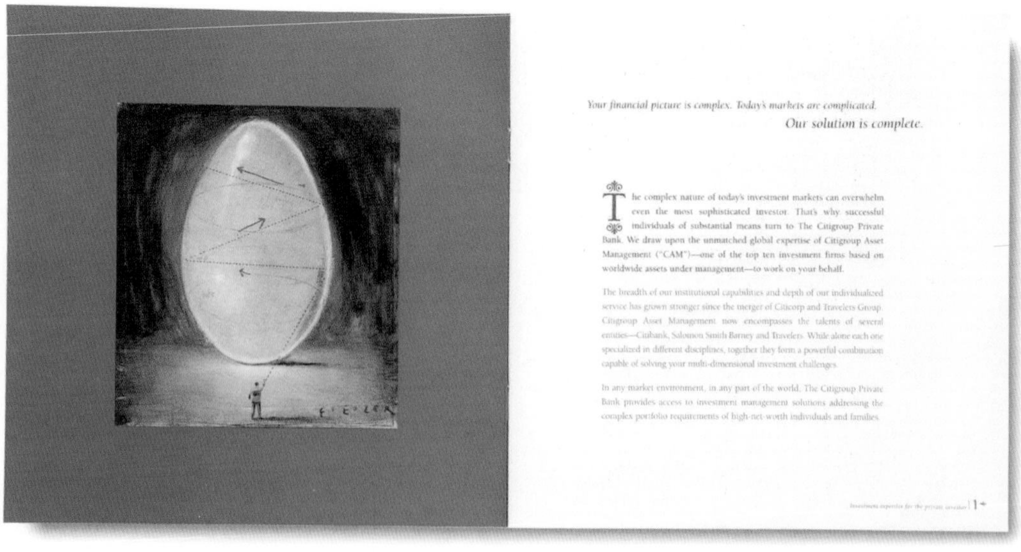

BANDUJO DONKER & BROTHERS

Citigroup Private Bank—Investment Expertise

ART DIRECTOR: Bob Brothers

DESIGNER: Laura Astuto

CLIENT: Citigroup Private Bank

TOOLS: Adobe Photoshop, QuarkXPress

MATERIALS: Mohawk Navajo

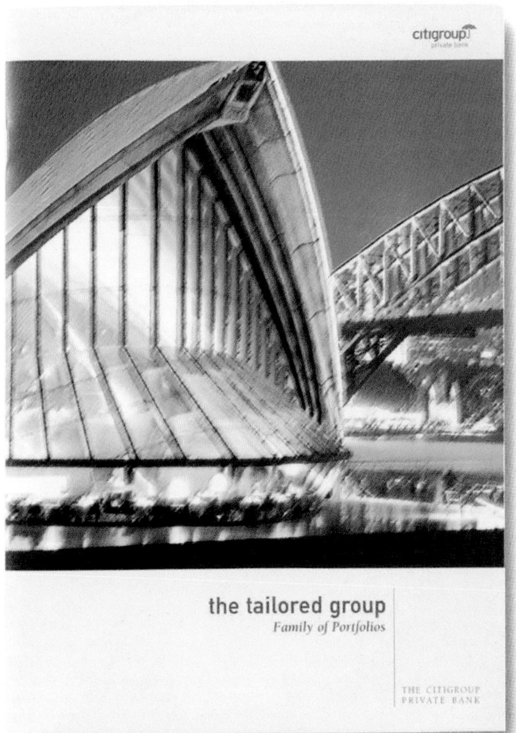

BANDUJO DONKER & BROTHERS

Citigroup Private Bank–The Tailored Group

ART DIRECTOR:	DESIGNER:	CLIENT:	TOOLS:	MATERIALS:
Bob Brothers	Laura Astuto	Citigroup Private Bank	Adobe Photoshop QuarkXPress	Mohawk Navajo

PENTAGRAM DESIGN/SF

Sales Brochure

ART DIRECTOR:
Kit Hinrichs

DESIGNER:
Laura Scott

CLIENT:
Muzak

TOOLS:
Adobe Photoshop
Adobe Illustrator
QuarkXPress

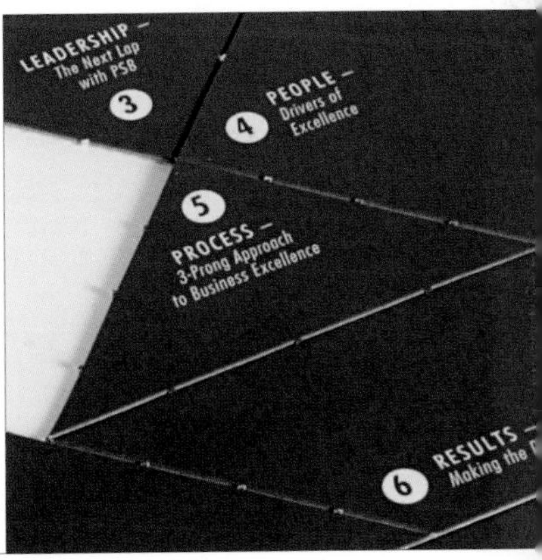

ZUCCHINI DESIGN PTE LTD

PSB Consulting Marketing Brochure

ART DIRECTOR:
Tew Sun Ne

DESIGNER:
Tew Sun Ne

CLIENT:
PSB Corporation

TOOLS:
Macromedia Freehand

MATERIALS:
Translucent PVC 012 mm (cover sleeve)
Centuri White 230 gsm (cover)
Aspire 130 gsm (text)

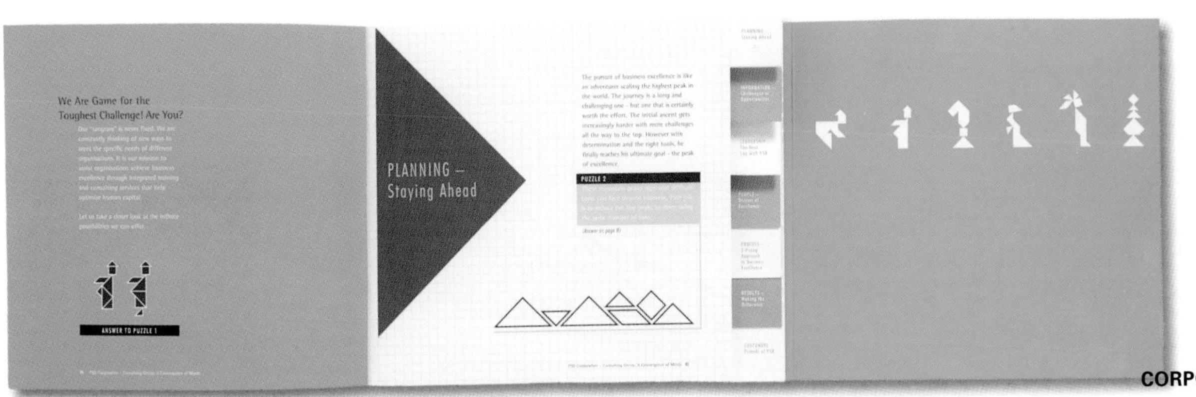

We Are Game for the Toughest Challenge! Are You?
ANSWER TO PUZZLE 1
PLANNING – Staying Ahead

BAUMANN & BAUMANN

Siemens Brand Elements

ART DIRECTORS:
Barbara and Gerd Baumann

DESIGNERS:
Barbara and Gerd Baumann

CLIENT:
Siemens AG Corporate Communications

TOOLS:
Adobe InDesign
Adobe Photoshop
Macromedia Freehand

MATERIALS:
Phoenix Motion

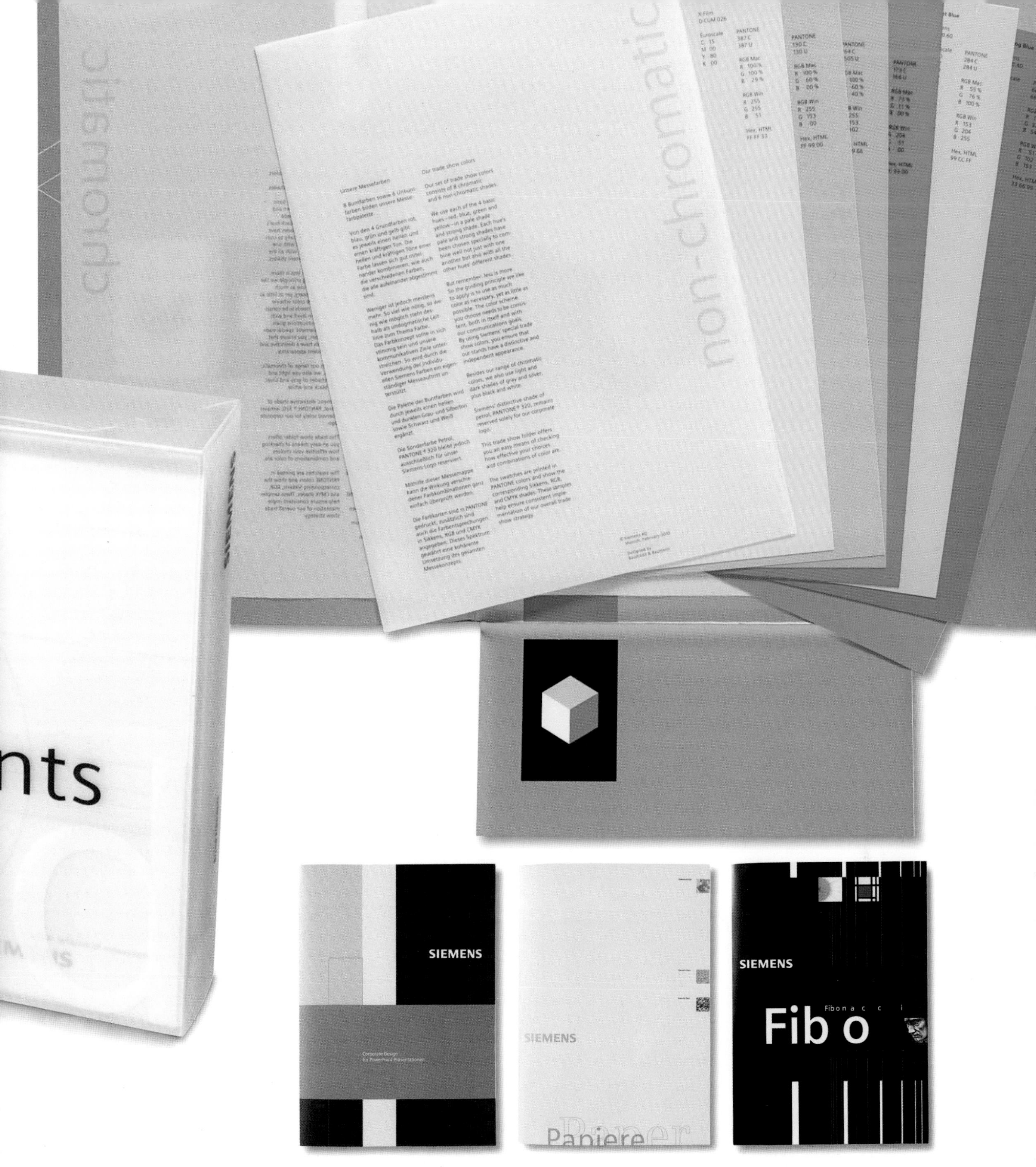
non-chromatic
SIEMENS
Corporate Design
für PowerPoint Präsentationen
SIEMENS
Papiere
SIEMENS
Fibonacci
Fib o

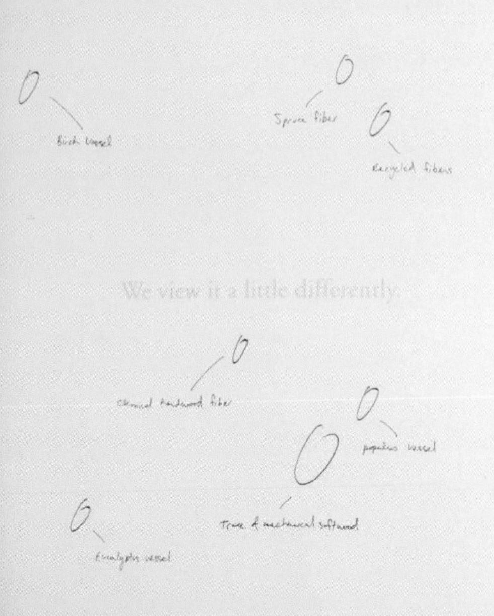

So you see, at Econotech Services, we are experts in seeing what others don't. Specifically in the areas of pulping, bleaching, pulp and paper testing, microscopy & wood technology, process chemical analyses and environmental analyses. And since the company was formed in 1972, we've grown to be one of the largest independent pulp and paper testing laboratories in the world.

Accurate, rapid and reliable results are key to our company's substantial expansion, as is the recognized knowledge of our staff. Our initial team of 11 experts has grown to include over 30 research professionals with expertise in chip testing, pulping, bleaching, pulp and paper testing, dissolving pulp evaluation, microscopy, environmental analysis and testing of process samples and liquors. Within a single 19,000 square foot facility, Econotech can perform over 400 analytical tests on everything from wood to finished product, around 100 tests on pulp and paper products and over 50 different microscopy tests.

Econotech's international clientele includes pulp and paper mills, equipment suppliers, chemical suppliers, consulting engineers and universities. In addition to providing unbiased, independent and confidential evaluations of new processes or chemicals, Econotech assists clients in the development of new equipment, the design of new mills and the evaluation of chemical costs involved in mill modernization. >>

me see this as a cover

HANGAR 18 CREATIVE GROUP

Econotech Brochure

DESIGNER: Kim Wolf

CLIENT: Econotech Services

TOOLS: QuarkXPress

MATERIALS: Cougar Opaque (text and cover)

04. MICROSCOPY AND WOOD TECHNOLOGY

07.98

PULP QUALITY IS DIRECTLY RELATED TO FIBER QUALITY

Microscopy is an indispensable testing discipline for the pulp and paper industry. The primary application is fiber analysis, which provides detailed evaluations of wood species and pulp type in paper, pulp and wood samples.

Contaminant identification is also a large portion of the work we do in the Microscopy Department. This provides valuable assistance in process troubleshooting. In addition to light microscopic techniques, we have access to scanning electron microscopy and Fourier Transform infra-red analysis. Digital photomicrographs enhance reports and provide instant visualization of contaminants and defects.

Microscopy is an art as much as a science and requires many years of training and experience to become proficient. The Microscopy Group has over 30 years combined experience in analyzing the untold variety of samples that are submitted. We have extensive reference resources including natural and man-made fibers, particle and contaminant samples and permanent slides. >>

ONLY 4% OF MAIL IS PERSONAL

HALLMARK LOYALTY

How to Stand Out in the Crowd: Profiting from Personalization

ART DIRECTOR:	**EDITORIAL DIRECTOR:**	**PHOTOGRAPHY:**	**CLIENT:**	**TOOLS:**	**MATERIALS:**
Christopher Huelshorst	Stacey Hsu	Ambrosi & Associates, Chicago	State Farm	QuarkXPress	Mohawk Superfine
DESIGNER:	**COPYWRITER:**	**PRINTER:**			
Christine Taylor	Janet Walnik	Nies Artcraft, St. Louis			

DIRECTIONS#3
TRENDS IN CSR REPORTING 2002-03
A JOINT REPORT BY SALTERBAXTER & CONTEXT
context
salterbaxter

SALTERBAXTER

Directions 3 Report

ART DIRECTOR:
Alan Delgado

DESIGNER:
Alan Delgado

CLIENT:
Salterbaxter

TOOLS:
QuarkXPress

MATERIALS:
Flockage cover

WEYMOUTH DESIGN

Sappi 2002 Annual Report Show

ART DIRECTOR:
Tom Laidlaw

DESIGNERS:
Robert Krivicich
Brad Lewthwaite

CLIENT:
Sappi Fine Paper
North America

TOOLS:
QuarkXPress
Adobe Photoshop

MATERIALS:
Sappi Fine Paper

CURRENTLY
THERE IS NO FDA APPROVED
MEDICAL TREATMENT WHICH
CREATES A SIGNIFICANT MEDICAL
AND MARKET OPPORTUNITY.

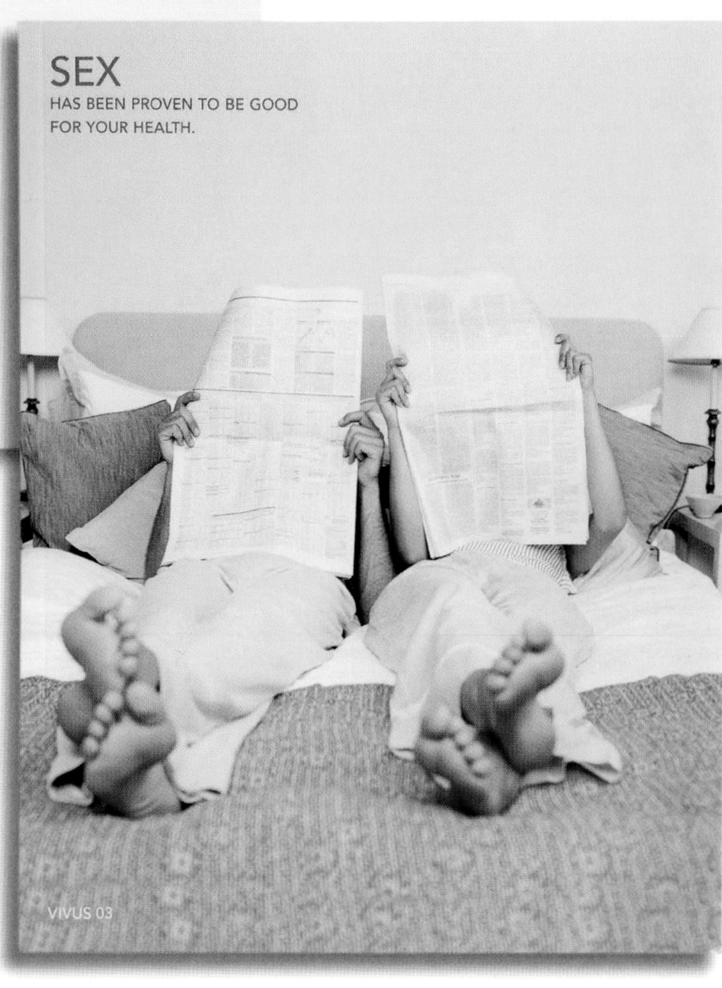

SEX
HAS BEEN PROVEN TO BE GOOD
FOR YOUR HEALTH.
VIVUS 03

HOWRY DESIGN ASSOCIATES

Viuus 2003 Annual Report

ART DIRECTOR:
Jill Howry

DESIGNER:
Ty Whittington

CLIENT:
Vivus Inc

TOOLS:
Adobe Photoshop
QuarkXPress

MATERIALS:
Utopia II matte 80 lb

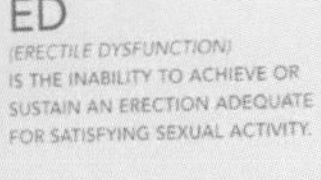

ED
(ERECTILE DYSFUNCTION)
IS THE INABILITY TO ACHIEVE OR
SUSTAIN AN ERECTION ADEQUATE
FOR SATISFYING SEXUAL ACTIVITY.

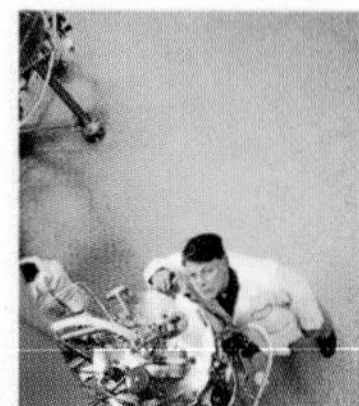

Millipore 2002 Annual Report
"For ABX-EGF we opted for an IgG2 subclass, and the challenge was to come up with an antibody that had suitable affinity and suitable selectivity for the cell-surface EGF receptor, so that it would have potential as a therapeutic. That antibody is now in clinical trials."

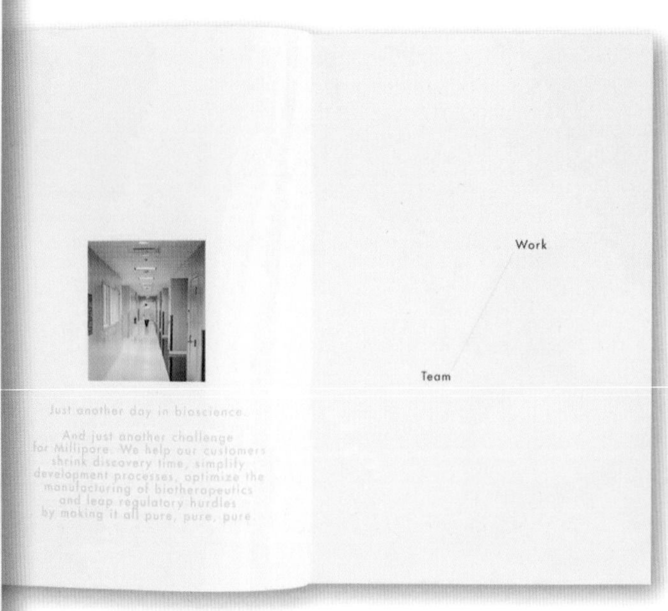

Work
Team
Just another day in bioscience.
And just another challenge for Millipore. We help our customers shrink discovery time, simplify development processes, optimize the manufacturing of biotherapeutics and leap regulatory hurdles by making it all pure, pure, pure.

WEYMOUTH DESIGN

Millipore AR 2003

ART DIRECTOR:	DESIGNER:	WRITER:	PHOTOGRAPHER:	TOOLS:	MATERIALS:
Michael Weymouth	Bob Kellerman	Tom Anderson	Michael Weymouth	Adobe Photoshop Adobe Illustrator QuarkXPress	100 lb Sappi McCoy matte (cover) 100 lb Sappi McCoy matte (text)

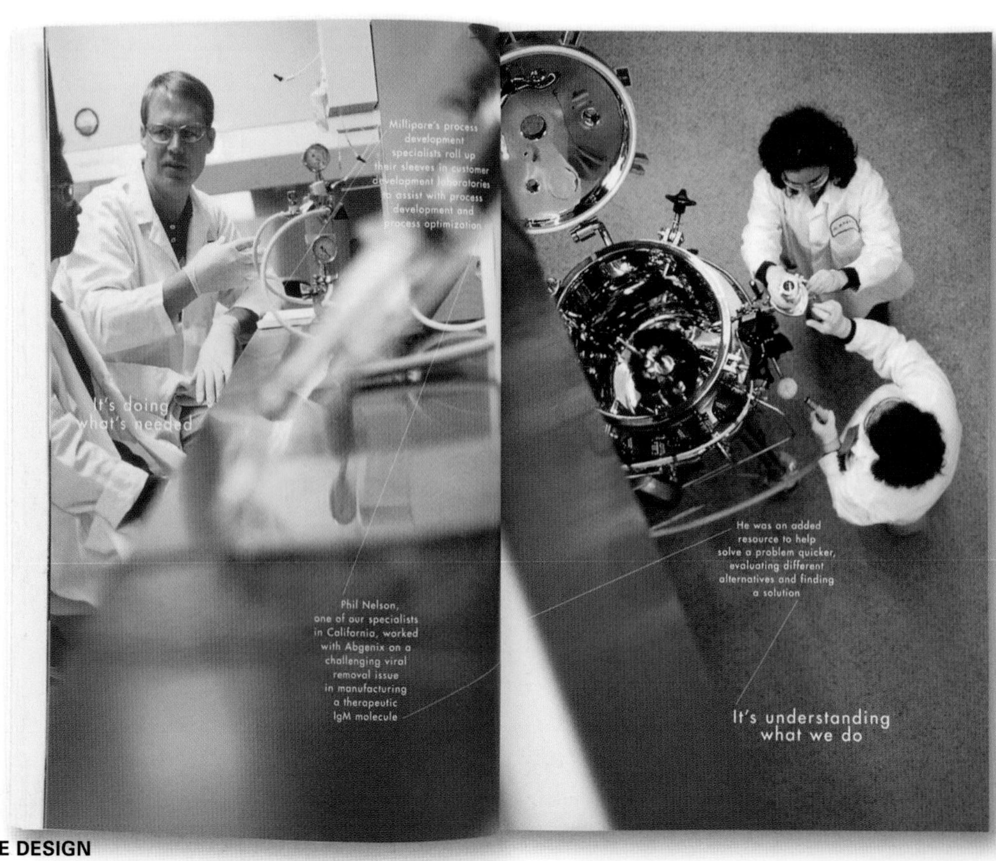

SALTERBAXTER

British Library Annual Report 2002-2003

ART DIRECTOR:	**DESIGNER:**	**CLIENT:**	**TOOLS:**	**MATERIALS:**
Penny Baxter	Hannah Griffiths	British Library	QuarkXPress	Hello Silk 150 gsm (text) Arjo Wiggins "Impressions Design" 300 gsm (cover)

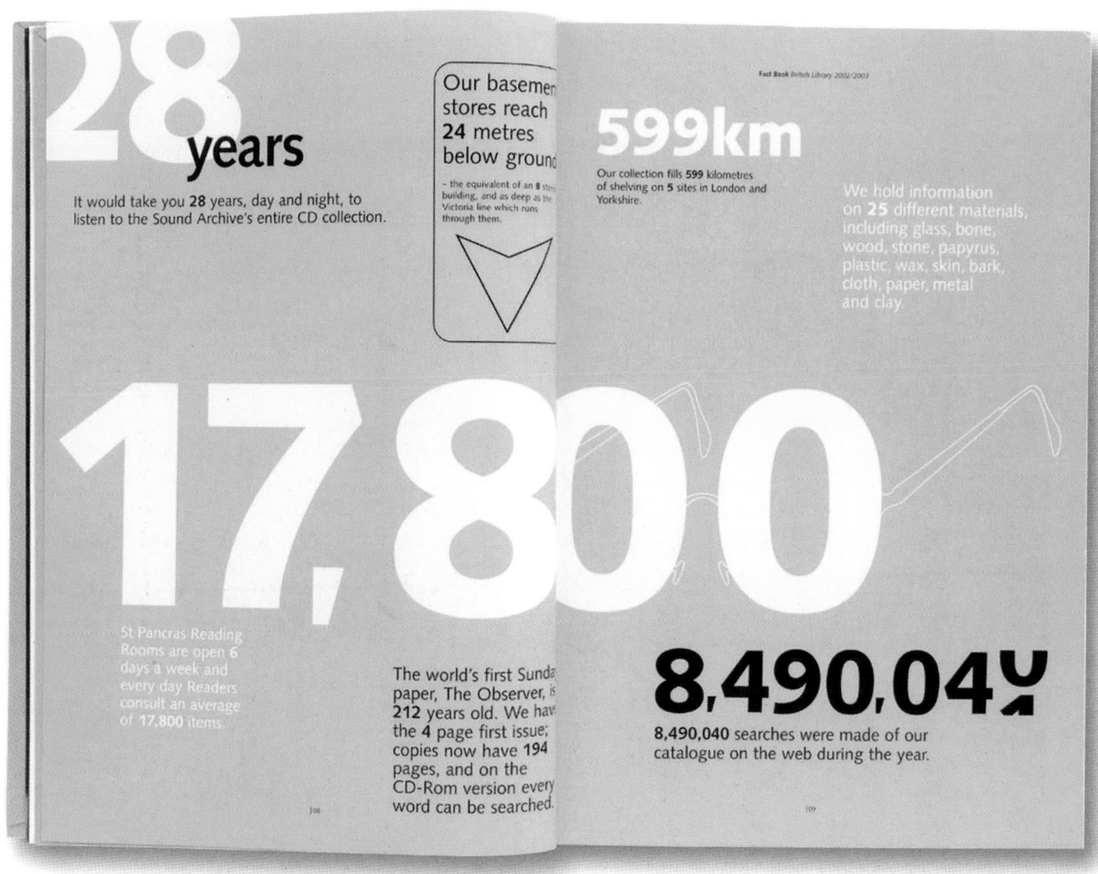

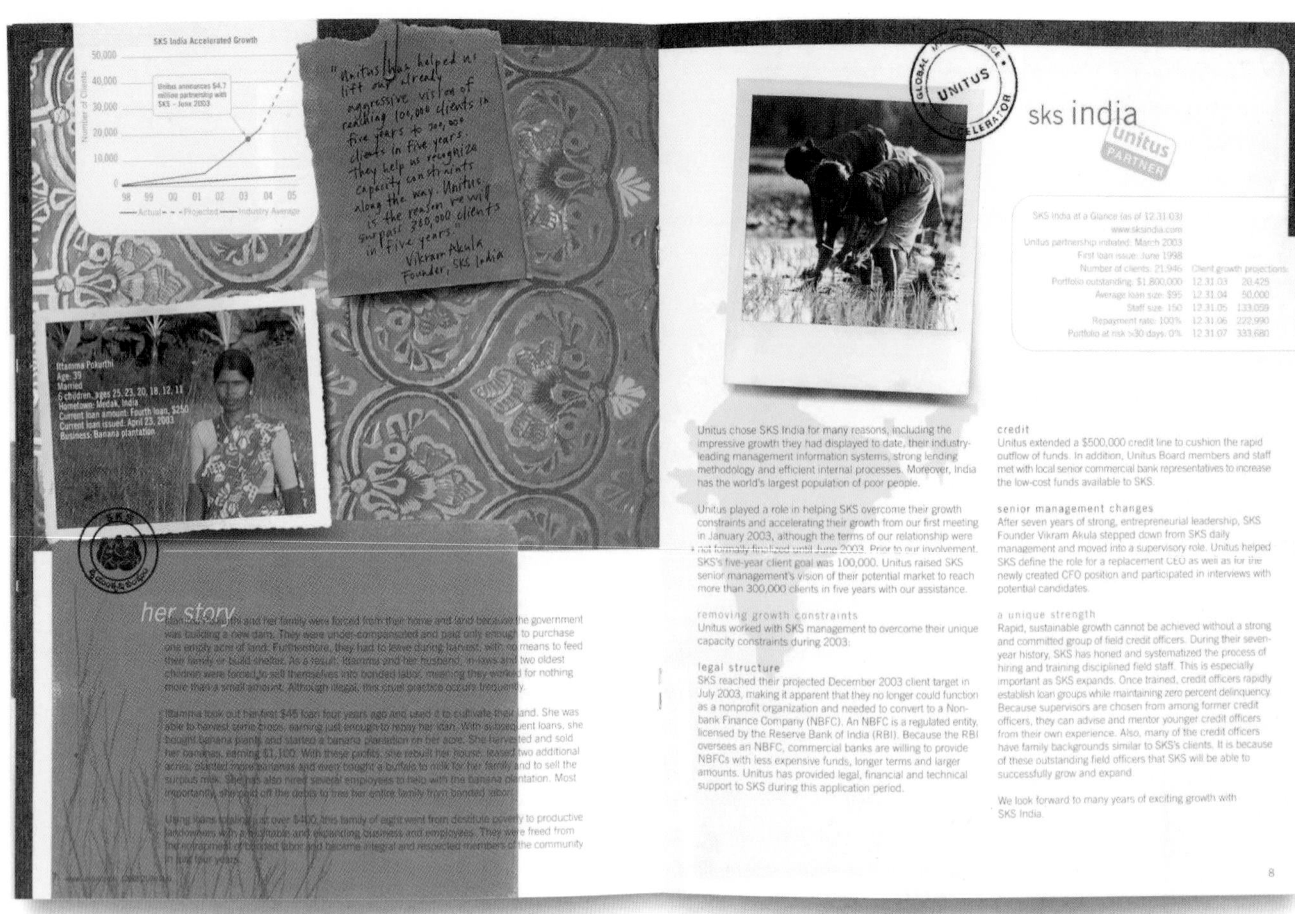

MONSTER DESIGN

Unitus Annual Report

ART DIRECTORS:
Theresa Monica
Hannah Wygal

DESIGNER:
Madeleine Eiche

CLIENT:
Unitus

TOOLS:
Adobe Photoshop
Macromedia Freehand
QuarkXPress

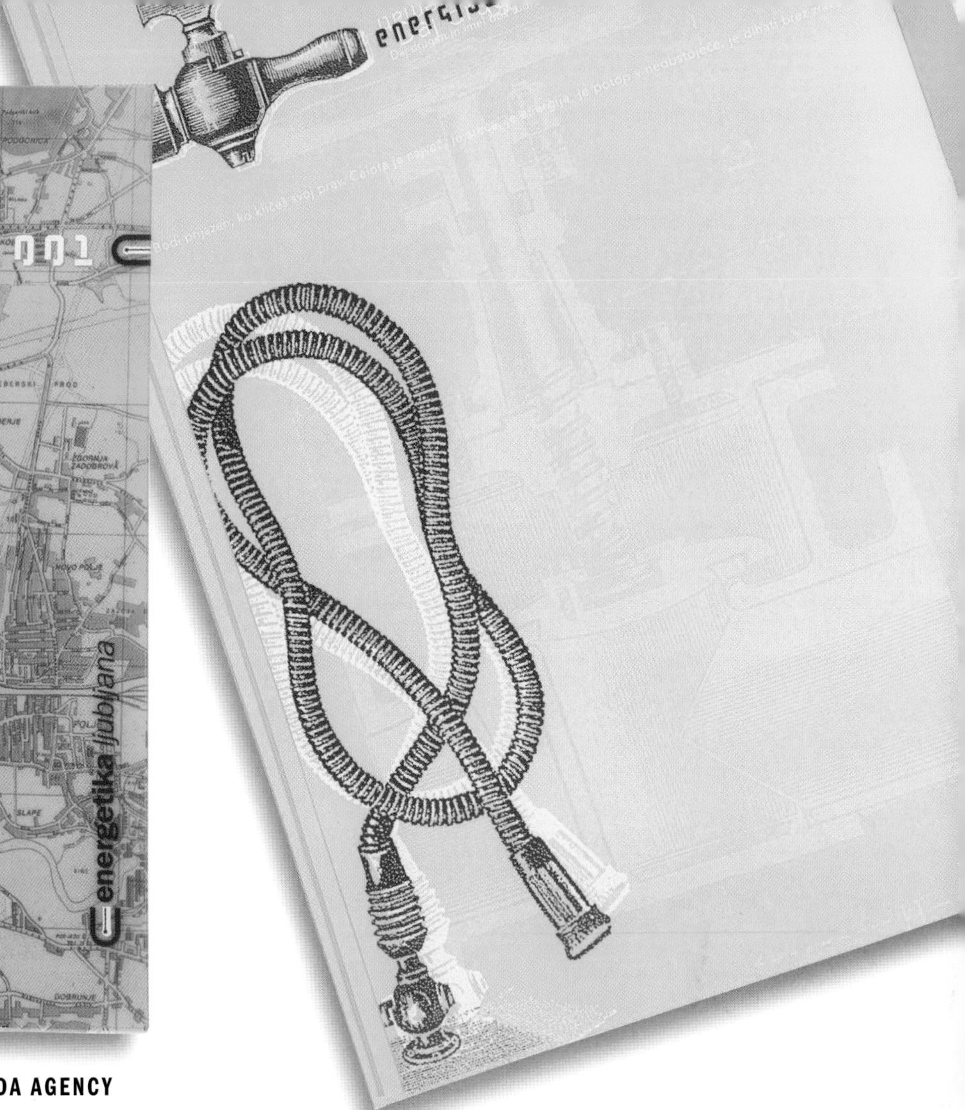

IMELDA AGENCY

Corporate Annual Report

Art Director:	Designer:	Client:	Materials:
Urukalo Saso	Urukalo Saso	Energetika Ljublyana	on offset

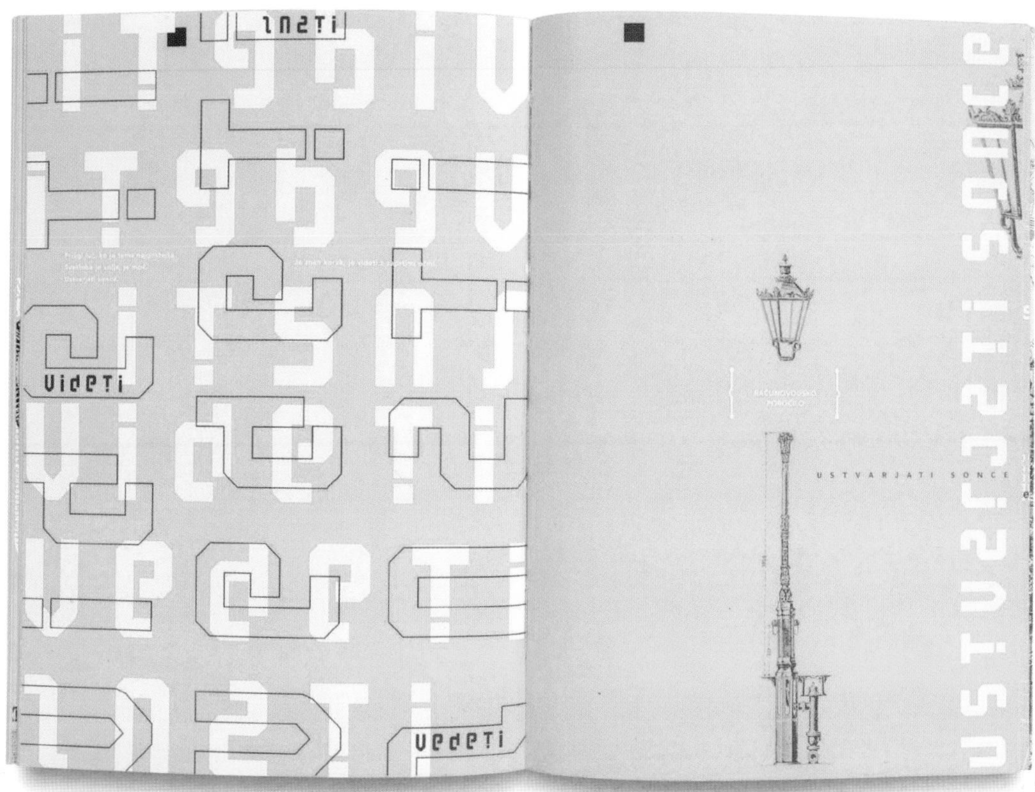

POPCORN INITIATIVE

KUA 2003 Annual Report—ON

ART DIRECTOR:
Chris Jones

DESIGNERS:
Chris Jones
Roger Wood

CLIENT:
Chris Gent, Kissimmee Utility Authority

TOOLS:
Adobe InDesign
Adobe Illustrator

MATERIALS:
Fox River
Coronado SST
Stipple 80 lb (cover)
formed rubber

HORNALL ANDERSON DESIGN WORKS, INC.

Tree Top 2003 Annual Report

ART DIRECTOR:
Katha Dalton

DESIGNERS:
Katha Dalton
Tiffany Place
John Anderle
Beckon Wyld

CLIENT:
Tree Top

TOOLS:
Adobe Photoshop
QuarkXPress

MATERIALS:
Mohawk 100 lb Superfine Text Smooth Ultrawhite (text)
Mohawk 80 lb Superfine Text Smooth Ultrawhite (inserts)
Mohawk 100 lb Superfine Cover Smooth Ultrawhite (cover)

WEYMOUTH DESIGN

Courier 2003 Annual Report

ART DIRECTOR:	DESIGNER:	CLIENT:	TOOLS:	MATERIALS:
Robert Krivicich	Aaron Haesaert	Courier Corporation	Adobe Photoshop Adobe Illustrator QuarkXPress	Sappi McCoy, Finch Opaque

1.
2.
3.
4.
5.
6.
7.
8.
9.
10.
pay attention
to shareholders
Chairman's Letter
37
Dear Shareholders, Customers, Employees and Friends: Another challenging year, finishing with another double-digit earnings increase. It's a story that never grows old. The challenges for Courier in fiscal 2003 were substantial, but so was our success as we applied our proven formula of focused strategy and enthusiastic, disciplined execution. People pitched in at every level of the company to overcome an adverse retail environment, delivering outstanding service that distinguished us from competitors and helped us to post a modest sales increase. At the same time, through innovations in technology, marketing, and process management, we were able to generate the solid earnings people have come to expect from Courier while laying the foundation for more top-line growth in the future.
Quantitative Highlights Included the Following:
— Income from continuing operations rose to a record $19.3 million, or $2.37 per diluted share on a post-split basis, up 18% from fiscal 2002 results of $16.3 million or $2.04 per diluted share. It was our seventh straight year of double-digit earnings growth.
$2.5M

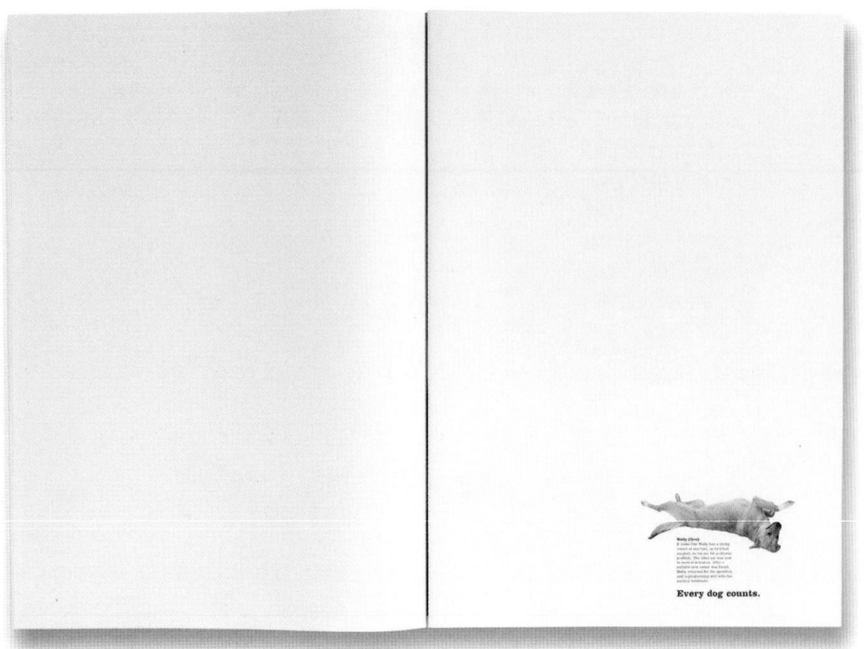

THE CHASE
Manchester Dogs' Home

Art Director:
Harriet Devoy
Designer:
Steve Royle
Client:
Manchester Dogs' Home
Software:
QuarkXPress, Adobe Illustrator, Adobe Photoshop
Paper/Materials:
Neptune Unique

6,796 dogs
Manchester Dogs' Home Annual Review 2001-2002

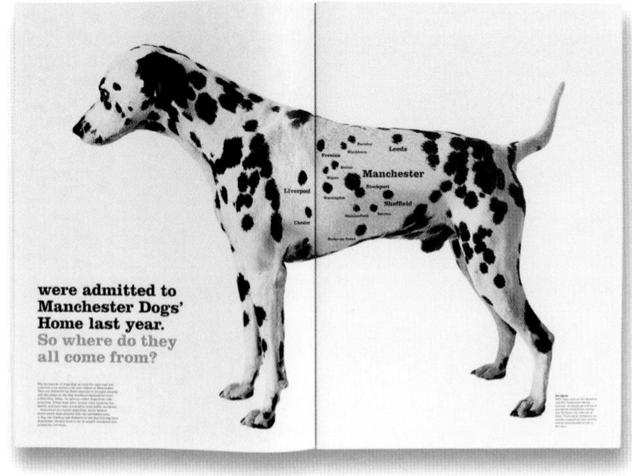

were admitted to Manchester Dogs' Home last year.
So where do they all come from?
Liverpool
Manchester
Leeds
Sheffield

9 out of 10 dogs were happily rehomed. That's 5,947 in total.

Chairmans' Report
What have we achieved this year?

WE BUILD UNDERSTANDING

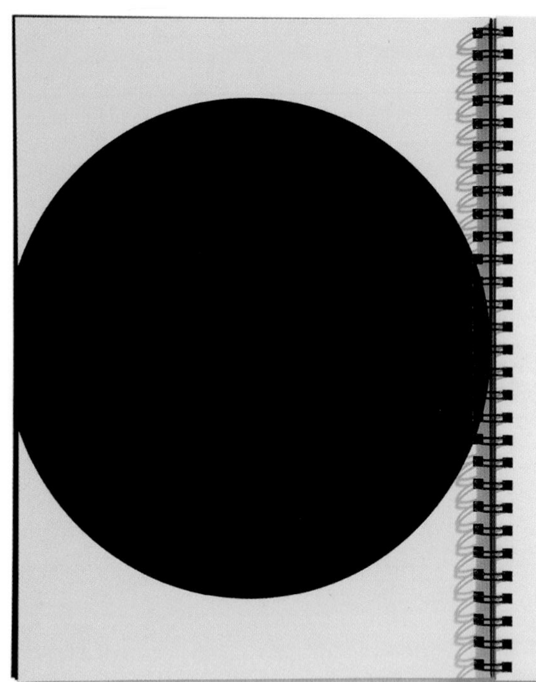

MESSAGE FROM THE PRESIDENT

When I sit down with my son and talk about his career plans, or how he views world issues, or... just life, I'm struck by the mind-boggling pace and extent of social change. The world his generation is growing up in is utterly unpredictable. Its distinguishing feature is an incredibly complicated environment of choice. Choice that is more promising, yet more forbidding, than anything my generation faced. What if you could genetically alter your unborn child? What if you had to undergo an eye scan each time you visited a bank, voted, or applied for insurance? What if the world had a CEO? And countries had no borders? These are questions confronted by no previous generation.

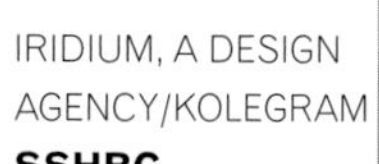

IRIDIUM, A DESIGN AGENCY/KOLEGRAM
SSHRC
Annual Report

Art Directors:
Jean-Luc Denat,
Mario L'Écuyer
Designers:
Mario L'Écuyer,
David Daigle
Client:
SSHRC
Software:
QuarkXPress,
Adobe Illustrator,
Adobe Photoshop
Paper/Materials:
Sappi Lustro Dull,
Domtar Cornwall
Pinweave, Rolland
Opaque Smooth

PRODUCT
AND SERVICE
BROCHURES

DESIGN FIRM › Kesselskramer
ART DIRECTOR › Erik Kessels
DESIGNER › Karen Heuter
ILLUSTRATORS/PHOTOGRAPHERS › Stang, Bianca Pilet
COPYWRITER › David Bell
CLIENT › Do
TOOLS (SOFTWARE/PLATFORM) › QuarkXPress, Apple Macintosh
PAPER STOCK/PRINTING PROCESS › Cyclus print
PRINTING PROCESS › Offset, sheet

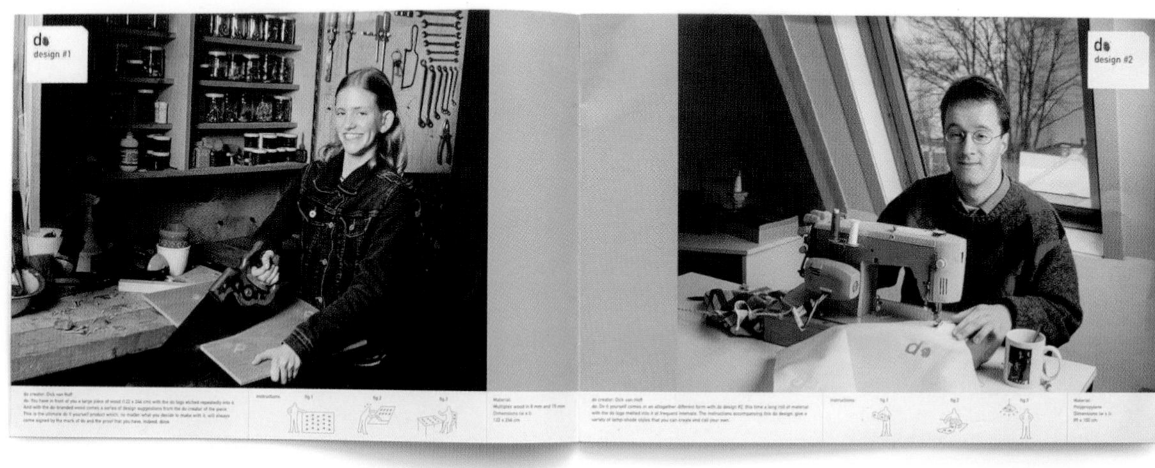

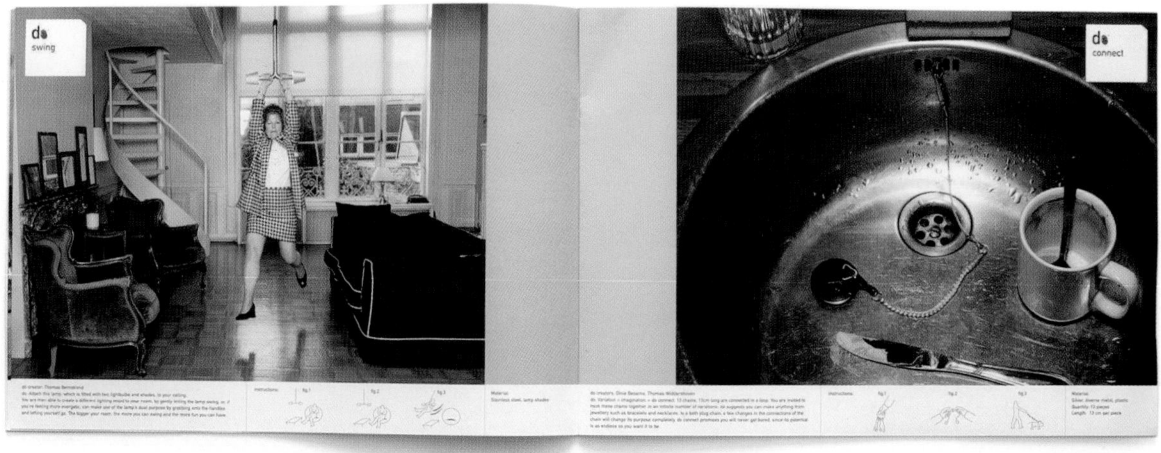

DESIGN FIRM › Zappata Diseñadores S.C.
ART DIRECTOR › Ibo Angulo
DESIGNER › Ibo Angulo
PHOTOGRAPHER › Ricardo Trabulsi
CLIENT › Laura Lavalle
TOOLS (SOFTWARE/PLATFORM) › Photoshop, Freehand
PRINTING PROCESS › Offset

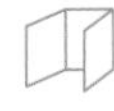

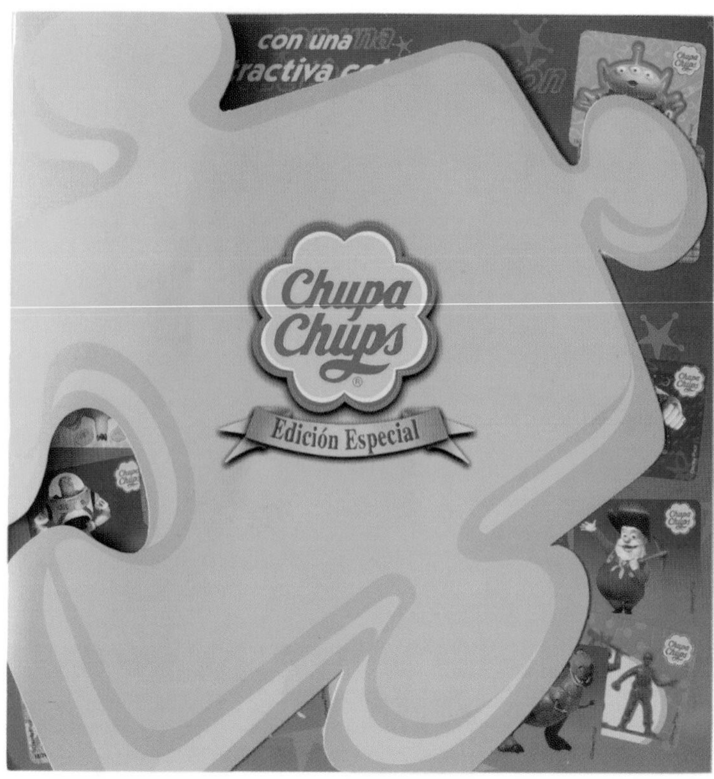

DESIGN FIRM › Zappata Diseñadores S.C.
ART DIRECTOR › Ibo Angulo
DESIGNER › Ibo Angulo
COPYWRITER › © Disney/Pixar
CLIENT › Cupa Chups
TOOLS (SOFTWARE/PLATFORM) › Adobe Illustrator
PRINTING PROCESS › Offset

DESIGN FIRM › 141 Singapore Pte Ltd.
ART DIRECTOR › Winnie Lee
DESIGNER › Wnnie Lee
ILLUSTRATORS/PHOTOGRAPHERS › Tomek and Eryk Photography Pty
COPYWRITER › Kok Chin Yin
CLIENT › Nokia Pte Ltd.
PAPER STOCK › Cover–112gsm GSK transparent paper; text–210 gsm Eagle Silhouette matt artcard
PRINTING PROCESS › Cover–3c x 0c; text–5c x 5c, solid matt artcard

DESIGN FIRM › Palmquist Creative
ART DIRECTORS › Kurt Palmquist, Kelly Bellcour
DESIGNERS › Kurt Palmquist, Kelly Bellcour
PHOTOGRAPHERS › Rob Wilke, Denver Bryan
COPYWRITER › Client
CLIENT › Field & Stream
TOOLS (SOFTWARE/PLATFORM) › Adobe Pagemaker, Illustrator, Macintosh
PAPER STOCK/PRINTING PROCESS › Frostbrite, 80 lb. book, white

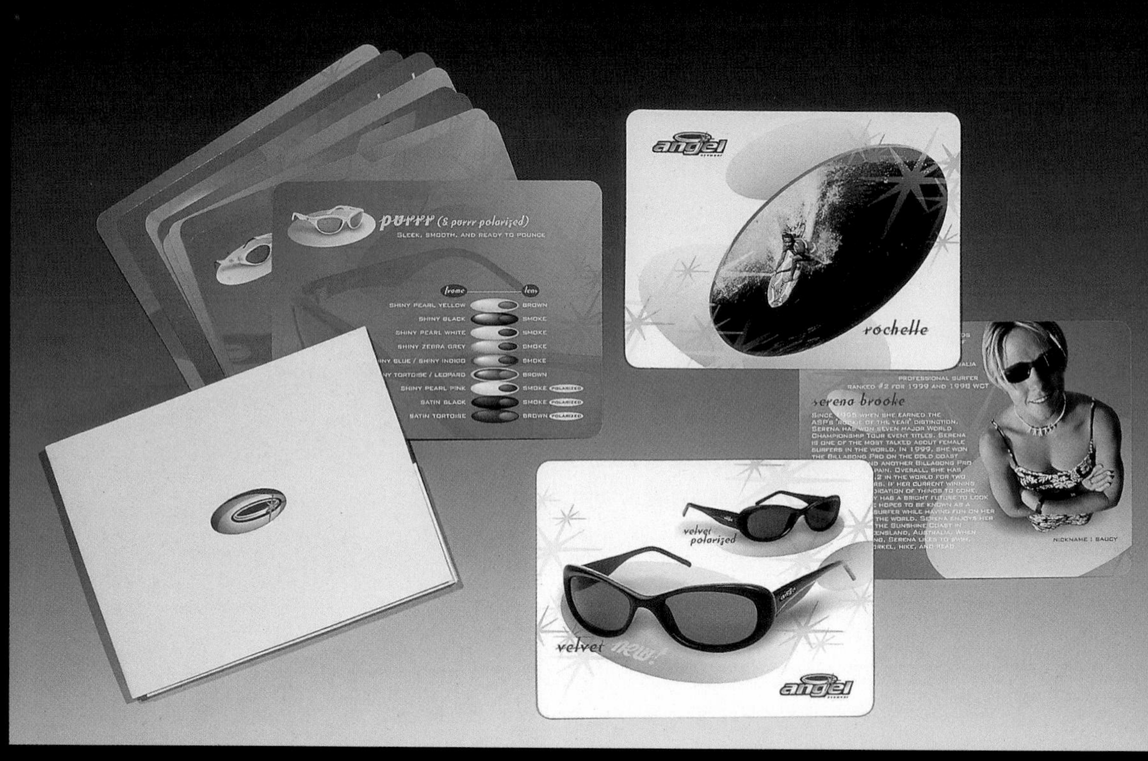

DESIGN FIRM › Alternatives
ART DIRECTOR › Julie Koch-Beinke
DESIGNER › Julie Koch-Beinke
ILLUSTRATOR/PHOTOGRAPHER › Various
CLIENT › Sungold Eyewear
TOOLS (SOFTWARE/PLATFORM) › Illustrator, Macintosh
PAPER STOCK › Metallic pearl white for cover, 100 lb. gloss cover
PRINTING PROCESS › Four-color process

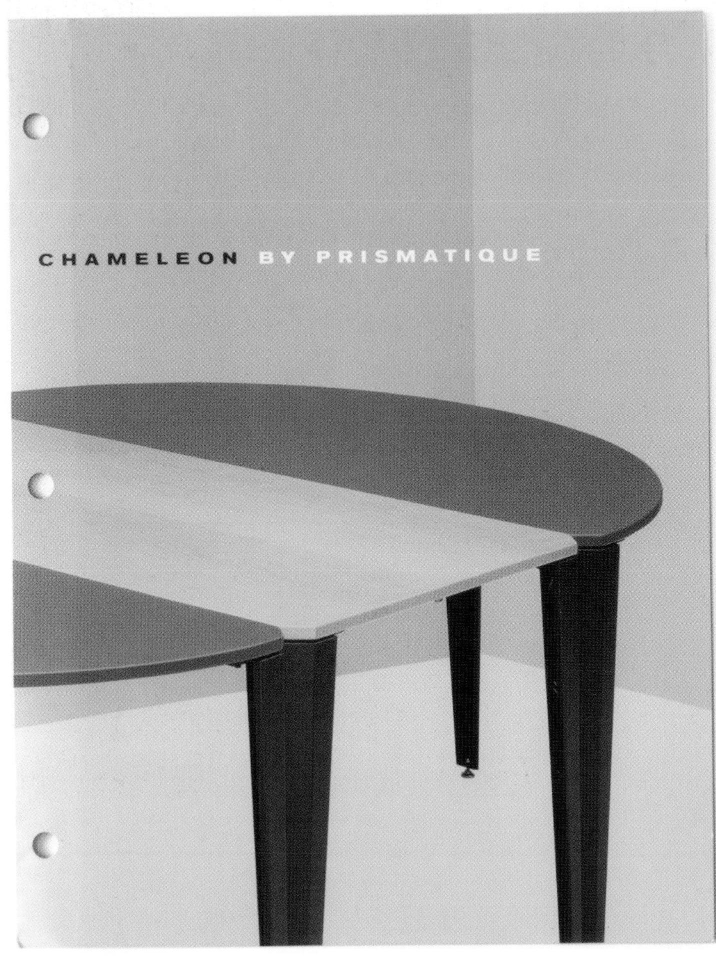

DESIGN FIRM › Dinnick & Howells
ART DIRECTOR › Jonathan Howells
DESIGNERS › Dwayne Dobson, Tracey Hanson
CLIENT › Prismatique
TOOLS (SOFTWARE/PLATFORM) › Macintosh G3, Illustrator, Photoshop

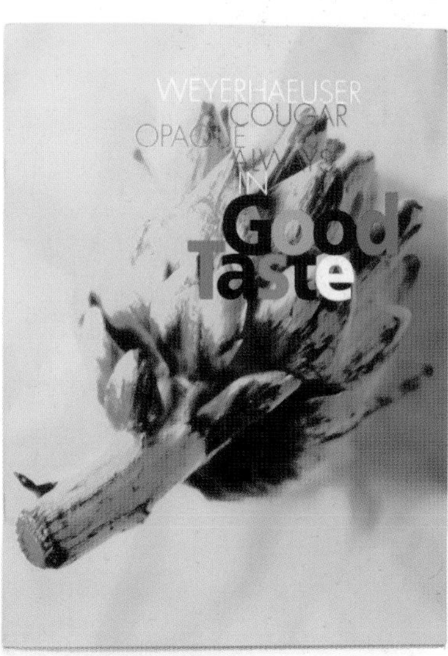

DESIGN FIRM › Sibley Peteet Design
ART DIRECTOR › Don Sibley
DESIGNERS › Don Sibley, Donna Aldridge
PHOTOGRAPHERS › Various
COPYWRITER › Don Sibley
CLIENT › Weyerhaeuser Paper
TOOLS (SOFTWARE/PLATFORM) › QuarkXPress, Macintosh
PAPER STOCK › Weyerhaeuser Cougar opaque

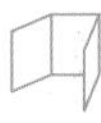

DESIGN FIRM > Creative Conspiracy, Inc.
ART DIRECTOR > Kris Hickcox
DESIGNER > Kris Hickcox
ILLUSTRATOR/PHOTOGRAPHER > Neil Hannum
CLIENT > Screaming Rhino Gift Market
TOOLS (SOFTWARE/PLATFORM) > QuarkXPress, Illustrator, Photoshop
PAPER STOCK/PRINTING PROCESS > Catalog: 80 lb. McCoy—text; 4/4 with bleeds—cover. Env: 80 lb. Gilbert Voice in Rye

DESIGN FIRM › Arias Associates
ART DIRECTOR › Mauricio Arias
DESIGNER › Mauricio Arias
ILLUSTRATORS/PHOTOGRAPHERS › Mike Halbert, Stefano Massei
COPYWRITER › Pottery Barn
CLIENT › Pottery Barn
TOOLS (SOFTWARE/PLATFORM) › QuarkXPress, Photoshop
PAPER STOCK › Champion Benefit, Mohawk superfine
PRINTING PROCESS › Lithography and letterpress

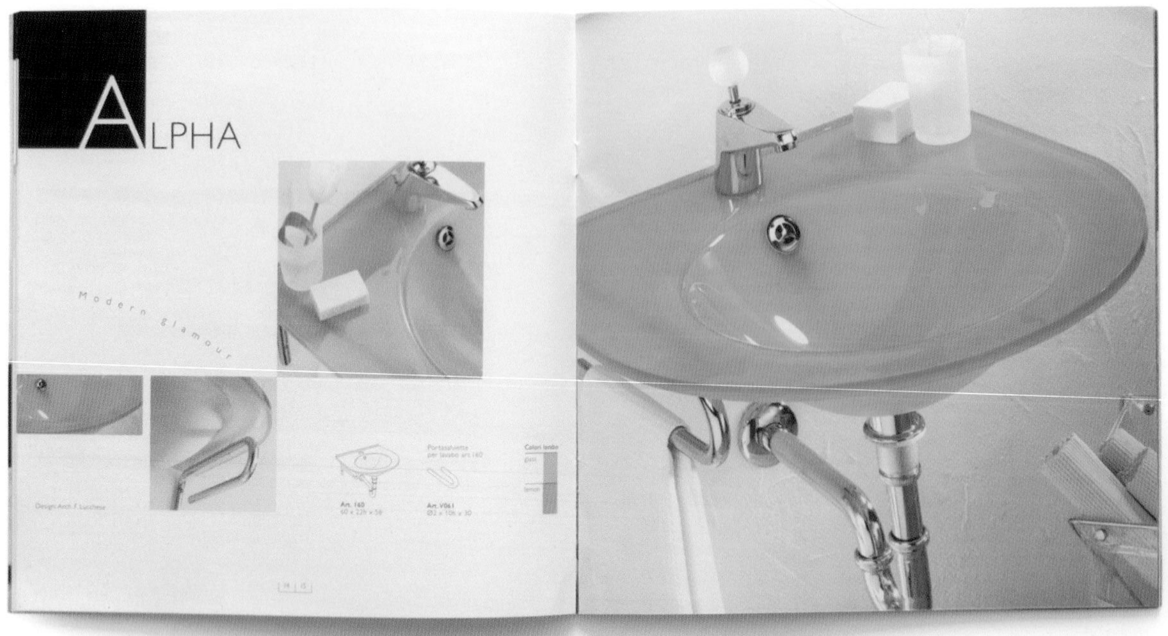

DESIGN FIRM › Giorgio Rocco Communications
ART DIRECTOR › Giorgio Rocco
DESIGNER › Giorgio Rocco
ILLUSTRATOR/PHOTOGRAPHER › Archives INDA
COPYWRITER › Elisabetta Campo
CLIENT › INDA spa, Italy
TOOLS (SOFTWARE/PLATFORM) › Macintosh, Photoshop, Freehand
PAPER STOCK › Burgo
PRINTING PROCESS › Four-color offset

DESIGN FIRM › Kan & Lau Design Consultants
ART DIRECTORS › Kan Tai-keung, Veronica Cheung, Mak Tsing Kuoh
DESIGNERS › Kan Tai-keung, Veronica Cheung, Mak Tsing Kuoh
COMPUTER ILLUSTRATOR › Ng Cheuk Bong
CLIENT › Rolex (HK) Ltd

DESIGN FIRM › Hand Made Group
ART DIRECTORS › Alessandro Esteri, Giona Maisrelli
DESIGNERS › Alessandro Esteri, Giona Maisrelli
ILLUSTRATOR/PHOTOGRAPHER › Alessandro Esteri
COPYWRITER › Verdiana Maggiorelli
CLIENT › Marco Pierguidi
TOOLS (SOFTWARE/PLATFORM) › QuarkXPress, Photoshop
PAPER STOCK › Garda
PRINTING PROCESS › Four-color

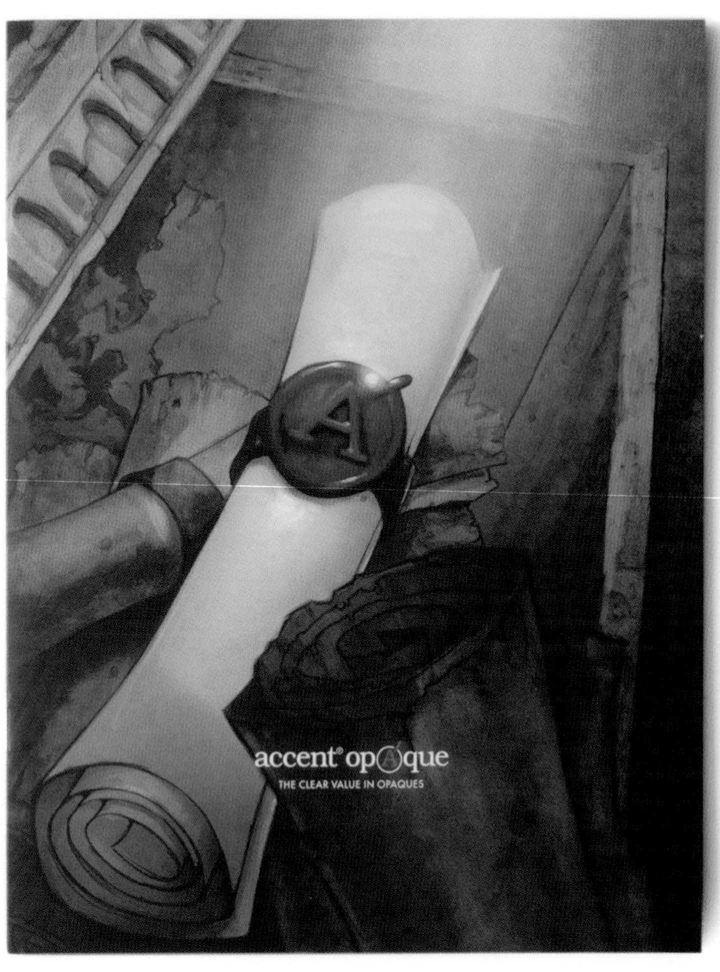

DESIGN FIRM › Oden Marketing and Design
CREATIVE DIRECTOR › Bret Terwilleger
DESIGNER › Michael Guthrie
ILLUSTRATOR › Michael Koelsch
PENCILS › Dean Zachary
COPYWRITER › Henry Ellis
CLIENT › Accent Opaque
PAPER STOCK › Williamson

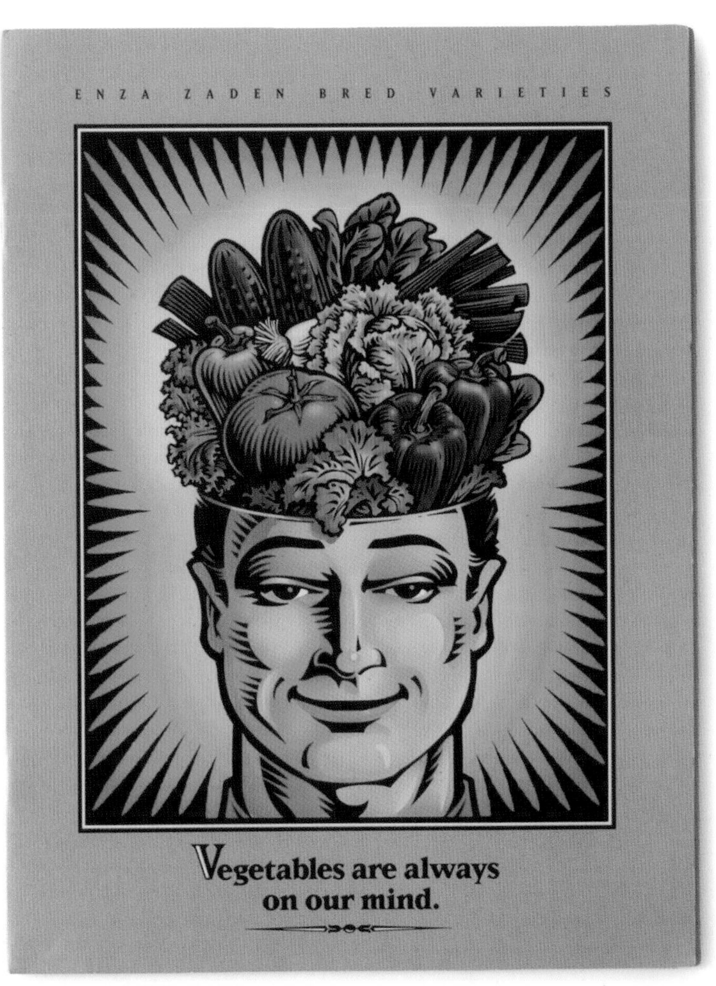

DESIGN FIRM › Lorenz Advertising
ART DIRECTOR › Glen Miranda
DESIGNER › Glen Miranda
ILLUSTRATORS/PHOTOGRAPHERS › Dan Thoner, various photographers
COPYWRITER › Carm Greco
CLIENT › Enza Zaden North America
TOOLS (SOFTWARE/PLATFORM) › QuarkXPress, Photoshop, Macintosh
PAPER STOCK › Simpson evergreen cord
PRINTING PROCESS › Five-color lithography

INTRODUCTION • HISTORY
We've come a long way in this business... all the way from Holland.

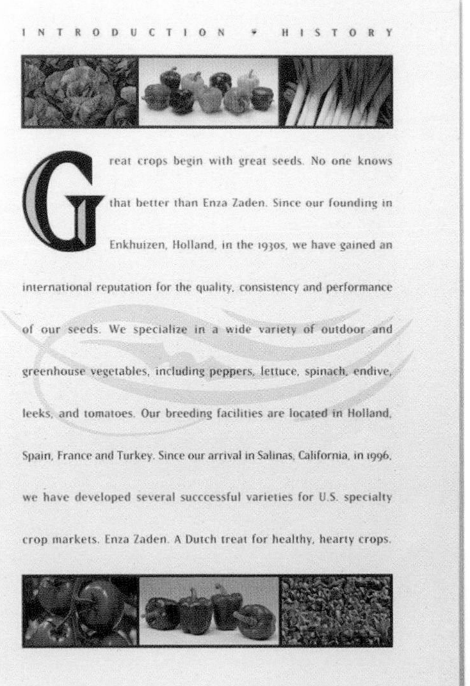

INTRODUCTION • HISTORY
Great crops begin with great seeds. No one knows that better than Enza Zaden. Since our founding in Enkhuizen, Holland, in the 1930s, we have gained an international reputation for the quality, consistency and performance of our seeds. We specialize in a wide variety of outdoor and greenhouse vegetables, including peppers, lettuce, spinach, endive, leeks, and tomatoes. Our breeding facilities are located in Holland, Spain, France and Turkey. Since our arrival in Salinas, California, in 1996, we have developed several succcessful varieties for U.S. specialty crop markets. Enza Zaden. A Dutch treat for healthy, hearty crops.

DESIGNFIRM > Lee Reedy Creative
ART DIRECTOR > Lee Reedy
DESIGNER > Heather Haworth
ILLUSTRATORS/PHOTOGRAPHERS > Bruce Wolf, Marshal Safron, Michael Peck
COPYWRITER > Carol Parsons
CLIENT > Hunter Douglas
TOOLS (SOFTWARE/PLATFORM) > QuarkXPress
PAPER STOCK > McCoy, laminated and U.V. coated

DESIGN FIRM › Tycoon Graphics
ART DIRECTOR › Tycoon Graphics
DESIGNER › Tycoon Graphics
PHOTOGRAPHER › Shoji Uchida
CLIENT › Abahouse International Co., Ltd.

DESIGN FIRM › Clarity Coverdale Fury
ART DIRECTOR › Jac Coverdale
DESIGNER › Jac Coverdale
ILLUSTRATORS › Bill Cook, Peter Sjn, Kate Thomessen, Time Life Books
PHOTOGRAPHER › Raymond Meeks
COPYWRITER › Jerry Fury
CLIENT › Millennium Import Co.
TOOLS (SOFTWARE/PLATFORM) › Illustrator, QuarkXPress, Photoshop, Macintosh
PAPER STOCK › Cover: 130 lb. Curtis back linen; text: 80 lb. Cougar natural smooth
PRINTING PROCESS › Cover: foil stamped, two-colors; text: offset, six-colors, two sides

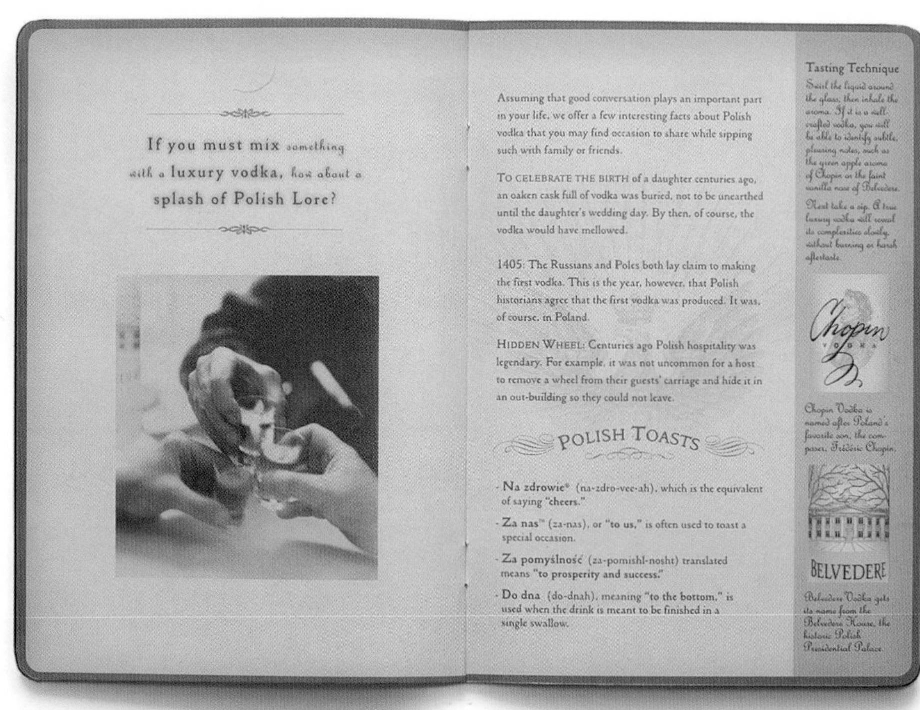

Naam: Johanna Kruize — Club: PSV

Merk: Whirlpool (via Philips)

Otto: Grasvlekken zet je in de week

7
360°
SEVEN CONTINENTS
THREE HUNDRED SIXTY DEGREE
PHOTOGRAPHY
EVEREN T. BROWN 360° IMAGES
ASIA
7
360°
SEVEN continents
THREE HUNDRED SIXTY DEGREE
PHOTOGRAPHY
GLOBAL IMAGE CATALOG BY EVEREN T. BROWN
NOTHING TOPS AN ORIGINAL!
EUROPE

DESIGN FIRM › Tracy Design Communications, Inc.
ART DIRECTOR › Jan Tracy
DESIGNER › Jan Tracy
ILLUSTRATOR/PHOTOGRAPHER › Jan Tracy
COPYWRITER › Katie Van Luchene
CLIENT › The Plaza Pavilion
TOOLS (SOFTWARE/PLATFORM) › QuarkXPress, Photoshop

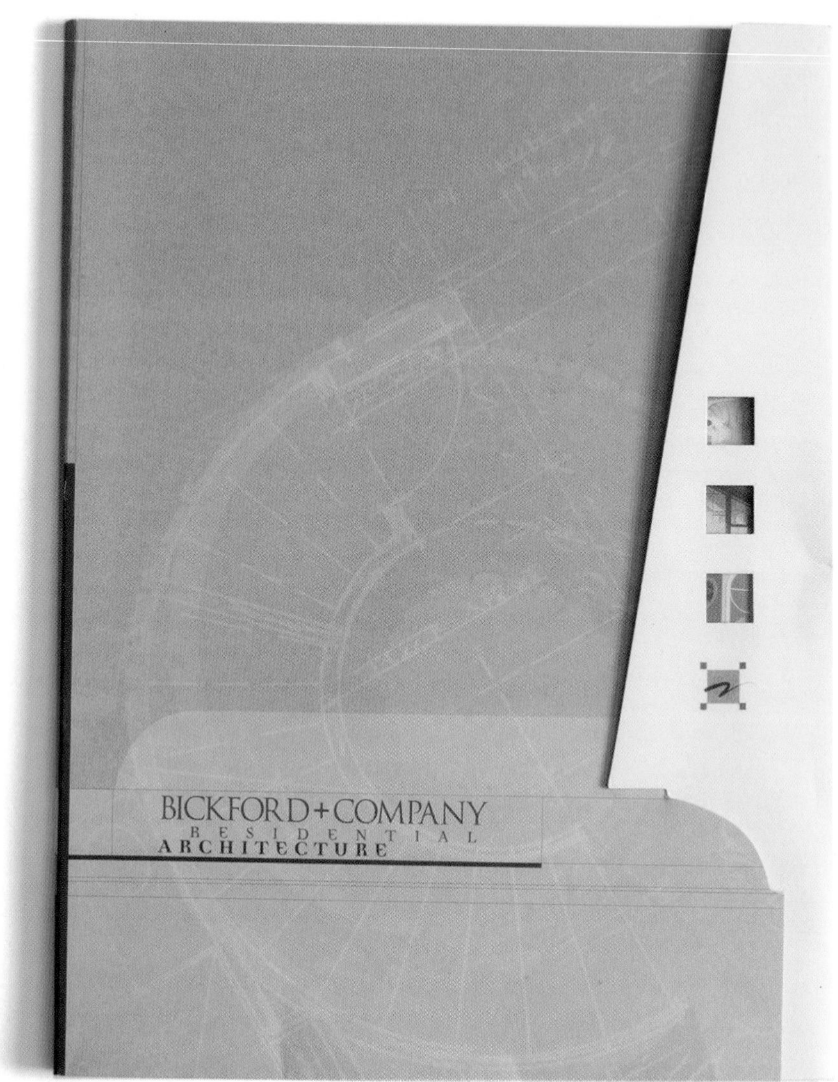

DESIGN FIRM › Tracy Design Communications, Inc.
ART DIRECTOR › Jan Tracy
DESIGNER › Anthony Magliano
ILLUSTRATORS/PHOTOGRAPHERS › Miscellaneous
COPYWRITER › Robin Zaplin
CLIENT › Bickford & Co.
TOOLS (SOFTWARE/PLATFORM) › QuarkXPress, Photoshop

DESIGN FIRM › IE Design
ART DIRECTOR › Marcie Carson
DESIGNER › Marcie Carson
CLIENT › Kern & Wooley LLP
TOOLS (SOFTWARE/PLATFORM) › Macintosh, Illustrator, Photoshop, QuarkXPress
PAPER STOCK/PRINTING PROCESS › Cover: Havana Structeras-Perla; text: Gilbert Oxford Cream
PRINTING PROCESS › Cover: two-color PMJS

DESIGN FIRM > ie design, Los Angeles
CREATIVE DIRECTOR > Marcie Carson
DESIGNER > Marcie Carson
CLIENT > Good Gracious Events

A boy named Devin had a box of dreams.
It was larger inside than out, it seemed,
for he pulled out a new dream every day,
he dreamed the dream, then tucked it away.
The dreams stayed nice and safe inside,
and no one could take them away if they tried.

DESIGN FIRM › Oden Marketing and Design
CREATIVE DIRECTOR › Bret Terwilleger
DESIGNER › Liz Fonville
ILLUSTRATOR › Bill Berry
COPYWRITERS › Liz Fonville, Sheperd Simmons
CLIENT › Boys and Girls Clubs of Greater Memphis

SOLUTIONS

www.osbornmaledon.com

DESIGN FIRM > After Hours Creative
ART DIRECTOR > After Hours Creative
DESIGNER > After Hours Creative
COPYWRITER > After Hours Creative
CLIENT > Osborn Maledon
TOOLS (SOFTWARE/PLATFORM) > Macintosh G4, Illustrator

COMPLEX

The best lawyers solve complicated problems in ways their clients can understand. • Osborn Maledon attorneys have the judgment, knowledge and experience to bring clarity to complex situations. You receive no-nonsense solutions to difficult business issues, from challenging litigation to mergers, acquisitions and public offerings. We know what it takes to get business done. And what it takes to help you achieve your goals. If everything were simple, your choice of a law firm wouldn't matter. When things get complicated, Osborn Maledon offers a clear solution.

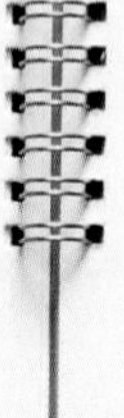

CREATIVE

By moving just one glass, arrange the top row to look like the bottom row.

Hydrothermal massage tubs in every room. A full range of
spa services. The finest comforts and amenities refresh the spirit

DESIGN FIRM › Arias Associates
ART DIRECTORS › Mauricio Arias, Maral Sarkis
DESIGNERS › Mauricio Arias, Maral Sarkis
COPYWRITER › Dawn Mortensen
CLIENT › Hotel Casa Del Mar
TOOLS (SOFTWARE/PLATFORM) › QuarkXPress, Photoshop, Illustrator
PAPER STOCK › Mohawk superfine and McCoy silk
PRINTING PROCESS › Lithography, embossing and letterpress

DESIGN FIRM › Arias Associates
ART DIRECTORS › Mauricio Arias, Maral Sarkis, Steve Mortensen, Stephanie Yee
DESIGNERS › Mauricio Arias, Maral Sarkis, Steve Mortensen, Stephanie Yee
ILLUSTRATOR/PHOTOGRAPHER › Fred Licht
COPYWRITER › Words by Design
CLIENT › Crescent Heights
TOOLS (SOFTWARE/PLATFORM) › QuarkXPress, Photoshop, Illustrator
PAPER STOCK › Starwhite Vicksburg
PRINTING PROCESS › Lithography, letterpress

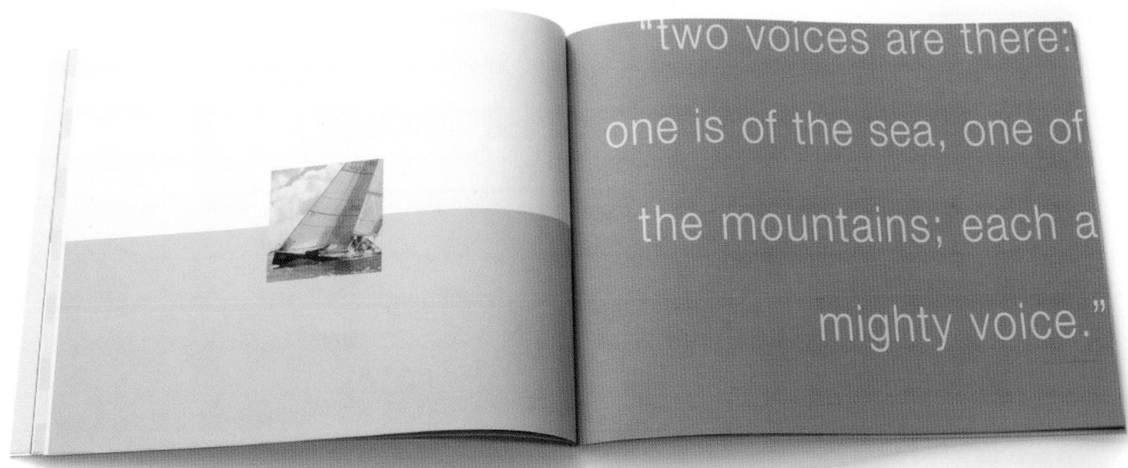
"two voices are there:
one is of the sea, one of
the mountains; each a
mighty voice."

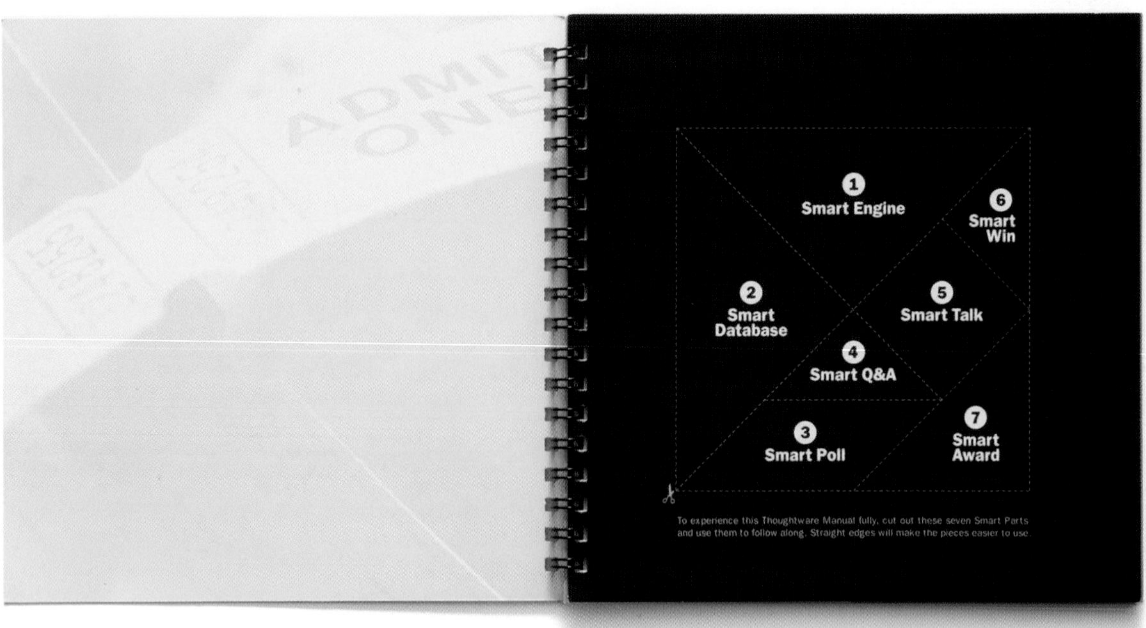

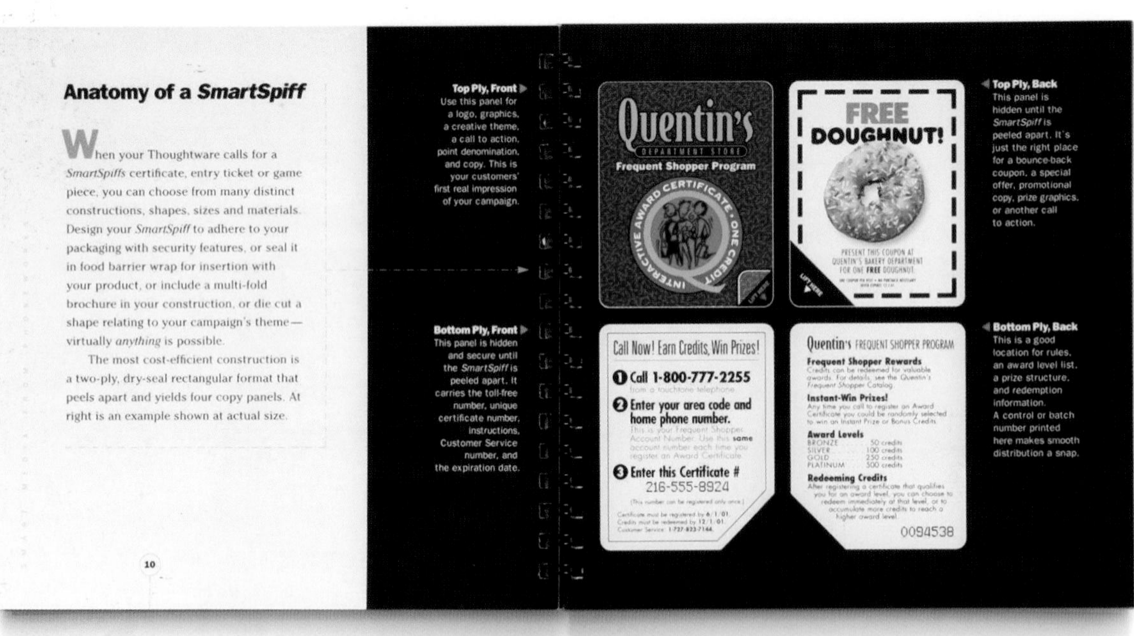

1 Smart Engine
2 Smart Database
3 Smart Poll
4 Smart Q&A
5 Smart Talk
6 Smart Win
7 Smart Award
To experience this Thoughtware Manual fully, cut out these seven Smart Parts and use them to follow along. Straight edges will make the pieces easier to use.

Anatomy of a *SmartSpiff*
When your Thoughtware calls for a *SmartSpiffs* certificate, entry ticket or game piece, you can choose from many distinct constructions, shapes, sizes and materials. Design your *SmartSpiff* to adhere to your packaging with security features, or seal it in food barrier wrap for insertion with your product, or include a multi-fold brochure in your construction, or die cut a shape relating to your campaign's theme—virtually *anything* is possible.
The most cost-efficient construction is a two-ply, dry-seal rectangular format that peels apart and yields four copy panels. At right is an example shown at actual size.
10
Top Ply, Front
Use this panel for a logo, graphics, a creative theme, a call to action, point denomination, and copy. This is your customers' first real impression of your campaign.
Bottom Ply, Front
This panel is hidden and secure until the *SmartSpiff* is peeled apart. It carries the toll-free number, unique certificate number, instructions, Customer Service number, and the expiration date.
Quentin's
Department Store
Frequent Shopper Program
FREE DOUGHNUT!
Call Now! Earn Credits, Win Prizes!
Call 1-800-777-2255
Enter your area code and home phone number.
Enter this Certificate #
216-555-8924
Quentin's FREQUENT SHOPPER PROGRAM
Frequent Shopper Rewards
Instant-Win Prizes!
Award Levels
Redeeming Credits
0094538
Top Ply, Back
This panel is hidden until the *SmartSpiff* is peeled apart. It's just the right place for a bounce-back coupon, a special offer, promotional copy, prize graphics, or another call to action.
Bottom Ply, Back
This is a good location for rules, an award level list, a prize structure, and redemption information.
A control or batch number printed here makes smooth distribution a snap.

DESIGN FIRM › Aspen Interactive
ART DIRECTOR › Ken Weightman
DESIGNER › Ken Weightman
CLIENT › Phoneworks
TOOLS (SOFTWARE/PLATFORM) › QuarkXPress, Adobe Photoshop, Macintosh
PAPER STOCK/PRINTING PROCESS › Four-color process and one match color

DESIGN FIRM › Sayles Graphic Design
ART DIRECTOR › John Sayles
DESIGNER › John Sayles
PHOTOGRAPHERS › David Crosby, Tony Smith
ILLUSTRATOR › John Sayles
COPYWRITER › Wendy Lyons
CLIENT › Greenville South Carolina Convention & Visitors Bureau
TOOLS (SOFTWARE/PLATFORM) › QuarkXPress, Macintosh
PRINTING PROCESS › Offset printed, includes tipped-on samples

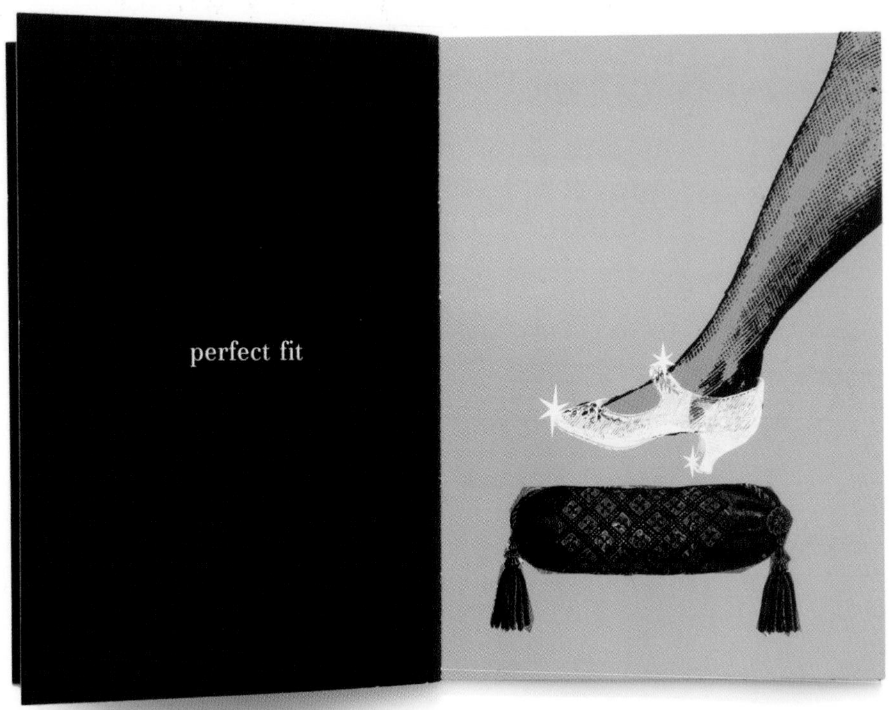

DESIGN FIRM › Sibley Peteet Design
ART DIRECTOR › Donna Aldridge
DESIGNER › Donna Aldridge
ILLUSTRATOR › Brandon Kirk
COPYWRITER › Don Sibley
CLIENT › Williamson Printing Company
TOOLS (SOFTWARE/PLATFORM) › QuarkXPress, Macintosh
PAPER STOCK › Strobe

DESIGN FIRM › Erbe Design
ART DIRECTOR › Maureen Erbe
DESIGNER › Maureen Erbe
ILLUSTRATOR › Allison Starcher
COPYWRITER › Maureen Gilmer
CLIENT › Monrovia
TOOLS (SOFTWARE/PLATFORM) › QuarkXPress
PRINTING PROCESS › Lithography

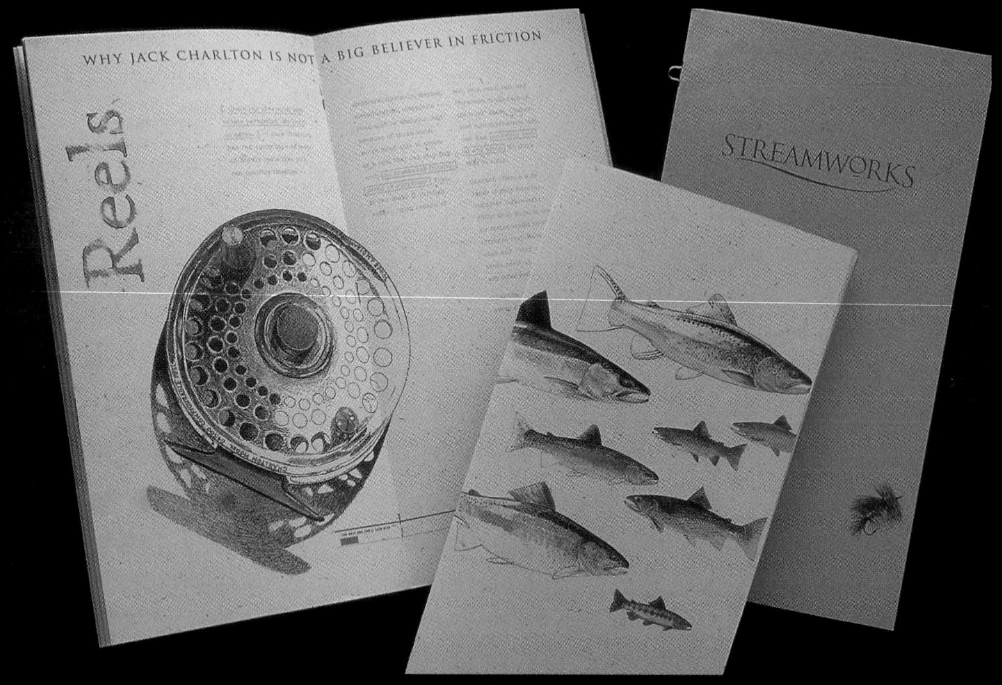

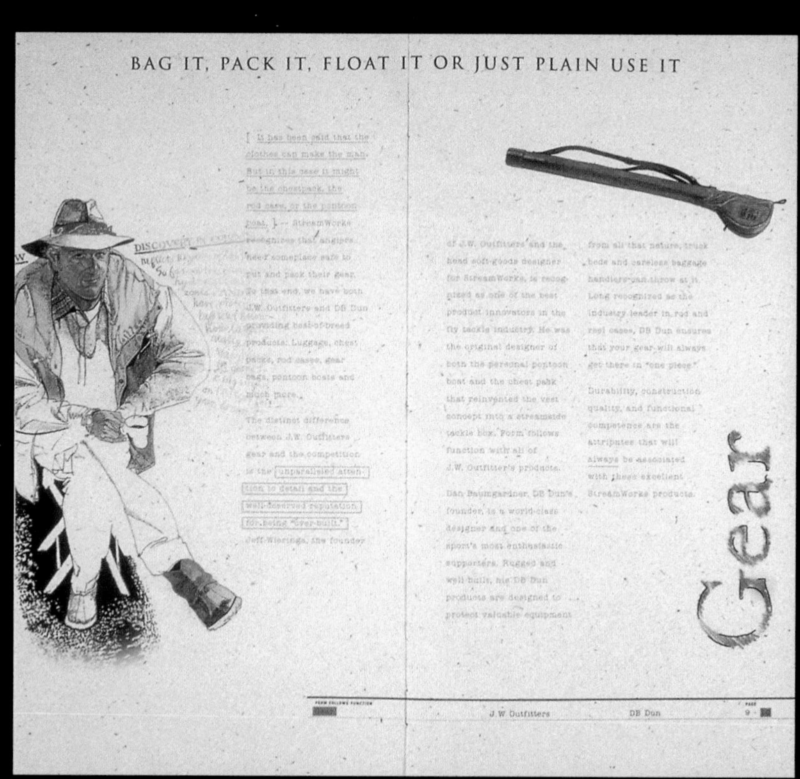

DESIGN FIRM > Hornall Anderson Design Works, Inc.
ART DIRECTOR > Jack Anderson
DESIGNERS > Jack Anderson, Belinda Bowling, Andrew Smith, Ed Lee
ILLUSTRATOR > Jack Unruh
COPYWRITERS > Various
CLIENT > Streamworks
TOOLS (SOFTWARE/PLATFORM) > QuarkXPress, Photoshop
PAPER STOCK > French Speckletone Kraft cover, natural text

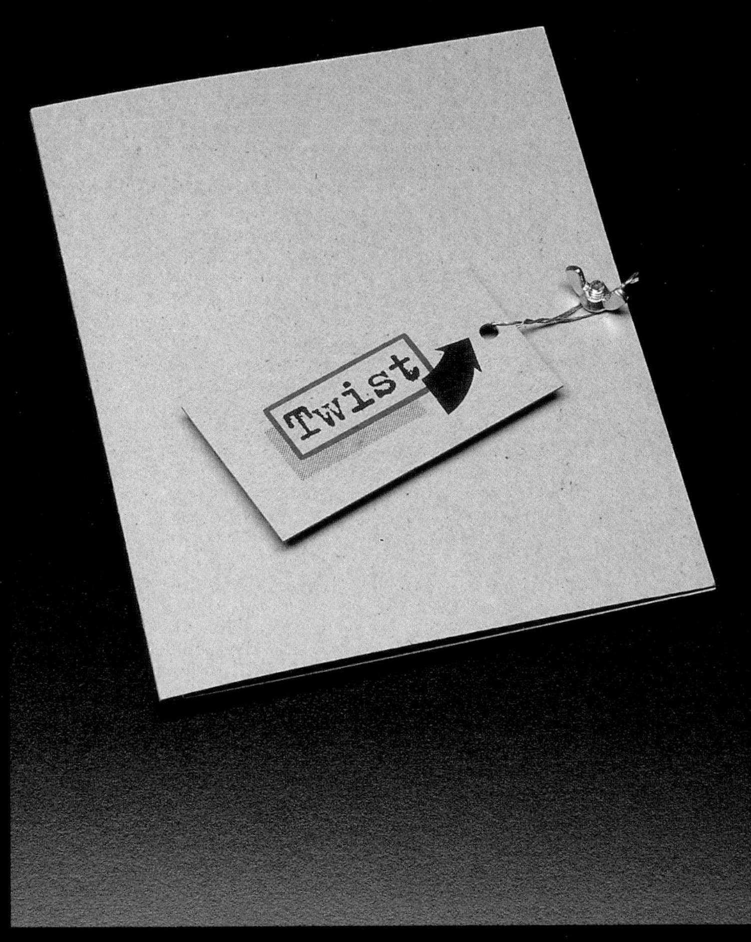

DESIGN FIRM › Lee Reedy Creative
ART DIRECTOR › Lee Reedy
DESIGNER › Lee Reedy
ILLUSTRATOR/PHOTOGRAPHER › Stock
COPYWRITER › Suzy Patterson
CLIENT › Travel Connections
TOOLS (SOFTWARE/PLATFORM) › QuarkXPress
PAPER STOCK › Chipboard
PRINTING PROCESS › Two-color

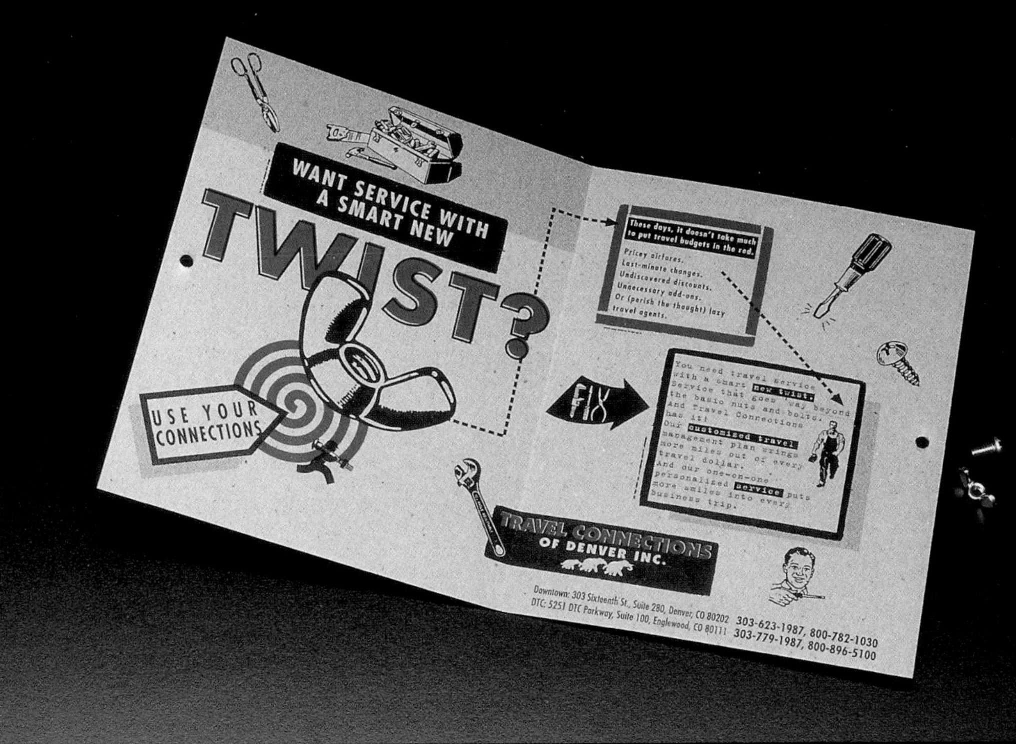

KO CRÉATION
S BY SHAN: COLLECTION 2002

CANADA

ART DIRECTOR:
POL BARIL

DESIGNERS:
ANNIE LACHAPELLE
POL BARIL

PHOTOGRAPHER:
JOËL DUMOULIN

CLIENT:
SHAN

SOFTWARE:
PHOTOSHOP
QUARKXPRESS

USINE DE BOUTONS
PIRELLI/DUCATI DFX RACING TEAM

Are you ready to meet us?
No velvet gloves for our opponents

ART DIRECTORS: LIONELLO BOREAN, CHIARA GRANDESSO
DESIGNER: LIONELLO BOREAN, CHIARA GRANDESSO
CLIENT: PIRELLI/DUCATI DFX RACING TEAM
PRINTING: CMYK + GOLD

ITALY

...but I demand maximum effort from them and I know they can give it
OK, I admit I have a rather particular way to run the set-up

MADE THOUGHT
SONNETI SPRING/SUMMER 2002
LOOK BOOK

ART DIRECTORS:
BEN PARKER
PAUL AUSTIN

DESIGNERS:
BEN PARKER
PAUL AUSTIN

PHOTOGRAPHER:
GEMMA BOOTH

CLIENT:
SONNETI

PRINTING:
PERIVAN

Spring/Summer 2002
Collections
Sonneti: Menswear
Apocalypse Then
Suedehead
Suburban Sports
Dirt X
Denim
wear
you're
at.®
Spring/Summer 2002 Collections
www.sonneti.com
Sonneti:

UK

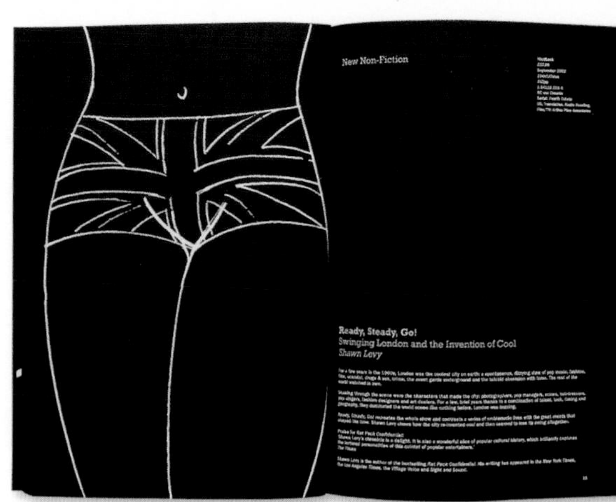

New Non-Fiction
Ready, Steady, Go!
Swinging London and the Invention of Cool
Shawn Levy

FROST DESIGN
FOURTH ESTATE CATALOG 2002

UK

ART DIRECTOR: VINCE FROST

DESIGNER: VINCE FROST

ILLUSTRATOR: MARION DEUCHARS

CLIENT: FOURTH ESTATE

MATERIALS: PAPER EPSILON NERO BY FENNER PAPER120GSM + 270GSM

PRINTING: SCREEN PRINTING BY LAUREN DISPLAYS

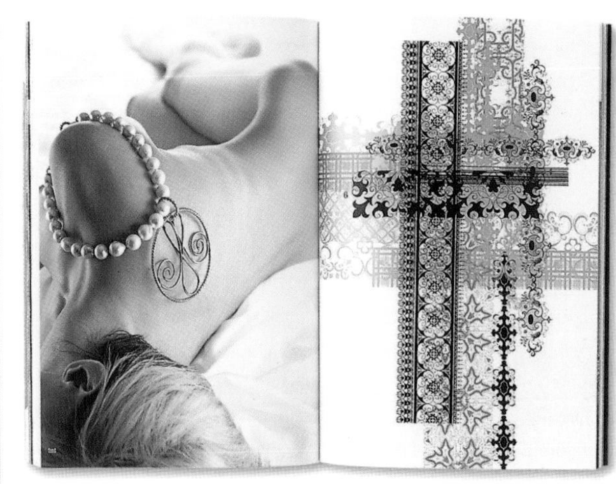

GERMANY

HEBE. WERBUNG & DESIGN
MAAS PRODUCT FOLDER

ART DIRECTOR:
REINER HEBE

DESIGNER:
STEFANIE WAHL

ILLUSTRATOR:
DOMINIK ZEHLE

CLIENT:
MAAS GOLDSMITH, STUTTGART

SOFTWARE AND HARDWARE:
QUARKXPRESS
MAC

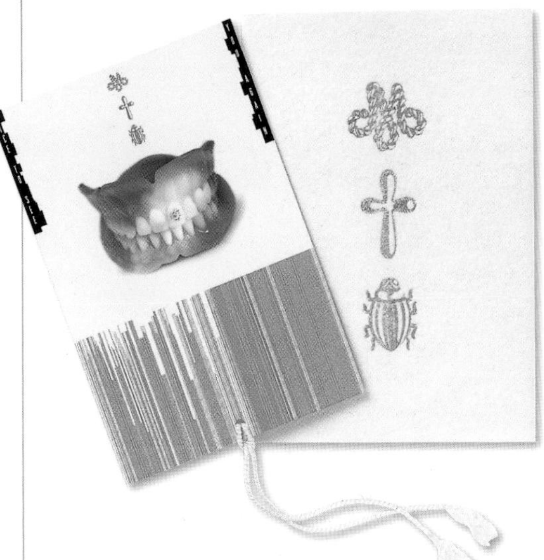

THE KITCHEN
DAY/NIGHT

UK

ART DIRECTORS:
ROB PETRIE
PHIL SIMS

What appears to be is what I deal with.
Sometimes, hum
the scene you
take a picture of
and it's lifeless,
you can take a pi
scratching his
great picture. I am a professional photographer by trade and an amateur photographer by vocation. Most of the time when I am out of the house I carry a small unobtrusive camera and I snap away obsessively at things that interest me and whatever I think would make a good picture.

USA

EMERSON, WAJDOWICZ STUDIOS

BRAVO ERWITT

museums
I go to museums to people watch. Because everyone there has gone to look and they are captured in a concentrated place, it is a particularly good thing. For a photographer, rather than fly casting, it's like shooting fish in a barrel. It is amazing how something which isn't much of anything becomes important when it's framed. Often the frames are more artistic than their contents. They are very reassuring, like the labels. Some people spend more time looking at the labels than at the work itself.
In the end all museums are interesting. Even when they're not.

ART DIRECTORS:
JUREK WAJDOWICZ
LISA LAROCHELLE

DESIGNERS:
JUREK WAJDOWICZ
LISA LAROCHELLE
MANNY MENDEZ

CLIENT:
DOMTAR

SOFTWARE:
QUARKXPRESS

MATERIALS:
BRAVO

PRINTING:
MACDONALD
PRINTING

If my pictures help some people to see things in a certain way, it's probably to look

at serious things non-seriously. Everything's serious. Everything's not serious.

C375
KREABAGNO BROCHURE

ROMA
Arte
Oval biçimli köşe duş tekneleri için tasarlanmış, 2 dışa açılır kapı ve 2 sabit panelden oluşan duş kabini.
Rounded shower enclosure with two pivot doors and two fixed panels for corner shower trays.

TURKEY

ART DIRECTOR: CEM ERUTKU

DESIGNER: SEMA DEMIRCIFT

PHOTOGRAPHERS: BULENT ERUTKU, EMRE IKIZLER

CLIENT: KREABAGNO

SOFTWARE: FREEHAND, PHOTOSHOP

MATERIALS: MODO

PRINTING: 4-COLOR OFFSET

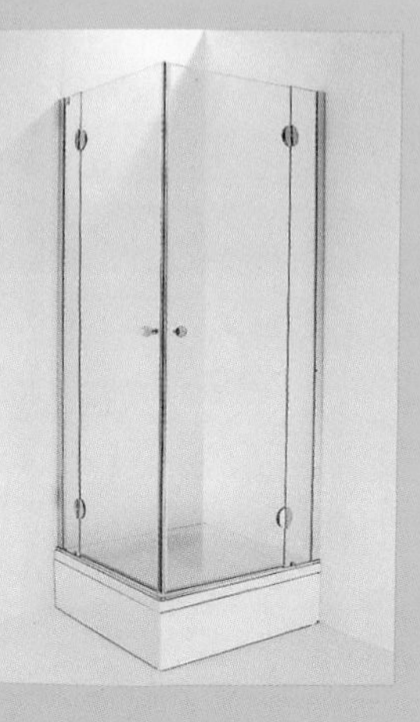

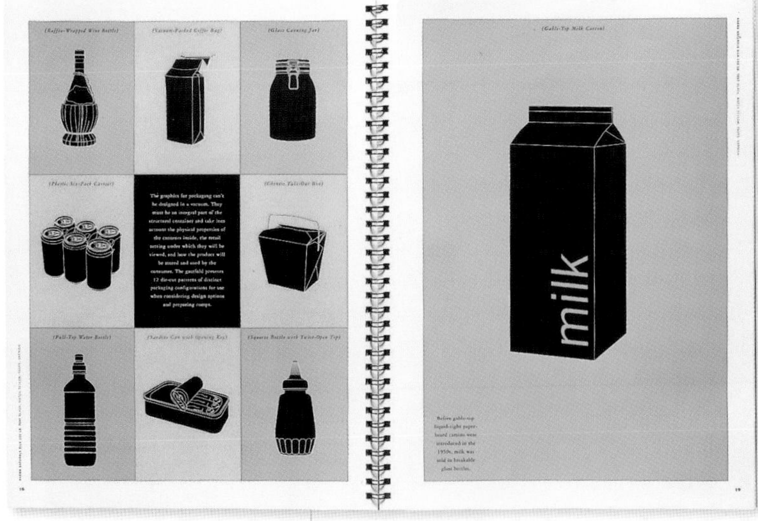

ART DIRECTOR:
KIT HINRICHS

DESIGNER:
MARIA WENZEL

CLIENT:
POTLATCH PAPER

SOFTWARE AND HARDWARE:
ILLUSTRATOR
PHOTOSHOP
MAC

MATERIALS:
POTLATCH

PRINTING:
ANDERSON,
LOS ANGELES

USA

PENTAGRAM SF
MCCOY REUNION

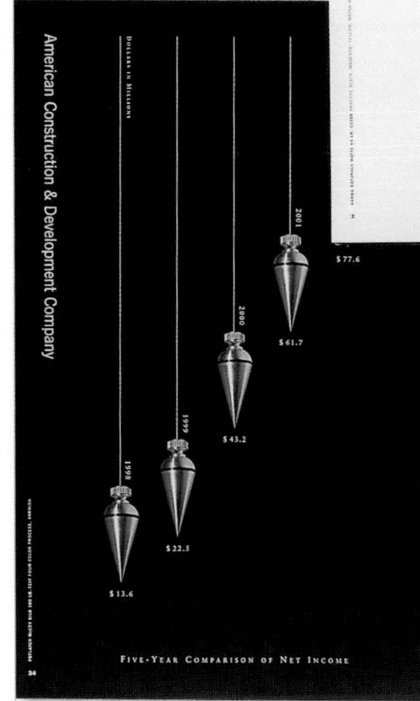

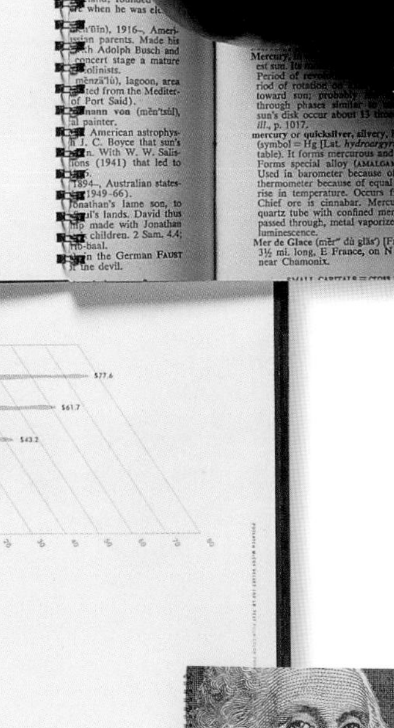

THE KITCHEN
NO BOOK

UK

GERMANY

Q
MISSION STRATAKOLOUR

ART DIRECTOR:
THILO VON DEBSCHITZ

DESIGNER:
MATTHIAS FREY

PHOTOGRAPHER:
MATTHIAS FREY

CLIENT:
ARJO WIGGINS GERMANY

SOFTWARE AND HARDWARE:
ILLUSTRATOR
QUARKXPRESS
MAC

MATERIALS:
STRATAKOLOUR

PRINTING:
GORIUS DRUCK & SERVICE

ART DIRECTOR:	DESIGNER:	CLIENT:	SOFTWARE AND HARDWARE:	MATERIALS:	PRINTING:
ANN WILLOUGHBY	TRENTON KENAGY	EL DORADO INC	QUARKXPRESS MAC	UNCOATED CHIPBOARD	IN-HOUSE

USA

WILLOUGHBY DESIGN GROUP

BARN BOOK

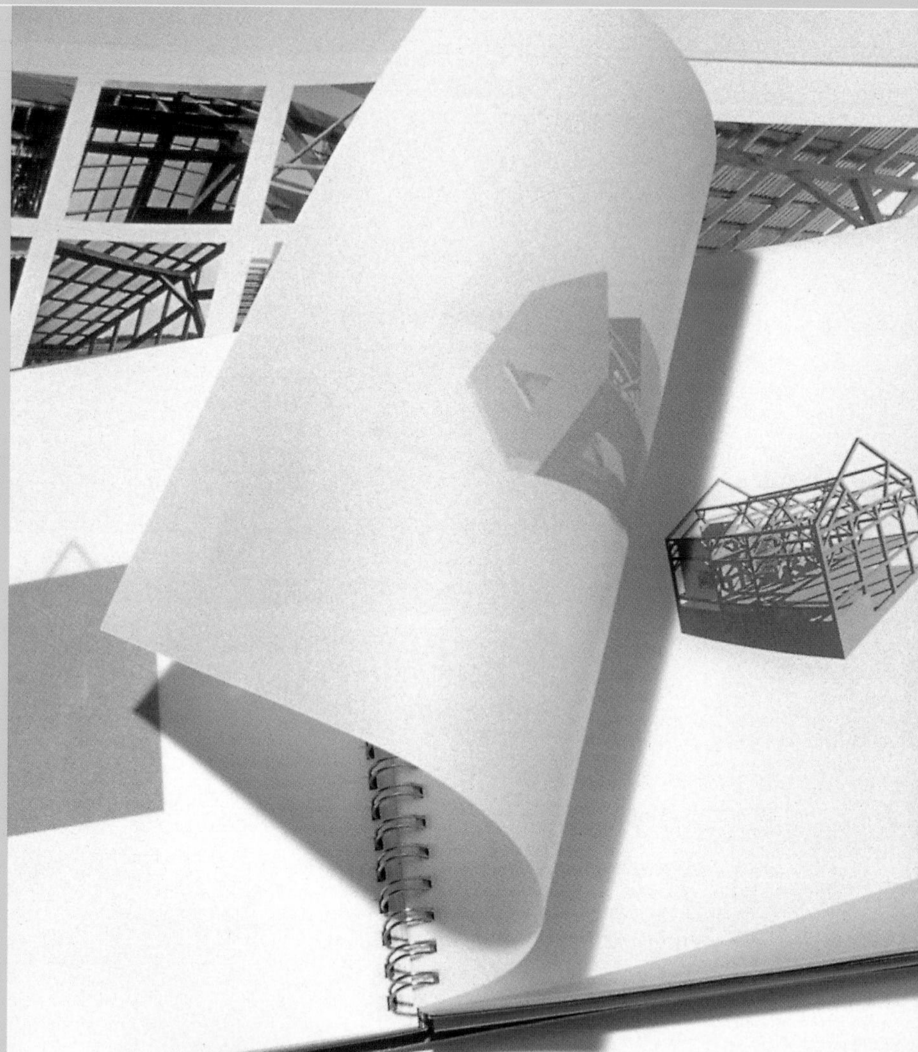

ART DIRECTORS:
MARIUS FAHRNER
UMUB ETTERLIG

DESIGNERS:
MARIUS FAHRNER
UMUB ETTERLIG

CLIENT:
DAHLER & COMPANY
PROJECT MARKETING

SOFTWARE:
FREEHAND

MATERIALS:
RÖMERTURM
CURTIS ESPARTO

PRINTING:
4-COLOR OFFSET

MARIUS FAHRNER DESIGN
AVANTGARDE

GERMANY

Afghanistan
Chris Steele-Perkins
The ageless rhythms of daily life in Afghanistan's fields, villages and towns are disrupted by war, displacement and natural disaster.
Stones: The Megaliths of England & Wales and the Stories Behind Them
David and Lai Ngan Corio
Stunning photography is accompanied by the fascinating variety of literature, opinions and fantasies inspired by the presence of ancient stones on the British landscape.
The Divine Frenzy: Ritual and Possession in Hindu Kerala
Pepita Seth
Illuminating photographs and texts chart the way in which the people of this region of southern India fuse with their land and their gods.
Carving the Mountains: The Marble Quarries of Carrara
Guido Buffoni and Stephen Cox
Guido Buffoni has photographed the marble quarries of northern Italy since the 1970s. His images are accompanied by an overview of Carrara's history by British sculptor Stephen Cox.

ROSE DESIGN ASSOCIATES, LTD
WESTZONE AUTUMN CATALOG

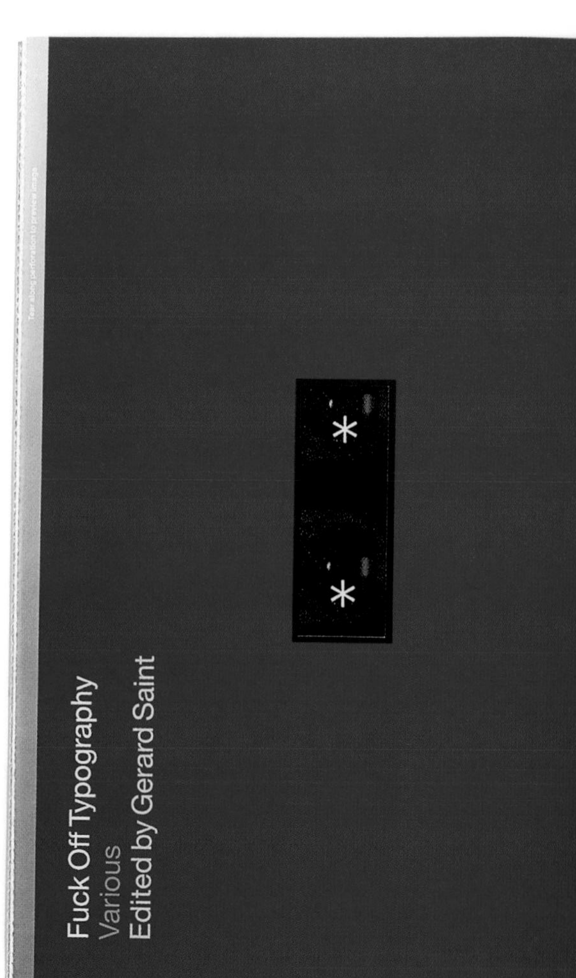

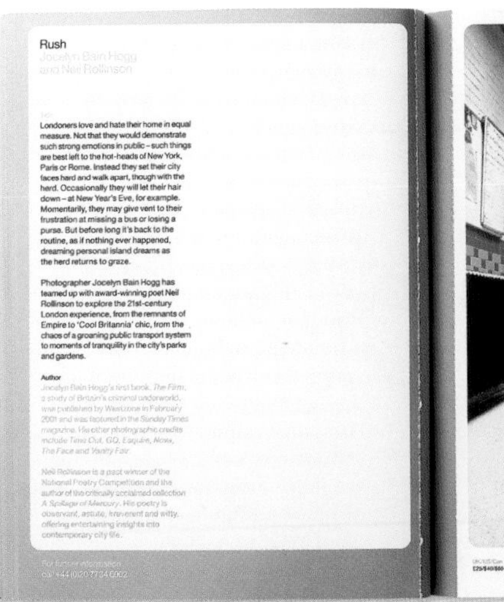

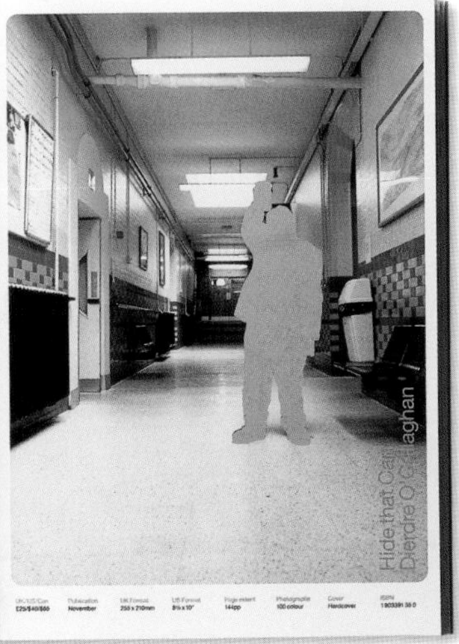

ART DIRECTOR: SIMON ELLIOTT

DESIGNER: SIMON ELLIOTT

CLIENT: WESTZONE PUBLISHING, LTD

SOFTWARE: ILLUSTRATOR, PHOTOSHOP, QUARKXPRESS

MATERIALS: VALLIANT SATIN ART

PRINTING: OFFSET LITHO

Fuck Off Typography
Various
Edited by Gerard Saint

Publication
June

Cover price
£40

Format
330mm x 265mm

Page extent
176

Illustrations
124 colour + b/w plates

Cover
Hardcover

ISBN
1 903391 21 0

Title
Fuck Off Typography invites prolific typographers, graphic designers and illustrators from the UK and international scene to trade visual insults. Peppered with expletives, *Fuck Off Typography* explores and offers insight into obscure taboo colloquialisms, and explores the creation of brand new, sharp-witted profanities expressed through the medium of typography.

Contributors include Paul Davis, Jasper Goodall, Dave Foldvari, Michael Gillette, Christophe Gowans, London design companies Form, Monster and many others, alongside their illustrious international contemporaries.

Author
Gerard Saint is an art director and co-founder of the London design group Big-Active.

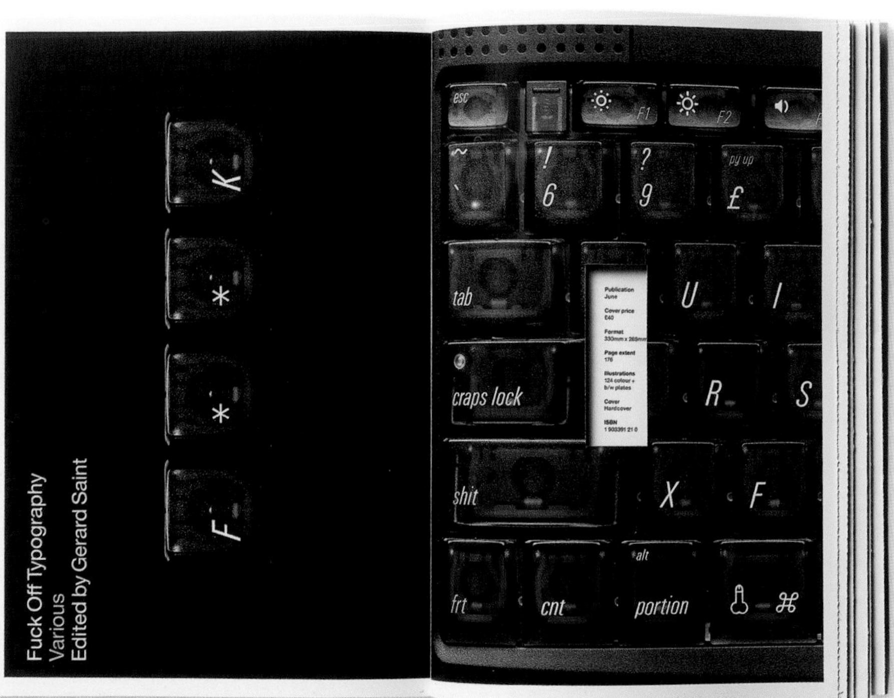

ART DIRECTOR:
VANESSA ECKSTEIN

DESIGNERS:
VANESSA ECKSTEIN
FRANCES CHEN

CLIENT:
NIENKAMPER

SOFTWARE:
ILLUSTRATOR

MATERIALS:
BECKETT

PRINTING:
LITHO

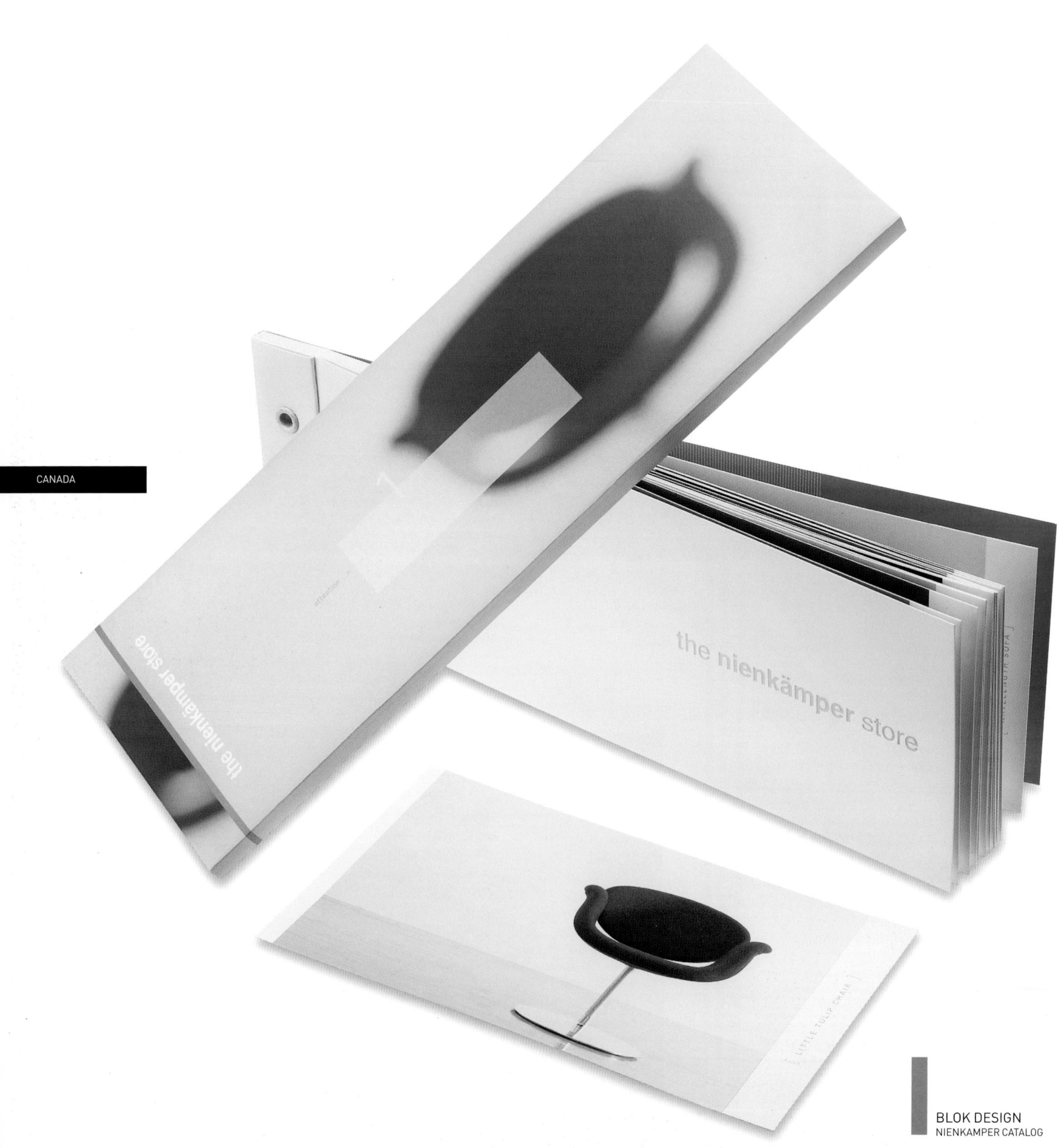

CANADA

BLOK DESIGN
NIENKAMPER CATALOG

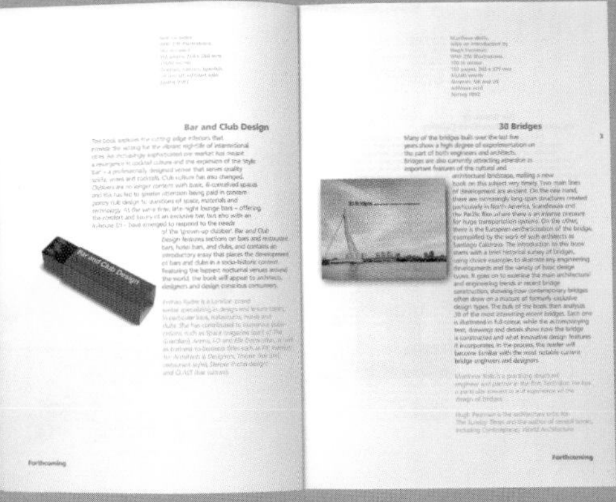

FROST DESIGN

LKP AUTUMN CATALOG 2001

UK

ART DIRECTOR:
VINCE FROST

DESIGNERS:
VINCE FROST
SONYA DYAKOVA

CLIENT:
LAURENCE KING
PUBLISHING LTD

MATERIALS:
NEW FORMATION
SUPERFINE 100GSM

PRINTING:
PRINCIPAL COLOR
(LITHO)

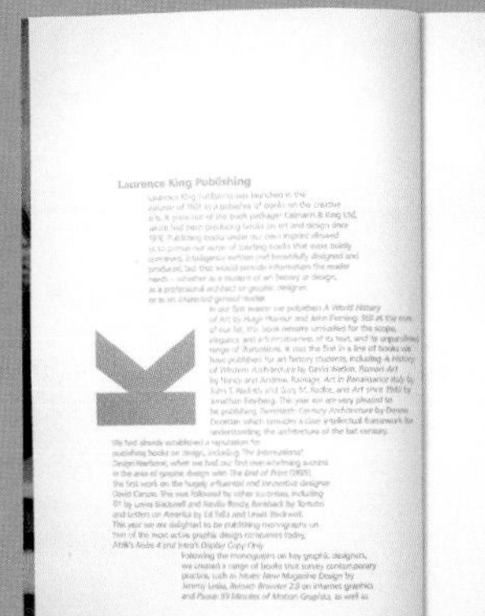

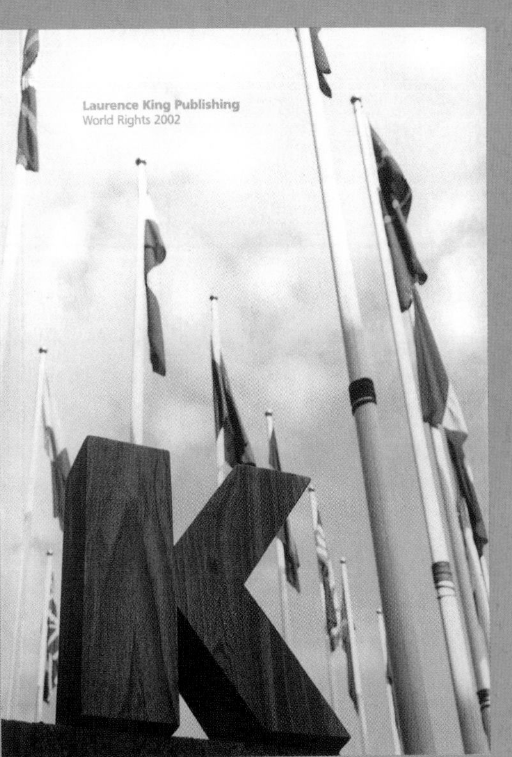

FABIO ONGARATO DESIGN
EXPRESSION PAPER PROMO

AUSTRALIA

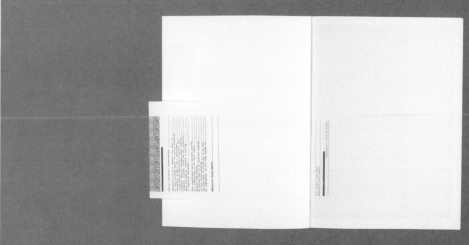

ART DIRECTOR: FABIO ONGARATO
DESIGNER: YARRA LAURIE
PHOTOGRAPHER: DEREK HENDERSON
CLIENT: K. W. DOGGETT
MATERIALS: EXPRESSION
PRINTING: GUNN & TAYLOR

ART DIRECTOR: JOHANNES PLASS

DESIGNER: KRISTINA DULLMANN

PHOTOGRAPHER: CARSTEN RAFFEL

CLIENT: SINNER SCHRADER

MATERIALS: ZANDERS MEDLEY PURE

PRINTING: DRUCKGEREI BRÜNNER

MUTABOR DESIGN

SINNER SCHRADER RECRUITING FLYER

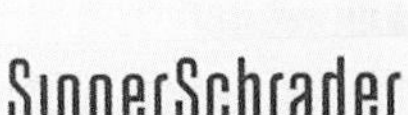

INTERACTIVATE your business

SinnerSchrader

| INTERACTIVATE your business |

GERMANY

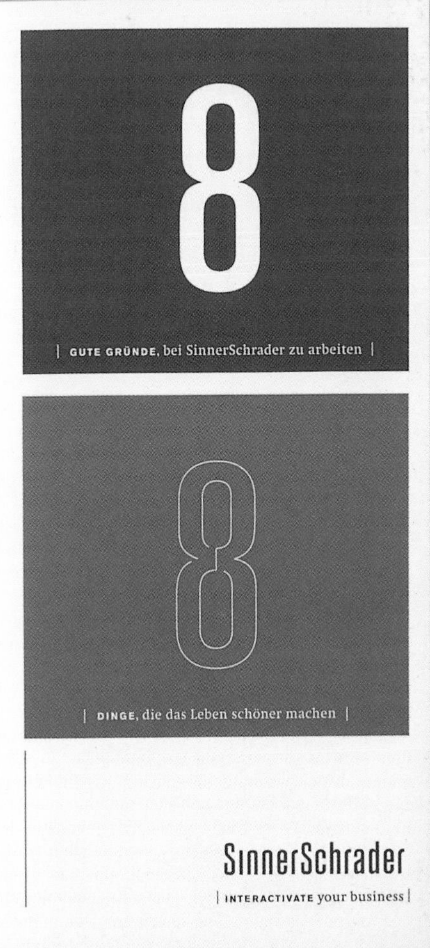

AJANS ULTRA

VAKKO SUPREFINE/
CHOCOLATTE BOOK

TURKEY

ART DIRECTOR:
NAZLI ONGAN

DESIGNER:
NAZLI ONGAN

PHOTOGRAPHER:
ABDULLAH
HEKIMHAN

CLIENT:
VAKKO

SOFTWARE:
FREEHAND

MATERIALS:
NONBRILLIANT
GLAZED PAPER

PRINTING:
4-COLOR OFFSET

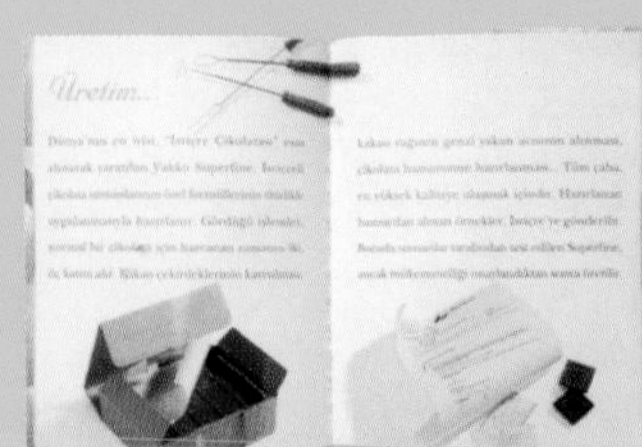

ART DIRECTOR:	DESIGNER:	CLIENT:	SOFTWARE:	MATERIALS:	PRINTING:
MARTIN STILLHART	MARTIN STILLHART	SKIM.COM	ILLUSTRATOR QUARKXPRESS	INVERCOAT 240GSM	OFFSET

SWITZERLAND

FAUXPAS
LEPORELLO

IRIDIUM, A DESIGN COMPANY

FACE TO FACE CATALOG

Our Vision

We are changing the way you communicate. We bring together video, voice and data over your IP, ATM or SONET network to enable interactive video communications and real-time video transport. Crystal clear video. Pure audio with exceptionally low delay. Flexible solutions to fit the way you work. With the quality of technologies like MPEG-2, and the reliability of a dedicated platform, Miranda Media Networks truly brings you **face to face**.

Changing the Face of Communication

Teach

Video expands the reach of educators and the ability of students to learn. With MPEG-2 technology from Miranda Media Networks, universities, schools, and professional colleges are using their resources more effectively. Video networks tie together statewide school systems, giving students better access to unique classes and greater flexibility in course schedules. Educators have access to best-in-class speakers who are no longer limited by geography or flight availability. Education is about expanding knowledge, and high quality video can provide the connectivity to make it happen.

Empowering Distance Learning

Live

The difference is quality. Medicine is a world of images, and their accuracy can mean life or death. Reliable, interactive MPEG-2 video enables doctors and specialists to learn, diagnose and treat today's patients more accurately and effectively. And video has become an invaluable part of the critically important teaching process for medical students and interns. In short - video communications can bring the knowledge of experts to those who need it.

Making a Difference in Diagnosis

CANADA

ART DIRECTOR: MARIO L'ÉCUYER

DESIGNER: JEAN-FRANÇOIS PLANTE

PHOTOGRAPHER: HEADLIGHT INNOVATIVE IMAGERY

CLIENT: MIRANDA MEDIA NETWORKS

SOFTWARE AND HARDWARE: ILLUSTRATOR, PHOTOSHOP, QUARKXPRESS, MAC 7500

MATERIALS: EUROART SILK

PRINTING: BEAUREGARD PRINTERS

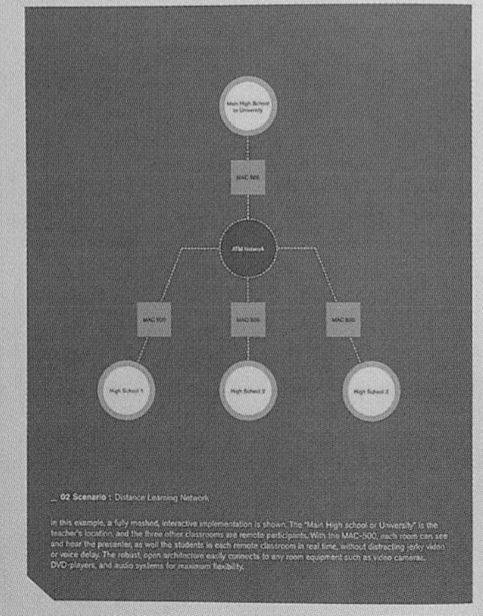

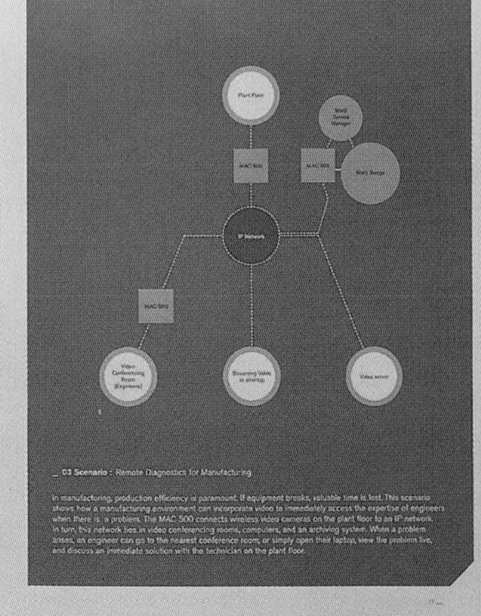

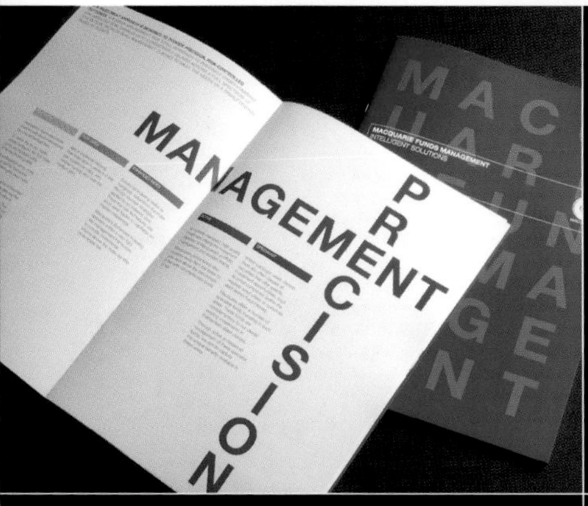

ART DIRECTOR: EMERY VINCENT DESIGN

DESIGNER: EMERY VINCENT DESIGN

CLIENT: MACQUARIE FUNDS MANAGEMENT

AUSTRALIA

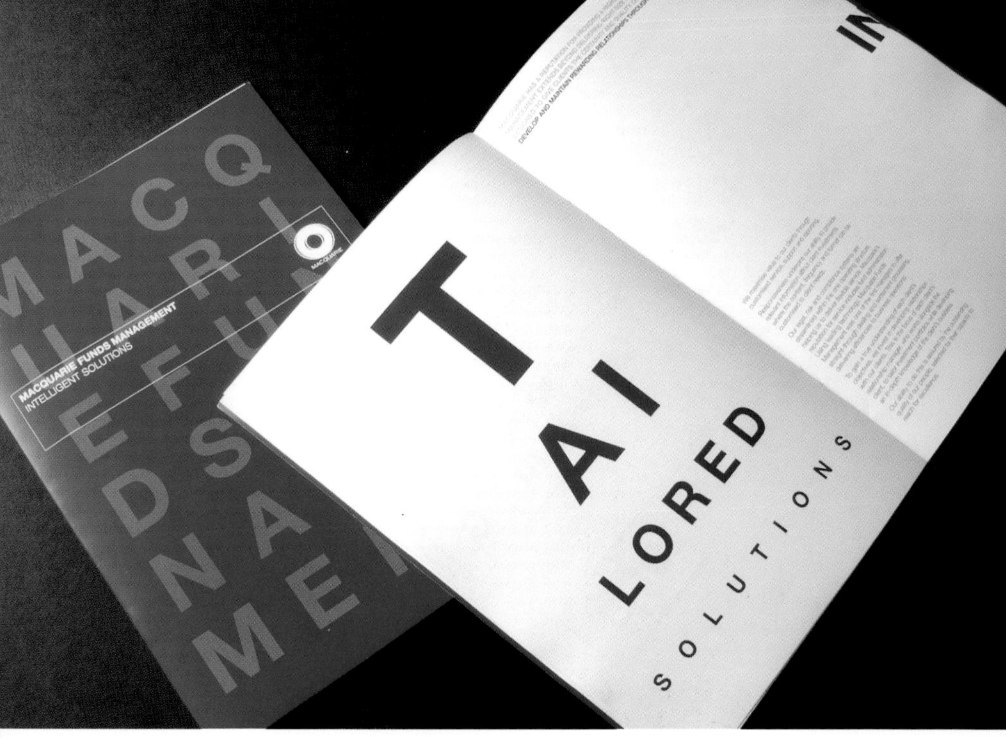

EMERY VINCENT DESIGN
INTELLIGENT SOLUTIONS

BAKKEN CREATIVE CO.

Vintners Inn Brochure

ART DIRECTOR:	DESIGNER:	CLIENT:	TOOLS:	MATERIALS:
Michelle Bakken	Gina Mondello	Vintners Inn	Adobe Illustrator	Strathmore Pastelle

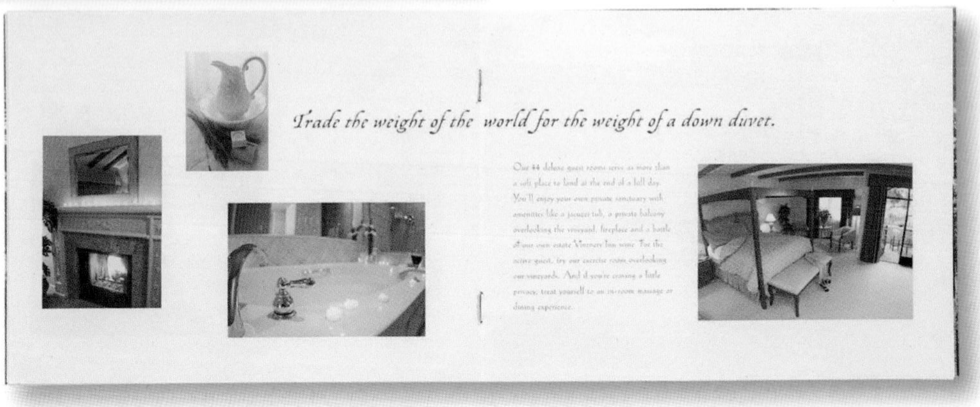

VOICE

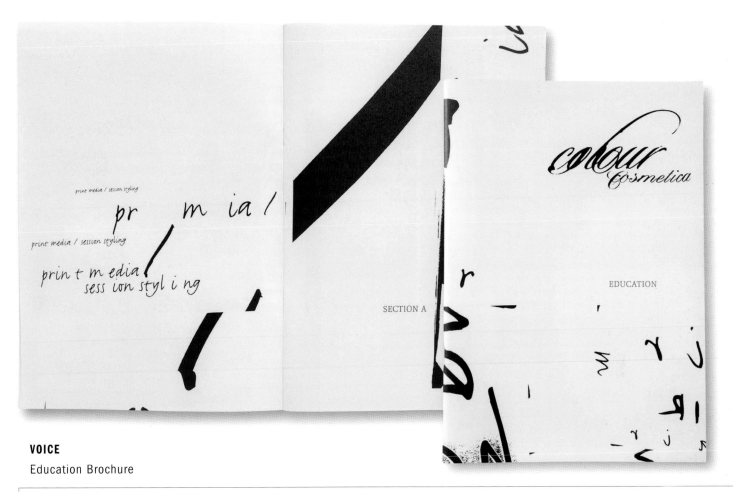

Education Brochure

ART DIRECTORS:
Anthony Deleo
Scott Carslake

DESIGNERS:
Anthony Deleo
Scott Carslake

CLIENT:
Colour Cosmetica

TOOLS:
Macromedia Freehand
QuarkXPress

MATERIALS:
Pacesetter Laser
250 gsm (cover)
Pacesetter Laser
110 gsm (text)

One&Only
Palmilla
Los Cabos, Mexico
The historic chapel, overlooking the resort's tropical grounds and beaches, exudes an aura of romance and enchantment that is perfect for weddings and renewal of vows.
Outdoor reception areas and contemporary conference facilities provide a choice of venues for all occasions, with the assurance that One&Only Palmilla's experienced staff will create an atmosphere of impeccable service and hospitality.

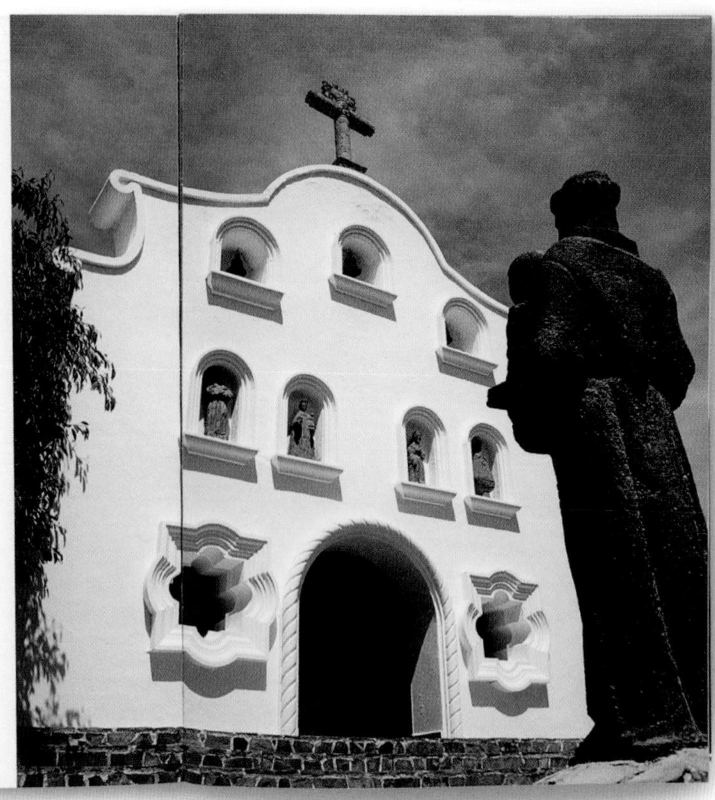

PENTAGRAM DESIGN/SF

Sales Brochure

ART DIRECTOR:
Brian Jacobs

DESIGNER:
Takayo Muroga

CLIENT:
One + Only Resorts

TOOLS:
Adobe Photoshop
Adobe Illustrator
QuarkXPress

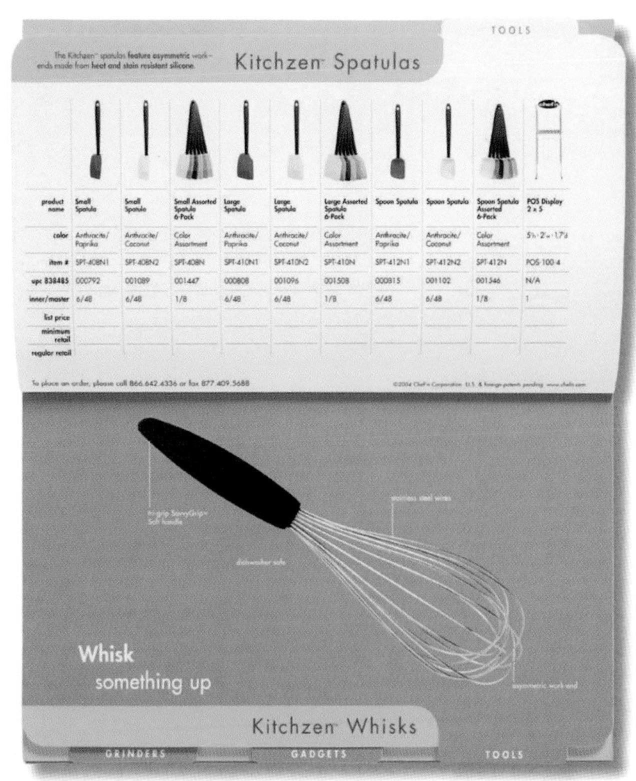

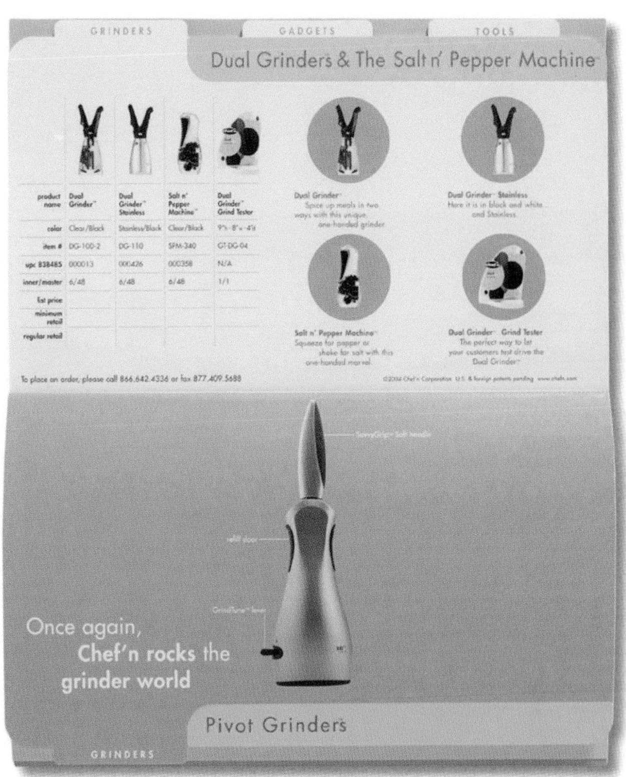

HORNALL ANDERSON DESIGN WORKS, INC.

Chef'n Catalog

ART DIRECTORS:	DESIGNERS:	CLIENT:	TOOLS:	MATERIALS:
Kathy Saito Jack Anderson Lisa Cerveny	Sonja Max Alan Copeland	Chef'n	Adobe Photoshop QuarkXPress	Mohawk Superfine 80 lb (cover)

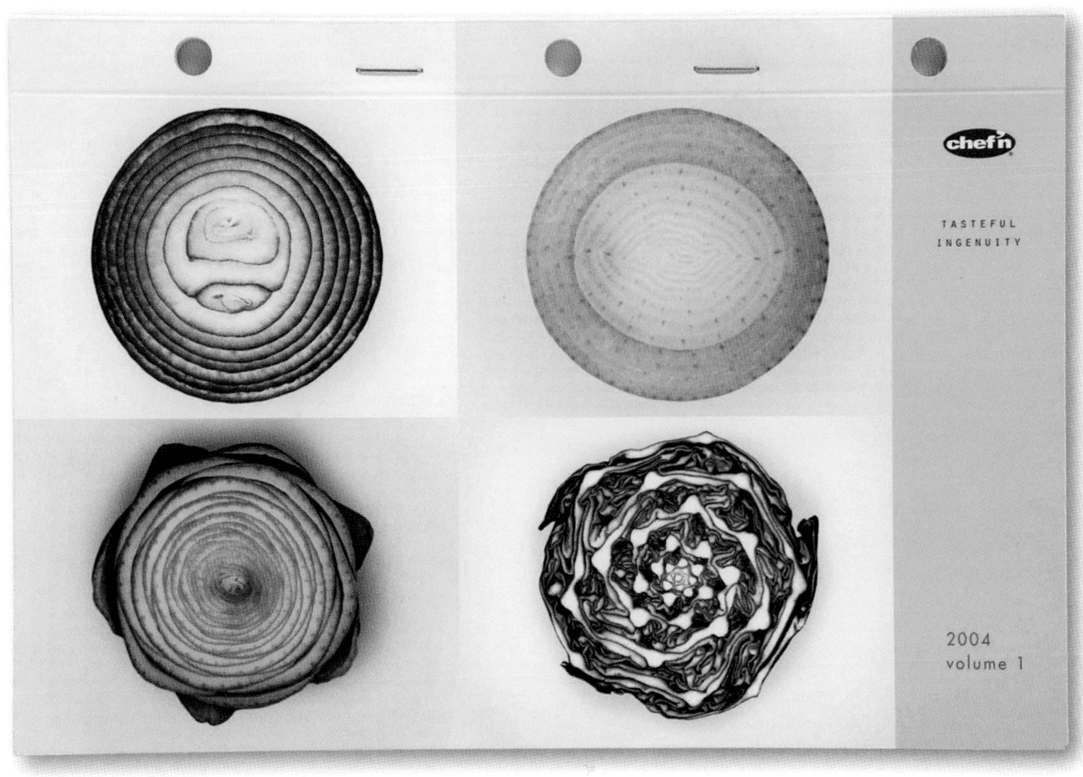

CF NAPA

Golden State Vineyards Brochure

ART DIRECTOR:
David Schuemann

DESIGNER:
CF Napa

CLIENT:
Golden State Vintners

TOOLS:
QuarkXPress

MATERIALS:
Paper with natural cork veneer

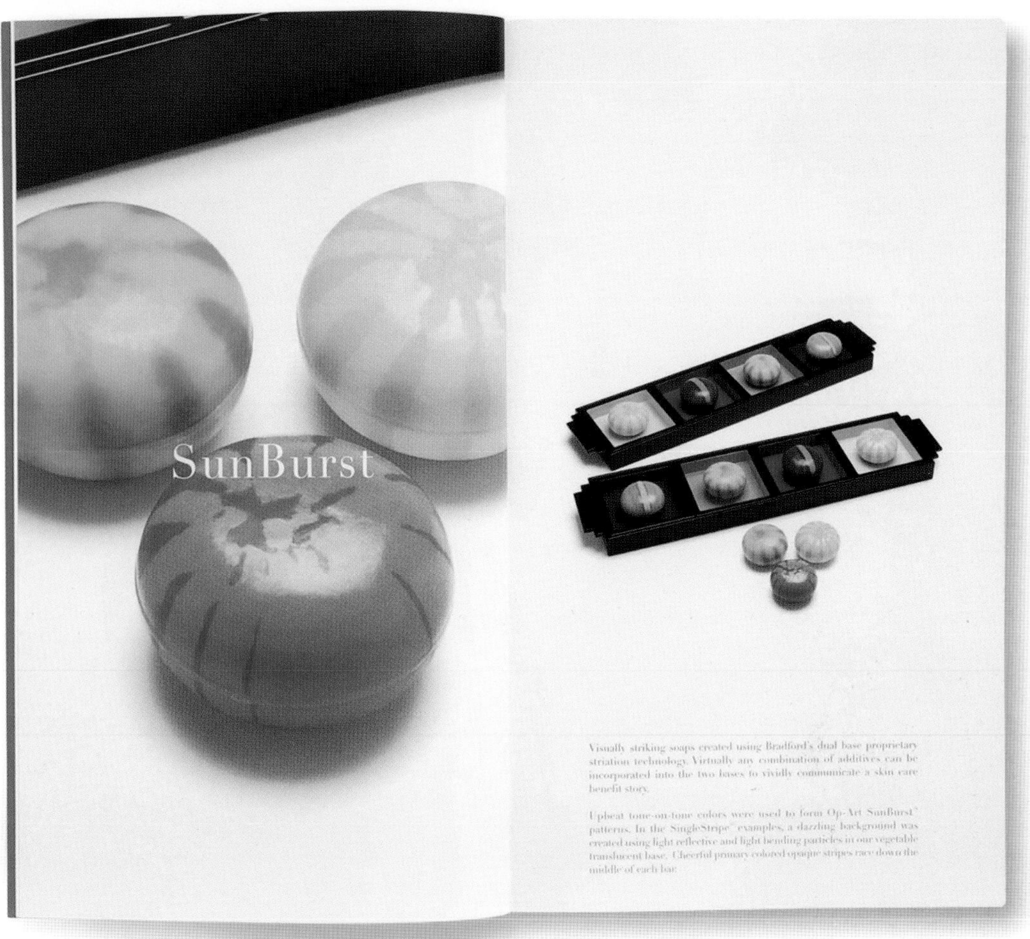

SunBurst
Visually striking soaps created using Bradford's dual base proprietary striation technology. Virtually any combination of additives can be incorporated into the two bases to vividly communicate a skin care benefit story.
Upbeat tone-on-tone colors were used to form Op-Art SunBurst patterns. In the SingleStripe examples, a dazzling background was created using light reflective and light bending particles in our vegetable translucent base. Cheerful primary colored opaque stripes race down the middle of each bar.

WEYMOUTH DESIGN

Bradford TrendScape Brochure

ART DIRECTOR:
Tom Laidlaw

DESIGNERS:
Arvi Raquel-Santos
Brad Lewthwaite

CLIENT:
Bradford Soap Works, Inc.

TOOLS:
QuarkXPress

MATERIALS:
Sappi McCoy Silk

Totally natural, uncolored, unfragranced soaps produced through the saponification of unusual blends of oils known to have beneficial effects on the skin. Eco-Ex is one of Bradford's new generation of soap bases. These formulas lather beautifully and leave the skin feeling silky-soft.
Tuscany Blend – Saponified from hazelnut, walnut, almond and coconut oils.
Polynesian Blend – Saponified from kukui nut, macadamia, almond and coconut oils.
Blue Ridge Mountain Blend – Saponified from pecan, walnut, peanut and coconut oils.
Moroccan Blend – Saponified from cashew, pistachio, walnut and coconut oils.

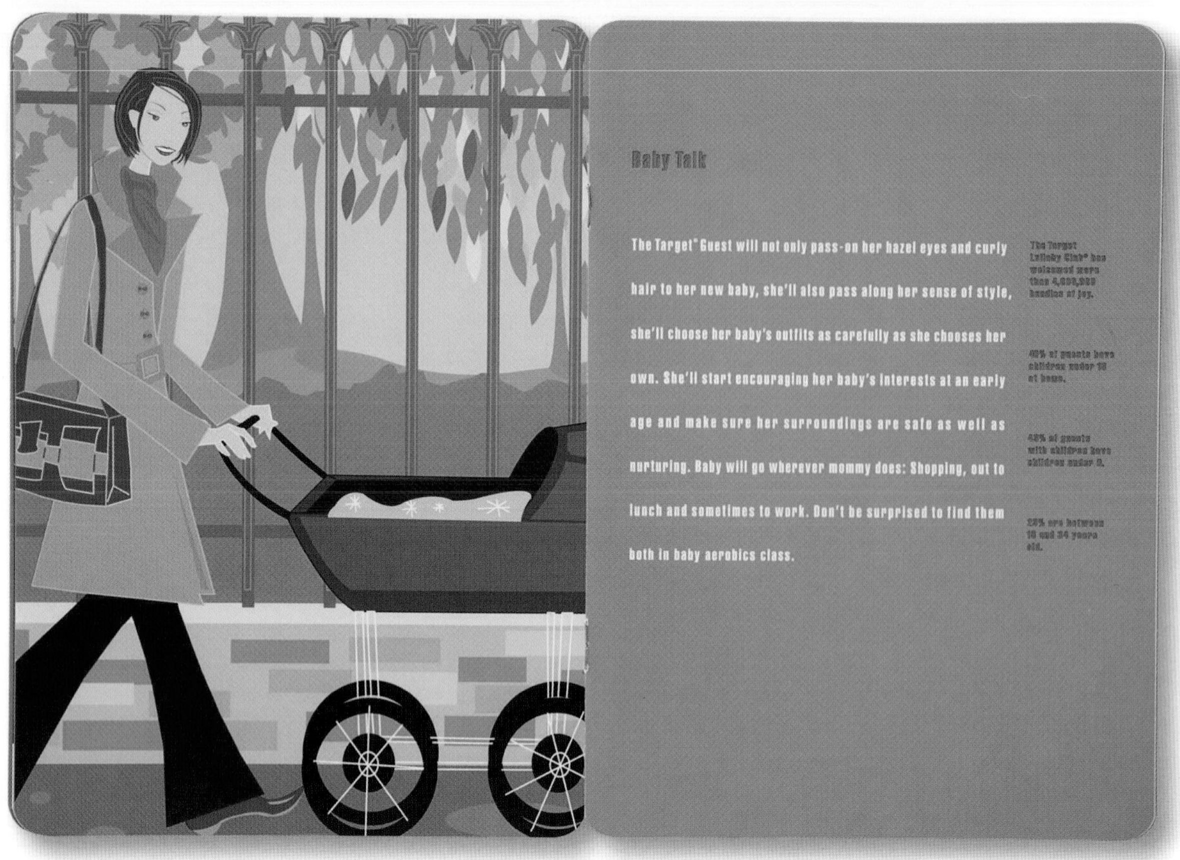

GRAPHICULTURE

Getting to Know . . .

ART DIRECTOR:	**CLIENT:**	**TOOLS:**	**MATERIALS:**
Cheryl Watson	Target	Adobe Illustrator QuarkXPress	dull coated stock

Who is The Core Guest?

Who shops at Target®? The answer is both simple and complex. She's a unique individual (80% are female) who's upscale (median household income of $54,000) and educated (40% have graduated from a 4-year college). When she's not working, you'll find her in her suburban home raising a family (40% have children) and pursuing a variety of interests (41% enjoy gardening). But she's much more than statistics. She's style conscious and aware of trends. She values her time and her opinions. And her life is about to change in a big way. Get to know her and you'll know what she's looking for.

Getting to know the Target® Guest

THE POINT GROUP

Upscale Real Estate Brochure

ART DIRECTOR:
David Howard

DESIGNER:
Cassandra Zimmerman

CLIENT:
W Hotel & Residences

TOOLS:
Adobe Photoshop
Adobe Illustrator
QuarkXPress

MATERIALS:
Domtar Solutions
Carrera white

Getting your message across the world is no easy task. There are many potential pitfalls. It's easy to use the wrong inflection, cause offence, or waste your money. When you're co-ordinating people and projects thousands of miles away, there's plenty of scope for misunderstandings.

Verbatim provides a total solution for companies who want to make their words count in different countries. Though we pride ourselves on the quality of our translation services, our comprehensive language management offer goes much further than just the words. It includes planning, production, logistics and distribution. So we can take a project all the way from the drawing board and right into your target audience's hands.

With Verbatim, you can be sure your words say the right thing at the right time.

Aa
> Could your life be made easier?
Few companies have the capability or resources to manage international communications. As well as careful co-ordination, they need local knowledge and dedicated teams in different parts of the world. But Verbatim knows how to smooth the whole process. We're experts in the field, and bring continuity and efficiency to even the most complex projects. Deal with us, and we can deal with everything else for you.

HAT-TRICK DESIGN

Verbatim Brochure

ART DIRECTORS:
Gareth Howat
David Kimpton
Jim Sutherland

DESIGNERS:
Jim Sutherland
Adam Giles

CLIENT:
Verbatim

TOOLS:
Adobe Photoshop
QuarkXPress

MATERIALS:
Skye Brilliant White

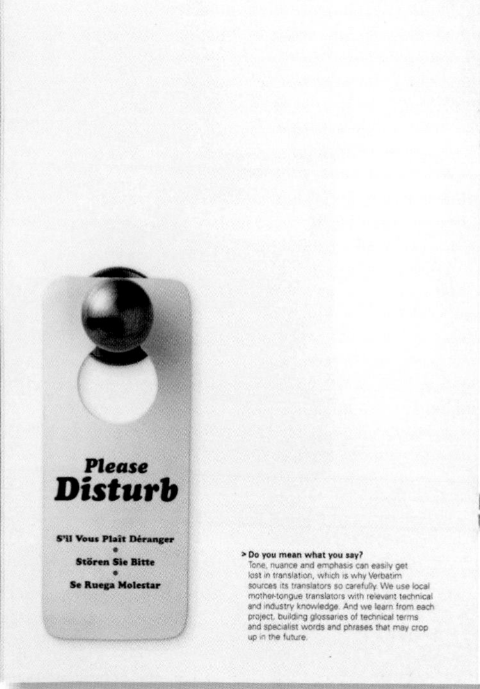

Please
Disturb
S'il Vous Plaît Déranger
Stören Sie Bitte
Se Ruega Molestar
> Do you mean what you say?
Tone, nuance and emphasis can easily get lost in translation, which is why Verbatim sources its translators so carefully. We use local mother-tongue translators with relevant technical and industry knowledge. And we learn from each project, building glossaries of technical terms and specialist words and phrases that may crop up in the future.

> Are your words digestible?
Mistranslations can be entertaining ('frozen codpiece' anybody?). But not when they affect your business. Verbatim makes sure that your messages come across loud, clear and consistently in different territories, in any media. This immediately shows you're serious, switched on and thorough. After all, the quality of your communication is a reflection of the quality of your product.
POOR TEA

MARIUS FAHRNER DESIGN

Kitchen Brochure for a Designer

ART DIRECTOR:
Marius Fahrner

DESIGNER:
Marius Fahrner

CLIENT:
Ulrike Urages

TOOLS:
Macromedia Freehand

MATERIALS:
Noblesse 300 g naturel
Classen Paper (cover)
Maxi Satin 200 g white
Igepa (text)

USINE DE BOUTONS

TRAVEL BOOK

ART DIRECTOR:
Lionello Borean

DESIGNERS:
Lionello Borean
Chiara Grandesso

CLIENT:
INVICTA SpA

TOOLS:
Adobe Illustrator

NO.PARKING

Presentation Brochure for Franchising Store (single sheets and folder)

ART DIRECTOR:	DESIGNER:	CLIENT:	TOOLS:	MATERIALS:
Caterina Romino	Caterina Romino	Iojo–Body Objects	QuarkXPress	Magnomatt 120 g

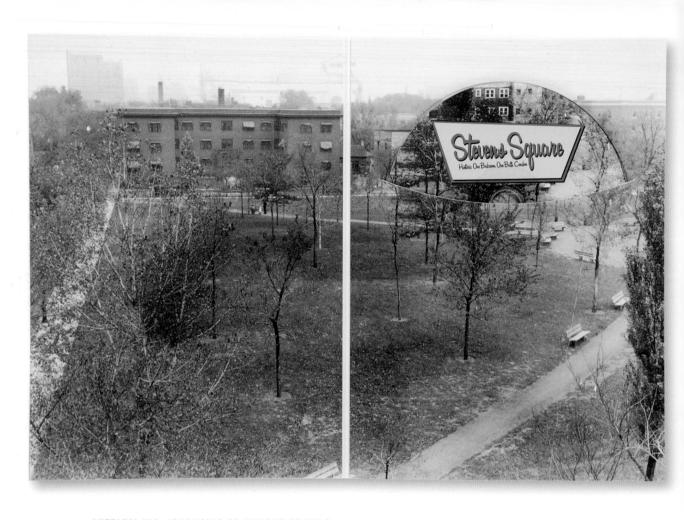

ANTFARM INC. (CHANGING TO KAMPER BRANDS)

Stevens Square Condos

DESIGNERS:	**CLIENT:**	**TOOLS:**
Dan Behrens Patrick Crowe	Real Estate Development Group	Adobe Photoshop Adobe Illustrator

ANTFARM INC.
(CHANGING TO KAMPER BRANDS)
Rossmor True Lofts

DESIGNERS:	CLIENT:	TOOLS:	MATERIALS:
Dan Behrens Patrick Crowe	PAK Properties	Adobe Photoshop Adobe Illustrator	four-color process Pantone 877 spot varnish

butter
cheese
cream
ice cream
milk
new dairy culture
yogurt
Dairy
The food of life

PERKS DESIGN PARTNERS

Dairy Culture Educational Kit

ART DIRECTOR:	DESIGNER:	CLIENT:	TOOLS:
Chris Perks	Maurice Lai	Dairy Australia	Adobe Illustrator QuarkXPress

GRAPHICULTURE

Swell—Simple Solutions

ART DIRECTOR:	CLIENT:	TOOLS:	MATERIALS:
Cheryl Watson	Target	Adobe Photoshop Adobe Illustrator QuarkXPress	coated paper

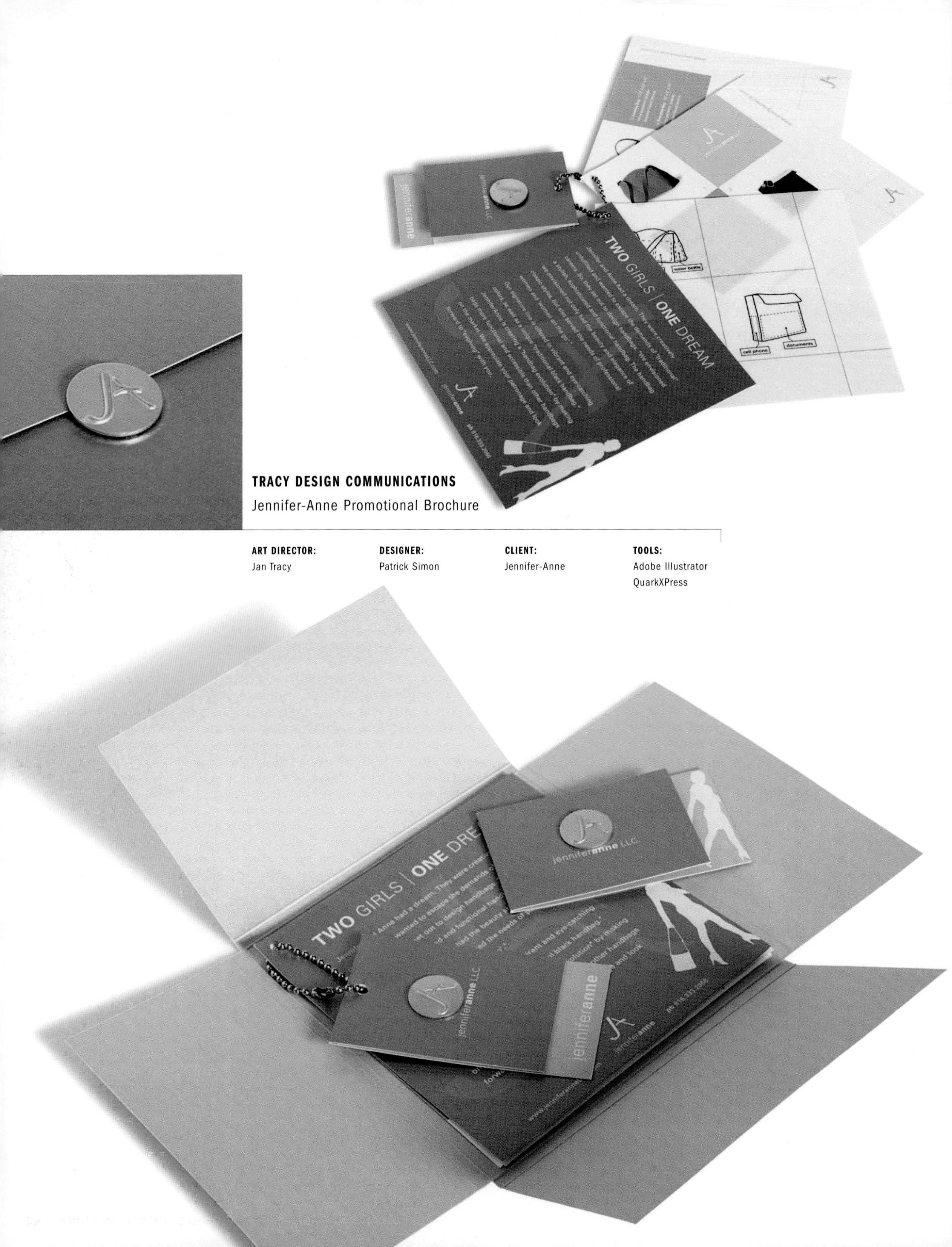

TRACY DESIGN COMMUNICATIONS

Jennifer-Anne Promotional Brochure

ART DIRECTOR:	**DESIGNER:**	**CLIENT:**	**TOOLS:**
Jan Tracy	Patrick Simon	Jennifer-Anne	Adobe Illustrator QuarkXPress

Tasman Bay Olives Ltd incorporates three olive groves - Beulah Olives, Nelson Olive Grove and Bethany Olive Grove, all situated on the Moutere clays in the Tasman Bay region of New Zealand. The Moutere clay is gaining increasing recognition for producing superior flavour for many types of horticultural crops such as wine, apples, and olives. The combination of these ideal growing conditions and high sunshine in the Nelson area results in a premium quality olive oil.
Tasman Bay Olives is primarily focused on the premium Italian varieties. Tests by the Cawthron Institute on Elovi Olive Oil show low acidity levels of between 0.05% to 0.17%.
ELOVI | OLIVE | OIL
the best of both worlds
Elovi

LLOYDS GRAPHIC DESIGN LTD

Olive Oil Producer Promotional Brochure

ART DIRECTOR:
Alexander Lloyd

DESIGNER:
Alexander Lloyd

CLIENT:
Tasman Bay Olives/Elovi Olive Oil

TOOLS:
Adobe Photoshop
Macromedia Freehand

MATERIALS:
matte textured stock
220 gsm

LISKA + ASSOCIATES, INC.

The Cass Gilbert Brochure

ART DIRECTOR:
Tanya Quick

DESIGNERS:
Tanya Quick
Fernando Munoz

CLIENT:
Douglas Elliman
The Cass Gilbert

TOOLS:
Adobe Photoshop
Adobe Illustrator
QuarkXPress

MATERIALS:
Mohawk Superfine soft white smooth 100 lb (cover)

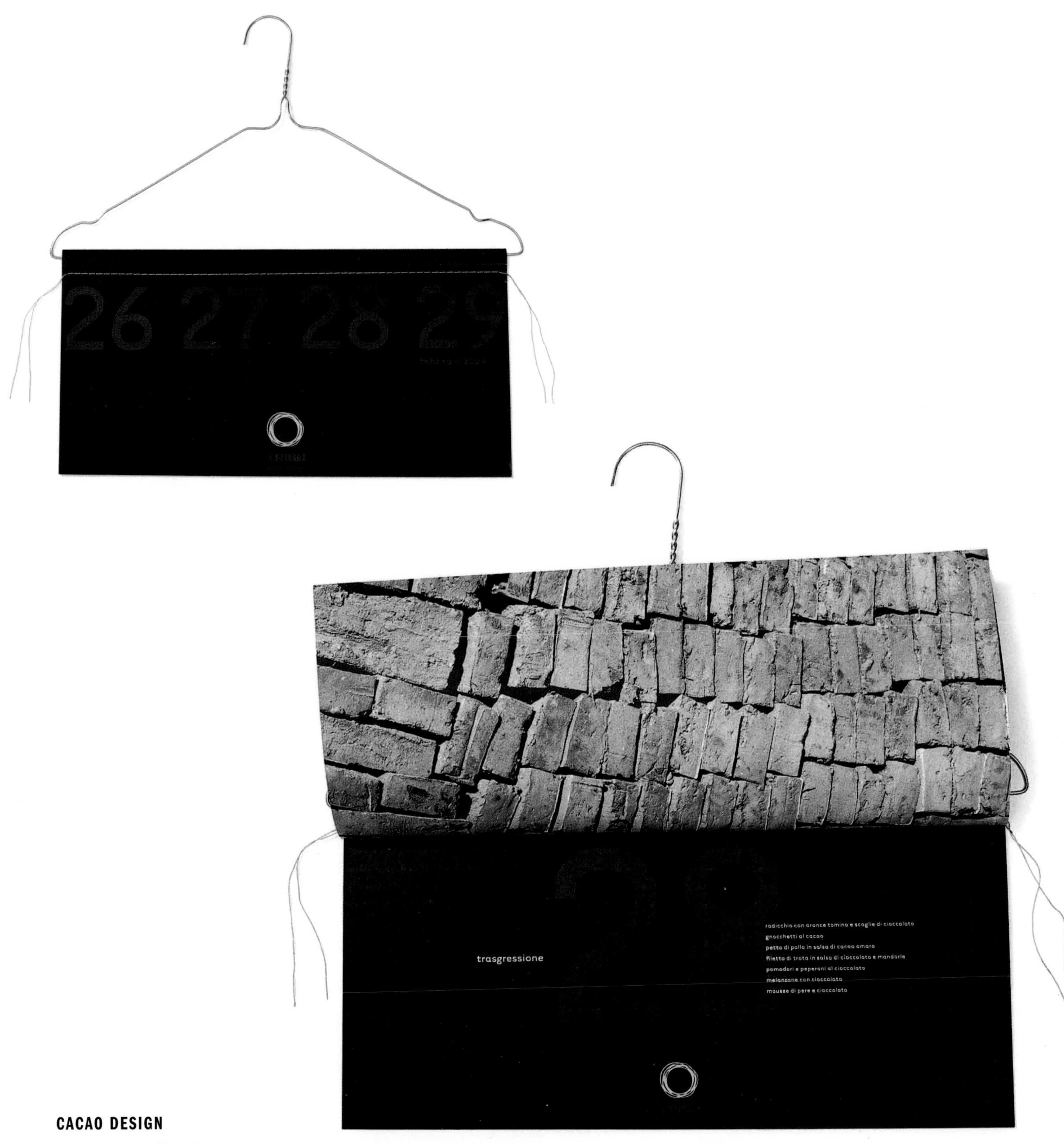

CACAO DESIGN

Events Menu/Brochure

ART DIRECTOR:	**DESIGNER:**	**CLIENT:**	**TOOLS:**
Creative Team	Anna Carbone	Tribu	Adobe InDesign

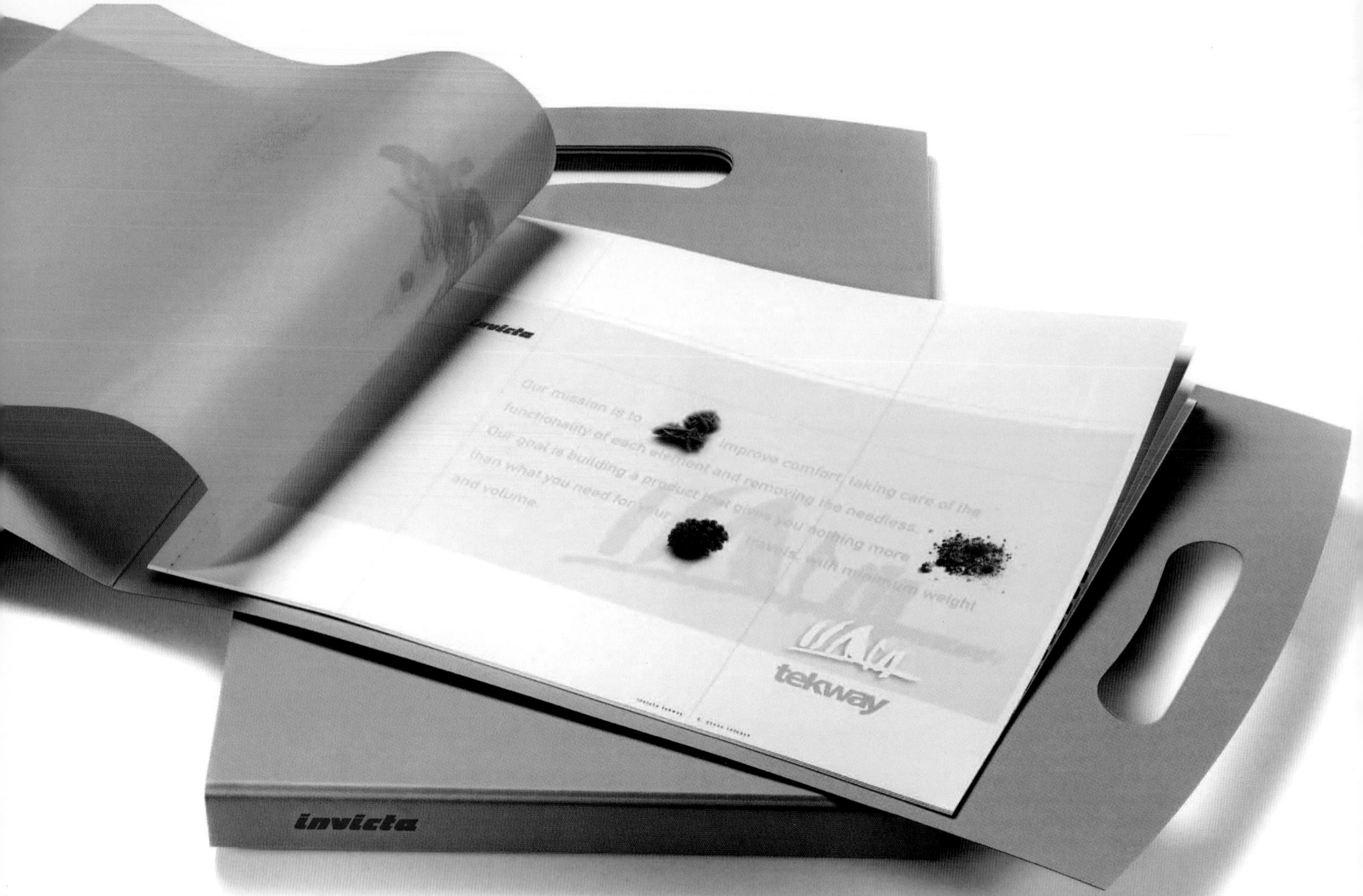

tekway
BorneoQuasar
AS3152 PAPUA

USINE DE BOUTONS

TEKWAY

ART DIRECTOR:	**DESIGNERS:**	**CLIENT:**	**TOOLS:**
Lionello Borean	Lionello Borean Chiara Grandesso	INVICTA SpA	Adobe Illustrator

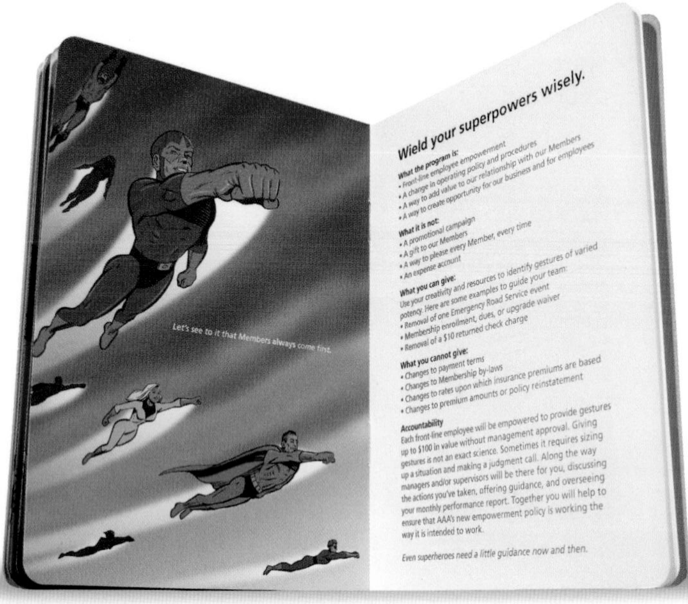

Let's see to it that Members always come first.
Wield your superpowers wisely.
What the program is:
• Front-line employee empowerment
• A change in operating policy and procedures
• A way to add value to our relationship with our Members
• A way to create opportunity for our business and for employees
What it is not:
• A promotional campaign
• A gift to our Members
• A way to please every Member, every time
• An expense account
What you can give:
Use your creativity and resources to identify gestures of varied potency. Here are some examples to guide your team:
• Removal of one Emergency Road Service event
• Membership enrollment, dues, or upgrade waiver
• Removal of a $10 returned check charge
What you cannot give:
• Changes to payment terms
• Changes to Membership by-laws
• Changes to rates upon which insurance premiums are based
• Changes to premium amounts or policy reinstatement
Accountability
Each front-line employee will be empowered to provide gestures up to $100 in value without management approval. Giving gestures is not an exact science. Sometimes it requires sizing up a situation and making a judgment call. Along the way managers and/or supervisors will be there for you, discussing the actions you've taken, offering guidance, and overseeing your monthly performance report. Together you will help to ensure that AAA's new empowerment policy is working the way it is intended to work.
Even superheroes need a little guidance now and then.

Question four:
Is the solution consistent with our values?

You've broken free of irksome approvals.
Now go make the world a better place.
About your new superpowers:
Frontline employees, like you, have been telling us lately that you'd like more power. But not just any powers ... special powers. Congratulations! Your super-signal was received and you now have the ability to create the most loyal and satisfied customers in the entire universe.
Wield your new power wisely: ask yourself the following questions before offering a AAA goodwill gesture. Interestingly enough, they're the same questions that managers used to ask themselves before granting approval. The difference is you can do it better, stronger, and faster.
Question One:
Is the solution good for business?
Consider the potential effect on our business of a Member's dissatisfaction. Is this a Member we should make a special effort to keep? Factors like the depth of a Member's relationship with AAA and the number of years he or she has been a Member can signal the importance of a little extra attention.
For example, a 15-year Member who insures both home and auto with us, and who frequently books trip through Travel Services, is a very valuable Member. It would make sense to increase the value of a goodwill gesture for a Member like this. On the other hand, if a Member makes frequent Emergency Road Service calls and insurance claims or if they have a history of payments returned by the bank, he or she may actually be costing us money and making a gesture of any sort may be inappropriate.
In the end, it comes down to how much benefit a Member offers AAA. In other words, do they deserve a superhero's rescue?

CSAA CREATIVE SERVICES
Your New Superpowers Booklet

Art Director:
Virginia Vovchuk
Designer:
Jeff Carino
Client:
CSAA Sales & Service
Software:
Adobe InDesign
Paper/Materials:
Starwhite Vicksburg (Fox River)

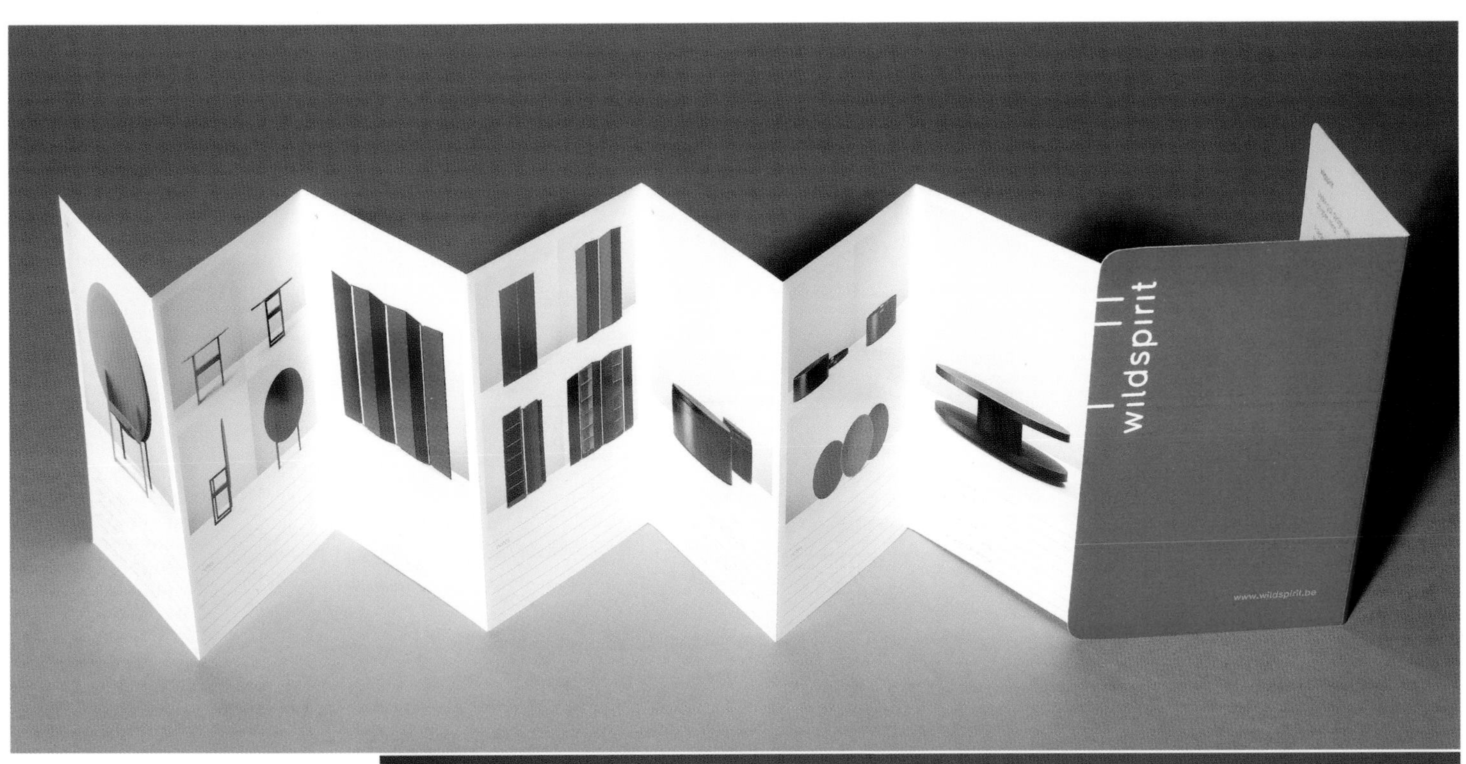

FLORE VAN RYN
Catalog / First Collection Wildspirit Furnitures

Art Director:
Flore Van Ryn
Designer:
Flore Van Ryn
Client:
Wildspirit
Software:
Adobe InDesign
Paper/Materials:
Coated matte 350 gsm (cover), 150 gsm (text)

HAMIET BLUIETT
Portraits of the Other Music
In my youth I saw alchemists, magicians, saints, downright holy men not like "oh my Lord", but "Lord have mercy". Drenched in spirit, these cats had the Holy Ghost like right now.
The reach and impact of this music, sometimes labeled free jazz, the new thing, avant garde, fire music, experimental or great blackness, has developed a much larger audience than what general media would have one believe. The music and its players are known in practically every country on earth. That's why the artists in this beautiful book are considered true pioneers and soldiers of the cause.
We are unquestionably heirs to the enormous legacy of Scott Joplin, Jelly Roll Morton, Louis Armstrong, Duke Ellington, Fletcher Henderson, Charlie Parker, Dizzy Gillespie, Thelonious Monk, Charles Mingus, John Coltrane, Miles Davis, Ornette Coleman and Sun Ra along with hundreds of other known and unknown giants of creative music.
The artists mentioned above I would call system deliverers. They are both spirit and conduit to the entire history of 20th century music. They were each able to change something about this world with their music. The life in the music expresses foremost a need for exploration. It is creativity in all of its profound intelligence, immediacy, rawness, and realness. Each of these photos reflects the energy of the improviser in a variety of moods. Bluiett, Malachi Favors, Billy Bang, Roscoe Mitchell, Fareed Haque, Ari Brown, Pharoah Sanders, Leo Smith, Cecil Payne are all cats that I truly love. I have the highest respect for their music and cultural contributions.

HARTFORD DESIGN, INC.
Jazz Masters Promotion

Art Director:
Tim Hartford
Designers:
Lisa Ermatinger, Judith Miller
Client:
Nimrod Systems
Software:
QuarkXPress
Paper/Materials:
Potlatch McCoy

SAGMEISTER INC.
Anni Kuan
Brochure, Gold

Art Director:
Stefan Sagmeister
Designer:
Ariane Spanari
Client:
Anni Kuan
Software:
Adobe CS
Paper/Materials:
Newsprint,
gold pieces

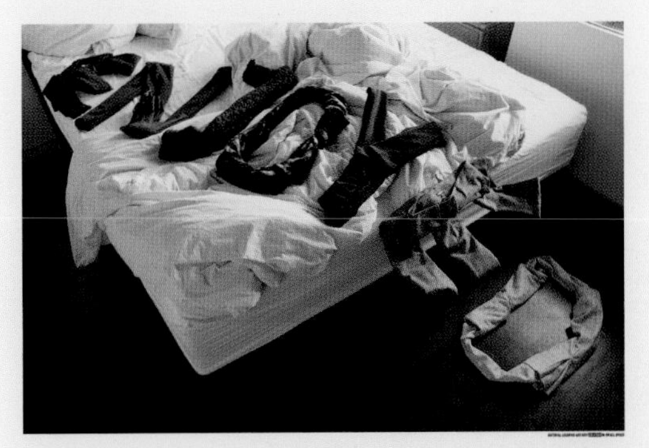

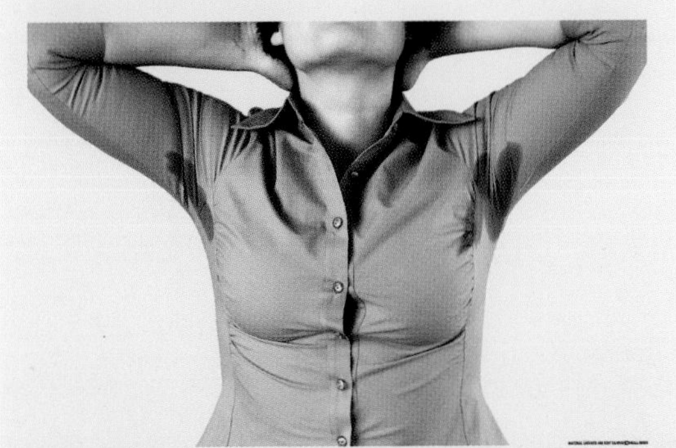

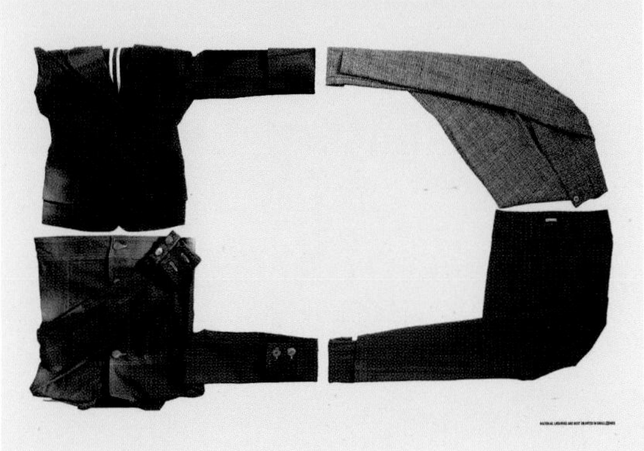

Swimming, fishing, sailing, hiking,
shopping, cooking, dancing...
We can hardly keep up with grandma!
But anyway, holidays are always
too short.

Knäckebröd, tomatoes, cheese, salad, yoghurt,
strawberries, butter, wine, soap...

-9-

HANDLAR'N

Our local grocery store

Donaldson

©THE WALT DISNEY COMPANY

The house on the 1001 lakes

a story by Donaldson

spring-summer 2004

FLORE VAN RYN

Donaldson / Fashion Catalog

Art Director:
Flore Van Ryn
Designer:
Flore Van Ryn
Client:
Donaldson
Software:
Adobe InDesign
Paper/Materials:
Munken Lynx 300 gsm (cover), 150 gsm (text)

while the boys
take it easy...

Daydreamin'
on the terrace

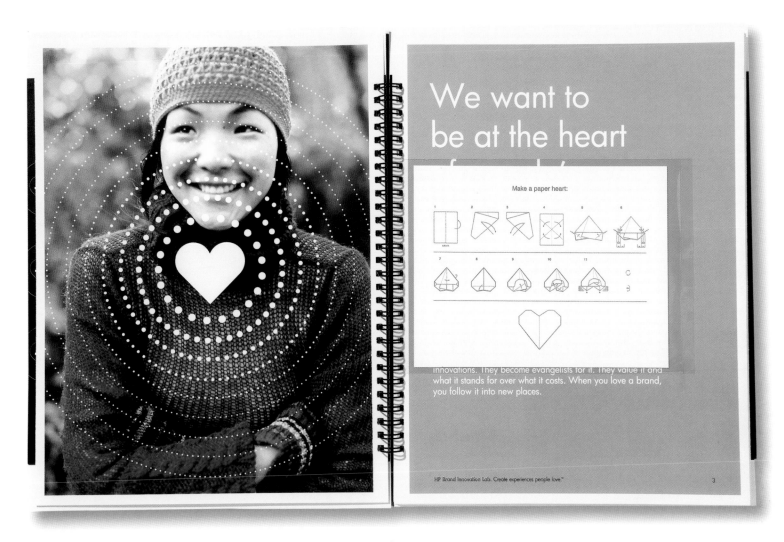

We want to
be at the heart

Make a paper heart:

innovations. They become evangelists for it. They value it and what it stands for over what it costs. When you love a brand, you follow it into new places.

HP Brand Innovation Lab. Create experiences people love.™ 3

MIRIELLO GRAFICO INC.
Hewlett Packard Brand Innovation

Designer:
Dennis Garcia
Client:
Hewlett Packard
Software:
Adobe Illustrator
Paper/Materials:
Carnival 80 lb text

300MILLION
Advocate Paper Works

Art Director:
Nigel Davies
Designer:
Natalie Turner
Client:
Tullis Russell
Software:
QuarkXPress, OSX
Paper/Materials:
Advocate

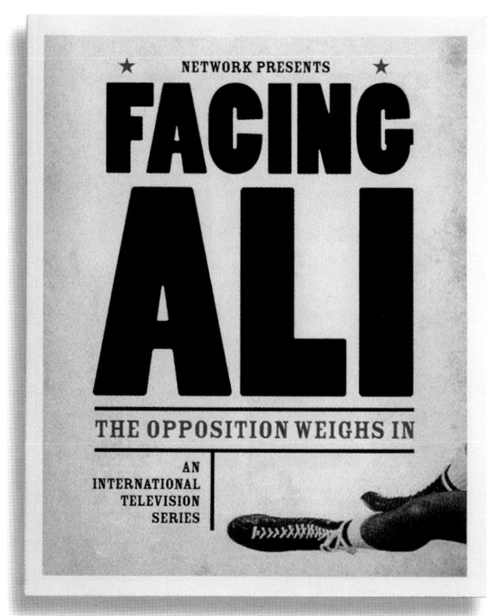

★ NETWORK PRESENTS ★
FACING
ALI
THE OPPOSITION WEIGHS IN
AN
INTERNATIONAL
TELEVISION
SERIES

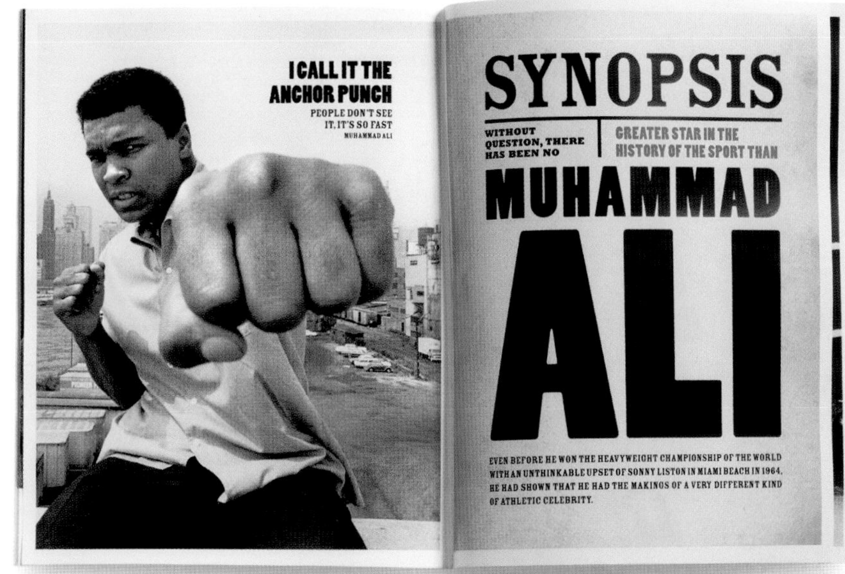

I CALL IT THE
ANCHOR PUNCH
PEOPLE DON'T SEE
IT, IT'S SO FAST
MUHAMMAD ALI
SYNOPSIS
WITHOUT
QUESTION, THERE
HAS BEEN NO
GREATER STAR IN THE
HISTORY OF THE SPORT THAN
MUHAMMAD
ALI
EVEN BEFORE HE WON THE HEAVYWEIGHT CHAMPIONSHIP OF THE WORLD WITH AN UNTHINKABLE UPSET OF SONNY LISTON IN MIAMI BEACH IN 1964, HE HAD SHOWN THAT HE HAD THE MAKINGS OF A VERY DIFFERENT KIND OF ATHLETIC CELEBRITY.

SUBPLOT
DESIGN INC.
Facing Ali

Art Directors:
Roy White,
Matthew Clarke
Designer:
Roy White
Client:
Network
Productions Inc.
Paper/Materials:
Pegasus

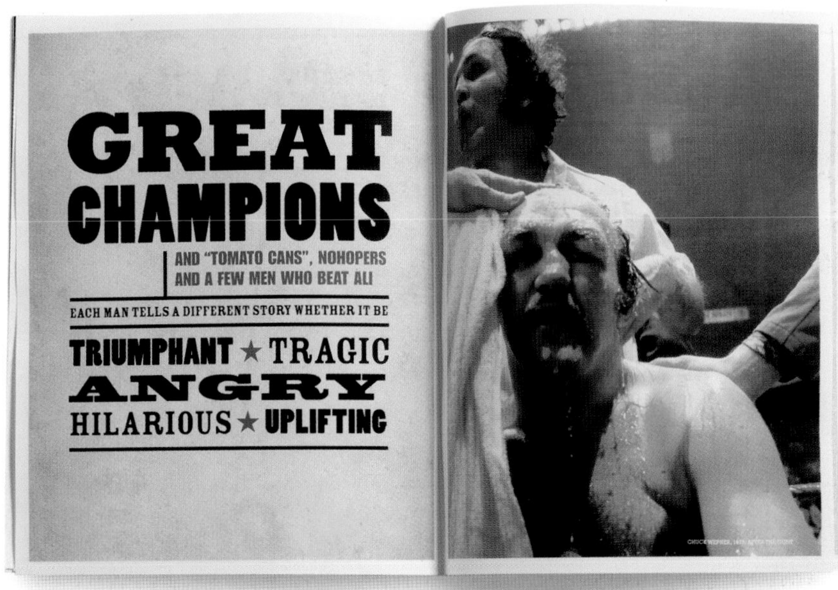

GREAT
CHAMPIONS
AND "TOMATO CANS", NOHOPERS
AND A FEW MEN WHO BEAT ALI
EACH MAN TELLS A DIFFERENT STORY WHETHER IT BE
TRIUMPHANT ★ TRAGIC
ANGRY
HILARIOUS ★ UPLIFTING

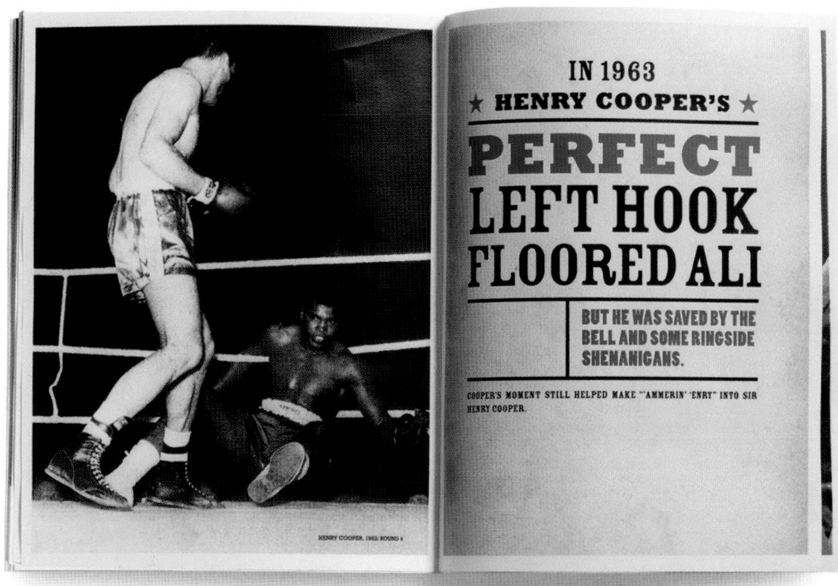

IN 1963
★ HENRY COOPER'S ★
PERFECT
LEFT HOOK
FLOORED ALI
BUT HE WAS SAVED BY THE
BELL AND SOME RINGSIDE
SHENANIGANS.
COOPER'S MOMENT STILL HELPED MAKE "AMMERIN' 'ENRY" INTO SIR HENRY COOPER.

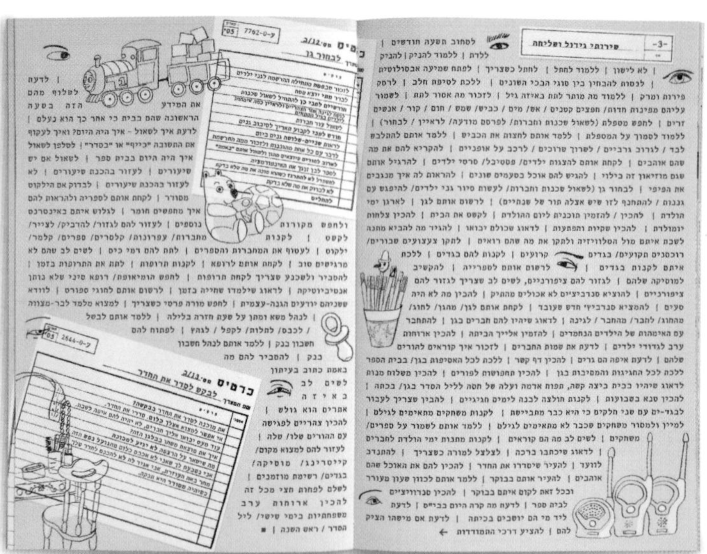

MICHAL GRANIT DESIGN STUDIO
Fashion Catalog

Art Director:
Michal Granit
Illustrator:
Orit Bergman
Client:
Comme il faut
Software:
Freehand,
Adobe Photoshop

BLOK DESIGN
Nienkamper Brochure

Art Director:
Vanessa Eckstein
Designer:
Vanessa Eckstein
Client:
Nienkamper
Paper/Materials:
Beckett Expression 130 lb

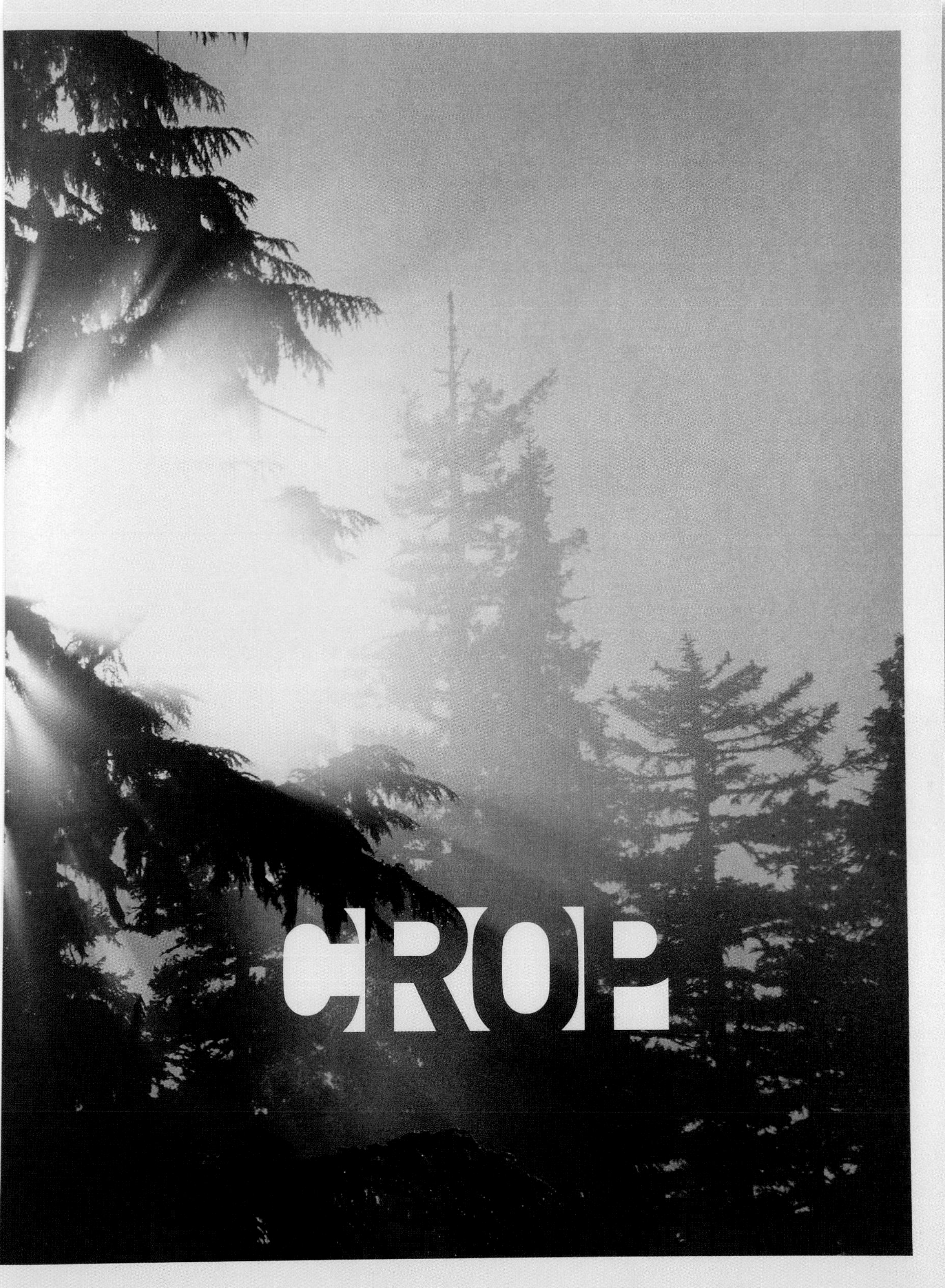

SEGURA INC.
Crop (Large Size Brochure)

Art Director:
Carlos Segura
Designers:
Carlos Segura,
Dave Weik,
Chris May,
Tnop
Client:
Corbis
Software:
Adobe InDesign,
Adobe Photoshop,
Adobe Illustrator

ICO DESIGN CONSULTANCY
Freehold Property Brochure

Art Director:
Andy Spencer
Designer:
Andy Spencer
Client:
Hammerson
Software:
Adobe InDesign
Paper/Materials:
Naturalis

Park Lane's most prestigious address
100 Park Lane is rich in architectural heritage.
In 1827, John William Ward, son of William Ward, Viscount Dudley and Ward, commissioned the architect William Atkinson to design and build the first Dudley home on this site.
The original Dudley House picture gallery, shown here in its former glory.

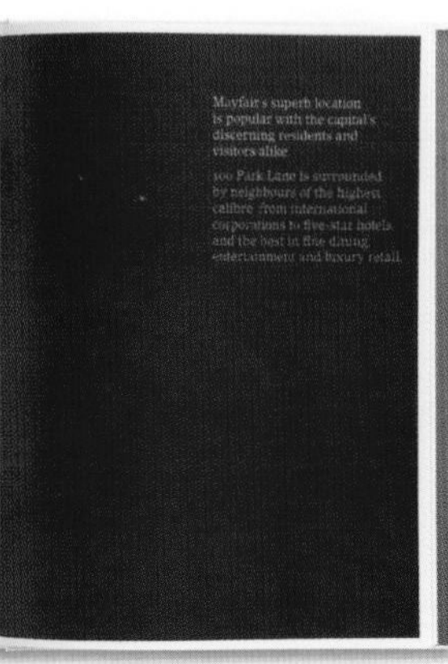

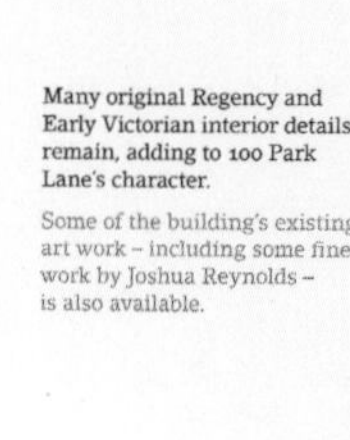

Many original Regency and Early Victorian interior details remain, adding to 100 Park Lane's character.
Some of the building's existing art work – including some fine work by Joshua Reynolds – is also available.

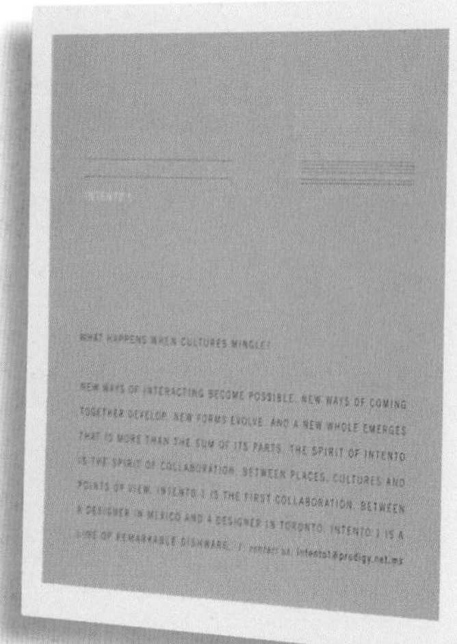

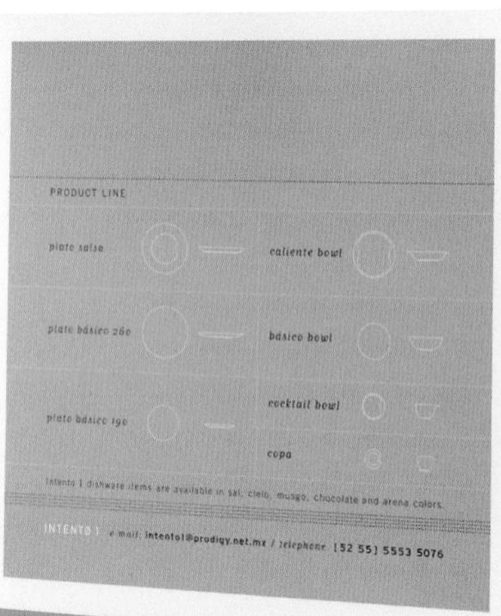

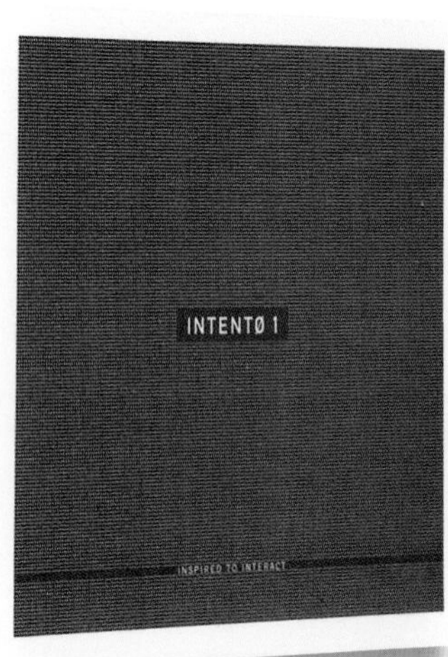

BLOK DESIGN
Intento 1

Art Director:
Vanessa Eckstein
Designers:
Vanessa Eckstein,
Mariana Contegni
Client:
Blok Design
Software:
Adobe Illustrator CS
Paper/Materials:
Starwhite, Sirus
Smooth, 130 lb (Fox
River)

KINETIC
SINGAPORE
Coral Island
Property Brochure

Art Directors:
Leng Soh, Pann Lim,
Roy Poh
Designers:
Leng Soh, Pann Lim,
Roy Poh
Client:
Hobee Group
Software:
Freehand,
Adobe Photoshop
Paper/Materials:
Matte art paper, card,
board

A LANDMARK CONCEPT WITHOUT EQUAL, A PRIME INVESTMENT OPPORTUNITY WITHOUT RIVAL
On the eastern end of the unspoiled island of Sentosa, located just off the southern coast of the thriving city-state of Singapore, within a stone's throw of the bustling central business district, an extraordinary residential enclave is in the midst of emerging.
Showcasing a unique concept that blends residential, commercial and marina facilities in the form of an integrated waterfront resort, Sentosa Cove introduces a truly magnificent oceanfront lifestyle and community without any equal in the region. Complete with its own fascinating Marina Village, the charming development stands in sharp contrast to the hustle and bustle of cosmopolitan, urban Singapore.

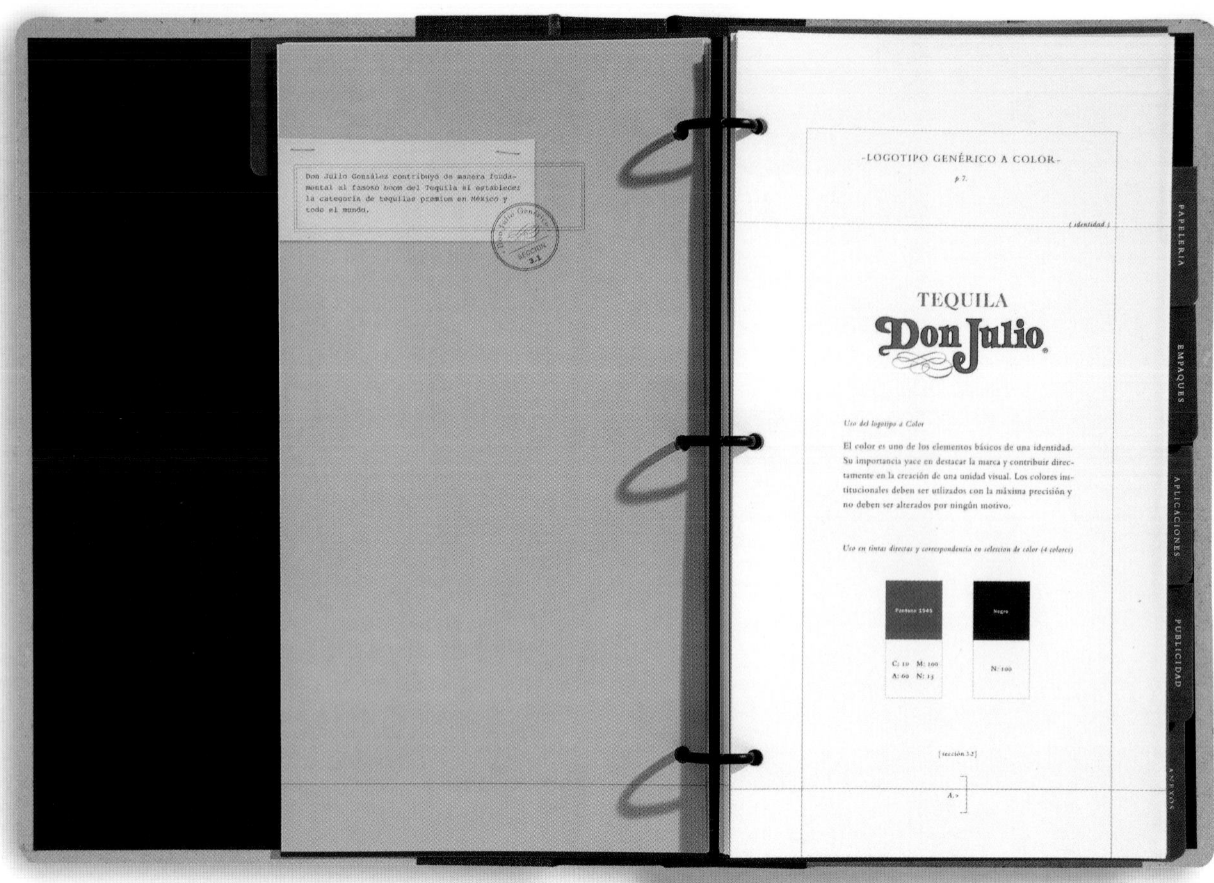

BLOK DESIGN

Don Julio

Art Director:
Vanessa Eckstein
Designers:
Vanessa Eckstein,
Vanesa Enriquez,
Mariana Contegni
Client:
Jose Cuervo
Software:
Adobe Illustrator
Paper/Materials:
Sundance Smoke and
Ultrawhite Smooth
(Fox River)

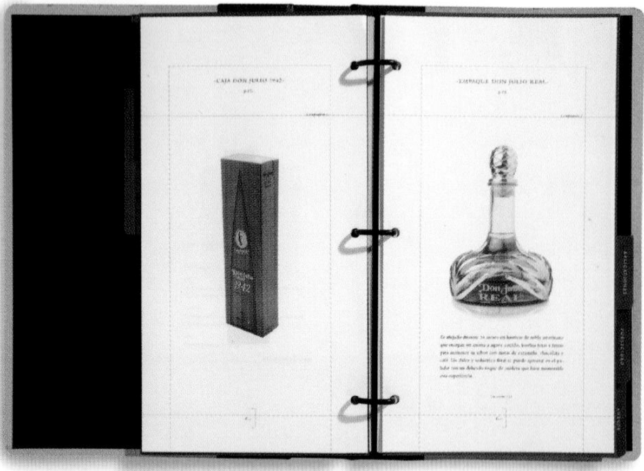

TAXI STUDIO LTD

Serious on the Outside...

Art Directors:
Ryan Wills,
Spencer Buck
Designers:
Alex Bane, Karl Wills,
Luke Manning,
Olly Guise
Client:
Science Museum
Software:
QuarkXPress,
Adobe Photoshop,
Adobe Illustrator
Paper/Materials:
Gardapat 13 150 gsm

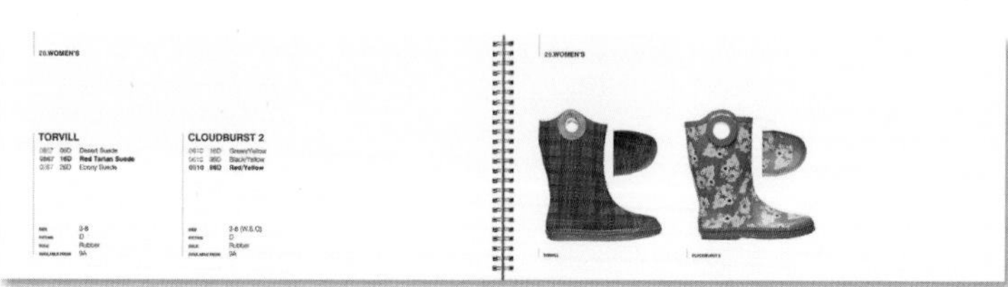

TAXI STUDIO LTD
Originals
Brochures

Art Director:
Ryan Wills
Designers:
Olly Guise,
Spencer Buck
Client:
Clarks
Software:
QuarkXPress

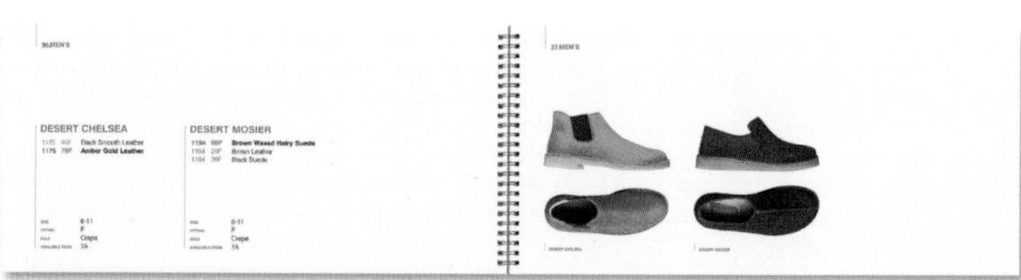

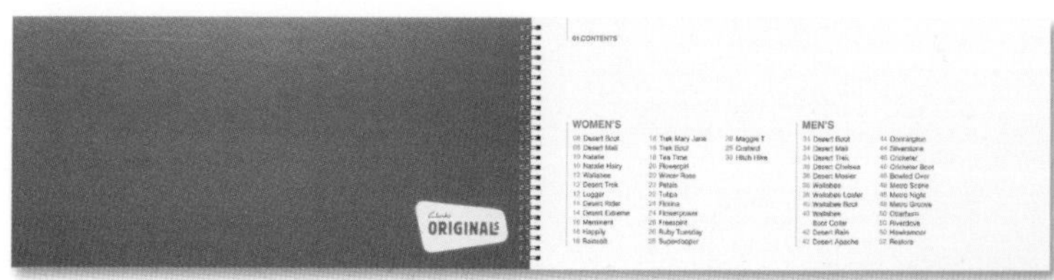

STILRADAR
The Grip Quadrants

Art Directors:
Raphael Pohland, Simone Winter
Designers:
Raphael Pohland, Simone Winter
Client:
Grip AG - Technische Textilkollktionen
Software:
Freehand
Paper/Materials:
Conqueror 160 gsm, 250 gsm

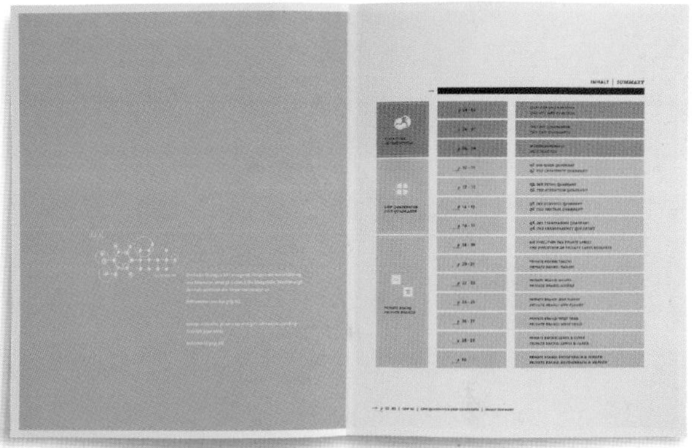

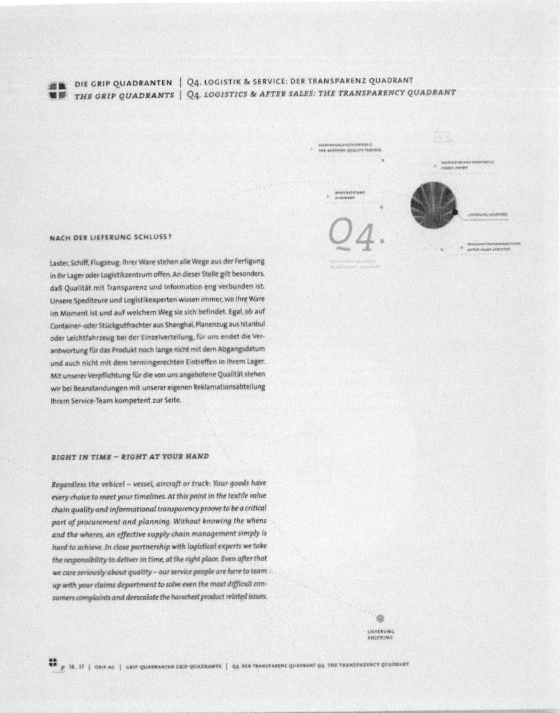

300MILLION

Naturalis Uncoated Brochure

Art Directors:
Nigel Davies,
Dom Bailey,
Martin Lawless
Client:
Tullis Russell
Software:
QuarkXPress, OSX
Paper/Materials:
Naturalis

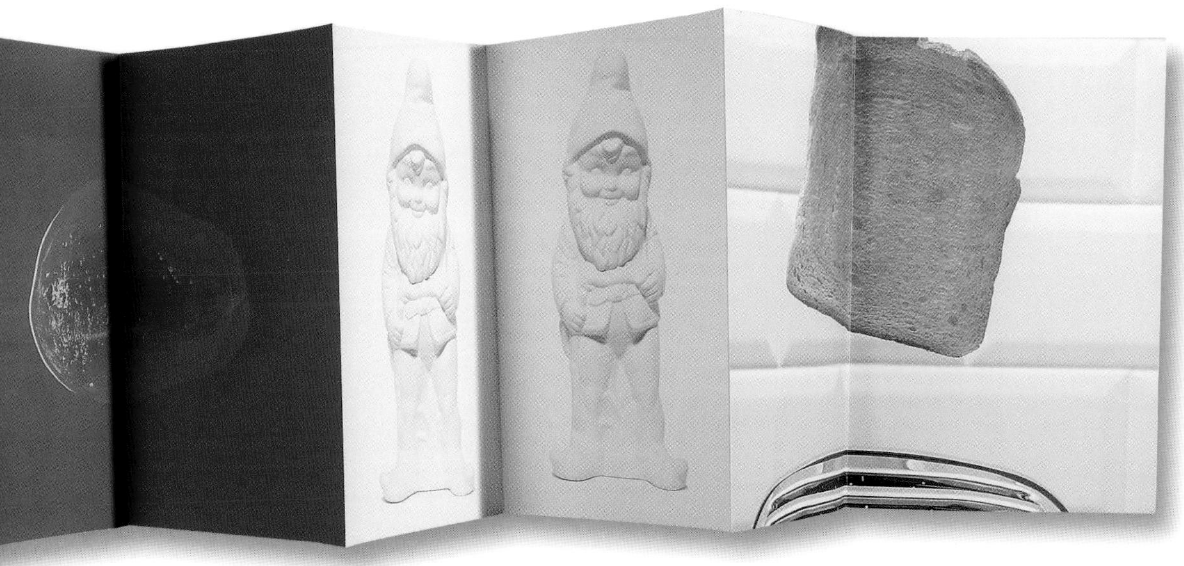

Le Mille
e una Carta
*The Thousand
and One Papers*

Double Face

BURGO

Double Face

BURGO

BRUNAZZI
& ASSOCIATI
**Brochures for
Burgo Papers**

Art Director:
Andrea Brunazzi
Designer:
Matteo Marucco
Client:
Cartiere Burgo
Software:
QuarkXPress,
Freehand
Paper/Materials:
Paper and cardboard

ALOOF DESIGN
Georgina Goodman Spring/ Summer

Art Director:
Sam Aloof
Designer:
Andrew Scrase
Client:
Georgina Goodman
Software:
Adobe Illustrator, Adobe Photoshop
Paper/Materials:
Colorplan & Zen GF Smith

The people are really nice here.

And other nasty rumors about us.

1

Summer associates are just as valued as partners.

careers.pillsburylaw.com

It's hard to know who to kiss up to.

CAHAN
& ASSOCIATES
Pillsbury Winthrop
Rumors Brochure

Art Director:
Bill Cahan,
Michael Braley
Designer:
Michael Braley
Client:
Pillsbury Winthrop
Shaw Pittman

3

You will work directly with clients early on in your career.

careers.pillsburylaw.com

Maybe not week one, but year one. Don't worry, we are behind you.

2

Summer associates are included in real deals.

careers.pillsburylaw.com

It isn't all filet mignon and box seats.

IAAH

Beyond the Sea Brochure

Art Director:
Nessim Higson
Designer:
Nessim Higson
Client:
Lion Gate Films
Software:
Adobe Photoshop, Adobe Illustrator

CEM ERUTKU
TASARIM
STUDYOSU - C375
Hotel Brochure

Art Director:
N. Cem Erutku
Designer:
N. Cem Erutku
Client:
Ourco Tourism
Software:
Adobe Photoshop,
Freehand
Paper/Materials:
Sappi 300 gsm

CAHAN
& ASSOCIATES
See: The Potential of Place, 2nd Issue

Art Directors:
Bill Cahan,
Todd Richards,
Steve Frykholm
Designers:
Todd Richards,
Nicholas Davison
Client:
Herman Miller
Paper/Materials:
International Papers
Via Recycled

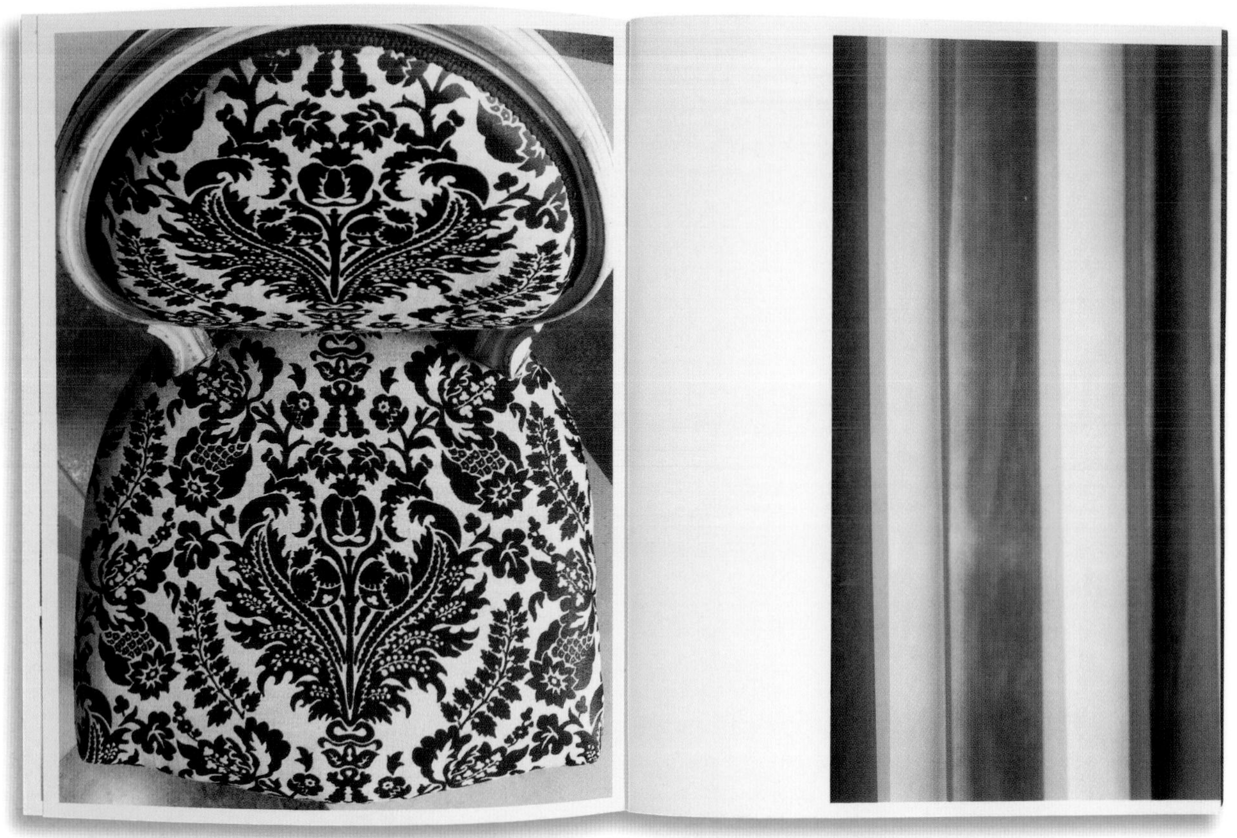

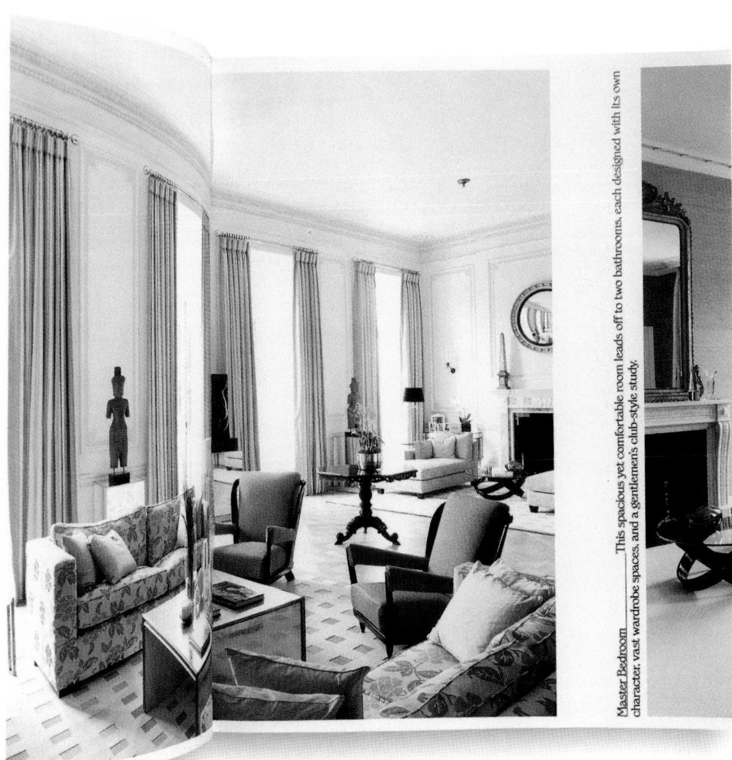

Master Bedroom
This spacious yet comfortable room leads off to two bathrooms, each designed with its own character, vast wardrobe spaces, and a gentlemen's club-style study.

ICO DESIGN CONSULTANCY
Freehold Property Brochure

Art Director:
Vivek Bhatia
Designer:
Vivek Bhatia
Client:
Bath + Bath
Software:
Adobe InDesign, Adobe Photoshop
Paper/Materials:
Naturalis, Curious (main brochure), Redeem, Curious (plans book), Flockage (box)

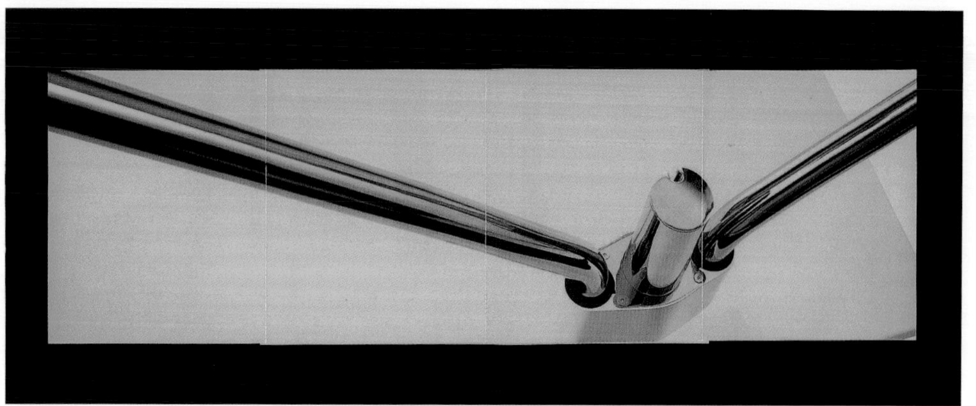

SEA

Staverton Brochure

Art Director:
Bryan Edmondson

Designer:
Stuart L Bailey

Client:
Staverton

Software:
QuarkXPress, Adobe Photoshop

Paper/Materials:
PVC (cover), Paralux (text)

PAST, PRESENT & FUTURE

DOWLING DESIGN & ART DIRECTION
Promotional Booklet

Art Director:
John Dowling
Designer:
John Dowling
Client:
Future Designs
Software:
QuarkXPress
Paper/Materials:
Neptune Unique (Fenner), Colorplan Ebony (GF Smith)

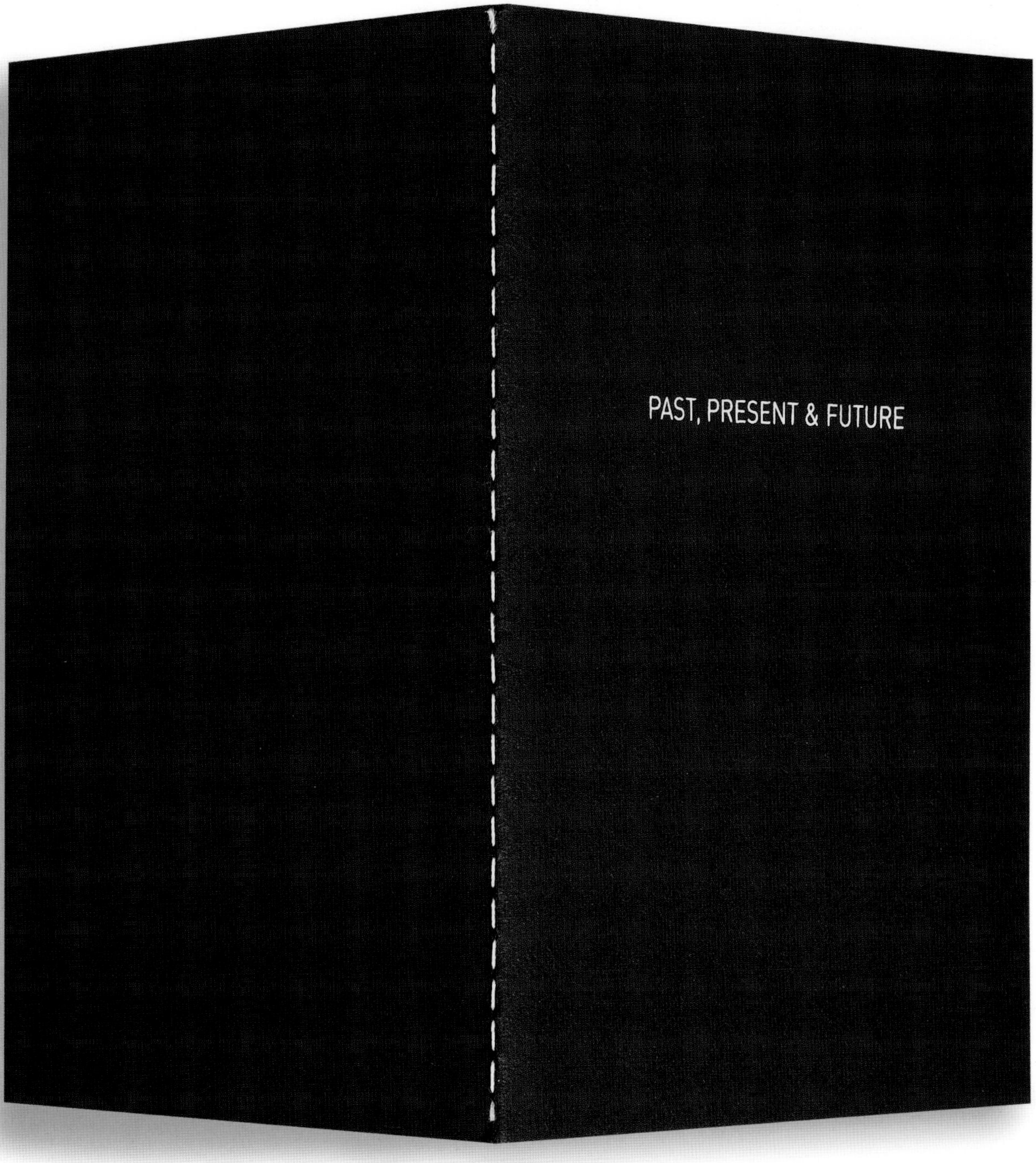

F
When we think of history, we think about the debt we owe to the inventor of the light bulb, Thomas Alva Edison.
A true pioneer, Edison gave us many inventions, including the phonograph, the kinescope, centralised power systems (electricity generators) and, of course, the light bulb... or did he?

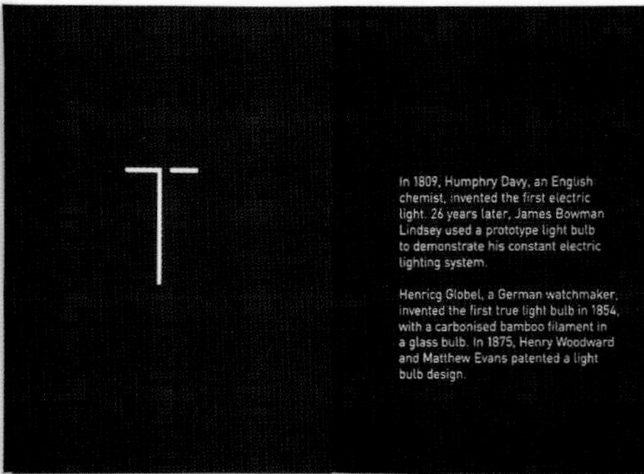

T
In 1809, Humphry Davy, an English chemist, invented the first electric light. 26 years later, James Bowman Lindsey used a prototype light bulb to demonstrate his constant electric lighting system.
Henricg Globel, a German watchmaker, invented the first true light bulb in 1854, with a carbonised bamboo filament in a glass bulb. In 1875, Henry Woodward and Matthew Evans patented a light bulb design.

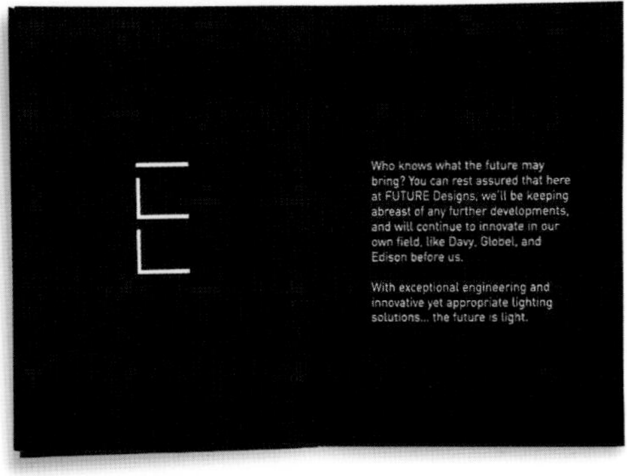

E
Who knows what the future may bring? You can rest assured that here at FUTURE Designs, we'll be keeping abreast of any further developments, and will continue to innovate in our own field, like Davy, Globel, and Edison before us.
With exceptional engineering and innovative yet appropriate lighting solutions... the future is light.

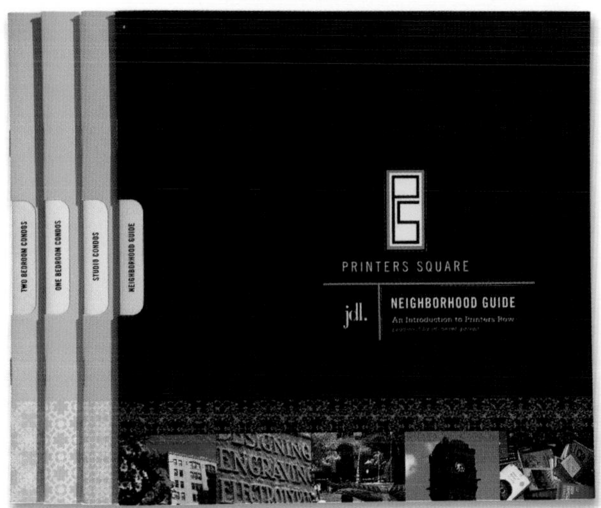

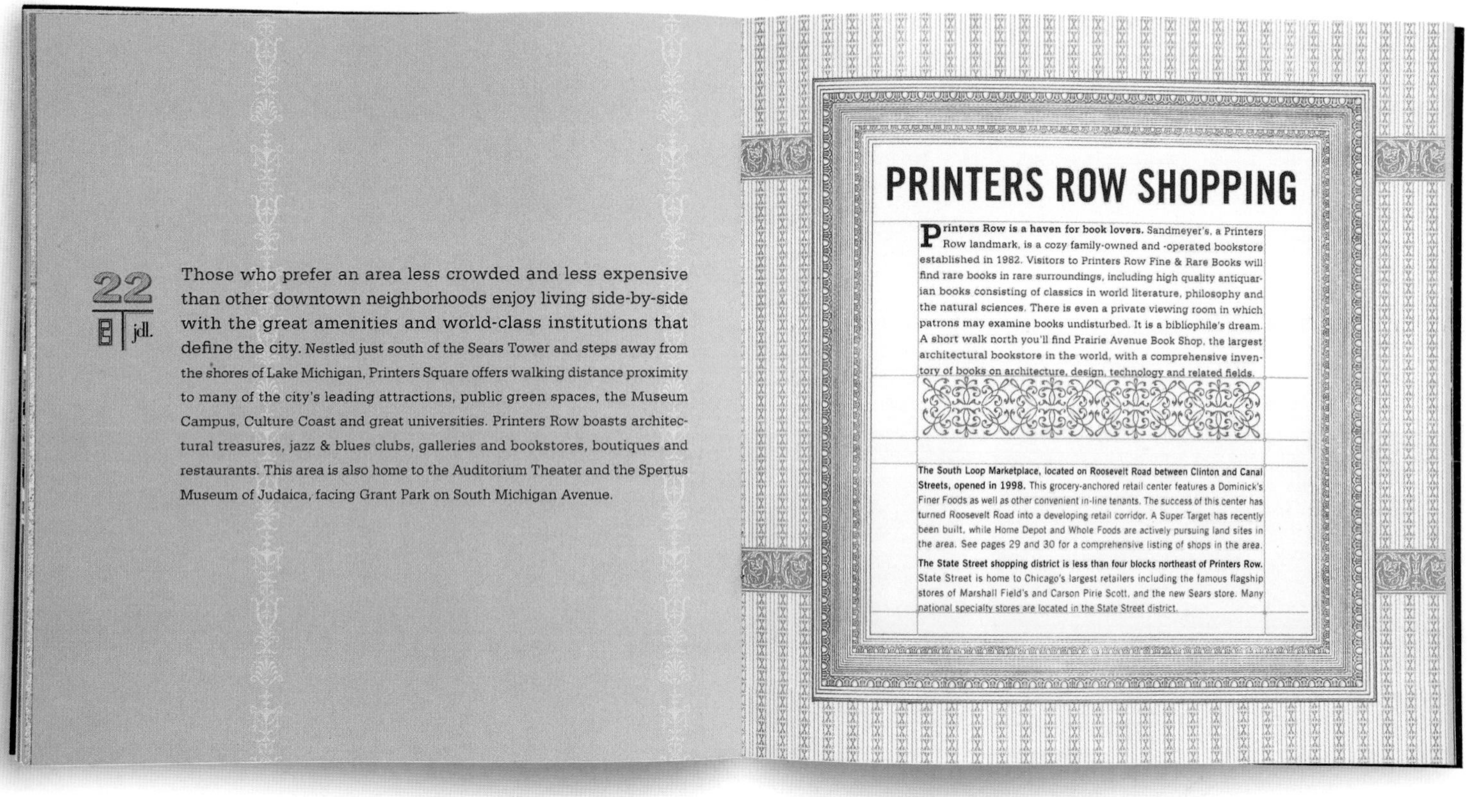

22

jdl.

Those who prefer an area less crowded and less expensive than other downtown neighborhoods enjoy living side-by-side with the great amenities and world-class institutions that define the city. Nestled just south of the Sears Tower and steps away from the shores of Lake Michigan, Printers Square offers walking distance proximity to many of the city's leading attractions, public green spaces, the Museum Campus, Culture Coast and great universities. Printers Row boasts architectural treasures, jazz & blues clubs, galleries and bookstores, boutiques and restaurants. This area is also home to the Auditorium Theater and the Spertus Museum of Judaica, facing Grant Park on South Michigan Avenue.

PRINTERS ROW SHOPPING

Printers Row is a haven for book lovers. Sandmeyer's, a Printers Row landmark, is a cozy family-owned and -operated bookstore established in 1982. Visitors to Printers Row Fine & Rare Books will find rare books in rare surroundings, including high quality antiquarian books consisting of classics in world literature, philosophy and the natural sciences. There is even a private viewing room in which patrons may examine books undisturbed. It is a bibliophile's dream. A short walk north you'll find Prairie Avenue Book Shop, the largest architectural bookstore in the world, with a comprehensive inventory of books on architecture, design, technology and related fields.

The South Loop Marketplace, located on Roosevelt Road between Clinton and Canal Streets, opened in 1998. This grocery-anchored retail center features a Dominick's Finer Foods as well as other convenient in-line tenants. The success of this center has turned Roosevelt Road into a developing retail corridor. A Super Target has recently been built, while Home Depot and Whole Foods are actively pursuing land sites in the area. See pages 29 and 30 for a comprehensive listing of shops in the area.

The State Street shopping district is less than four blocks northeast of Printers Row. State Street is home to Chicago's largest retailers including the famous flagship stores of Marshall Field's and Carson Pirie Scott, and the new Sears store. Many national specialty stores are located in the State Street district.

FIREBELLY DESIGN
Real Estate Development Brochure

Art Director:
Dawn Hancock
Designers:
Dawn Hancock, Aaron Shimer, Antonio Garcia
Client:
JDL Development Corp.
Software:
Adobe Photoshop, Adobe Illustrator, Adobe InDesign
Paper/Materials:
New Leaf Reincarnation Matte

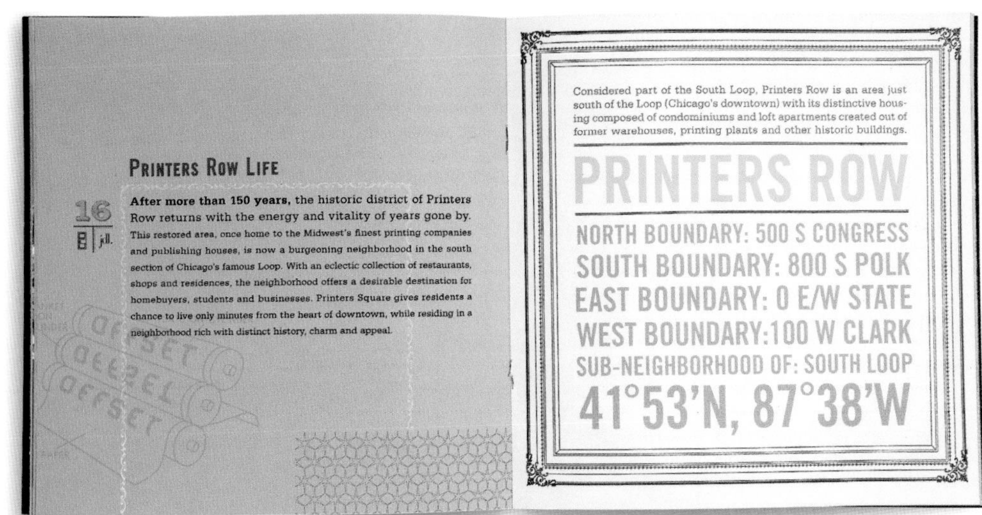

PRINTERS ROW LIFE
16
After more than 150 years, the historic district of Printers Row returns with the energy and vitality of years gone by. This restored area, once home to the Midwest's finest printing companies and publishing houses, is now a burgeoning neighborhood in the south section of Chicago's famous Loop. With an eclectic collection of restaurants, shops and residences, the neighborhood offers a desirable destination for homebuyers, students and businesses. Printers Square gives residents a chance to live only minutes from the heart of downtown, while residing in a neighborhood rich with distinct history, charm and appeal.
OFFSET
Considered part of the South Loop, Printers Row is an area just south of the Loop (Chicago's downtown) with its distinctive housing composed of condominiums and loft apartments created out of former warehouses, printing plants and other historic buildings.
PRINTERS ROW
NORTH BOUNDARY: 500 S CONGRESS
SOUTH BOUNDARY: 800 S POLK
EAST BOUNDARY: 0 E/W STATE
WEST BOUNDARY:100 W CLARK
SUB-NEIGHBORHOOD OF: SOUTH LOOP
41°53'N, 87°38'W

TABLE OF CONTENTS
PRINTERS ROW SYNOPSIS
DURING THE DAY, the neighborhood is an easy walk to offices in the Loop, off Michigan Avenue, or the LaSalle Street financial centers. After hours, the district is alive with anything from restaurants, pubs, and blues clubs to coffee shops and bookstores.
It boasts famous blues clubs, eclectic music venues and neighborhood taverns. Its annual book fair, the Chicago Tribune Printers Row Book Fair, gathers authors, poets, speakers and, of course, a great selection of books.
Printers Row is also walking distance to the Spertus Museum of Judaica, the newly reconstructed Soldier Field and Chicago's Museum Campus, with the Field Museum, Adler Planetarium and Shedd Aquarium just blocks away.
PRESS No 2

ATELIER WORKS
Made in UK
(Promotion for
Product Designers)

Art Director:
John Powner
Designer:
A. Browne
Client:
Factory Design
Software:
Adobe Photoshop,
QuarkXPress

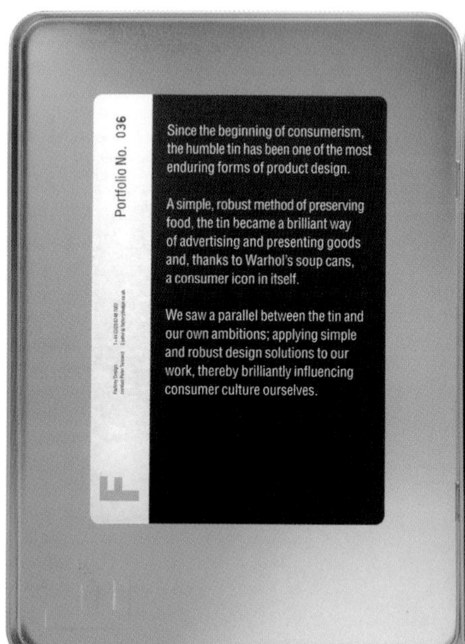

Portfolio No. 036
Since the beginning of consumerism, the humble tin has been one of the most enduring forms of product design.
A simple, robust method of preserving food, the tin became a brilliant way of advertising and presenting goods and, thanks to Warhol's soup cans, a consumer icon in itself.
We saw a parallel between the tin and our own ambitions; applying simple and robust design solutions to our work, thereby brilliantly influencing consumer culture ourselves.
F

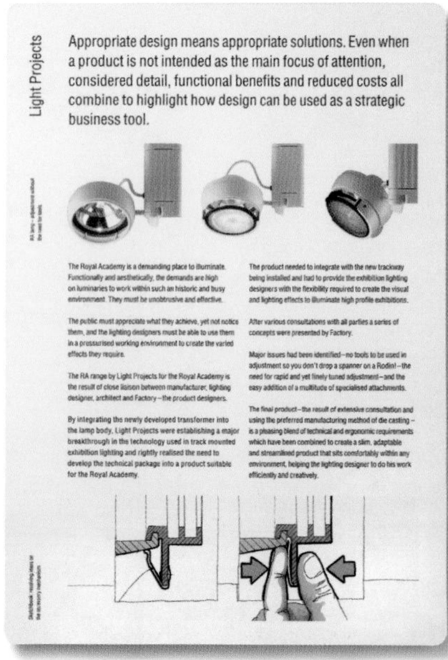

Light Projects
Appropriate design means appropriate solutions. Even when a product is not intended as the main focus of attention, considered detail, functional benefits and reduced costs all combine to highlight how design can be used as a strategic business tool.

NINA DAVID
KOMMUNIKA-
TIONSDESIGN
Font Report

Art Director:
Nina David
Designer:
Nina David
Client:
Font-o-Rama
Software:
QuarkXPress,
Adobe Photoshop,
Adobe Illustrator
Paper/Materials:
Splendorgel

KAMPER BRANDS

Brochure for Factory Conversion into Lofts

Art Director:
Patrick Crowe
Designers:
Dan Behrens,
Sarah Anderson
Client:
Trio Development
Software:
Adobe Illustrator,
Adobe Photoshop
Paper/Materials:
130 lb Cougar Double Thick Cover

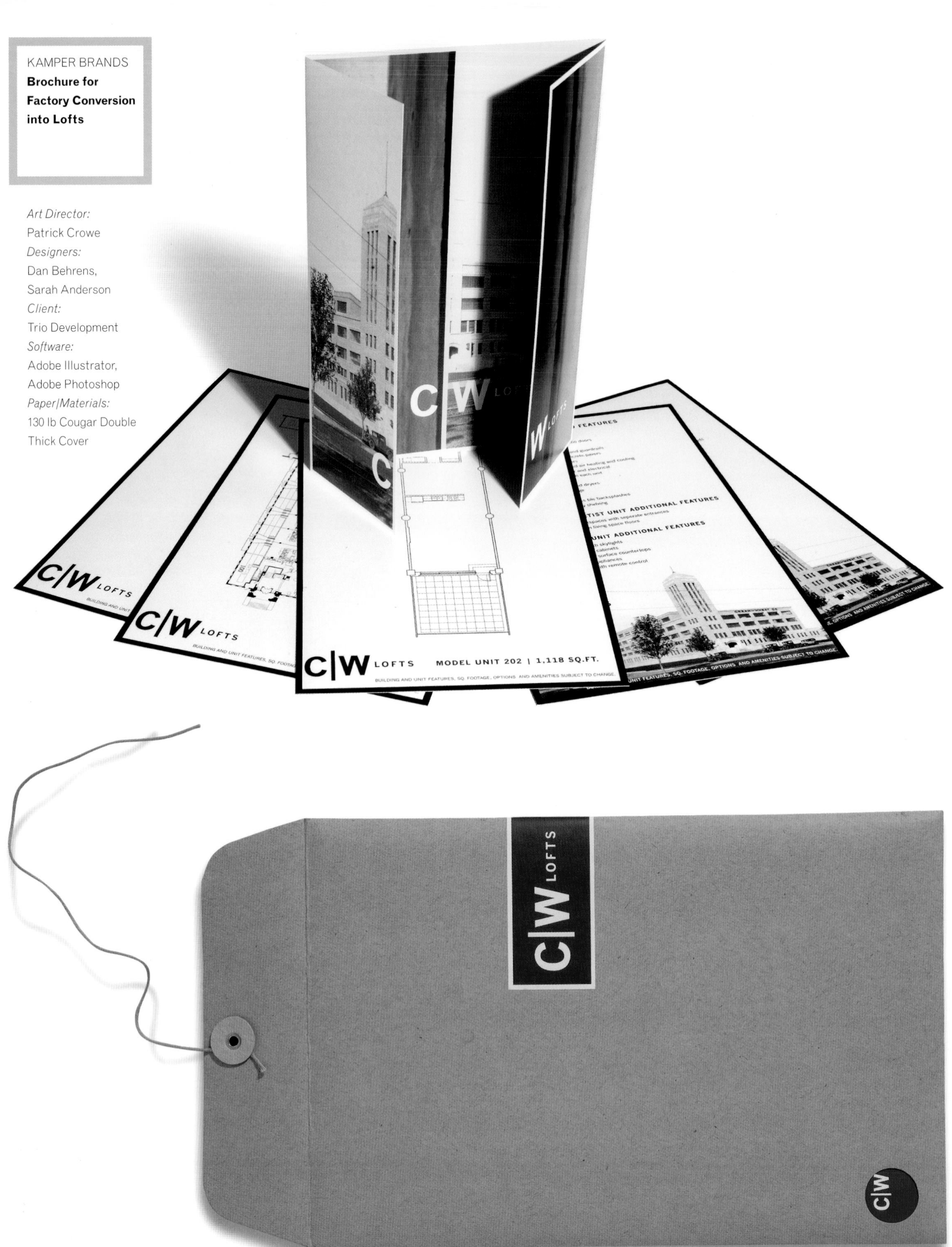

KAMPER BRANDS
Brochure for Condominium Project

Art Director:
Patrick Crowe
Designer:
Sladjana Dirakovi
Client:
The Wall Company
Software:
Adobe Illustrator, Adobe Photoshop
Paper/Materials:
Domtar Proterra (Coastal Whites), cotton bag

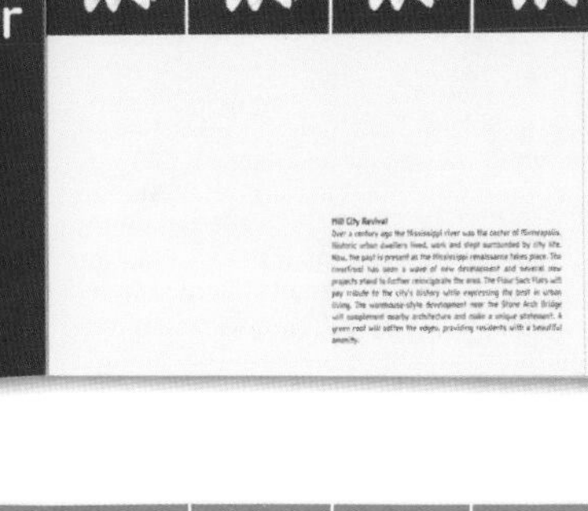

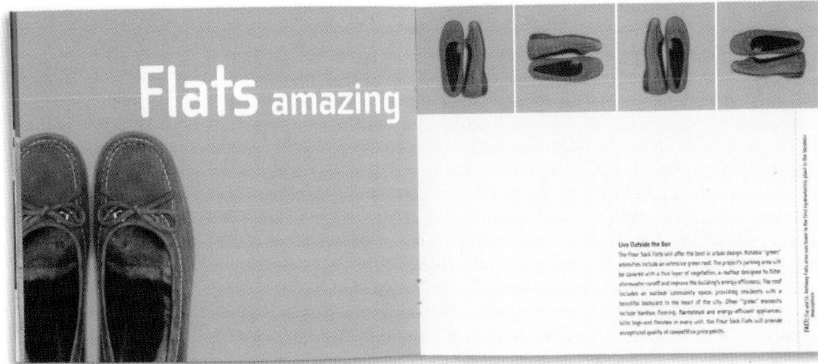

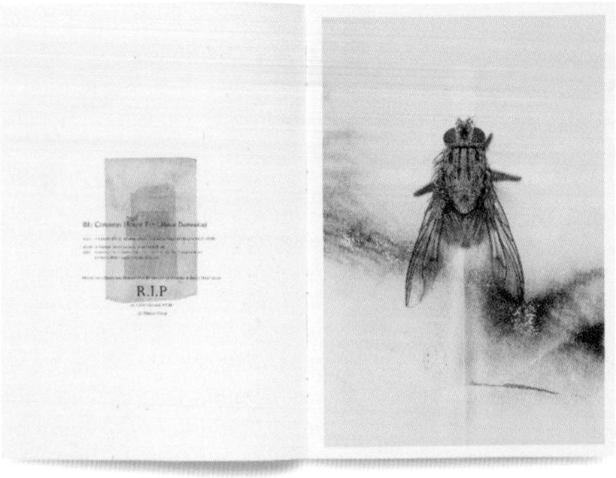

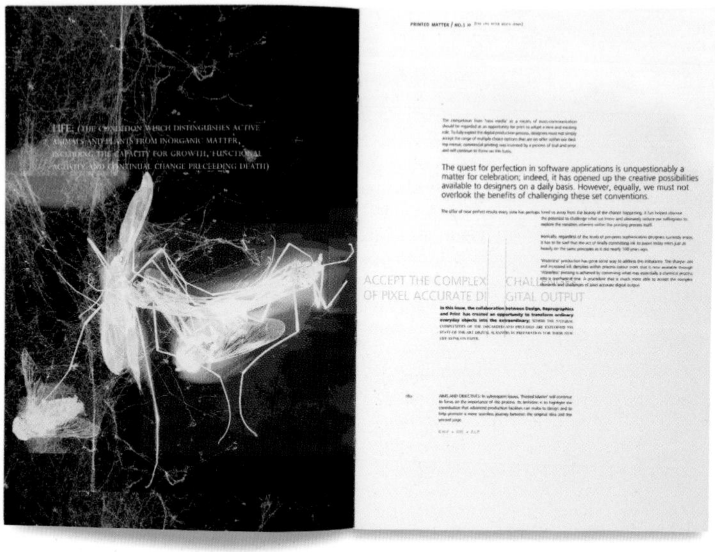

RUSSELL
WARREN-FISHER
Printed Matter
No.1

Art Director:
Russell Warren-Fisher
Designer:
Russell Warren-Fisher
Client:
Ripe/Park Lane
Software:
QuarkXPress,
Adobe InDesign,
Adobe Photoshop
Paper/Materials:
Consort Royal

SEA

Beyon Brochure

Art Director: Bryan Edmondson
Designer: Stuart L Bailey
Client: Beyon
Software: QuarkXPress, Adobe Photoshop
Paper/Materials: Construction board (cover), PhoenixMotion Xenon (text)

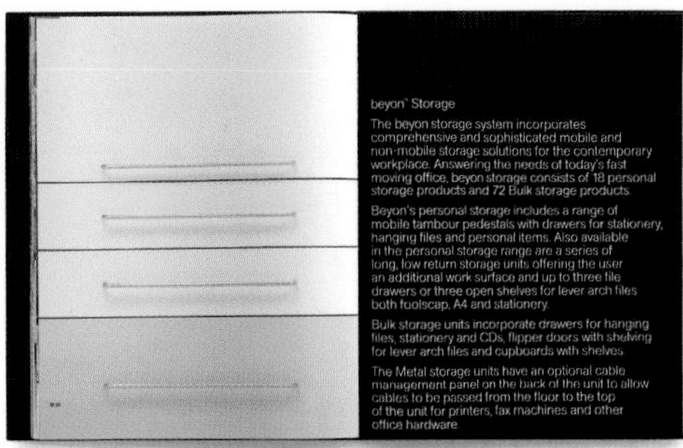

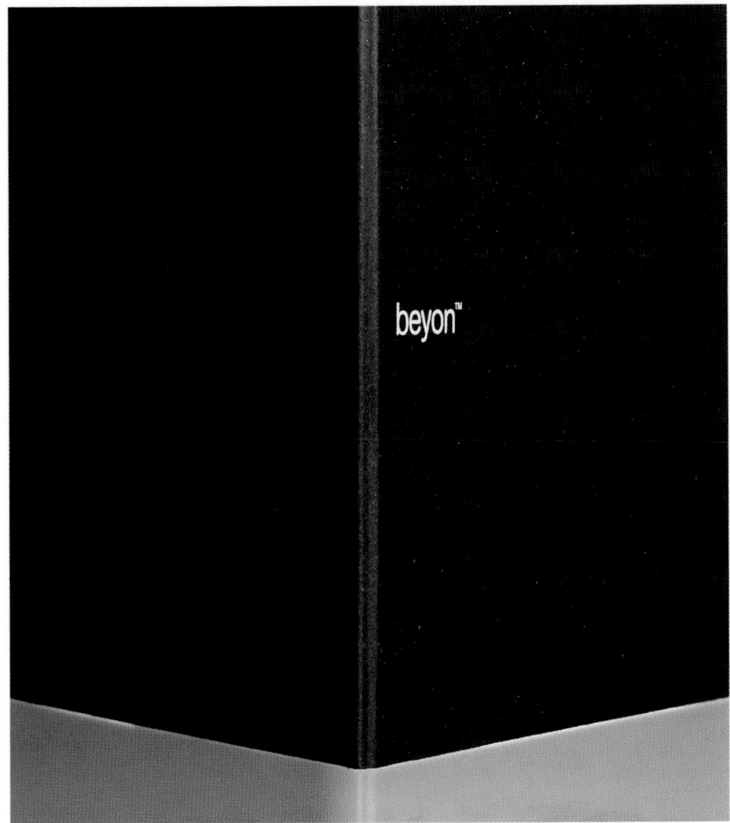

beyon™ philosophy

To create working environments which are open and inviting, that inspire and motivate, creating feelings of confidence.

Designing clean and contemporary furniture that captures the essence of the modern with the substance and beauty of the classic.

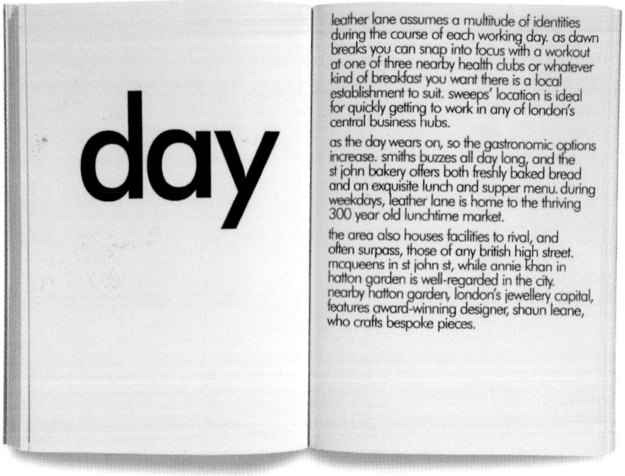

day

leather lane assumes a multitude of identities during the course of each working day. as dawn breaks you can snap into focus with a workout at one of three nearby health clubs or whatever kind of breakfast you want there is a local establishment to suit. sweeps' location is ideal for quickly getting to work in any of london's central business hubs.

as the day wears on, so the gastronomic options increase. smiths buzzes all day long, and the st john bakery offers both freshly baked bread and an exquisite lunch and supper menu. during weekdays, leather lane is home to the thriving 300 year old lunchtime market.

the area also houses facilities to rival, and often surpass, those of any british high street. mcqueens in st john st, while annie khan in hatton garden is well-regarded in the city. nearby hatton garden, london's jewellery capital, features award-winning designer, shaun leane, who crafts bespoke pieces.

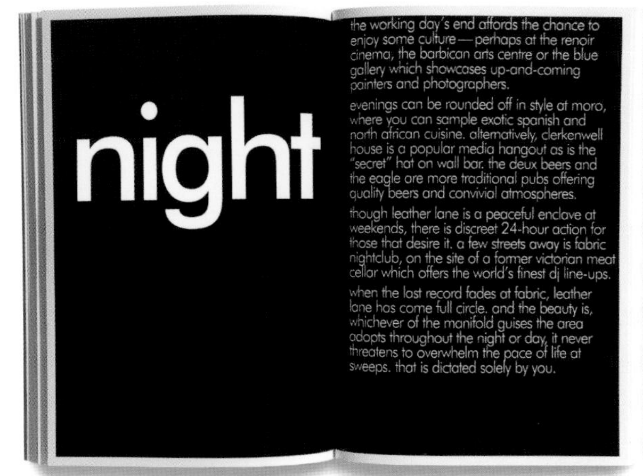

night
the working day's end affords the chance to enjoy some culture—perhaps at the renoir cinema, the barbican arts centre or the blue gallery which showcases up-and-coming painters and photographers.
evenings can be rounded off in style at moro, where you can sample exotic spanish and north african cuisine. alternatively, clerkenwell house is a popular media hangout as is the "secret" hat on wall bar. the deux beers and the eagle are more traditional pubs offering quality beers and convivial atmospheres.
though leather lane is a peaceful enclave at weekends, there is discreet 24-hour action for those that desire it. a few streets away is fabric nightclub, on the site of a former victorian meat cellar which offers the world's finest dj line-ups.
when the last record fades at fabric, leather lane has come full circle. and the beauty is, whichever of the manifold guises the area adopts throughout the night or day, it never threatens to overwhelm the pace of life at sweeps. that is dictated solely by you.

STUDIO
MYERSCOUGH
Sweeps Loft Apartments EC1

Art Director:
Morag Myerscough
Designer:
Morag Myerscough
Photographer:
Richard Learoyd
Client:
Derwent Valley

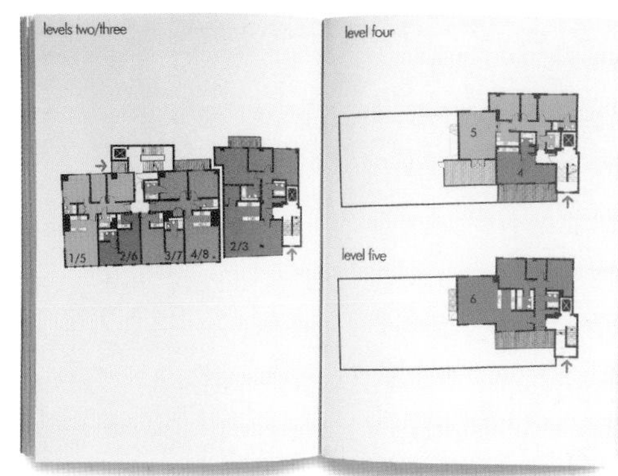

Hull
GF Smith
Lockwood Street
Hull HU2 OHL
Telephone
01482 323 503
Facsimile
01482 223 174
Email
info@gfsmith.com
www.gfsmith.com
London
GF Smith
2 Leathermarket
Weston Street
London SE1 3ET
Telephone
020 7407 6174
Facsimile
020 7403 1037
Email
london@gfsmith.com
Paper from GF Smith
Printed on
Monadnock 148gsm
Produced
12/04
Paper from GF Smith
White Book
Smith
Paper from GFSmith

SEA

White Book

Art Director:
Bryan Edmondson
Designer:
Ryan Jones
Client:
GF Smith
Software:
QuarkXPress,
Adobe Photoshop
Paper/Materials:
Mixed stock

DOWLING DESIGN & ART DIRECTION
Product Brochure

Art Director:
John Dowling
Designer:
John Dowling
Photographer:
Steve Rees
Client:
Robert Welch
Software:
QuarkXPress
Paper/Materials:
Millenium Silk (Fenner)

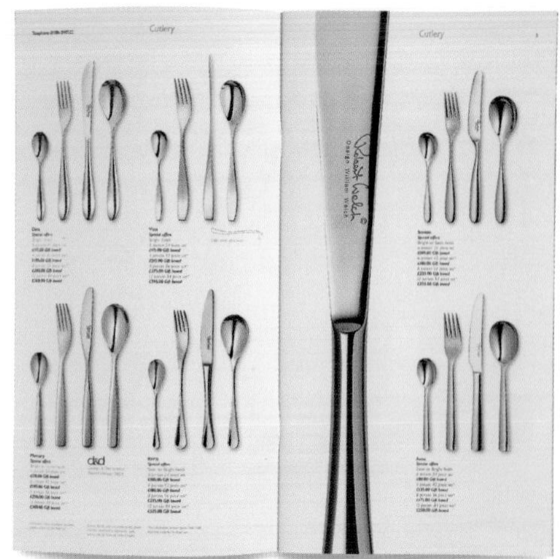

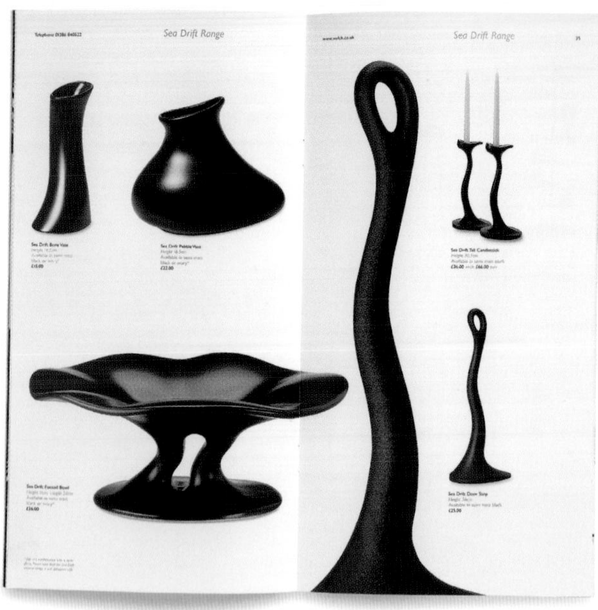

HGV

Wallace Collection Corporate/Wedding Brochure

Art Director:
Pierre Vermeir
Designer:
Tommy Taylor
Client:
Wallace Collection
Software:
Adobe Photoshop, QuarkXPress
Paper/Materials:
Zanders Medley

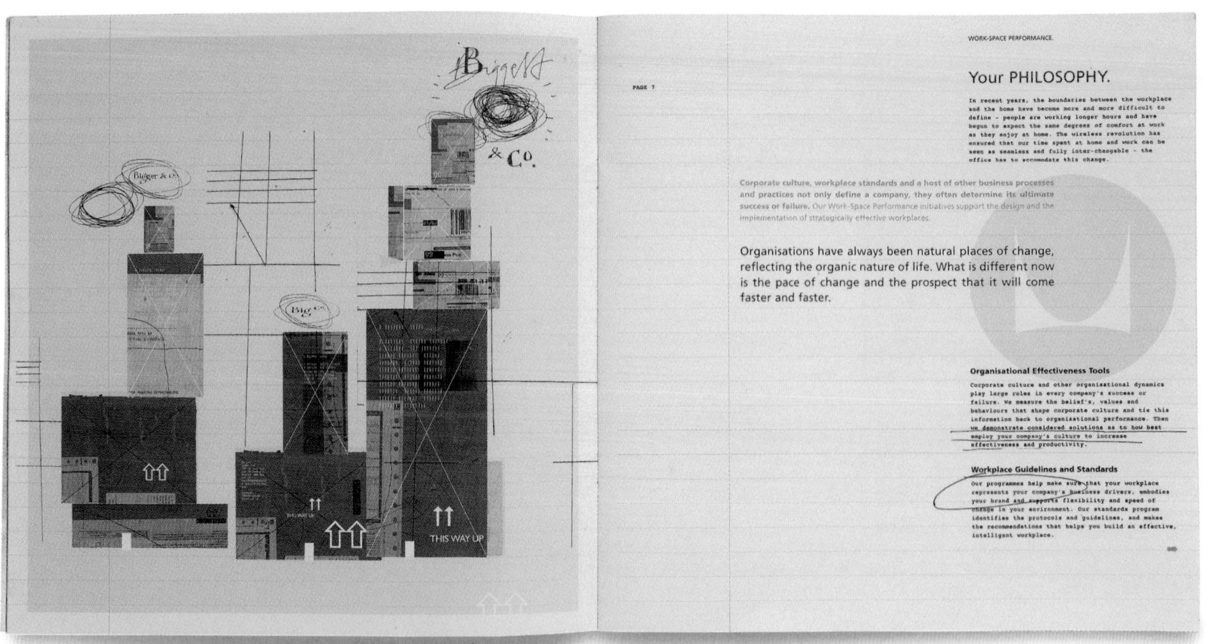

RUSSELL WARREN-FISHER

Workplace Intelligence Brochure

Designer:
Russell Warren-Fisher
Client:
Herman Miller
Software:
QuarkXPress, Adobe Photoshop
Paper/Materials:
Redeem

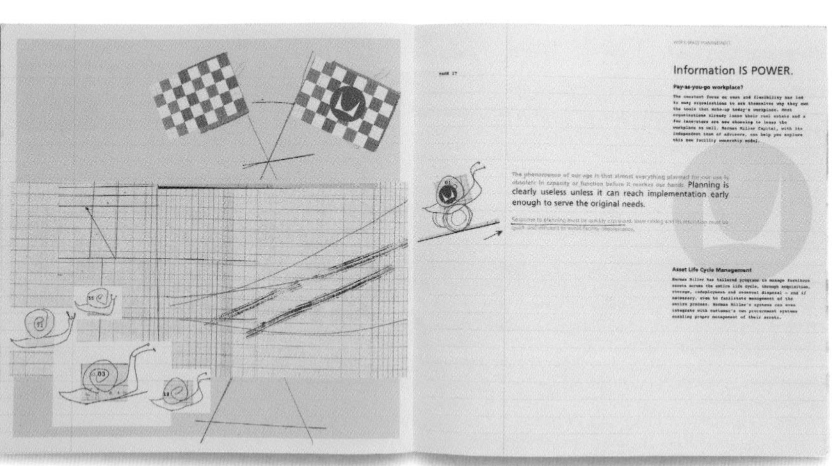

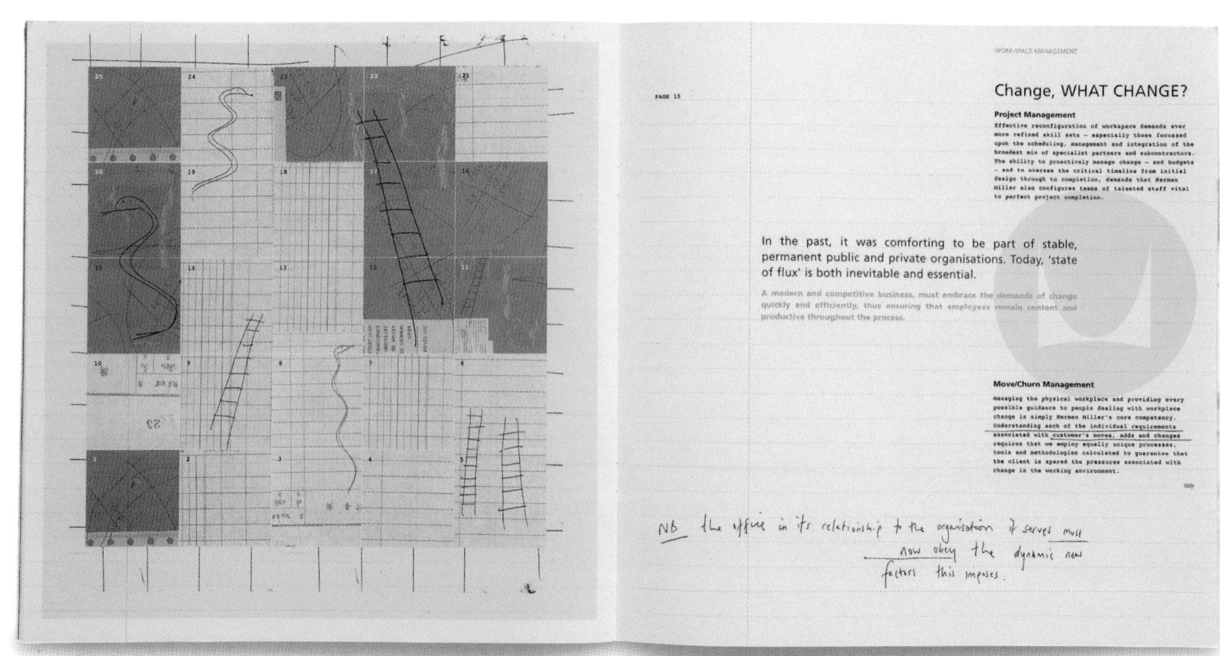

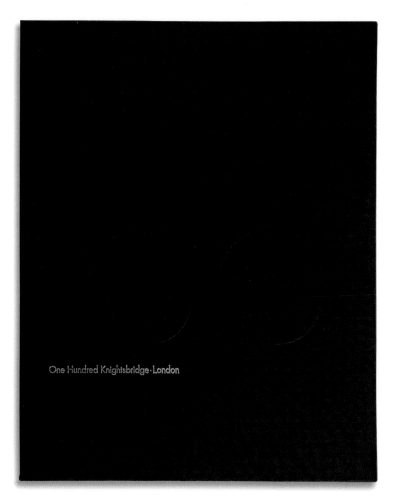

NB:STUDIO

One Hundred Knightsbridge

Art Directors:
Nick Finney, Ben Stott, Alan Dye
Client:
Land Securities

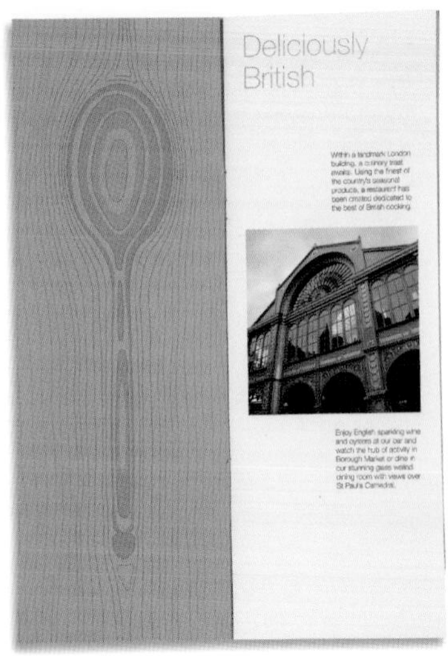

HGV

Roast

Art Director:
Pierre Vermeir
Designer:
Pierre Vermeir
Client:
Roast Restaurant
Software:
Adobe Illustrator,
Adobe InDesign
Paper/Materials:
Splendorgel Extra
White (Popset Fawn)

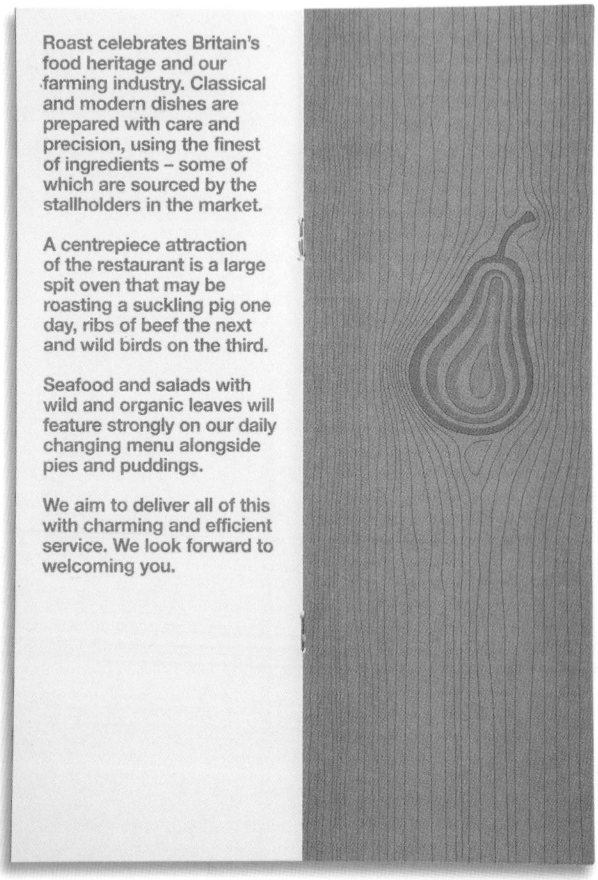

Roast celebrates Britain's food heritage and our farming industry. Classical and modern dishes are prepared with care and precision, using the finest of ingredients – some of which are sourced by the stallholders in the market.
A centrepiece attraction of the restaurant is a large spit oven that may be roasting a suckling pig one day, ribs of beef the next and wild birds on the third.
Seafood and salads with wild and organic leaves will feature strongly on our daily changing menu alongside pies and puddings.
We aim to deliver all of this with charming and efficient service. We look forward to welcoming you.

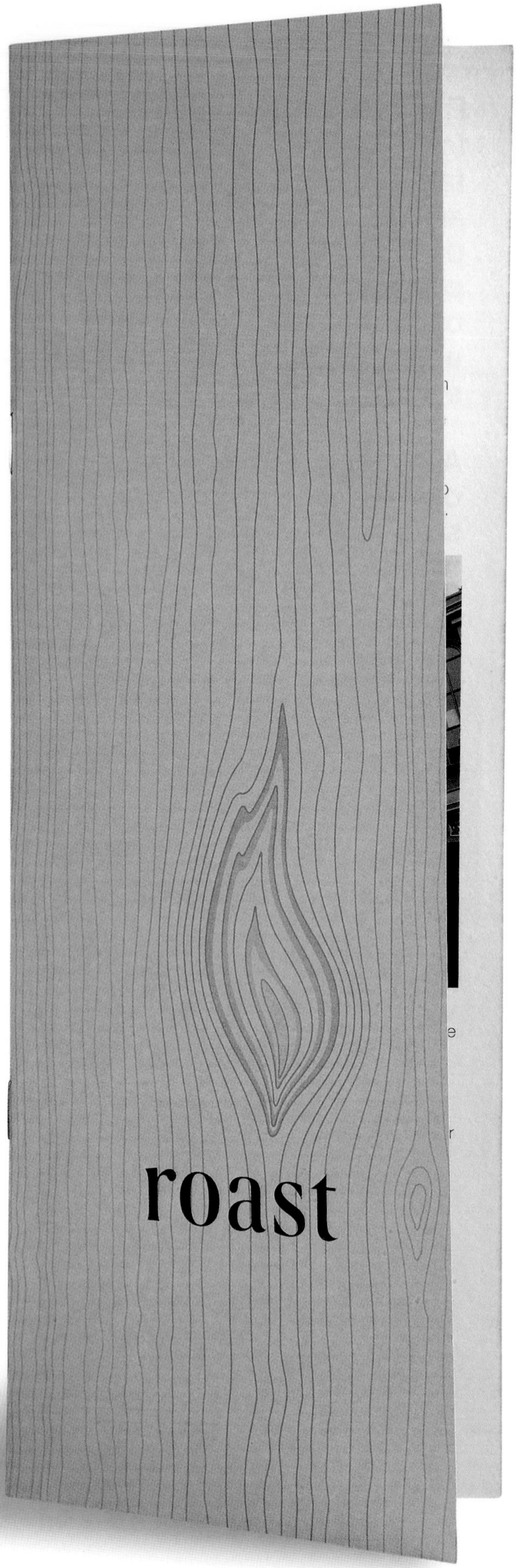

STUDIO
MYERSCOUGH
Conran Shop
Furniture

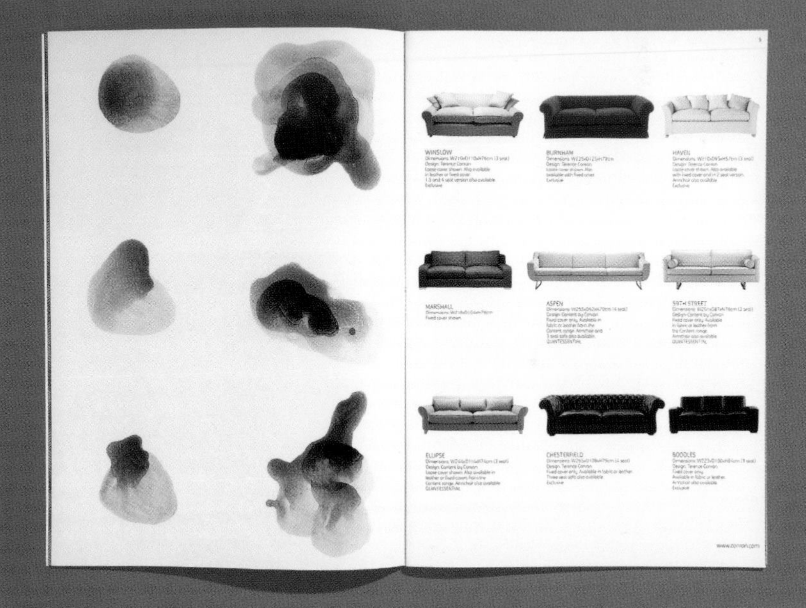

Art Director:
Morag Myerscough
Designer:
Morag Myerscough
Photographer:
Richard Learoyd
Client:
Conran Shop,
Polly Dickens
& Terence Conran

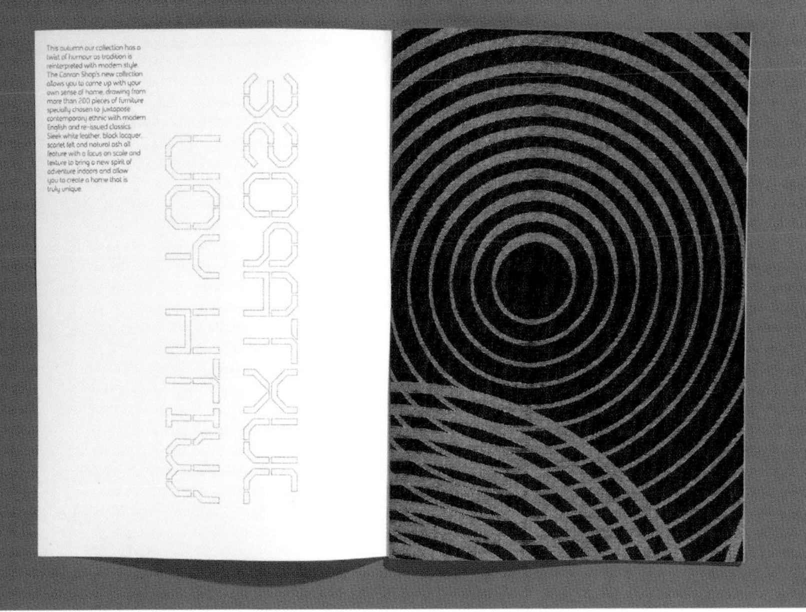

PENTAGRAM DESIGN, LONDON
Edmund De Waal Catalogue

Art Director:
Angus Hyland
Client:
Blackwell: De Waal

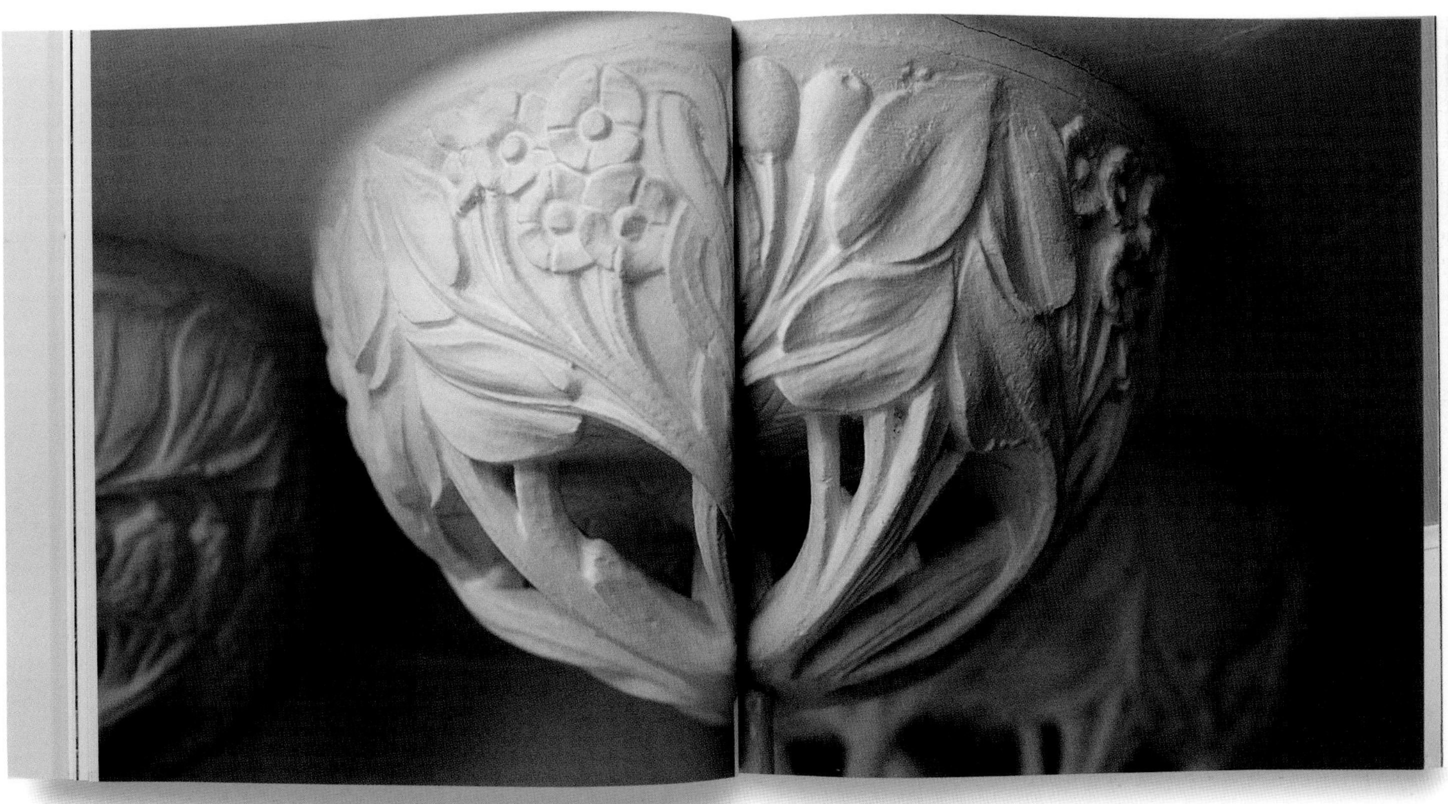

STUDIO
MYERSCOUGH
Tea Building

Art Director:
Morag Myerscough
Designers:
Morag Myerscough,
Chris Merrick
Photographer:
Richard Learoyd
Client:
Derwent Valley

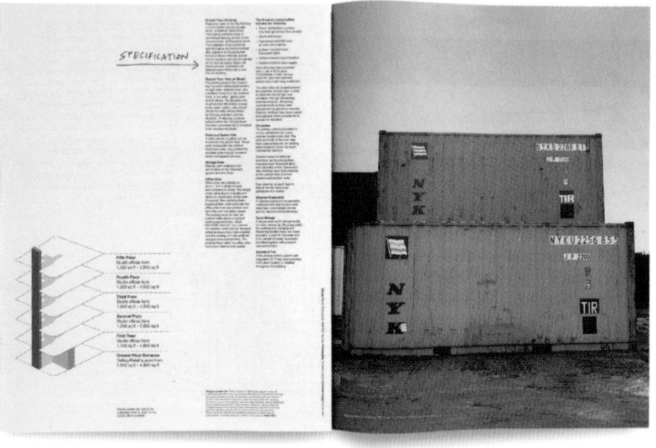

k!
The end is nigh. Burn all the books. Words are done for. Pictures are the future. If you believe everything you read, you wouldn't be reading. Books would be doorstops and brochures would be shelved. And as for direct mail and magazines, the less said about them the better. But the truth is different.
ink! is a team of copywriters, journalists and communication strategists who believe words can still have a huge impact. We work with design agencies and businesses offering strategic advice for their literature, writing words that jump off the page and making every letter count. Starting here.

MYTTON WILLIAMS
Ink! Promotional Brochure

Art Director:
Bob Mytton
Designer:
Tracey Bowes
Client:
Ink! Copywriters
Software:
Adobe InDesign
Paper/Materials:
Challenger Offset
120 gsm

Words are a little like icebergs. Beneath the elegant bits on the surface is an unseen force holding everything together. In writing, this is the thought behind the words; the strategy that makes your communication stand out.
So before we put pen to paper, we pause for a while.
And take a moment to fully understand your aims and challenges, your company's brand values and tone of voice, your audience's attitudes and behaviour. At these opening stages, our strategic thought can really add value. Then, when everything's in place, we start to write.
think

MIKE LACKERSTEEN DESIGN
Beat

Art Director:
Mike Lackersteen
Designer:
Mike Lackersteen
Client:
Heart
Paper/Materials:
Matrisse Avorio (cover), Neptune Unique Fenner Paper (text)

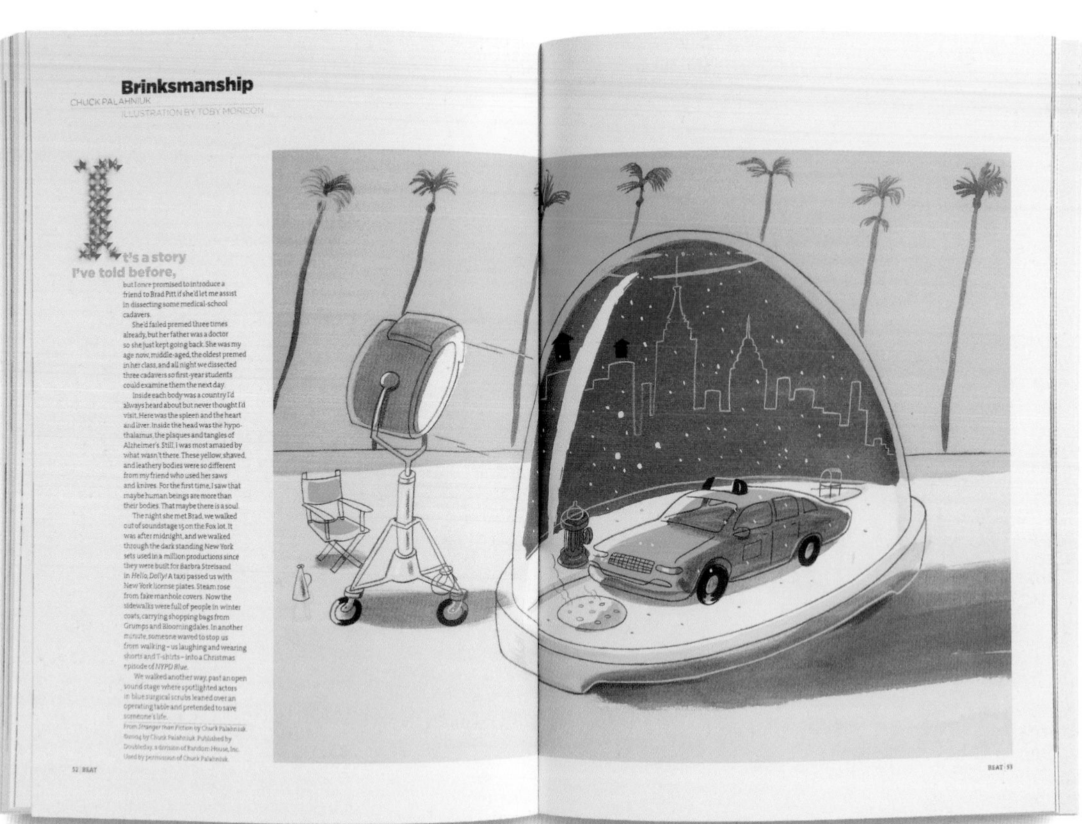

Brinksmanship

CHUCK PALAHNIUK

ILLUSTRATION BY TOBY MORISON

It's a story I've told before, but I once promised to introduce a friend to Brad Pitt if she'd let me assist in dissecting some medical-school cadavers.

She'd failed premed three times already, but her father was a doctor so she just kept going back. She was my age now, middle-aged, the oldest premed in her class, and all night we dissected three cadavers so first-year students could examine them the next day.

Inside each body was a country I'd always heard about but never thought I'd visit. Here was the spleen and the heart and liver. Inside the head was the hypothalamus, the plaques and tangles of Alzheimer's. Still, I was most amazed by what wasn't there. These yellow, shaved, and leathery bodies were so different from my friend who used her saws and knives. For the first time, I saw that maybe human beings are more than their bodies. That maybe there is a soul.

The night she met Brad, we walked out of soundstage 15 on the Fox lot. It was after midnight, and we walked through the dark standing New York sets used in a million productions since they were built for Barbra Streisand in *Hello, Dolly!* A taxi passed us with New York license plates. Steam rose from fake manhole covers. Now the sidewalks were full of people in winter coats, carrying shopping bags from Grumps and Bloomingdales. In another minute, someone waved to stop us from walking – us laughing and wearing shorts and T-shirts – into a Christmas episode of *NYPD Blue*.

We walked another way, past an open sound stage where spotlighted actors in blue surgical scrubs leaned over an operating table and pretended to save someone's life.

From Stranger than Fiction by Chuck Palahniuk. ©2004 by Chuck Palahniuk. Published by Doubleday, a division of Random House, Inc. Used by permission of Chuck Palahniuk.

52 | BEAT

...like all expatriate New Yorkers, I am drawn back, as an ant to its hole. I left New York but the city never let me go

From the moment I learned of the attack, I felt an urgent need to be home, home in the city of my bones, home among my people

Memories of Brooklyn

...of wonder and love

...of sheer luxury and taste

PENTAGRAM
DESIGN, LONDON
One & Only
Brochure

Art Director:
John Rushworth
Client:
One & Only

...of excitement and discovery
One&Only Kanuhura

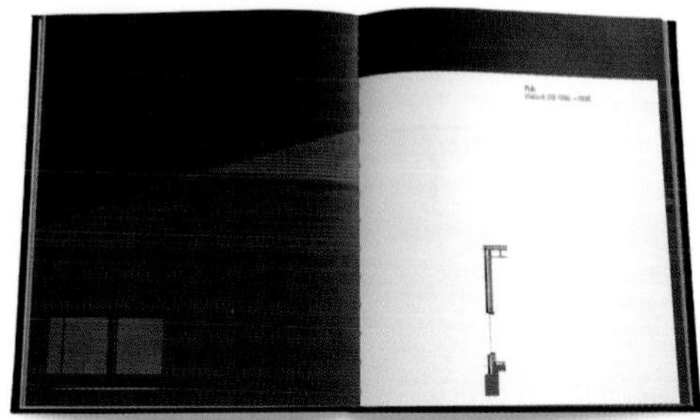

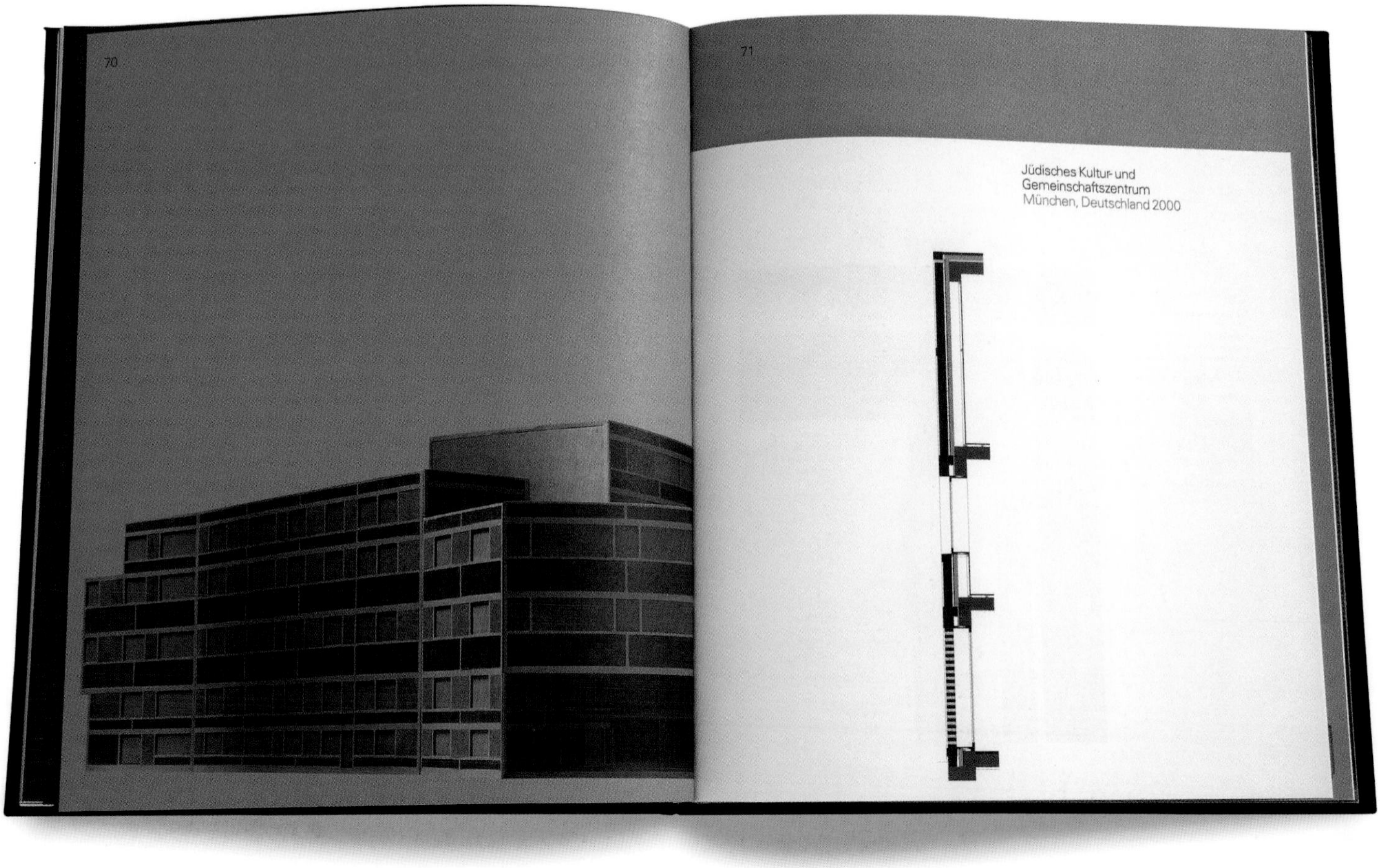

70

71

Jüdisches Kultur- und
Gemeinschaftszentrum
München, Deutschland 2000

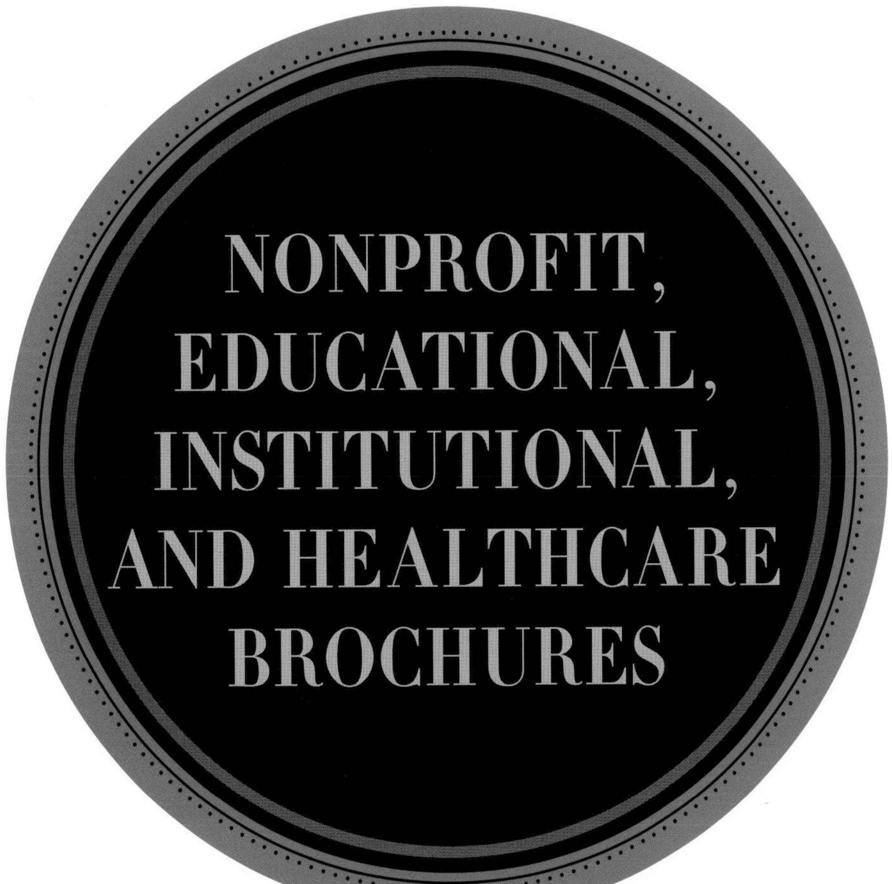
NONPROFIT,
EDUCATIONAL,
INSTITUTIONAL,
AND HEALTHCARE
BROCHURES

DESIGN FIRM › O & J Design Inc.
ART DIRECTORS › Barbara Olejniczak, Lia Camera Mariscal
DESIGNERS › Barbara Olejniczak, Lia Camera Mariscal
ILLUSTRATOR/PHOTOGRAPHER › David Radler
COPYWRITERS › Kalen Blinn, Mimi Koren
CLIENT › Isabella Geriatric Center
TOOLS (SOFTWARE/PLATFORM) › QuarkXpress
PAPER STOCK/PRINTING PROCESS › Cover: three-color; interior: two-color

DESIGN FIRM › Zappata Diseñadores S.C.
ART DIRECTOR › Ibo Angulo
DESIGNER › Ibo Angulo
CLIENT › Nuevo Mundo University
TOOLS (SOFTWARE/PLATFORM) › Photoshop, Freehand, Macintosh
PRINTING PROCESS › Offset, couche

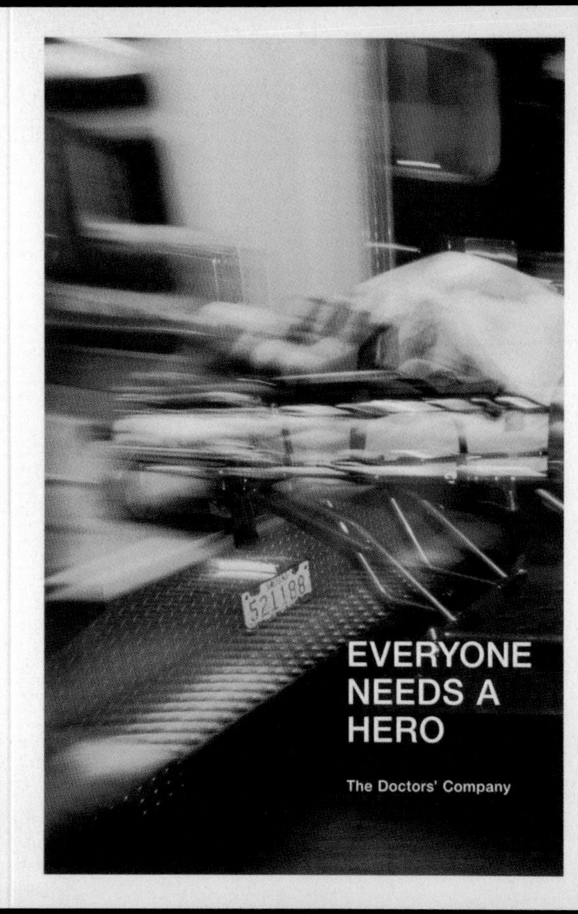

DESIGN FIRM › Oh Boy, A Design Company
ART DIRECTOR › David Salanitro
DESIGNER › Ryan Mahar
PHOTOGRAPHER › Scott Goldsmith
COPYWRITERS › Susan Wilkinson, Dana Cooper-The Doctors' Company
CLIENT › The Doctors' Company
PAPER STOCK › Superfine, ultra white smooth

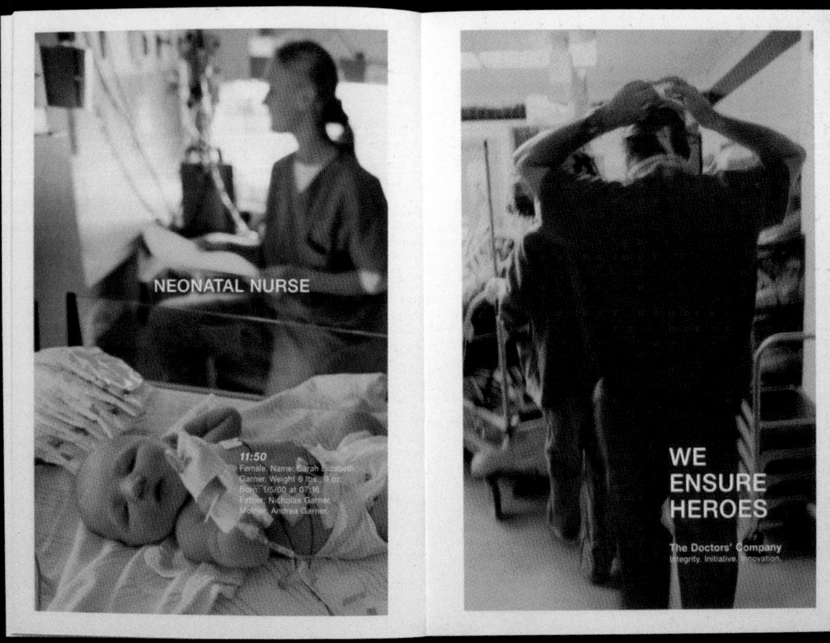

DESIGN FIRM > Shamlian Advertising
ART DIRECTOR > Brian DiRienzi
DESIGNER > Brian DiRienzi
CLIENT > ESF Summer Camps
TOOLS (SOFTWARE/PLATFORM) > Photoshop, Macintosh
PAPER STOCK/PRINTING PROCESS > 4/4

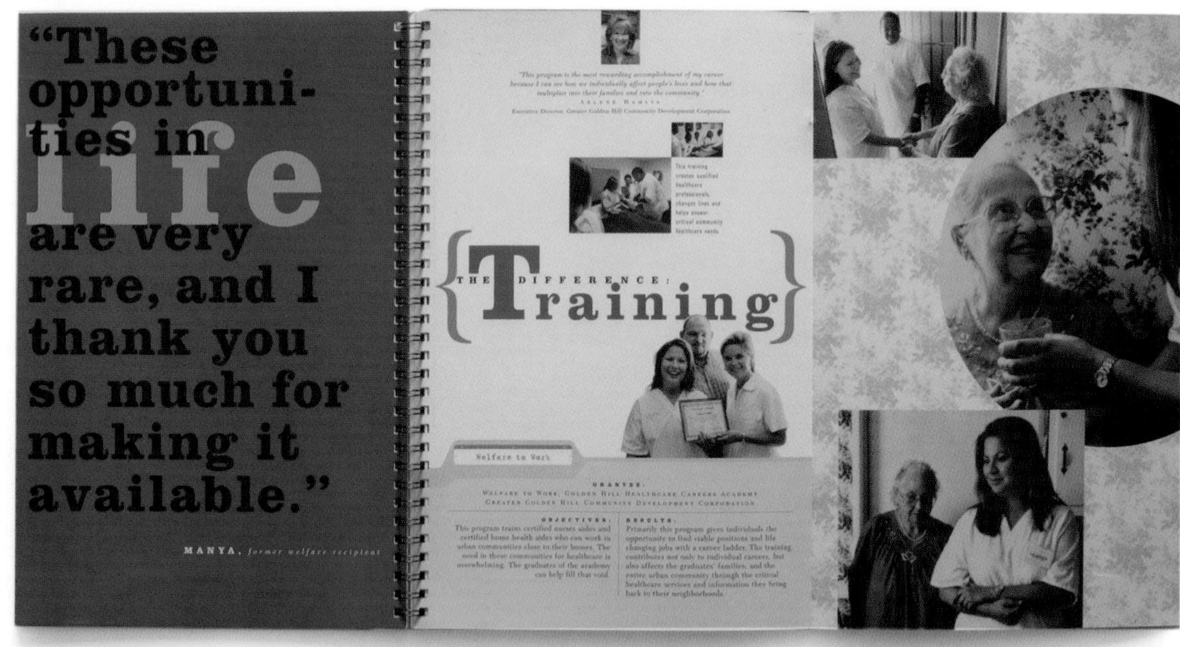

DESIGN FIRM > Gee + Chung Design
ART DIRECTOR > Earl Gee
DESIGNERS > Earl Gee, Fani Chung
PHOTOGRAPHER > Steve Jost
COPYWRITERS > Stephanie Lasenza, Gary Hawk
CLIENT > Alliance Healthcare Foundation
TOOLS (SOFTWARE/PLATFORM) > QuarkXPress, Adobe Illustrator, Photoshop
PAPER STOCK > Potlatch Karma natural 100 lb. text, French Paper Co., Speckletone Madero beach white 70 lb. text
PRINTING PROCESS > Offset lithography, blind embossing

DESIGN FIRM › Oh Boy, A Design Company
ART DIRECTOR › David Salanitro
DESIGNER › Alice Chang
PHOTOGRAPHER › Tony Stone Images
COPYWRITER › Son Rant
CLIENT › Thap!
PAPER STOCK › Caress eggshell 80 lb.
PRINTING PROCESS › Offset, sheet fed

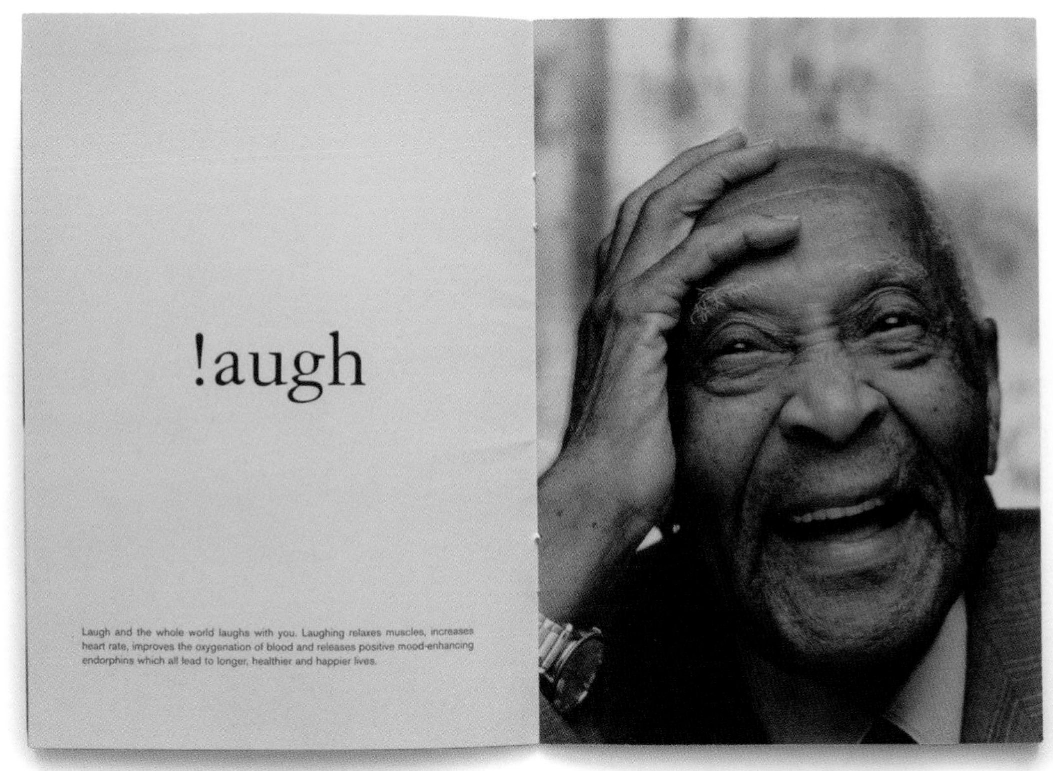

!augh
Laugh and the whole world laughs with you. Laughing relaxes muscles, increases heart rate, improves the oxygenation of blood and releases positive mood-enhancing endorphins which all lead to longer, healthier and happier lives.

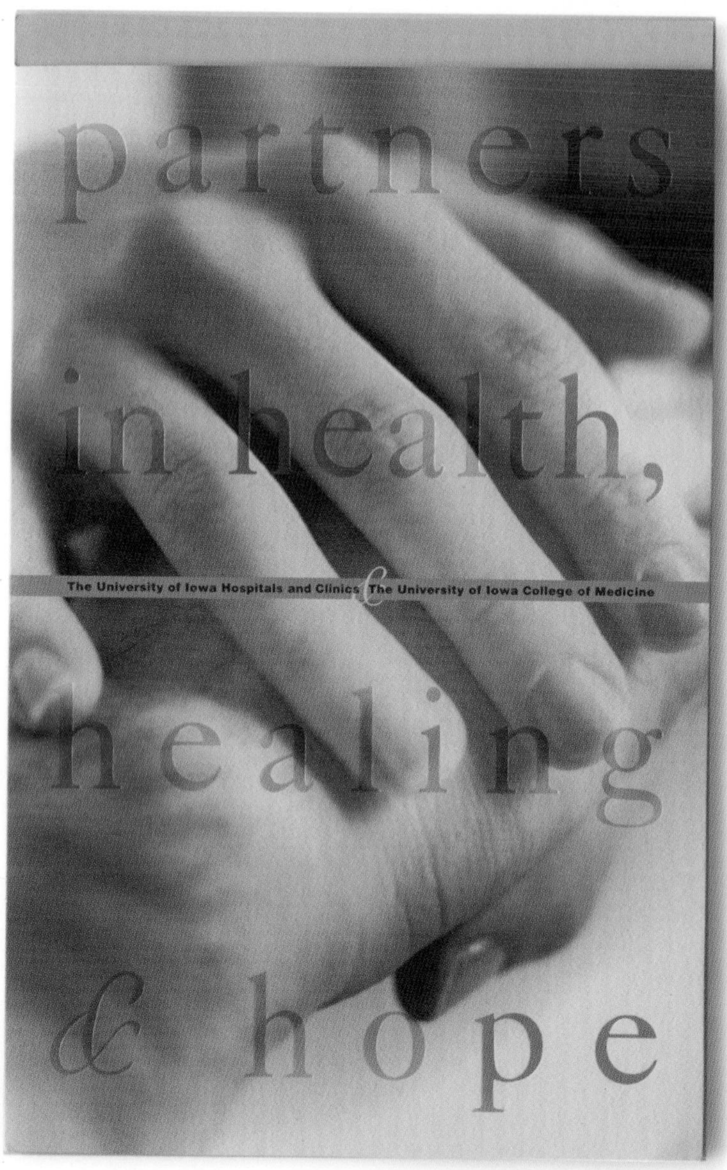

partners
in health,
The University of Iowa Hospitals and Clinics & The University of Iowa College of Medicine
healing
& hope

DESIGN FIRM › University of Iowa Foundation
ART DIRECTOR › Theresa Black
DESIGNER › Theresa Black
ILLUSTRATORS/PHOTOGRAPHERS › Jon Van Allen, Diane Hill, Reggie Morrow
COPYWRITER › Claudia Reinhardt
CLIENT › VI Foundation
TOOLS (SOFTWARE/PLATFORM) › Pagemaker, Photoshop, Macintosh
PAPER STOCK › Gilbert Voice
PRINTING PROCESS › Three PMS colors

FAMILY MEDICINE
continuing
excellence

partners
in health,
healing
& hope
continuing
excellence

DESIGN FIRM › SamataMason
ART DIRECTOR › Greg Samata
DESIGNER › Kevin Kureger
PHOTOGRAPHERS › Sandro, Martha Brock
CLIENT › WITS (Working in the Schools)
TOOLS (SOFTWARE/PLATFORM) › QuarkXPress, Macintosh
PAPER STOCK › French Speckletone Chipboard, Appleton Utopia two matt and Springhill Incentive
PRINTING PROCESS › Offset printing, sheet fed

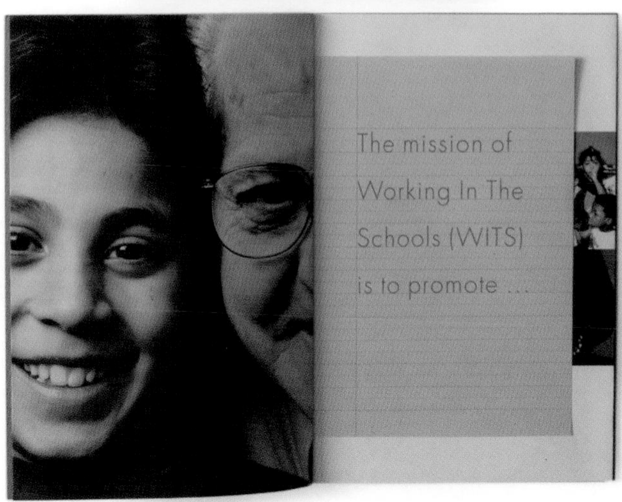

The mission of
Working In The
Schools (WITS)
is to promote ...

DESIGN FIRM > Danette Angerer
ART DIRECTOR > Danette Angerer
DESIGNER > Danette Angerer
ILLUSTRATORS/PHOTOGRAPHERS > Mike Schlotterback, Mark Trade, Rod Bradley, Michael Ask, Jeff Schmatt
COPYWRITER > Elinor Day
CLIENT > Brucemore
TOOLS (SOFTWARE/PLATFORM) > Pagemaker, Macintosh
PAPER STOCK > Dust cover: Environment Desert Storm. Cover: Environment Sedona Red.
Flysheet: U.V./Ultra II sepia interior. Interior stock: Sterling satin.
PRINTING PROCESS > Four-color process, PMS 876 metallic and spot dull varnish
PRINTER > Garner Printing, Des Moines, IA

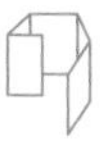

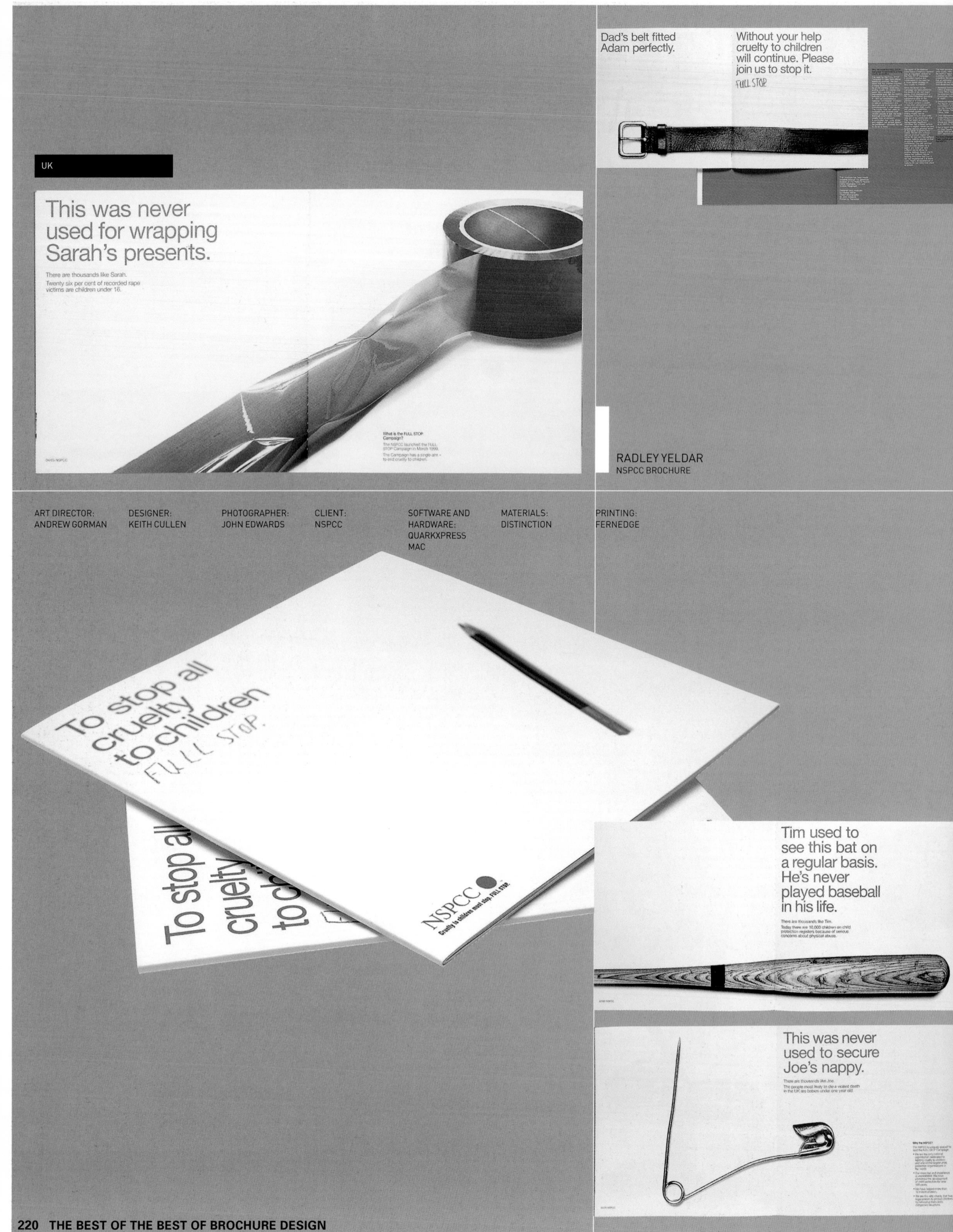

Dad's belt fitted Adam perfectly.
Without your help cruelty to children will continue. Please join us to stop it.
FULL STOP
This was never used for wrapping Sarah's presents.
There are thousands like Sarah.
Twenty six per cent of recorded rape victims are children under 16.
What is the FULL STOP Campaign?
To stop all cruelty to children
FULL STOP.
NSPCC
Cruelty to children must stop. FULL STOP.
Tim used to see this bat on a regular basis. He's never played baseball in his life.
There are thousands like Tim.
This was never used to secure Joe's nappy.
There are thousands like Joe.

UK

RADLEY YELDAR
NSPCC BROCHURE

ART DIRECTOR: ANDREW GORMAN
DESIGNER: KEITH CULLEN
PHOTOGRAPHER: JOHN EDWARDS
CLIENT: NSPCC
SOFTWARE AND HARDWARE: QUARKXPRESS MAC
MATERIALS: DISTINCTION
PRINTING: FERNEDGE

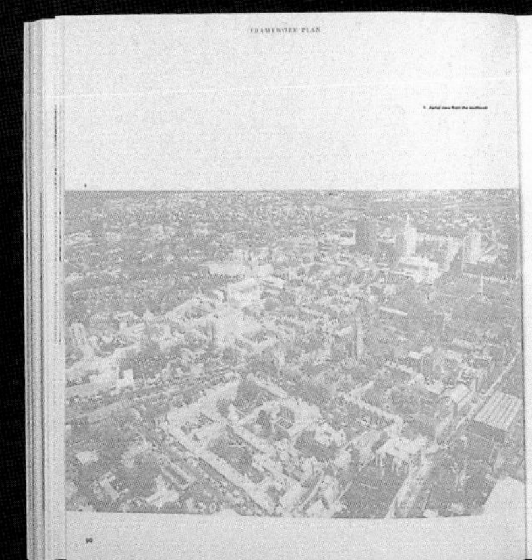

FRAMEWORK PLAN

Photographs showing existing character of the Crown/George area
1 High-rise housing
2 Shared City and University retail area

the Route 34/Oak Street Connector to Chapel Street. A joint effort by the City and Yale could significantly enhance the area by improving the streetscape and expanding arts-related uses, medical uses (both office and clinical), restaurants, retail stores, shops and studios that support the performing and visual arts. Development and improvements should focus on the York and College Street corridors. Yale already has an important presence in this area. It owns several parcels on York Street between Chapel and High Streets. University Towers houses many Yale-related tenants and the Medical Center leases space north of the Route 34/Oak Street Connector. The retail space between George Street and the Air Rights Garage has a high turnover rate that might decrease if quality stores moved in. The University should propose to the City that it convert York and College Streets to two-way traffic, and that it undertake landscaping and lighting programs to improve vehicular access and the pedestrian experience for everyone in the area. Physical improvements and building development along these corridors would reinforce connections between the Central Campus and Medical Center.

These two opportunities, especially when undertaken through joint planning projects by the City of New Haven and the University, would enhance the City and move each significantly closer to the common goal of more fully blending Yale's environment with that of its neighbors.

2

88

CAMPUS FRAMEWORK SYSTEMS

Uses
Built Form
Landscape and Open Space
Circulation
Pedestrian
Vehicular
Bicycles
Parking
Signage
Lighting
Neighborhood Interface

89

POULIN + MORRIS

YALE UNIVERSITY: A FRAMEWORK FOR CAMPUS

ART DIRECTOR: L RICHARD POULIN

DESIGNER: AMY KWON

CLIENT: COOPER, ROBERTSON & PARTNERS

SOFTWARE: QUARKXPRESS

MATERIALS: MOHAWK SUPERFINE

PRINTING: UNIVERSAL PRINTING

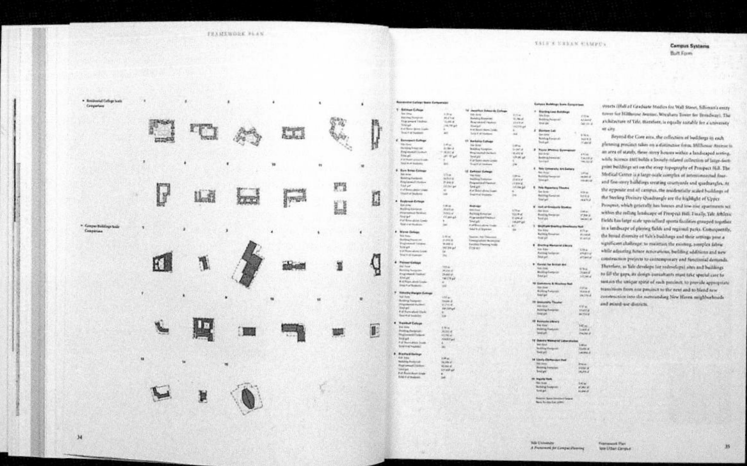

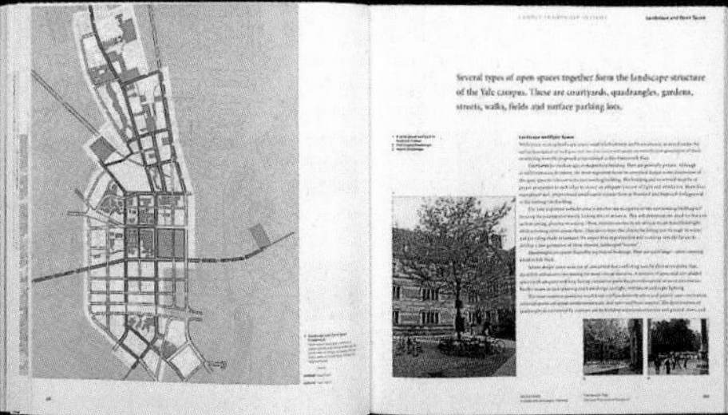

CLARK CREATIVE GROUP
THE STANFORD CARDINAL 90–00

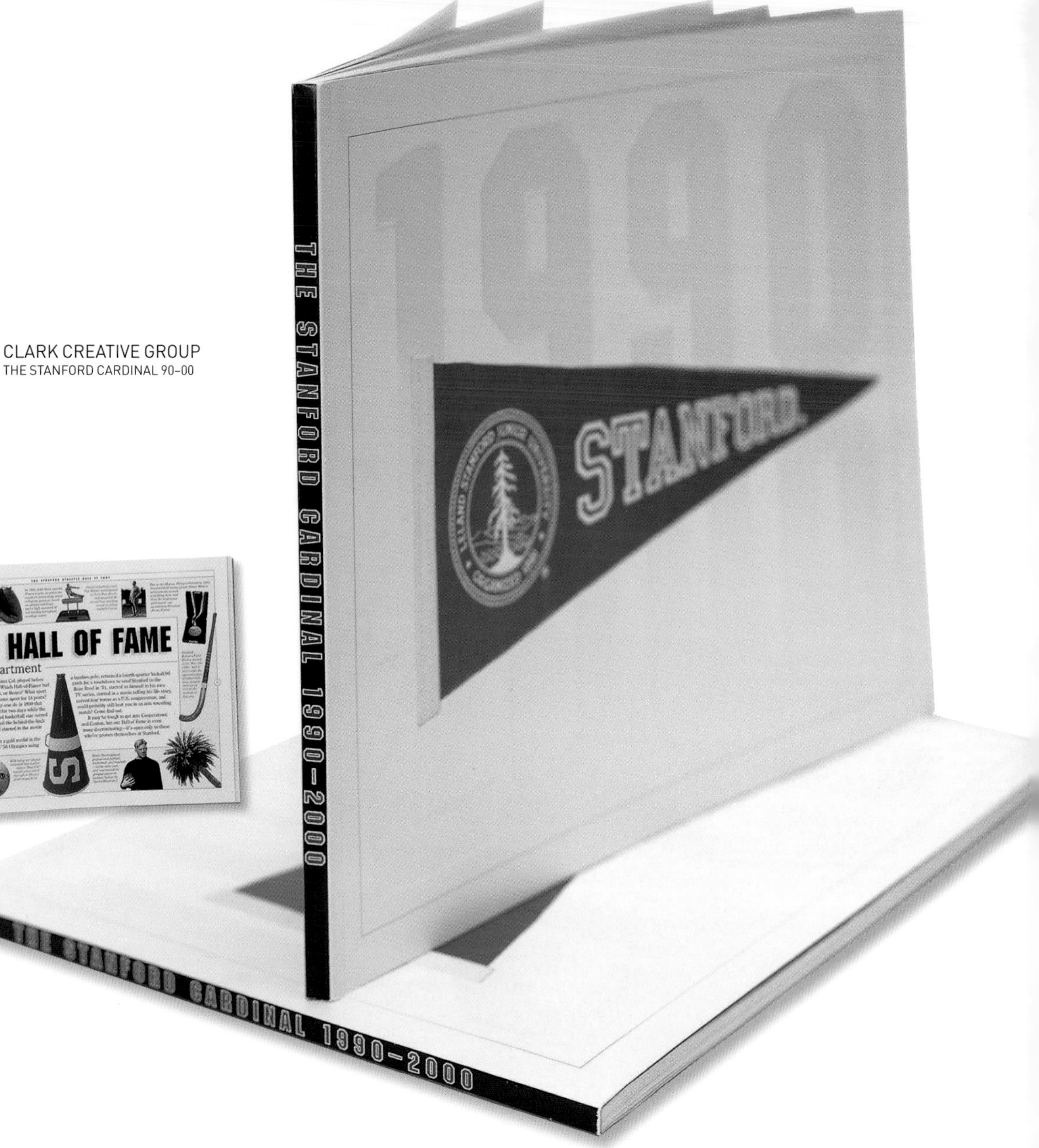

USA

ART DIRECTOR:
ANNEMARIE CLARK

DESIGNER:
NOREEN REI FUKUMORI

CLIENT:
STANFORD ATHLETIC DEPT

SOFTWARE:
ILLUSTRATOR
PHOTOSHOP
QUARKXPRESS

MATERIALS:
CENTURA

PRINTING:
HEMLOCK PRINTERS

CHENG DESIGN
TEACHERS AS SCHOLARS 2001–2002

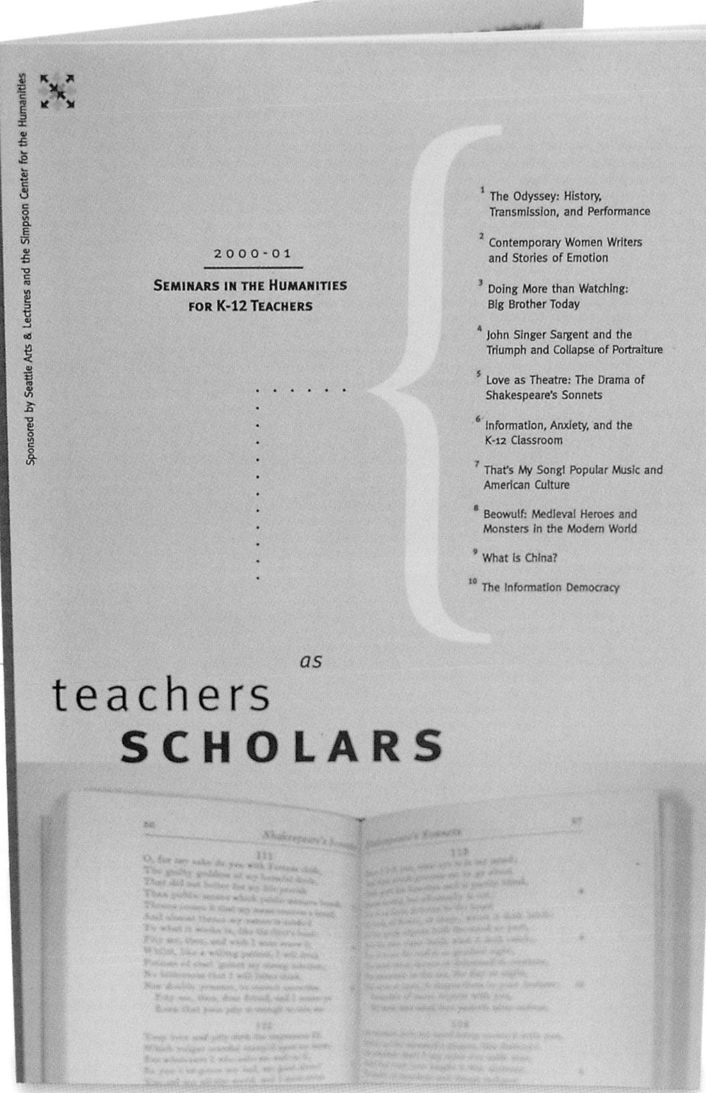

Sponsored by Seattle Arts & Lectures and the Simpson Center for the Humanities
2000-01
Seminars in the Humanities for K-12 Teachers
1 The Odyssey: History, Transmission, and Performance
2 Contemporary Women Writers and Stories of Emotion
3 Doing More than Watching: Big Brother Today
4 John Singer Sargent and the Triumph and Collapse of Portraiture
5 Love as Theatre: The Drama of Shakespeare's Sonnets
6 Information, Anxiety, and the K-12 Classroom
7 That's My Song! Popular Music and American Culture
8 Beowulf: Medieval Heroes and Monsters in the Modern World
9 What is China?
10 The Information Democracy
teachers as SCHOLARS

DESIGNER:
KAREN CHENG

CLIENT:
SEATTLE ARTS
AND LECTURES

SOFTWARE:
ILLUSTRATOR
PHOTOSHOP
QUARKXPRESS

MATERIALS:
FINCH FINE
COVER + TEXT

PRINTING:
2 PMS COLORS

USA

USA

M
Mission Guadalupe Alternative Programs fosters learning, personal growth and skill development in those individuals who are not well served by mainstream educational institutions.

Survivors
CLASS OF 2000
Imagine attending high school while you are pregnant or getting yourself and your child ready for school every morning. Imagine arriving in this country as a teenager and having to learn a second language while taking academic courses required for graduation. Imagine getting a year or more behind your classmates in school, but persevering and graduating anyway. Imagine the pressure and honor of being the first person in your family to graduate.
The 23 students who made up the GAP graduating class of 2000 have lived through situations that some of us can only imagine. They are a group of survivors and left high school just a few weeks ago as seasoned, confident young adults ready to seize their futures. To a person, they know how to set and achieve goals, use their resources, help one another. They are ready. In their words, GAP has been a small place where they got individual attention, where teachers were cool, and where students got along well together. It is a nice thing to think about now that they are gone and we look forward to the beginning of another school year.

ART DIRECTOR: WILLIAM HOMAN

DESIGNER: WILLIAM HOMAN

CLIENT: GUADALUPE ALTERNATIVE PROGRAM

MATERIALS: CLASSIC CREST

PRINTING: CUSTOM COLOR PRINTING

WILLIAM HOMAN DESIGN
GUADALUPE ALTERNATIVE PROGRAM

Milestones of the millennium As we move forward into the next century, our goal is to be prepared to meet the needs of all current and future GAP students. We have grown from a one-room house to a building with programs that provide multiple educational opportunities for youth and adults. We have reached many milestones this year. On an academic level, our students' scores improved substantially over last year. Culturally, through collaborations and partnerships, students have learned about the richness and diversity of others, the importance of tradition and the need to respect each other. They continue to prepare for the technological advances of the future and the need for communication and computer skills. We can achieve these goals because of the commitment and dedication of the staff. Congratulations to Sister Anna Louise Wilson, who will be celebrating her fiftieth anniversary as a School Sister of Notre Dame. She has worked at GAP for 25 years. Her contributions to GAP have been legendary. She has received numerous awards, but what is more important to her is the contact she makes with students in her art classes. The board has diligently worked this year to provide the resources for staff members to create an environment that allows each student to reach his or her potential. A new strategic plan has been adopted to position us for the future. We remain committed to the mission of GAP. Karen Thompson, Chair, GAP Board of Directors

Sister Ann
This annual report reviews the year 1999 and, we hope, shows that this agency is secure financially and solid as an educational institution–as it always has been. It also celebrates the graduating class of 2000 and the teachers and support staff who had so much to do with the success of our new-century graduates. We appreciate them and their talents and we also, and in the same breath, appreciate you and your support of GAP. In a unique way, your dedication to our mission is felt here every day, helping us create a place where learning and opportunity are realities.
Thanks

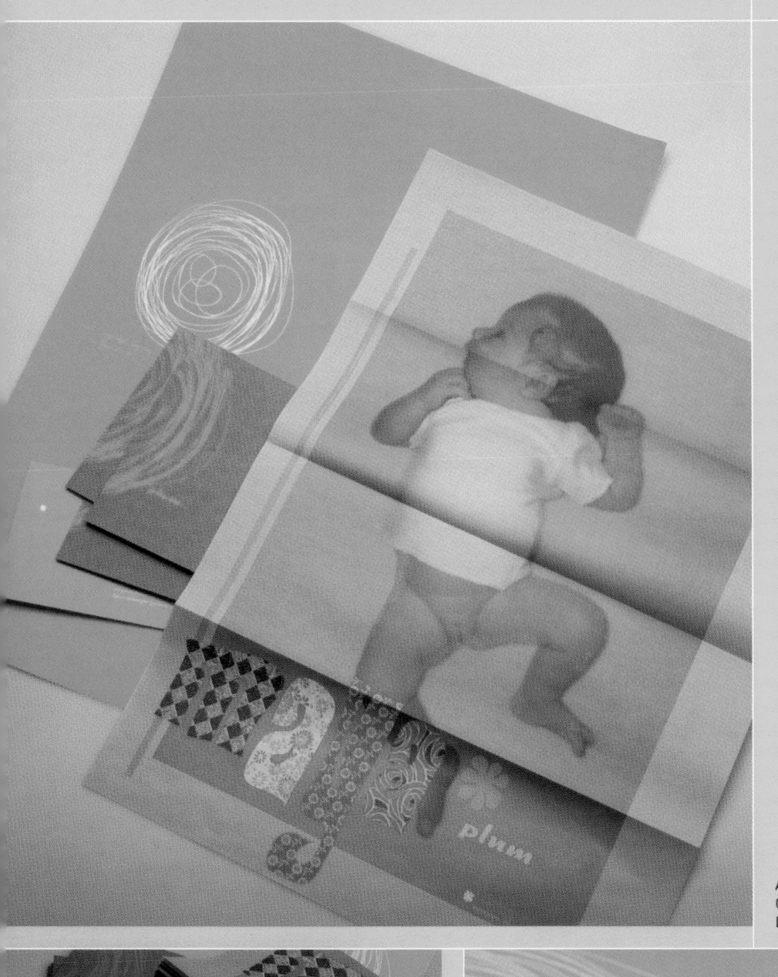

ART DIRECTORS:	DESIGNERS:	CLIENT:	MATERIALS:	PRINTING:
CHIARA GRANDESSO LIONELLO BOREAN	CHIARA GRANDESSO LIONELLO BOREAN	CHIARA GRANDESSO LIONELLO BOREAN	ENVELOPE WITH EMBOSSED PRINT	CMYK + GOLD INK + 1 PANTONE

USINE DE BOUTONS
MAYAPLUM BIRTH
ANNOUCEMENT

ITALY

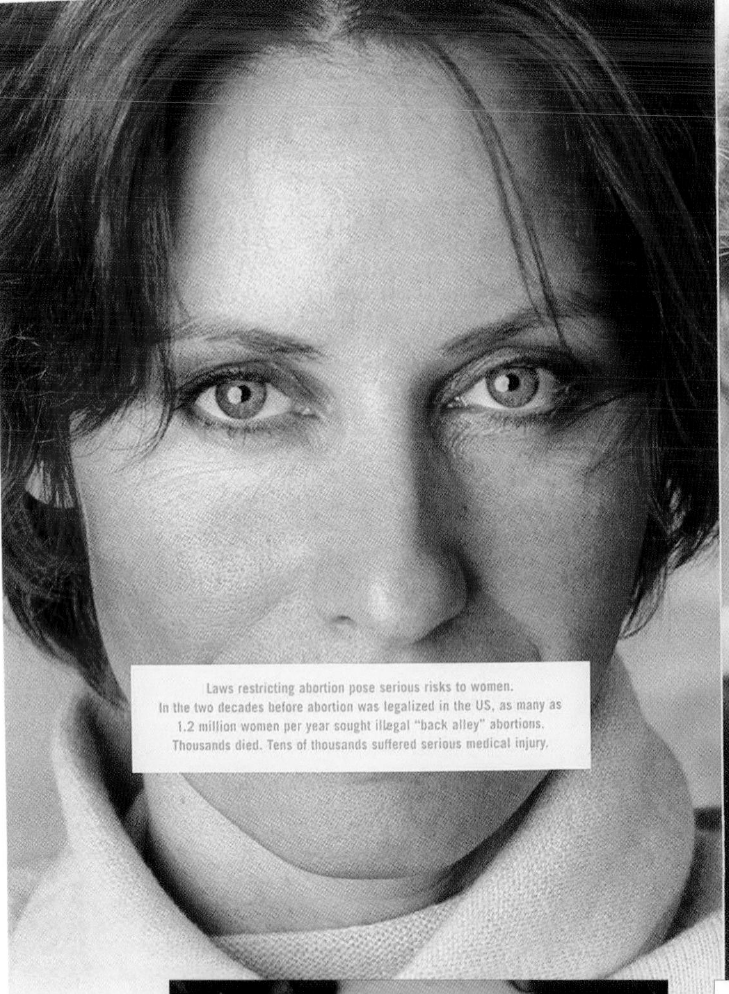

Laws restricting abortion pose serious risks to women.
In the two decades before abortion was legalized in the US, as many as 1.2 million women per year sought illegal "back alley" abortions.
Thousands died. Tens of thousands suffered serious medical injury.

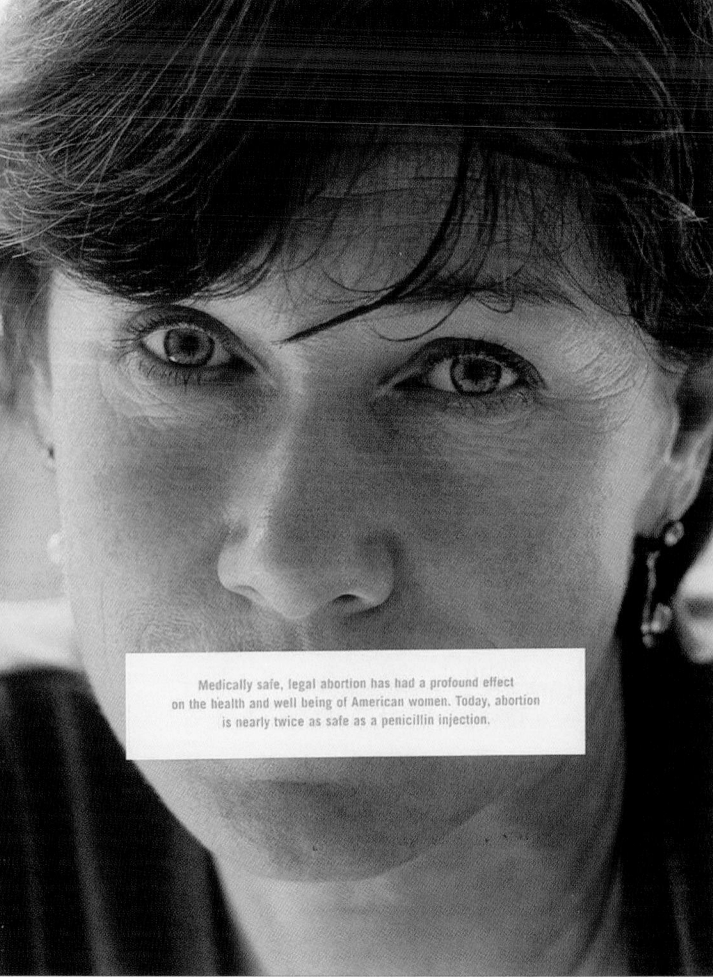

Medically safe, legal abortion has had a profound effect on the health and well being of American women. Today, abortion is nearly twice as safe as a penicillin injection.

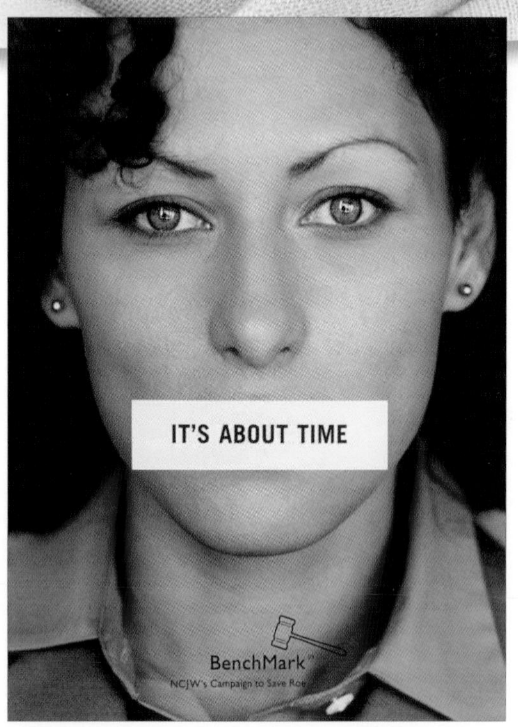

NCJW'S VOICE:

THE VOICE OF THE JEWISH COMMUNITY

FOR OVER A CENTURY THE NATIONAL COUNCIL OF JEWISH WOMEN HAS BEEN AT THE FOREFRONT OF SOCIAL CHANGE – COURAGEOUSLY TAKING A PROGRESSIVE STANCE ON ISSUES SUCH AS REPRODUCTIVE FREEDOM. TODAY, NCJW IS THE LEADING JEWISH ORGANIZATION FIGHTING TO PROTECT THAT FREEDOM.

As Jews, we understand what it means to have fundamental rights and liberties stripped away.

WE CANNOT BE SILENT ON THIS ISSUE

92% OF THE JEWISH COMMUNITY IS PRO-CHOICE

IT IS TIME TO BRING THE POWER AND THE VOICE OF THAT COMMUNITY TOGETHER

Reproductive rights are closely tied to religious freedom. Women have the right to be respected as moral decision-makers, able to make choices based on their own beliefs and traditions. For the courts to impose one religion's view on all of us defies the very meaning of religious liberty.

NCJW'S BENCHMA
ALREADY TAKING

EDUCATING AND MOBILIZING

LEADING PRO-CHOICE RALLIES ACROSS THE COUNTRY

BUILDING STATE COALITIONS

FLYING KEY LEADERS AND SP TO MEET WITH SENATORS

EMPOWERING ONLINE ACTIVIS AN INTERACTIVE WEB SITE

NOW, IT'S

LOG ON TO WWW.BE AND JOIN BENCHMARK

AND PARTNERS

It's About Time: NCJW's Campaign to Save Roe

ART DIRECTOR:	DESIGNER:	CLIENT:	TOOLS:	MATERIALS:
David Schimmel	Susan Brzozowski	National Council of Jewish Women	Adobe Photoshop QuarkXPress	Productolith

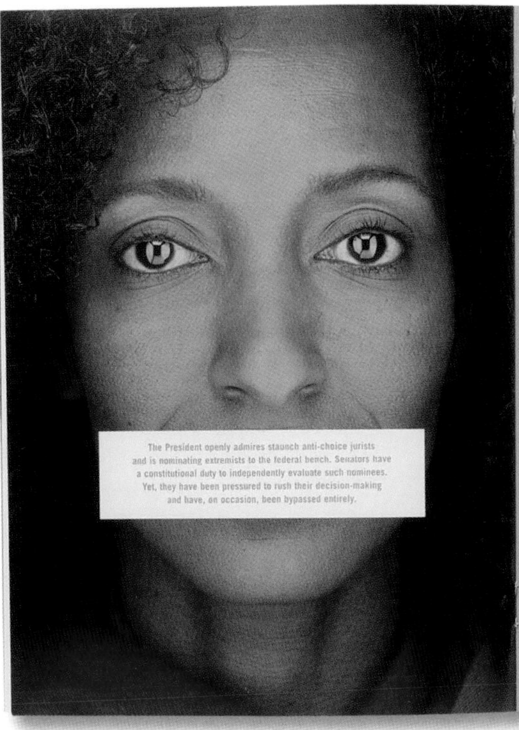

The President openly admires staunch anti-choice jurists
and is nominating extremists to the federal bench. Senators have
a constitutional duty to independently evaluate such nominees.
Yet, they have been pressured to rush their decision-making
and have, on occasion, been bypassed entirely.

THE EROSION OF FREEDOM IS A SLIPPERY SLOPE. IF WE LOSE REPRODUCTIVE RIGHTS, OTHER CORE RIGHTS–LIKE RELIGIOUS LIBERTY AND CIVIL RIGHTS–MAY BE CLOSE BEHIND.

THE FUTURE WILL BE SET BY JUDGES WHO HOLD LIFETIME SEATS ON THE FEDERAL BENCH. ANTI-CHOICE JUDGES ARE ALREADY ATTACKING THE RIGHT TO ABORTION. AND MORE ANTI-CHOICE NOMINEES ARE WAITING IN THE WINGS–POSITIONED TO RENDER DECISIONS THAT WILL DEFINE FREEDOM FOR GENERATIONS TO COME.

FIND YOUR VOICE. IT'S TIME TO SPEAK OUT AND FIGHT BACK. ON JANUARY 22, 1973 THE SUPREME COURT AFFIRMED WOMEN'S CONSTITUTIONAL RIGHT TO ABORTION IN ITS LANDMARK *ROE V. WADE* RULING.

TODAY THIS RIGHT IS UNDER ATTACK IN COURTROOMS ACROSS THE COUNTRY. YOU CAN DO SOMETHING ABOUT IT. TAKE ACTION TODAY, BEFORE IT'S TOO LATE.

MIRKO ILIĆ CORP.

Massachusetts Lesbian & Gay Bar Association Brochures

ART DIRECTOR: Mirko Ilić

CLIENT: Massachusetts Lesbian & Gay Bar Association

TOOLS: QuarkXPress

GEORGE TSCHERNY, INC.

Hurra! We Made It—Brochure

ART DIRECTOR:	**DESIGNERS:**	**PHOTOGRAPHER:**	**CLIENT:**	**TOOLS:**	**MATERIALS:**
Siles H. Rhodess	George Tscherny Matthew Cocco	Joseph Sinnot	School of Visual Arts	Adobe Photoshop QuarkXPress	Centura white dull white 80 lb (cover)

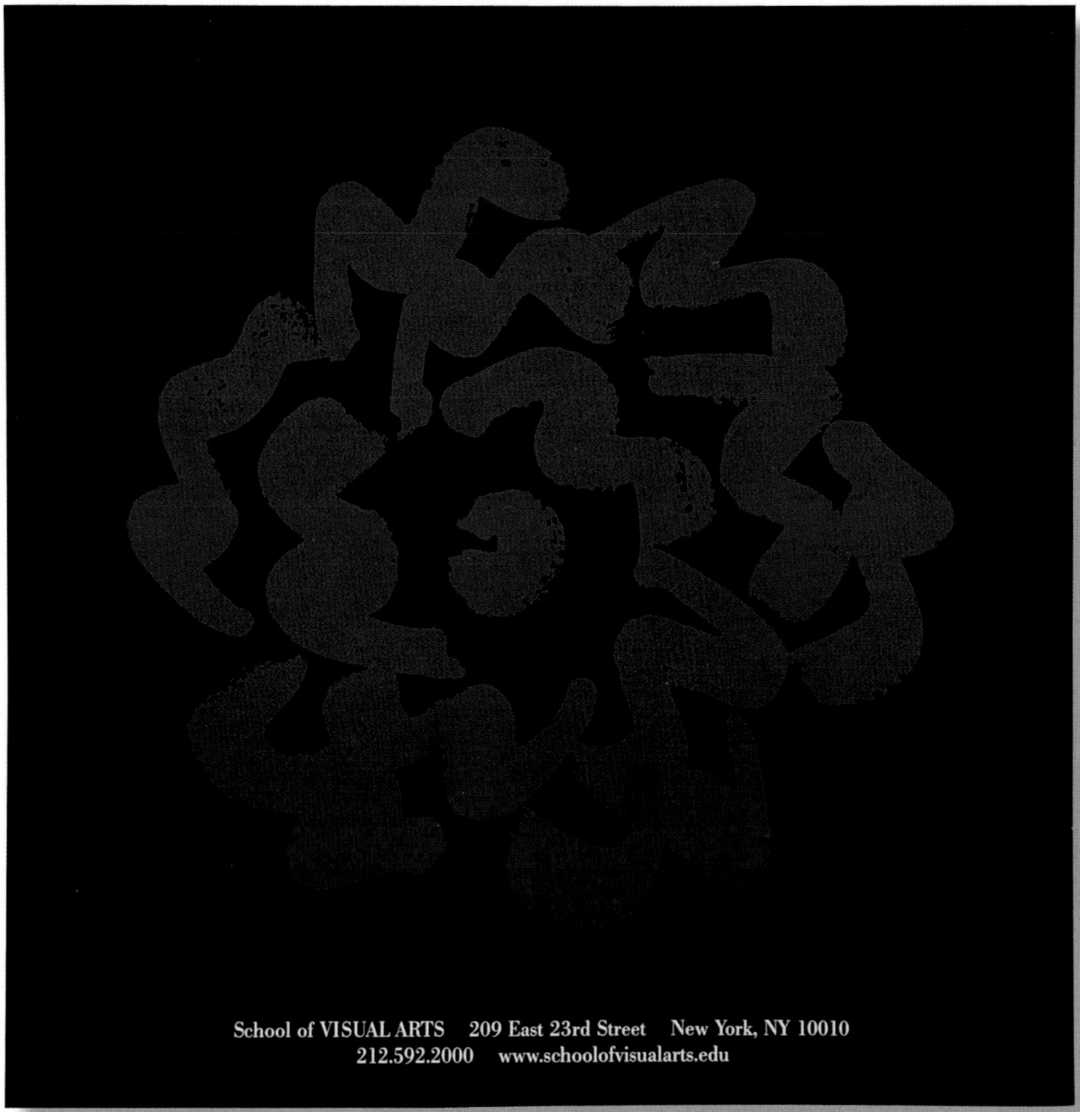

School of VISUAL ARTS 209 East 23rd Street New York, NY 10010
212.592.2000 www.schoolofvisualarts.edu

HAT-TRICK DESIGN

The Graduate Pioneer Programme

ART DIRECTORS:
Gareth Howat
David Kimpton
Jim Sutherland

DESIGNERS:
David Kimpton
Jamie Ellul
Mark Wheatcroft

CLIENT:
Nesta

TOOLS:
Adobe Photoshop
QuarkXPress

MATERIALS:
Naturalis

RUTGERS UNIVERSITY

Rutgers Study Abroad—Recruitment Brochure

ART DIRECTOR:	DESIGNER:	CLIENT:	TOOLS:	MATERIALS:	MATERIALS:
John Van Cleaf	John Van Cleaf	Rutgers Study Abroad	Adobe Photoshop QuarkXPress	French Paper Durotone Butcher, off white 100 lb (cover)	Finch Vanilla Fine 105 lb (text)

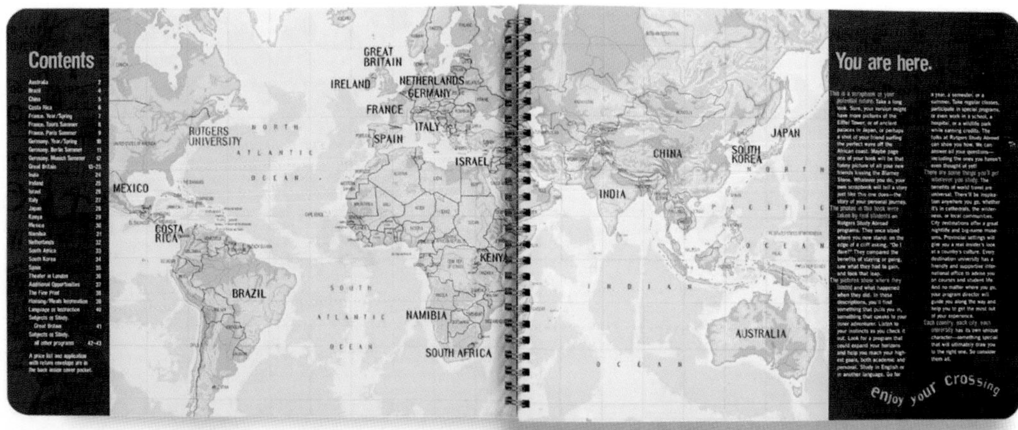

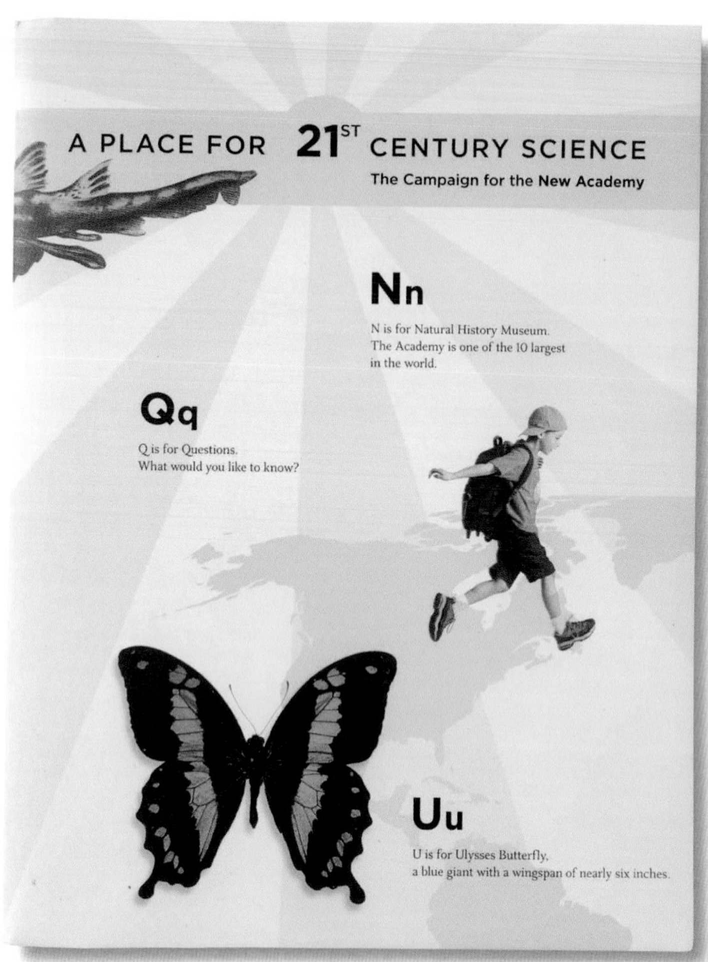

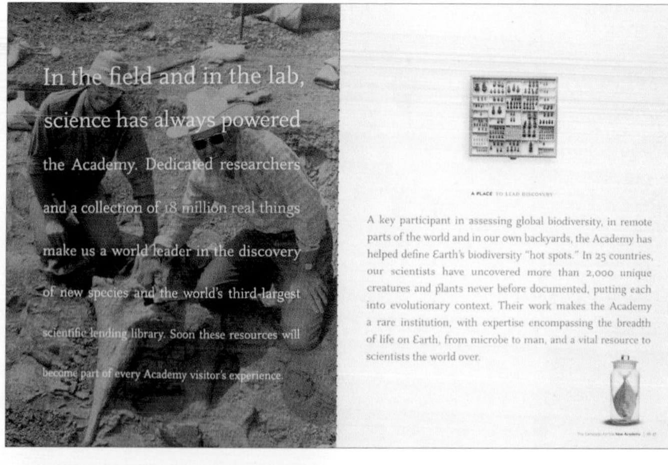

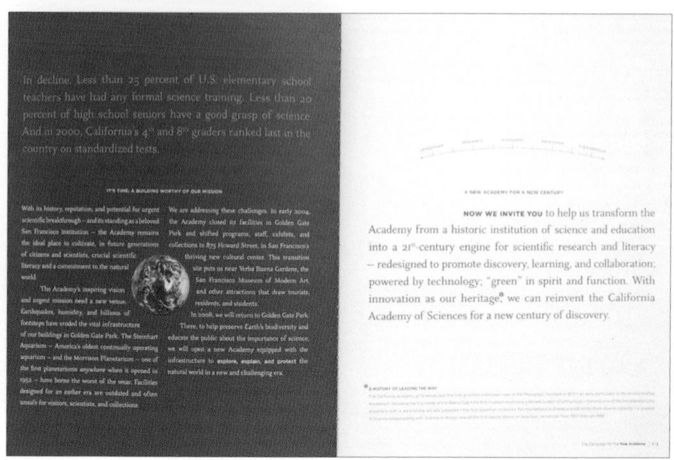

ALTERPOP

California Academy of Sciences Brochure

ART DIRECTOR:	DESIGNER:	CLIENT:	TOOLS:
Dorothy Remington	Christopher Simmons	California Academy of Sciences	Adobe Photoshop Adobe InDesign

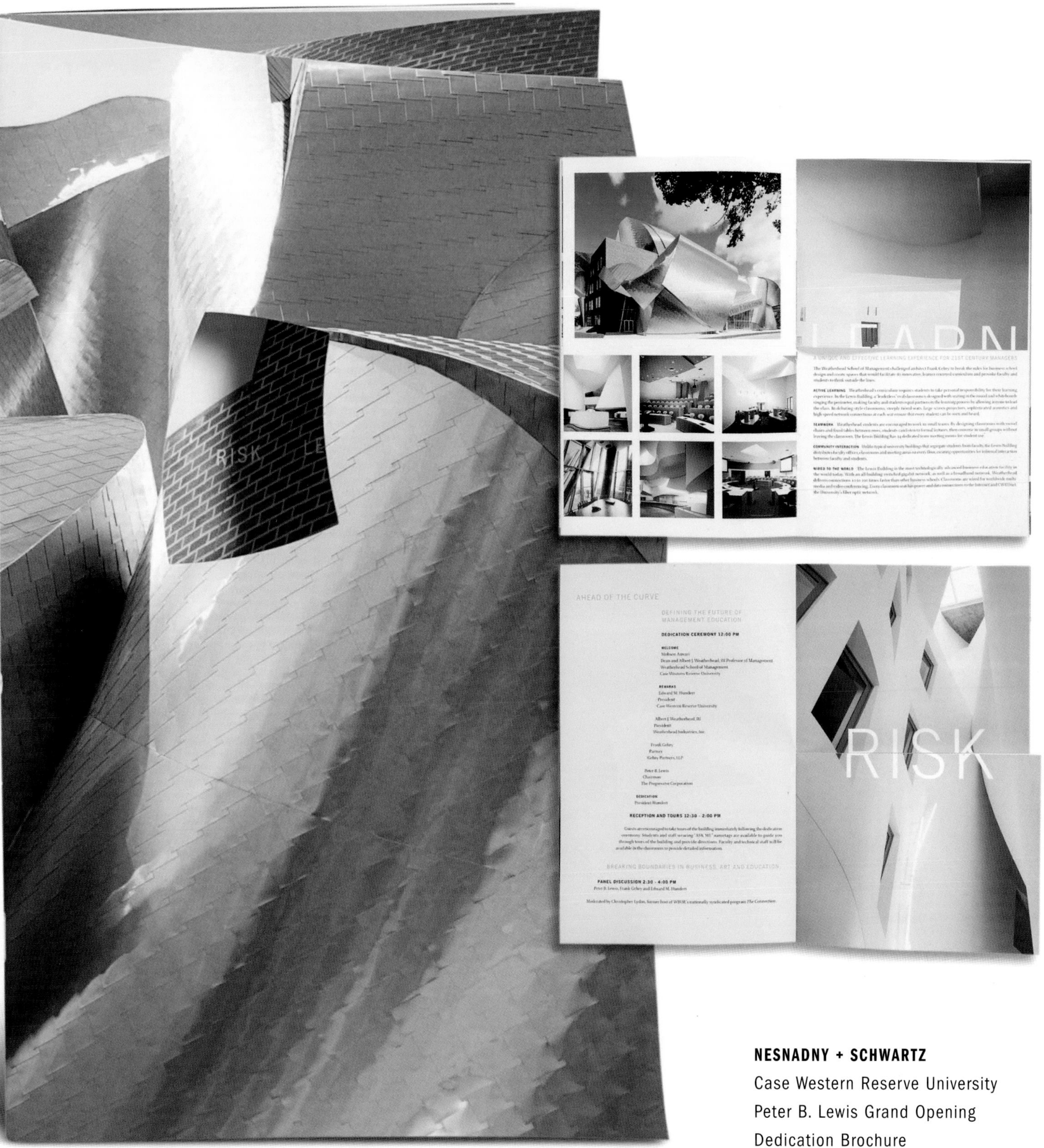

NESNADNY + SCHWARTZ

Case Western Reserve University
Peter B. Lewis Grand Opening
Dedication Brochure

ART DIRECTORS:
Mark Schwartz
Michelle Moehler
Gregory Oznowich
Stacie Ross

DESIGNERS:
Michelle Moehler
Gregory Oznowich
Stacie Ross

CLIENT:
Case Western Reserve University and Weatherhead School of Management

TOOLS:
Adobe Photoshop
Adobe Illustrator
QuarkXPress

MATERIALS:
Mohawk Option
Kromekoteplus
Benefit

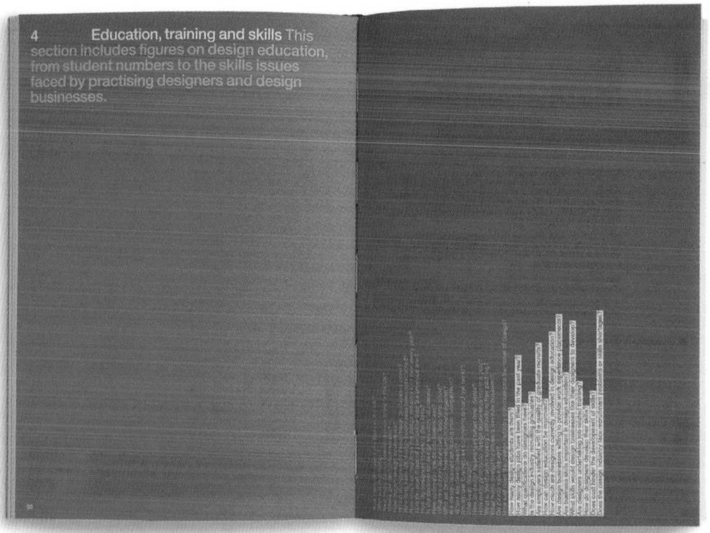

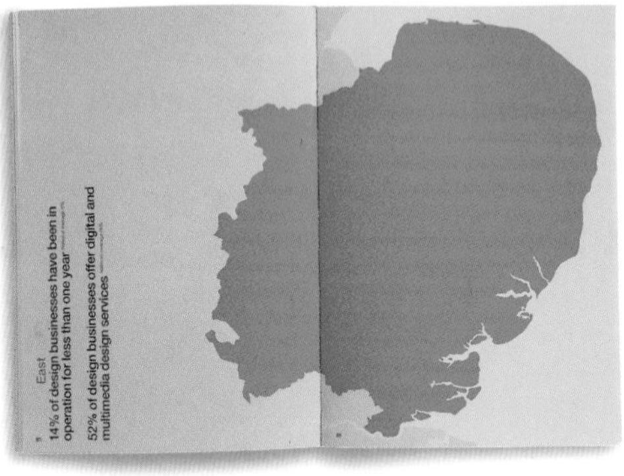

CARTLIDGE LEVENE

The Business of Design, Design Industry Research

Art Director:
Ian Cartlidge
Designer:
Cartlidge Levene
Client:
Design Council
Software:
Adobe InDesign
Paper/Materials:
Howard Smith (cover), Think White (text), McNaughton Cyclus (text)

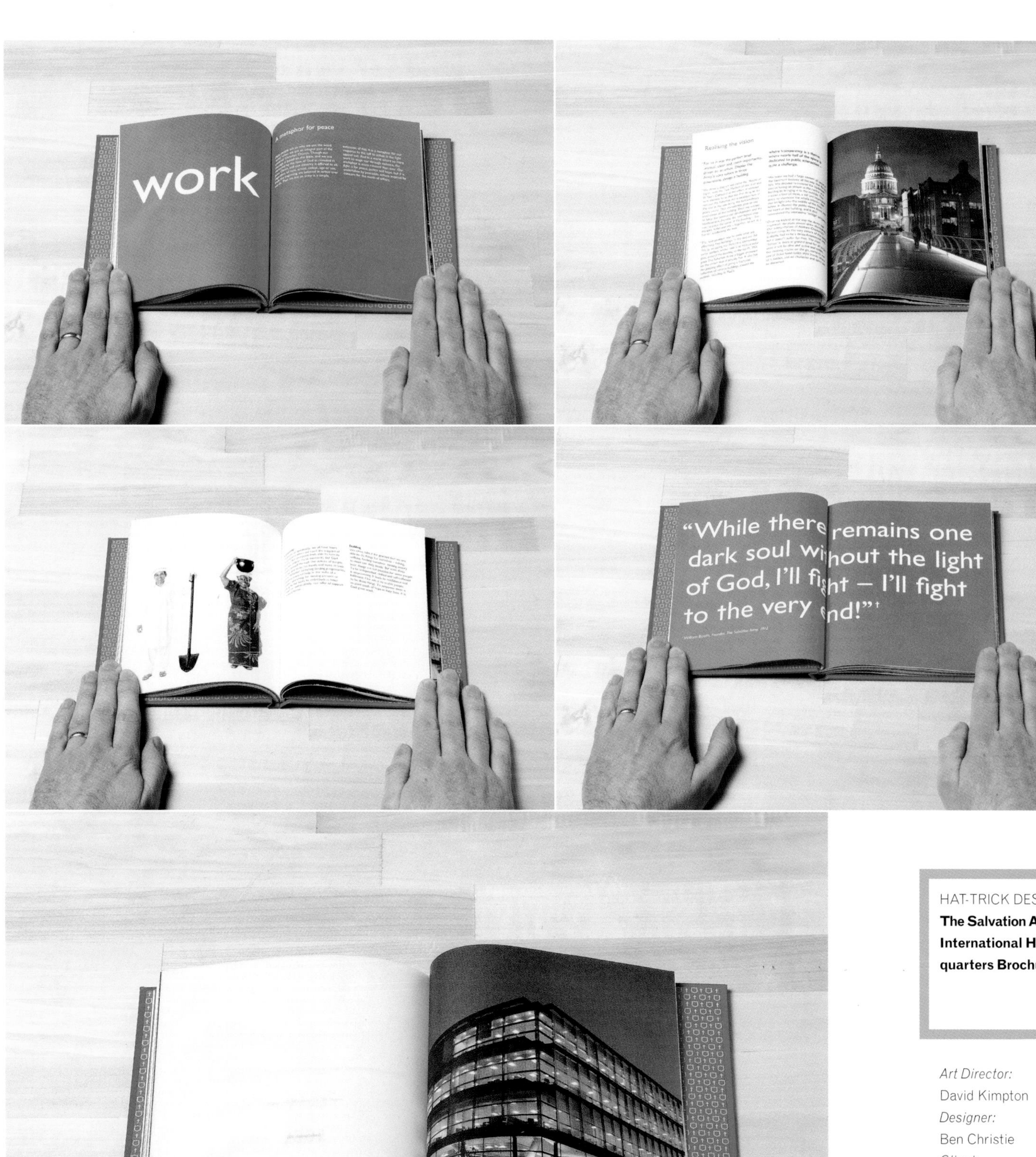

HAT-TRICK DESIGN

The Salvation Army International Headquarters Brochure

Art Director:
David Kimpton
Designer:
Ben Christie
Client:
The Salvation Army
Software:
QuarkXPress
Paper/Materials:
Bible Paper

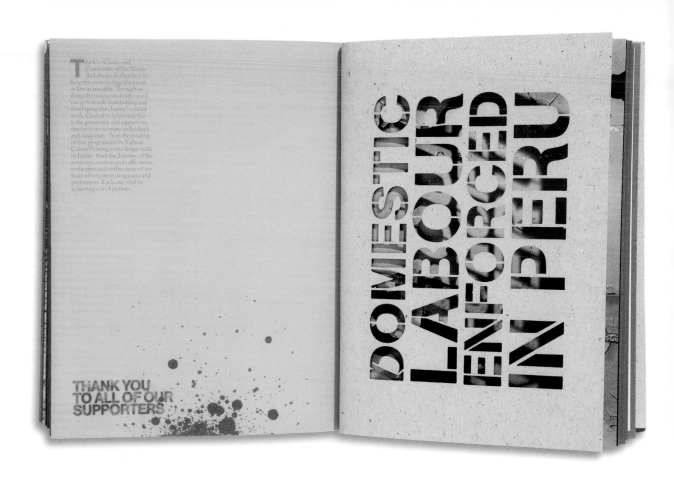
The Co-Chairs and Committee of The Magic Ball always do their best to keep the costs to stage the event as low as possible. Through so doing the maximum funds raised can go towards maintaining and developing the charity's crucial work. Central to achieving this is the generosity and support we receive from so many individuals and companies - from the printing of this programme by Fulmar Colour Printing to the design work by Inaria - from the donation of the resources, auction and raffle items to the time and enthusiasm of our team of volunteers, magicians and performers. Each one vital to achieving our objectives.
THANK YOU TO ALL OF OUR SUPPORTERS
DOMESTIC LABOUR ENFORCED IN PERU

Anti-Slavery is committed to eliminating all forms of slavery in today's world. Slavery, servitude and forced labour are violations of individual freedom, which deny basic dignity and fundamental human rights. Anti-Slavery supports today's fight for tomorrow's freedom by exposing current cases of slavery and campaigning for their eradication, supporting the initiatives of local organisations to release people, supporting the prevention and rehabilitation of child domestic workers, and pressing for more effective implementation of international laws against slavery.
David Simpson
Honorary Life Member,
Anti-Slavery International
ANTI-SLAVERY INTERNATIONAL'S MISSION

INARIA

Colors of the World

Art Directors:
Andrew Thomas,
Debora Berardi
Designers:
Andrew Thomas,
Debora Berardi
Client:
Anti-Slavery
International
Paper/Materials:
Hanno Art Silk
200 gsm (text),
Hanno Art Gloss
320 gsm (cover)

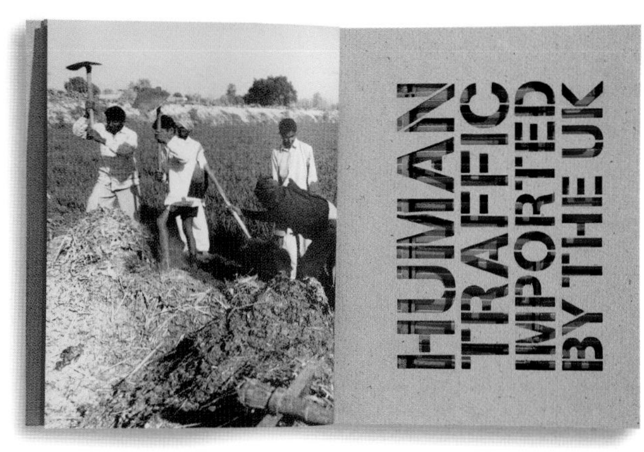

POULIN + MORRIS INC.

Brooklyn Botanic Garden, Master Plan

Designers:
L. Richard Poulin, Anna Crider
Client:
Brooklyn Botanic Garden
Software:
Adobe InDesign
Paper/Materials:
Sappi, Lustro Dull

HARVARD BUSINESS SCHOOL
you can hear it in the voices of the students...
Harvard Business School is a community of people engaged in many activities focused on one purpose—developing leaders.
HBS PROVIDES US THE OPPORTUNITY TO SIT IN A CLASSROOM WITH PEOPLE FROM SO MANY COUNTRIES WHO INFORM OUR UNDERSTANDING OF THE ISSUES THAT FACE THEIR HOMES. I'VE REALIZED HOW SMALL A SLICE OF GLOBAL LIFE I'D EXPERIENCED AND HOW MANY THINGS EXIST ABOUT WHICH I'D LIKE TO KNOW MORE.
William D. Bahm MBA 2004
New York, New York

STOLTZE DESIGN

Harvard Business School Admissions Brochure

Art Director:
Clifford Stoltze
Designer:
Roy Burns
Client:
Harvard Business School
Software:
QuarkXPress
Paper/Materials:
Finch Fine

KOLEGRAM
Canadian Archive Association Promotion

Designer:
Gontran Blais
Client:
Library & Archives Canada
Paper/Materials:
Domtar Titanium and Proterra

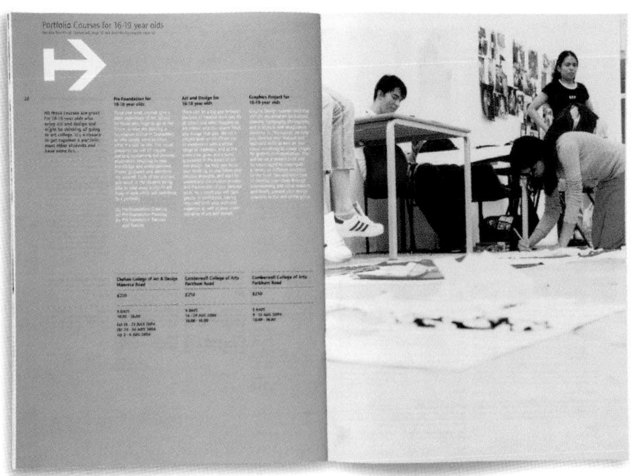

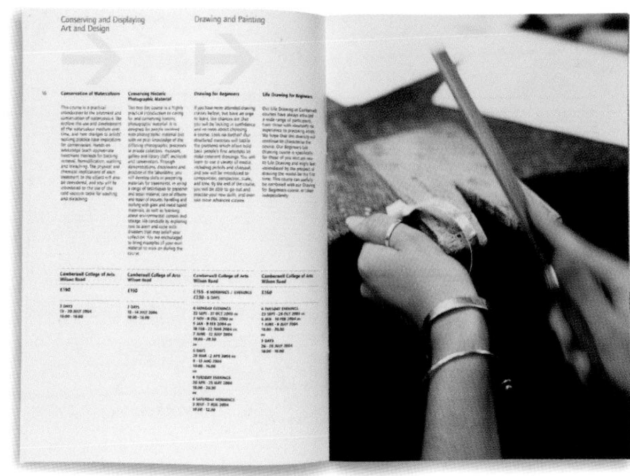

RB-M
Camberwell & Chelsea Short Courses Brochure

Art Director:
Richard Bonner-Morgan
Designer:
Richard Bonner-Morgan
Photographer:
Richard Learoyd
Client:
London Artscom Limited
Software:
QuarkXPress
Paper/Materials:
Nimrod Silk

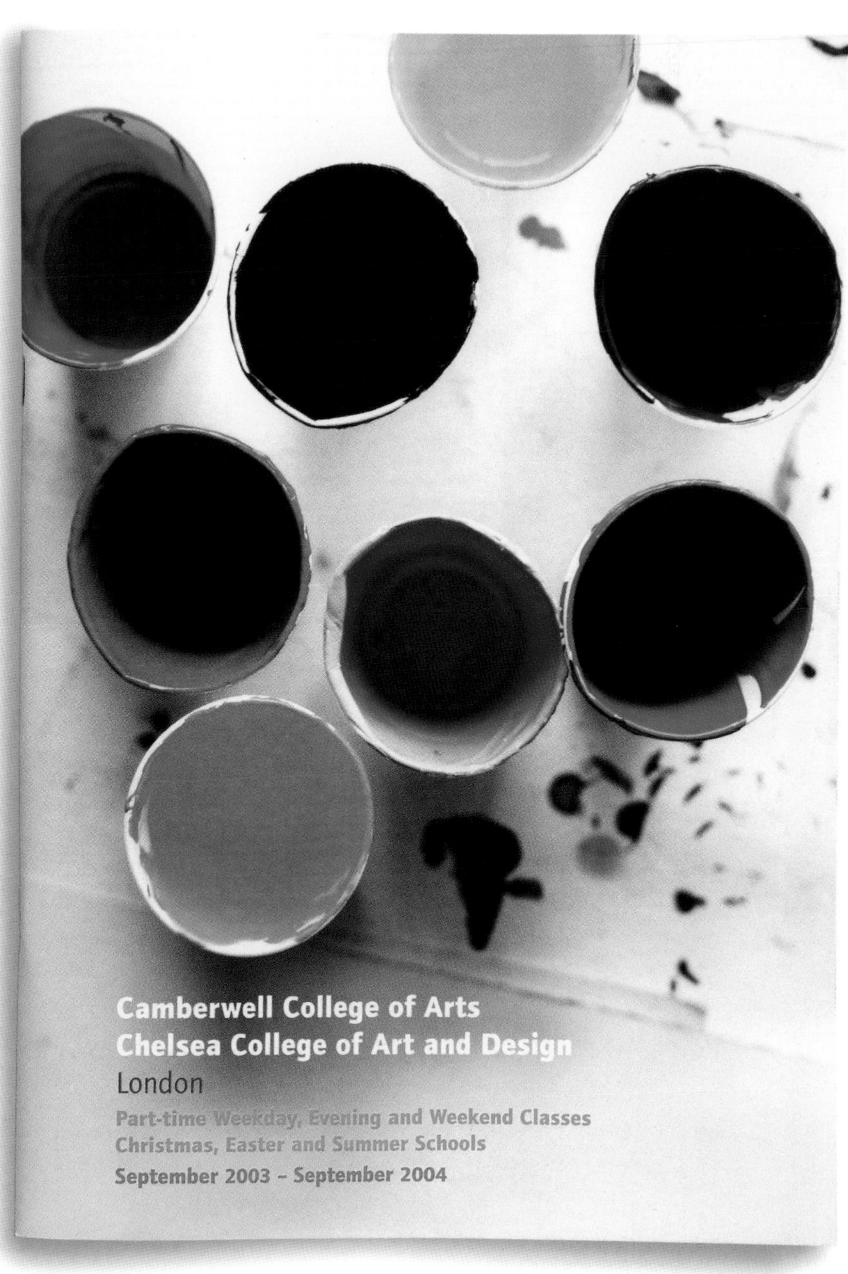

Camberwell College of Arts
Chelsea College of Art and Design
London
Part-time Weekday, Evening and Weekend Classes
Christmas, Easter and Summer Schools
September 2003 – September 2004

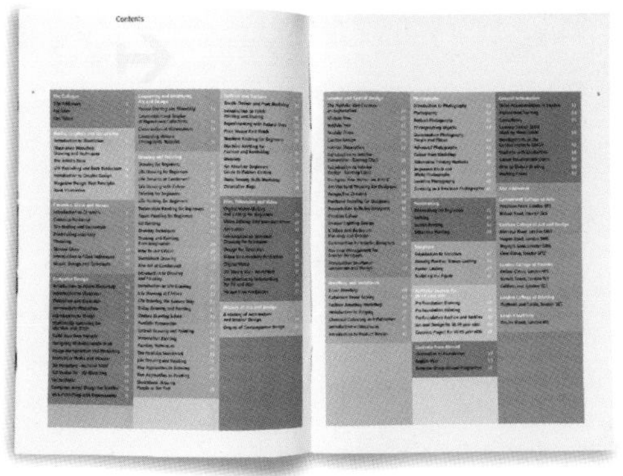

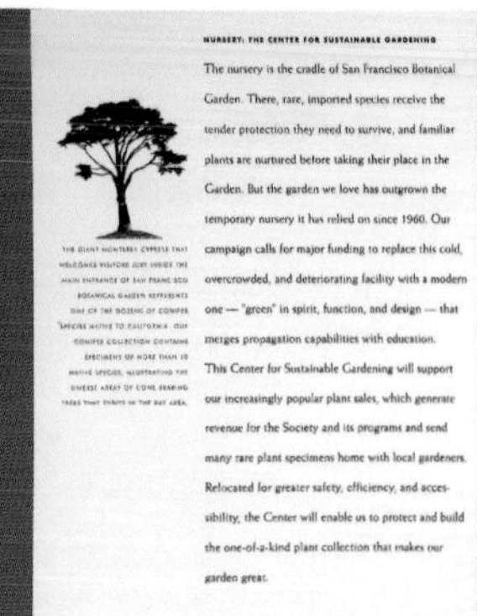

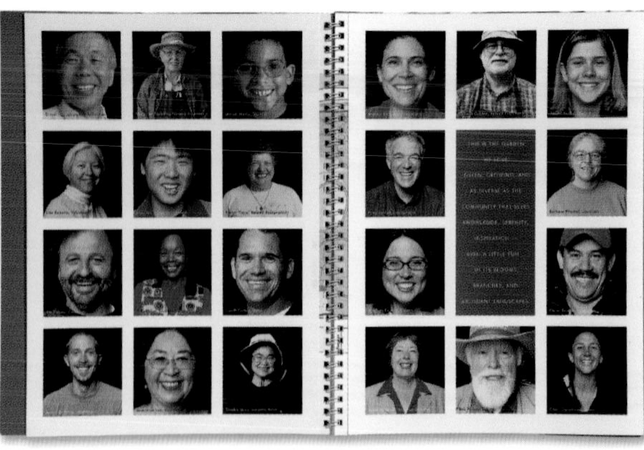

PENTAGRAM DESIGN,
SAN FRANCISCO
San Francisco Botanical Garden

Art Director:
Kit Hinrichs
Designers:
Belle How,
Jessica Siegel
Client:
The San Francisco Botanical Garden Association
Software:
Adobe InDesign

Think about what makes a city great: Is it the spirit and outlook of its people? Its geography? Its history? San Francisco, a great city by any measure, has it all — including one inspiring resource no great city should be without: a botanical garden where people can experience nature, learn about plants and the environment, relax, and seek respite from urban life. Since 1940, San Francisco Botanical Garden at Strybing Arboretum has embodied all that makes San Francisco great — a jewel-like setting, a mild climate in which diversity thrives, a conservation spirit, and a sensibility that cherishes beauty and seeks to share it with others. For the people of the Bay Area, this unique garden is more than a place in Golden Gate Park. It's a place in our hearts, a familiar backdrop for the times of our lives. On its daisy-dotted meadows, we've picnicked or sat sketching a magnificent magnolia in bloom. On its meandering paths, we've contemplated life's big issues, answered a child's questions about nature, or sought inspiration for a home garden, even if it's a window box. However we experience it, this garden reminds us that connecting with and protecting nature — whether we're dedicated gardeners or just admirers of Earth's diverse beauty — makes us more alive. For 50 years, the Botanical Garden Society has augmented public funding to make San Francisco Botanical Garden great. Now, with your help, we can turn San Francisco's garden — the garden we love — into one of the world's finest botanical gardens. This opportunity is unique and perishable, and the time to seize it is now, while we have a vision of what our great city's garden can become and the talented team to bring that vision to life.

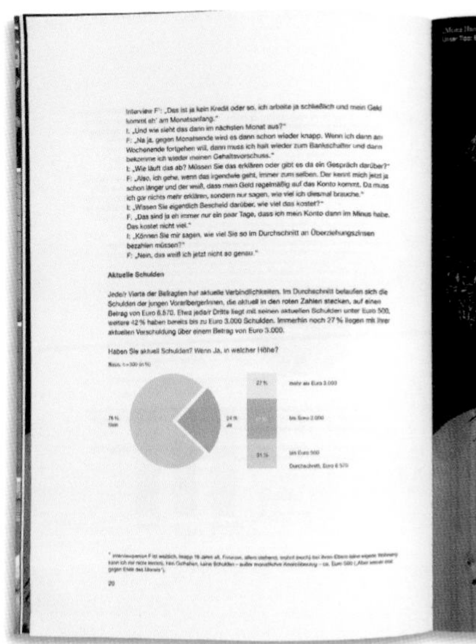

SÄGENVIER DESIGN KOMMUNIKATION

Attention Schulden Falle

Art Director:
Sigi Ramoser
Designers:
Klaus Österle,
Oli Ruhm,
Silvia Keckeis
Client:
AK Vorarlberg

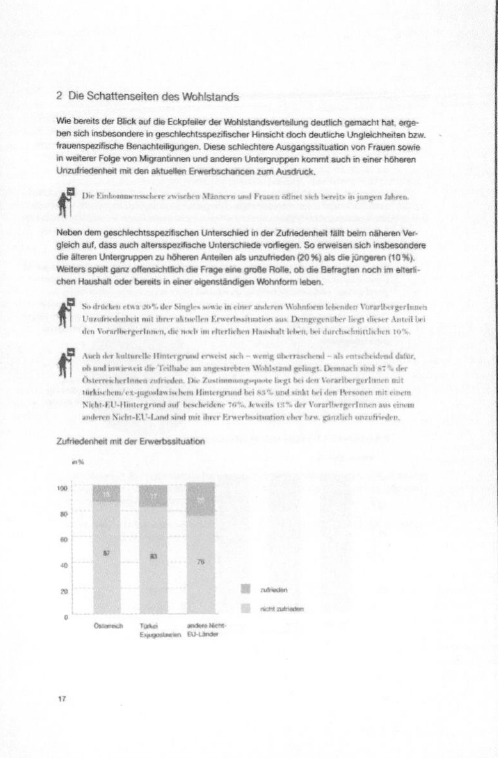

'I was attracted by the one-year programme and the opportunity to experience French and Asian culture. In a world that continues to get closer, INSEAD stands out as an example of how students and faculty drawn from across the globe can come together to make an unforgettable experience. When I came to INSEAD a year ago, I never expected to leave with the diversity and depth of friendships I have today'. **Monisha Dillon, 25 (United Kingdom)**

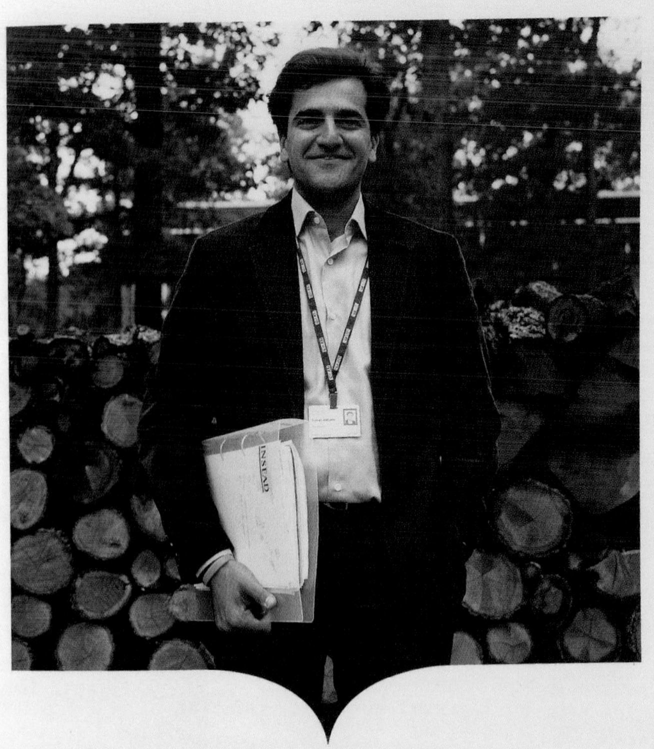

'I chose INSEAD because of the diversity of the student body. I had good friends who were alums who spoke highly of the place. Also, I had met their friends and felt they were broadminded and internationally orientated. The ability to move geographies and, at my relatively mature age, the one year programme, also appealed to me. It was a good choice exceeding my expectations'. **Saman Ahsani, 31 (Iran)**

NB:STUDIO
Insead
MBA Program

Art Directors:
Nick Finney, Ben Stott, Alan Dye
Designer:
Daniel Lock
Client:
Insead

One year to earn your place among our alumni.
Patricia Sharma-Inglis

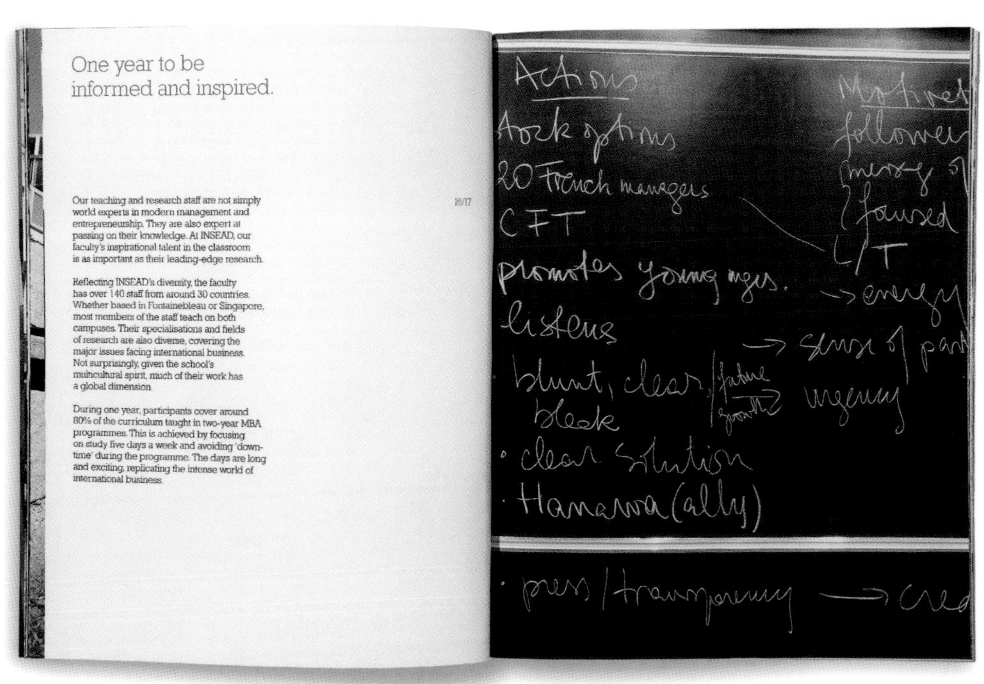
One year to be informed and inspired.
Our teaching and research staff are not simply world experts in modern management and entrepreneurship. They are also expert at passing on their knowledge. At INSEAD, our faculty's inspirational talent in the classroom is as important as their leading-edge research.
Reflecting INSEAD's diversity, the faculty has over 140 staff from around 30 countries. Whether based in Fontainebleau or Singapore, most members of the staff teach on both campuses. Their specialisations and fields of research are also diverse, covering the major issues facing international business. Not surprisingly, given the school's multicultural spirit, much of their work has a global dimension.
During one year, participants cover around 80% of the curriculum taught in two-year MBA programmes. This is achieved by focusing on study five days a week and avoiding 'down-time' during the programme. The days are long and exciting, replicating the intense world of international business.
16/17

Building the Jubilee School
Everyone and the Architect

Building Sights
Building Sights is a campaign to involve the public in building projects. Run by Arts Council England and the Commission for Architecture and the Built Environment (CABE), Building Sights is an award scheme to celebrate the best examples of public involvement and a website that provides practical information and ideas about how to go about it.

This book is the story of a new school in Tulse Hill, Brixton, London. It comes in two parts;

Part One
How the process was shared

Part Two
How the school was designed

Awards for the school

Aug 2001
RSA Art for Architecture Award

Aug 2003
RIBA Regional Award

Sept 2003
Short-listed for the Prime Minister's Better Public Building Award

Sept 2003
Short-listed for a Building Construction Industry Award

Part One

A guide to sharing the process – getting everyone involved in the process of creating a new building.

STUDIO MYERSCOUGH
Jubilee

Art Director:
Morag Myerscough
Designers:
Morag Myerscough, David Lowbridge
Client:
Arts Council England, CABE & Allford, Hall, Monaghan, Morris

SELF-
PROMOTIONAL
BROCHURES

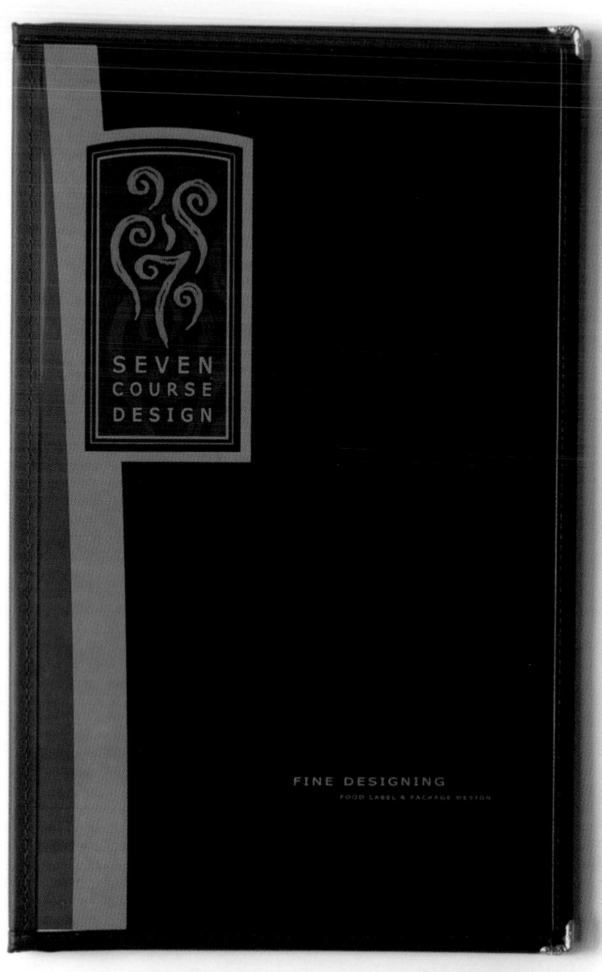

DESIGN FIRM › Graif Design
ART DIRECTOR › Matt Graif
DESIGNER › Matt Graif
CLIENT › Seven Course Design
TOOLS (SOFTWARE/PLATFORM) › Illustrator 9.0
PAPER STOCK › Neenah Paper Co.
PRINTING PROCESS › Offset printing

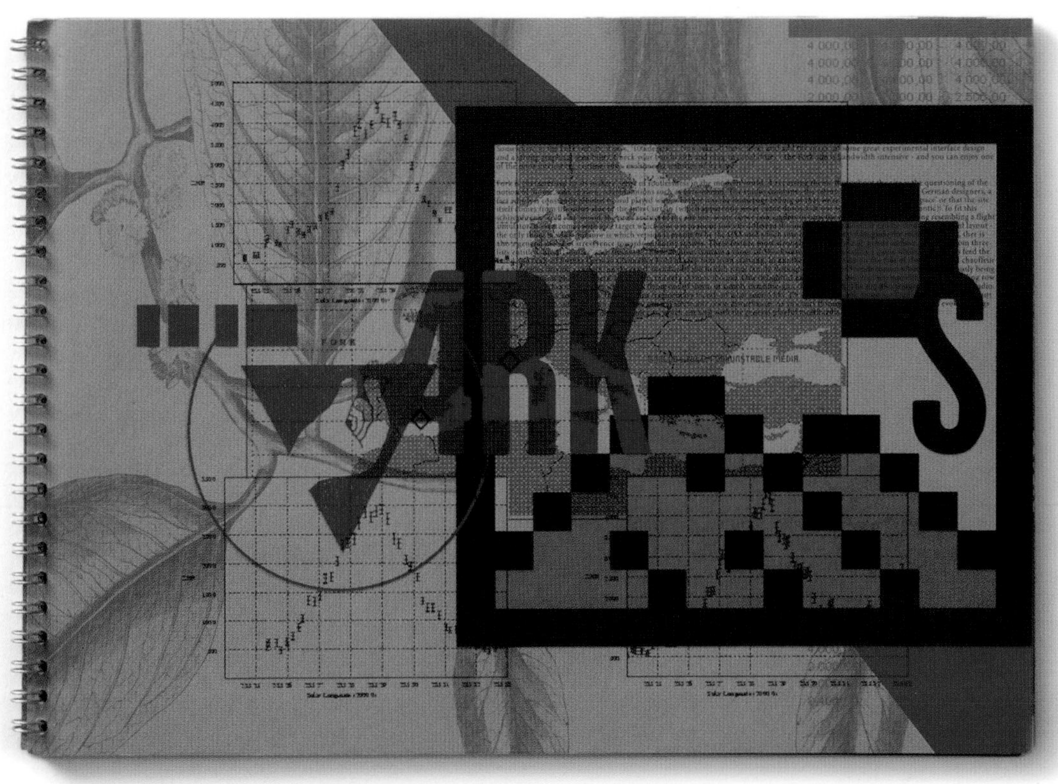

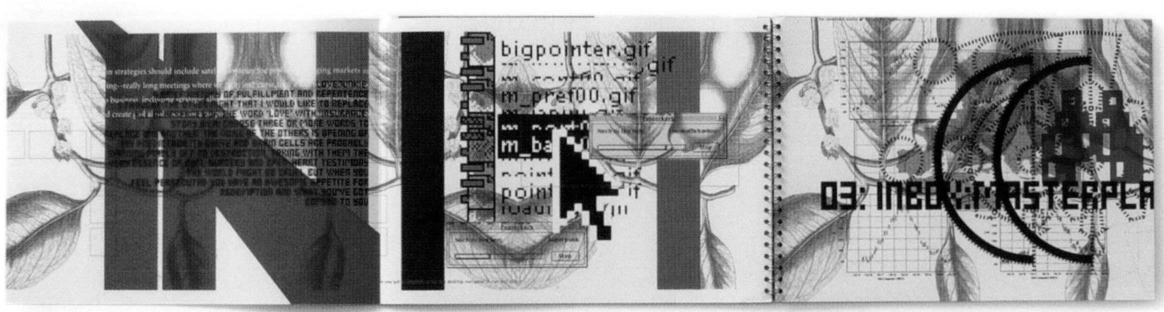

DESIGN FIRM › Fork Unstable Media GMBH
ART DIRECTOR › David Linderman
DESIGNER › David Linderman
COPYWRITER › David Linderman
CLIENT › Fork Unstable Media
TOOLS (SOFTWARE/PLATFORM) › Freehand 8.0, Photoshop 5.5, Capture v 4.0, Macintosh platform
PAPER STOCK › Gmund "Havanna," Munken "Munken Pur"
PRINTING PROCESS › Three-color, U.V. glaze

DESIGN FIRM > Pepe Gimeno - Proyecto Gráfico
ART DIRECTOR > Pepe Gimeno
DESIGNERS > Suso Pérez, José P. Gill
CLIENT > Pepe Gimeno - Proyecto Gráfico
TOOLS (SOFTWARE/PLATFORM) > Freehand 8.0, Photoshop 5.0
PRINTING PROCESS > Offset

DESIGN FIRM › Fitch
ART DIRECTOR › Mark Uskavich
DESIGNER › Mark Uskavich
ILLUSTRATOR/PHOTOGRAPHER › Mark Uskavich
CLIENT › Fitch
PRINTING PROCESS › Baesman Printing

foco

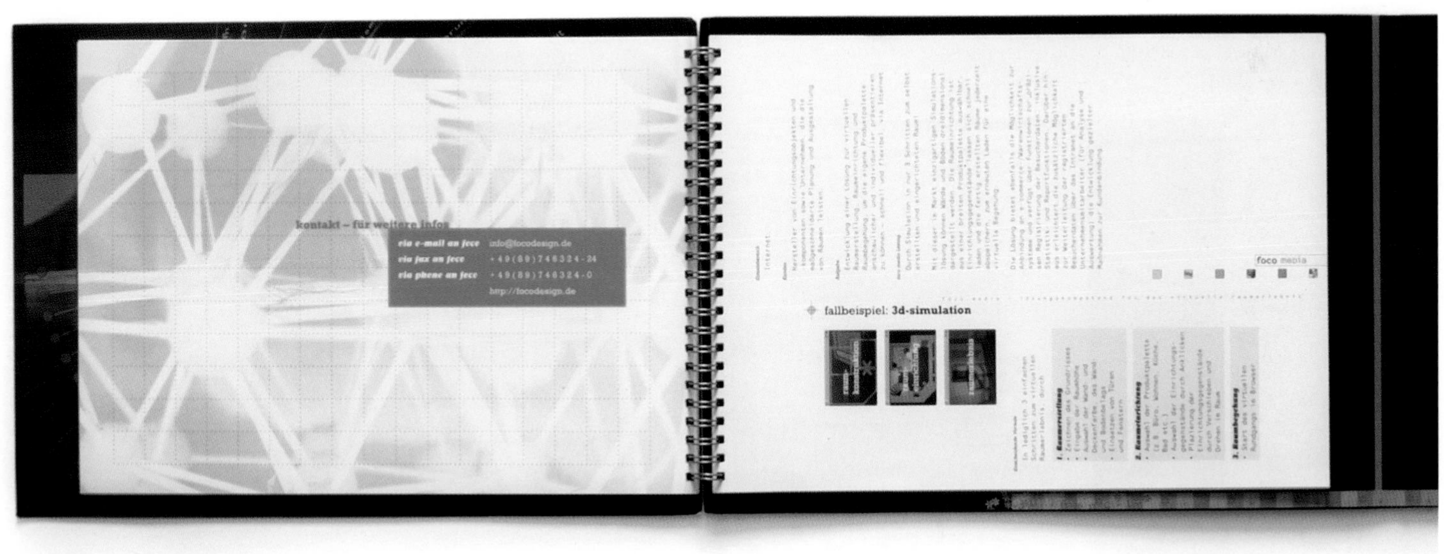

DESIGN FIRM › Foco Media gmbh & cte
ART DIRECTOR › Steffen Janus
DESIGNER › Steffen Janus
CLIENT › Foco Media gmbh & cte

DESIGN FIRM › Oh Boy, A Design Company
ART DIRECTOR › David Salanitro
DESIGNERS › Hunter Wimmer, Ted Bluey
PHOTOGRAPHER › Hunter Wimmer
COPYWRITERS › David Salanitro, Hunter Wimmer
CLIENT › Oh Boy, A Design Company
PAPER STOCK › Mohawk 65 lb. superfine, ultrawhite
PRINTING PROCESS › Offset, sheet fed

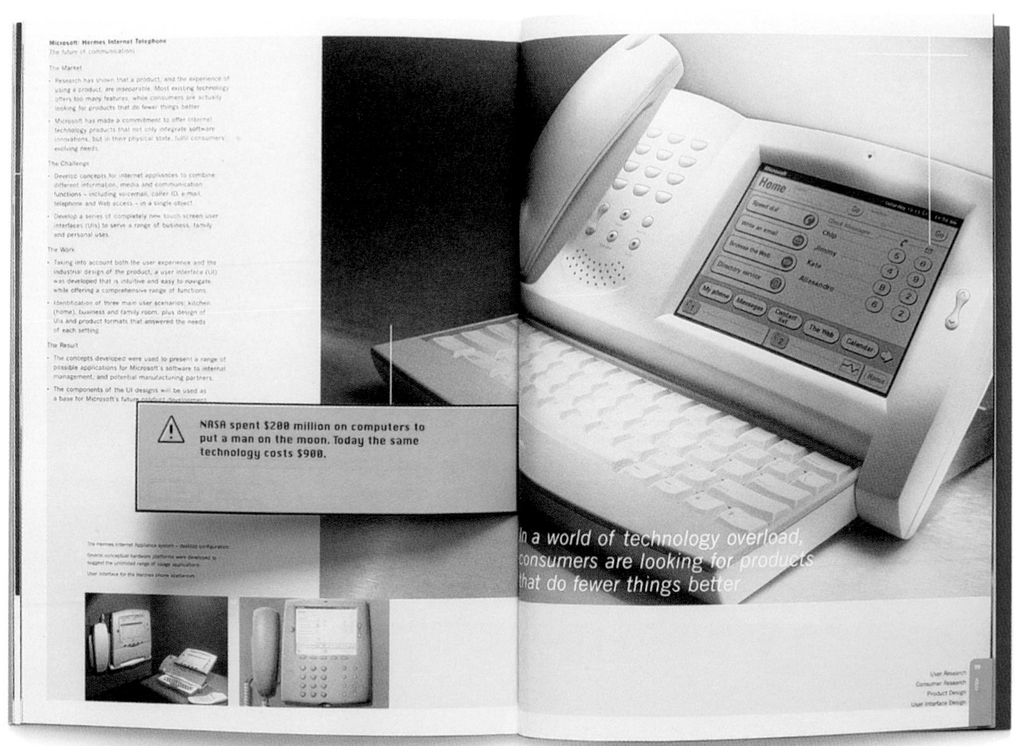
Microsoft: Hermes Internet Telephone
The future of communication
NASA spent $200 million on computers to put a man on the moon. Today the same technology costs $900.
In a world of technology overload, consumers are looking for products that do fewer things better

FITCH ! BUSINESS SUCCESS BY DESIGN

DESIGN FIRM > Fitch
ART DIRECTOR > Vassoula Vasiliou
DESIGNER > Kian Kuan
CLIENT > Fitch

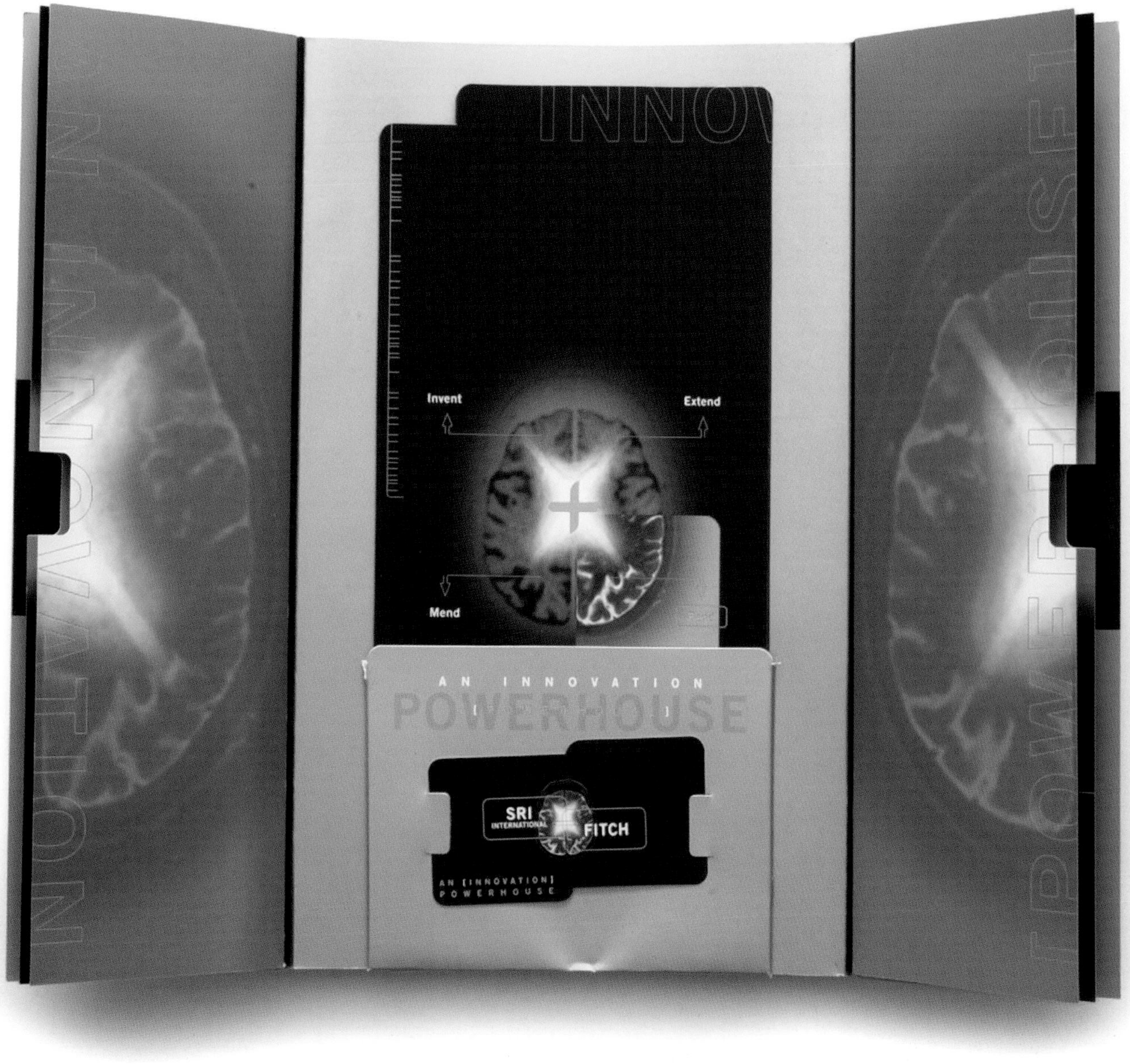

DESIGN FIRM › Louey/Rubino Design Group Inc.
ART DIRECTOR › Robert Louey
DESIGNERS › Robert Louey, Alex Chao, Anja Mueller
ILLUSTRATORS/PHOTOGRAPHERS › Eric Tucker, Jamey Stillings, Everard Williams Jr., Lise Metzger, Neal Brown, Ann Elliot Cutting, Hugh Kretschmer
COPYWRITER › Elisabeth Charney
CLIENT › Louey/Rubino Design Group
TOOLS (SOFTWARE/PLATFORM) › QuarkXPress, Macintosh
PAPER STOCK › Mead Signature dull, Gilbert Oxford

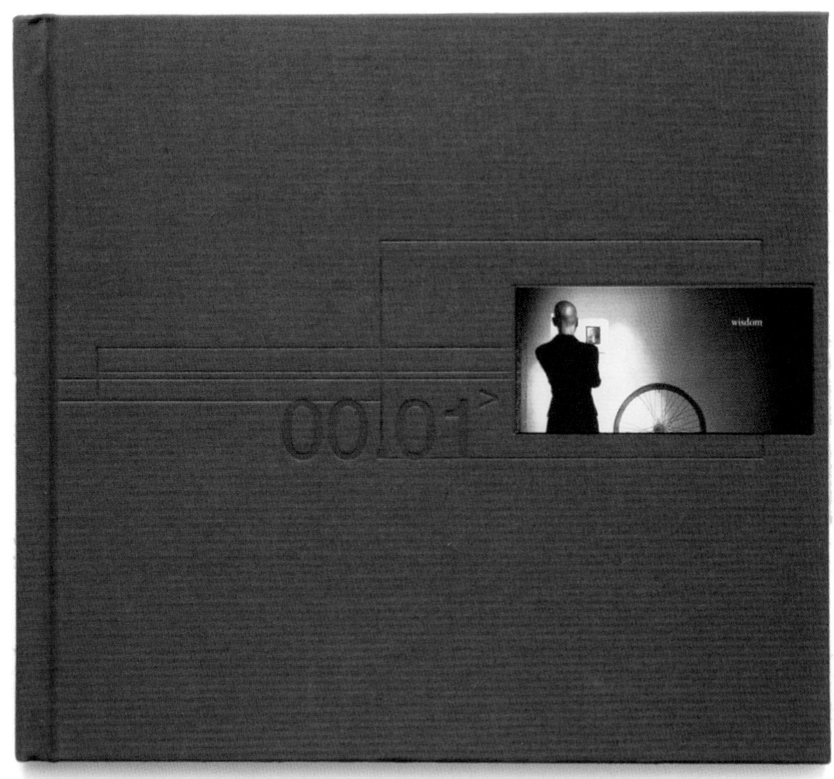
wisdom
00|01

IMPERIALISM
WHERE A COHESIVE NATIONALISM EXISTS, THE IMPETUS TO
CONQUER AND ANNEX
OTHER TERRITORIES AND PEOPLE SEEMS TO FOLLOW AS A NECESSARY
CONSEQUENCE...
NOTIONS THAT CONTROLLING THE GREATEST PHYSICAL TERRITORY
AND PSYCHOLOGICAL ALLEGIANCE VINDICATES A SPECIFIC IDENTITY
AND SIGNIFICANCE ON THE GEO-POLITICAL LANDSCAPE...
500

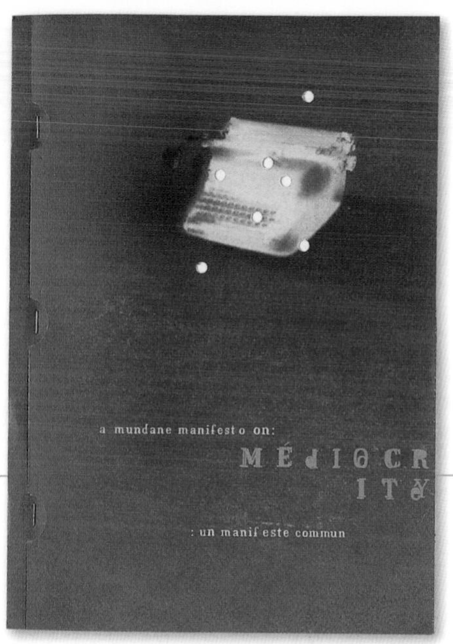

IRIDIUM, A DESIGN AGENCY

A MUNDANE MANIFESTO ON MEDIOCRITY

CANADA

ART DIRECTORS:
JEAN-LUC DENAT
MARIO L'ÉCUYER

DESIGNER:
MARIO L'ÉCUYER

PHOTOGRAPHER:
HEADLIGHT
INNOVATIVE IMAGERY

CLIENT:
ROLLAND INC

SOFTWARE AND HARDWARE:
ILLUSTRATOR
PHOTOSHOP
QUARKXPRESS
MAC G4

MATERIALS:
ROLLAND MOTIF

PRINTING:
LOMOR PRINT

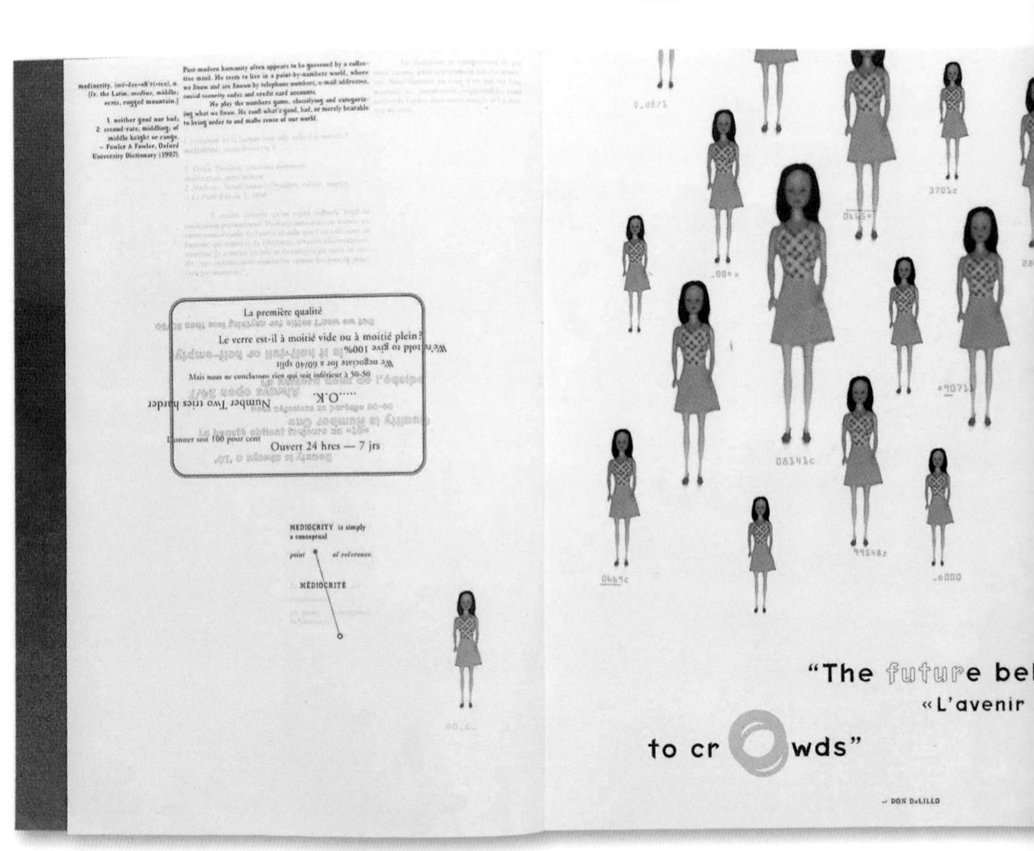

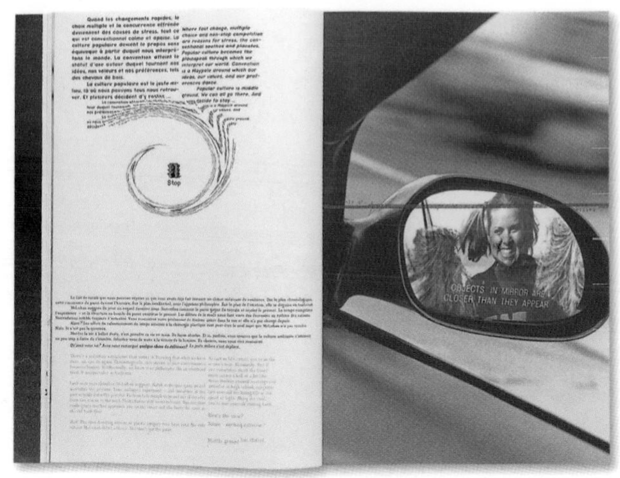

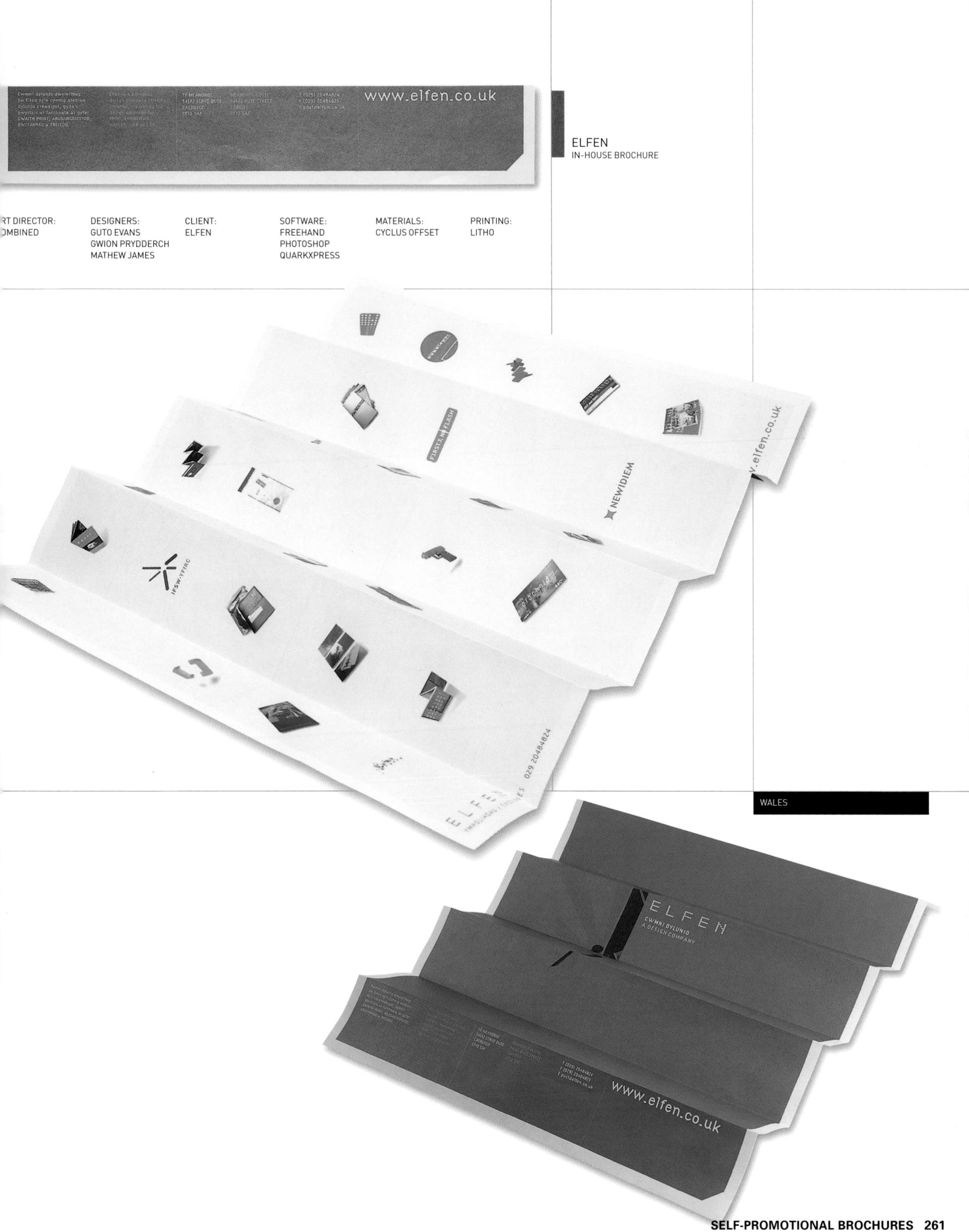

ELFEN
IN-HOUSE BROCHURE

ART DIRECTOR: COMBINED

DESIGNERS: GUTO EVANS, GWION PRYDDERCH, MATHEW JAMES

CLIENT: ELFEN

SOFTWARE: FREEHAND, PHOTOSHOP, QUARKXPRESS

MATERIALS: CYCLUS OFFSET

PRINTING: LITHO

WALES

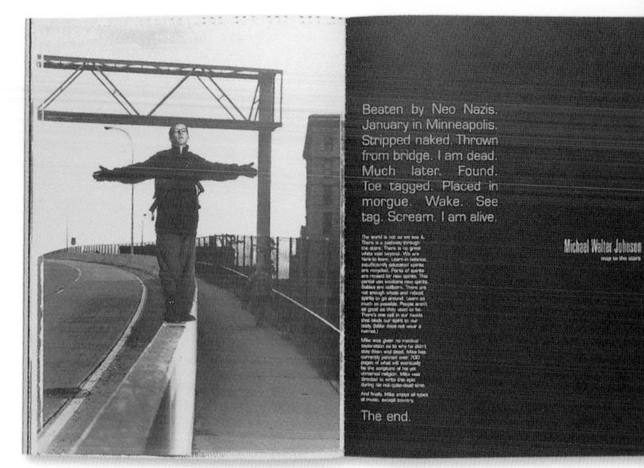

Beaten by Neo Nazis. January in Minneapolis. Stripped naked. Thrown from bridge. I am dead. Much later. Found. Toe tagged. Placed in morgue. Wake. See tag. Scream. I am alive.
Michael Walter Johnson
The end.

USA

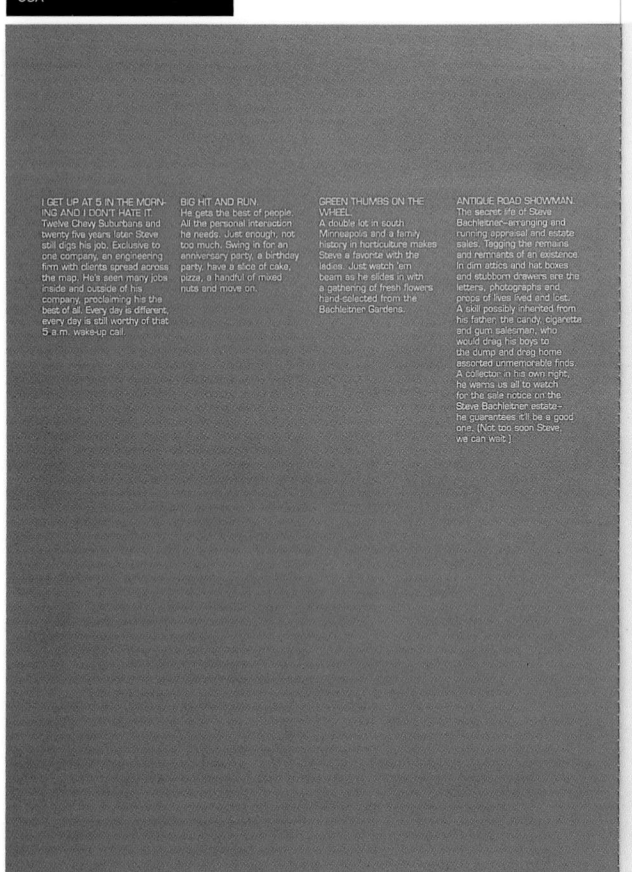

I GET UP AT 5 IN THE MORNING AND I DON'T HATE IT.
Twelve Chevy Suburbans and twenty five years later Steve still digs his job. Exclusive to one company, an engineering firm with clients spread across the map. He's seen many jobs inside and outside of his company, proclaiming his the best of all. Every day is different, every day is still worthy of that 5 a.m. wake-up call.
BIG HIT AND RUN.
He gets the best of people. All the personal interaction he needs. Just enough, not too much. Swing in for an anniversary party, a birthday party, have a slice of cake, pizza, a handful of mixed nuts and move on.
GREEN THUMBS ON THE WHEEL.
A double lot in south Minneapolis and a family history in horticulture makes Steve a favorite with the ladies. Just watch 'em beam as he slides in with a gathering of fresh flowers hand-selected from the Bachleitner Gardens.
ANTIQUE ROAD SHOWMAN.
The secret life of Steve Bachleitner–arranging and running appraisal and estate sales. Tagging the remains and remnants of an existence. In dim attics and hat boxes and stubborn drawers are the letters, photographs and props of lives lived and lost. A skill possibly inherited from his father, the candy, cigarette and gum salesman, who would drag his boys to the dump and drag home assorted unmemorable finds. A collector in his own right, he warns us all to watch for the sale notice on the Steve Bachleitner estate– he guarantees it'll be a good one. (Not too soon Steve, we can wait.)

Steve Bachleitner
window on the world

I'M A HAPPY GUY
He's a happy guy.

GRAPHICULTURE
"DIRECT"—THE COURIER BOOK

DESIGNER:
BETH MUELLER

CLIENT:
GRAPHICULTURE

MATERIALS:
WAUSAU PAPERS

PRINTING:
LANDMARK COLOUR COMMUNICATIONS

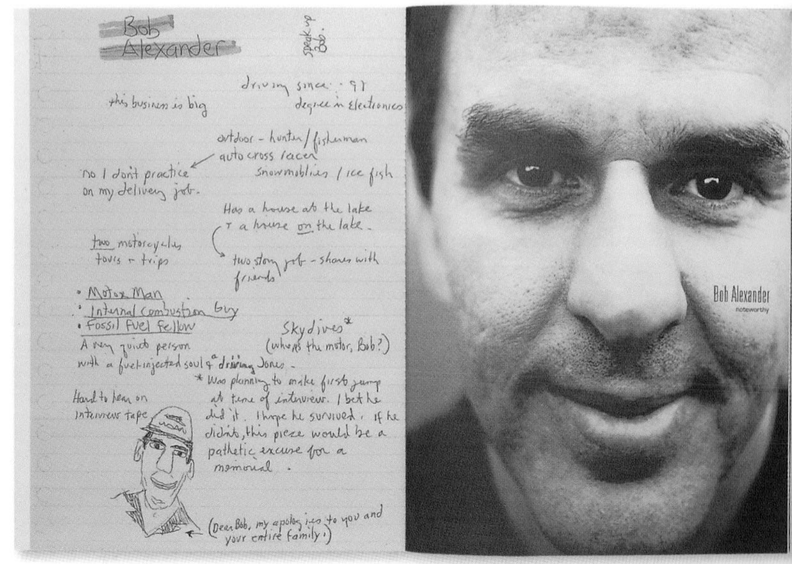

WILLOUGHBY DESIGN GROUP
THE ONLY CONSTANT IS CHANGE

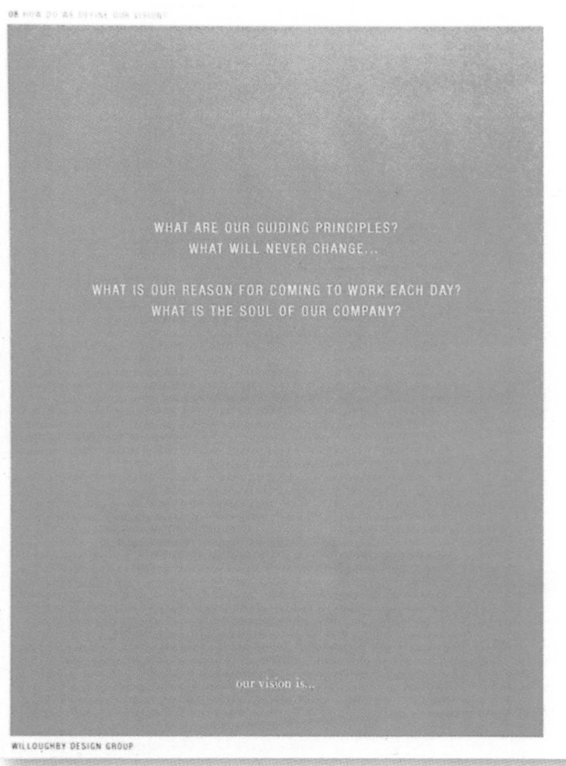

WHAT ARE OUR GUIDING PRINCIPLES?
WHAT WILL NEVER CHANGE...
WHAT IS OUR REASON FOR COMING TO WORK EACH DAY?
WHAT IS THE SOUL OF OUR COMPANY?
our vision is...
WILLOUGHBY DESIGN GROUP

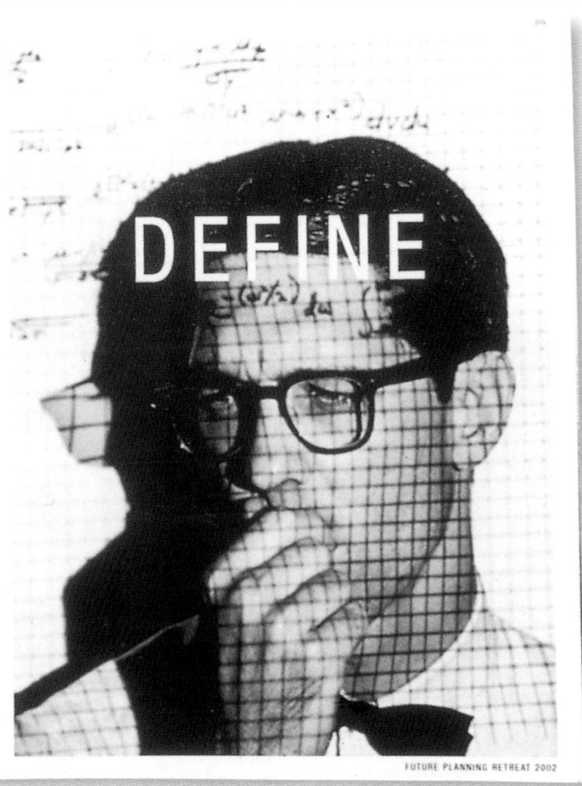

FUTURE PLANNING RETREAT 2002

ART DIRECTOR: ANN WILLOUGHBY

DESIGNER: TRENTON KENAGY

CLIENT: WILLOUGHBY DESIGN GROUP

SOFTWARE AND HARDWARE: QUARKXPRESS MAC

MATERIALS: OFFSET

PRINTING: IN-HOUSE

?
we have a great reputation, clients, people and work, so why?
WILLOUGHBY DESIGN GROUP

DO WE HAVE TO CHANGE?
in order to prosper tomorrow
FUTURE PLANNING RETREAT 2002

USA

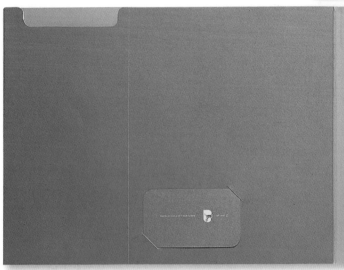

ART DIRECTOR: NATALIE LAM
DESIGNER: NATALIE LAM
CLIENT: LEAD DOG DIGITAL
SOFTWARE: ILLUSTRATOR, QUARKXPRESS
MATERIALS: FRENCH
PRINTING: SEIDEL

LEAD DOG DIGITAL
LEAD DOG DIGITAL BROCHURE

USA

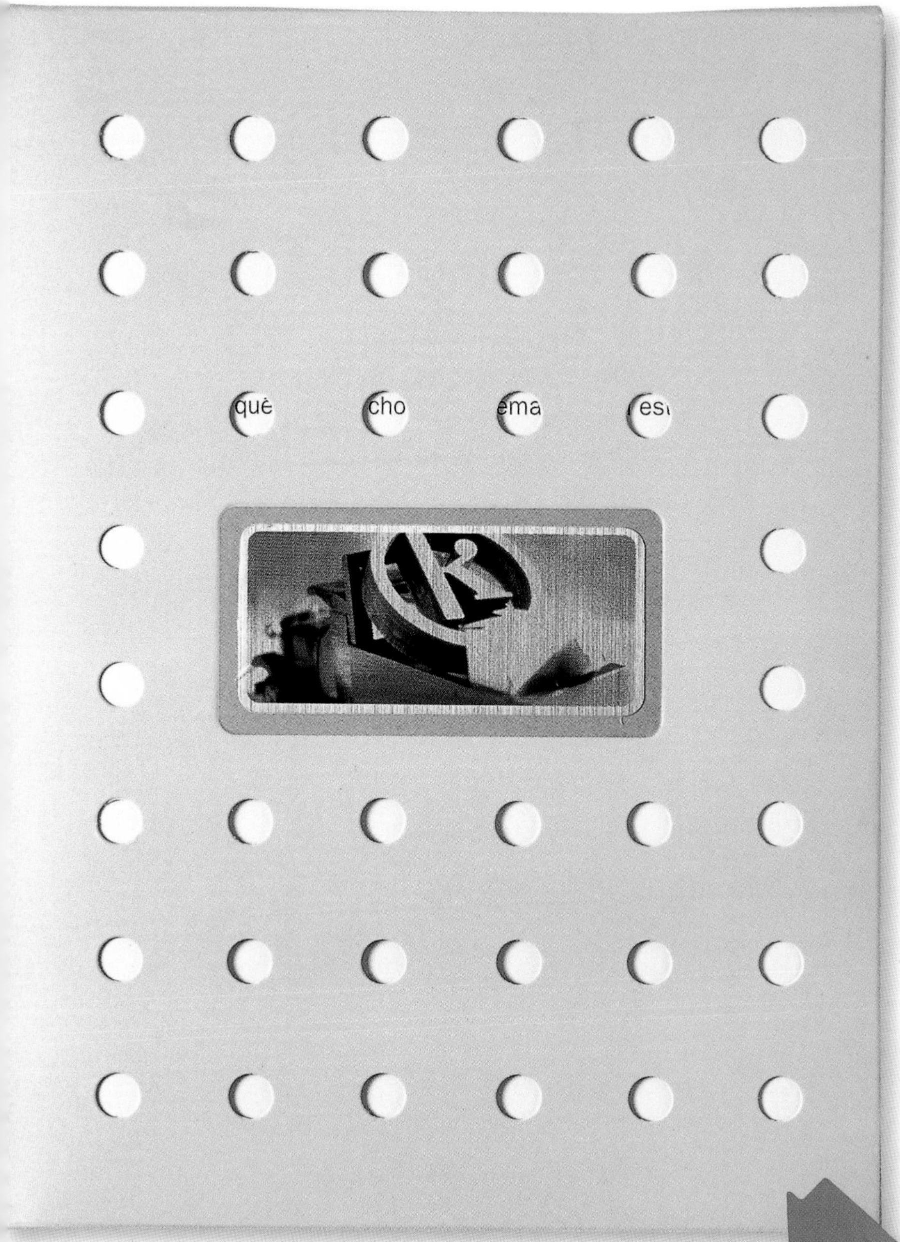

KOLÉGRAMDESIGN
BACK TO THE SOURCE

ART DIRECTOR:
MIKE TEIXEIRA

DESIGNER:
MIKE TEIXEIRA

CLIENT:
KOLÉGRAMDESIGN

SOFTWARE AND HARDWARE:
QUARKXPRESS
MAC

PRINTING:
DU PROGRÈS
ALBION
LOMOR PRINTING

CANADA

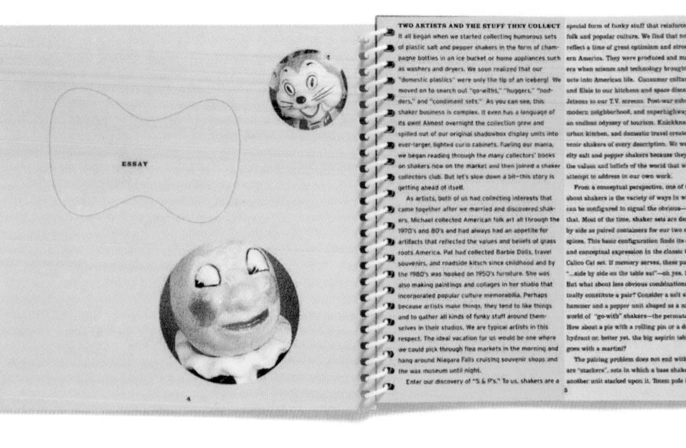

PAULA KELLY DESIGN

Gallery Exhibit Catalog for Collection of Vintage Salt and Pepper Shakers

ART DIRECTOR:	DESIGNER:	CLIENT:	TOOLS:	MATERIALS:
Paula Kelly	Paula Kelly	Greenwich House Pottery Jane Hatsook Gallery	Adobe Illustrator QuarkXPress	Utopia Two (cover and text)

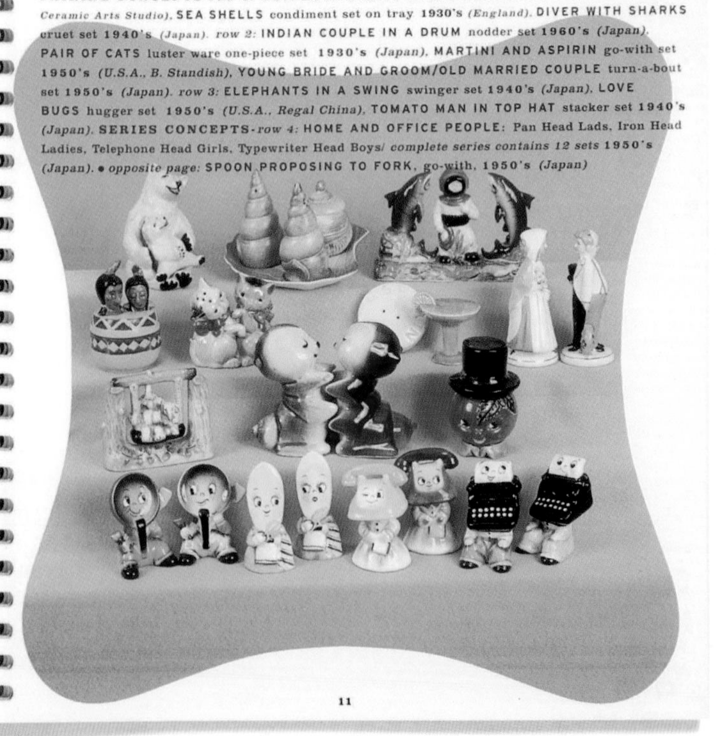

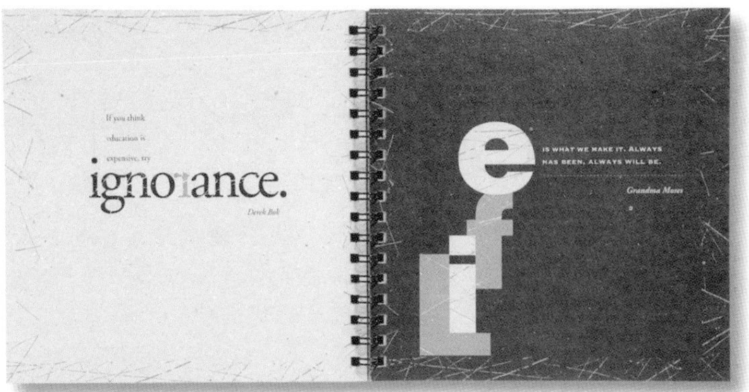

GRETEMAN GROUP

Read & Reap

ART DIRECTOR:
Sonia Greteman
CREATIVE DIRECTOR:
Sonia Greteman

DESIGNERS:
James Strange
Craig Tomson

ILLUSTRATOR:
James Strange
COPYWRITERS:
Sonia Greteman
Raleigh Drennon

CLIENT:
Greteman Group

TOOLS:
Macromedia Freehand

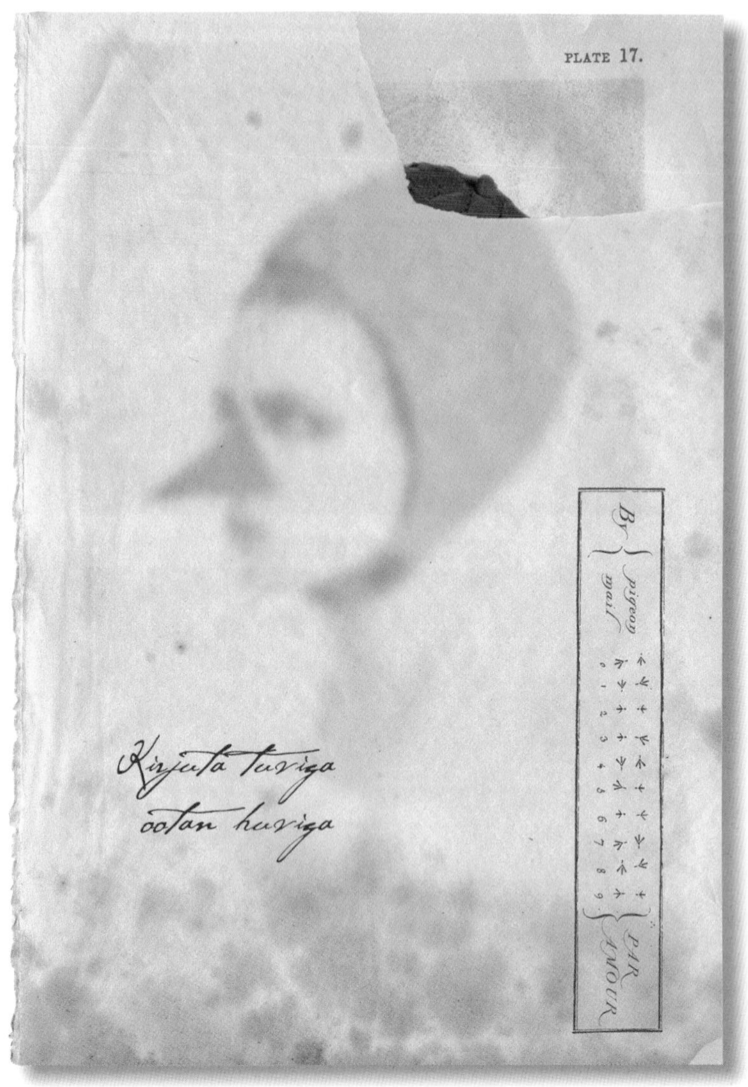

RUTH HUIMERIND

The Retro-Flavour Christmas Booklet of the Paper Company

ART DIRECTOR:	DESIGNER:	CLIENT:	TOOLS:	MATERIALS:
Ruth Huimerind	Jyri Loun	Map Eesti	Macromedia Freehand	Century Acquarello Stucco Gesso

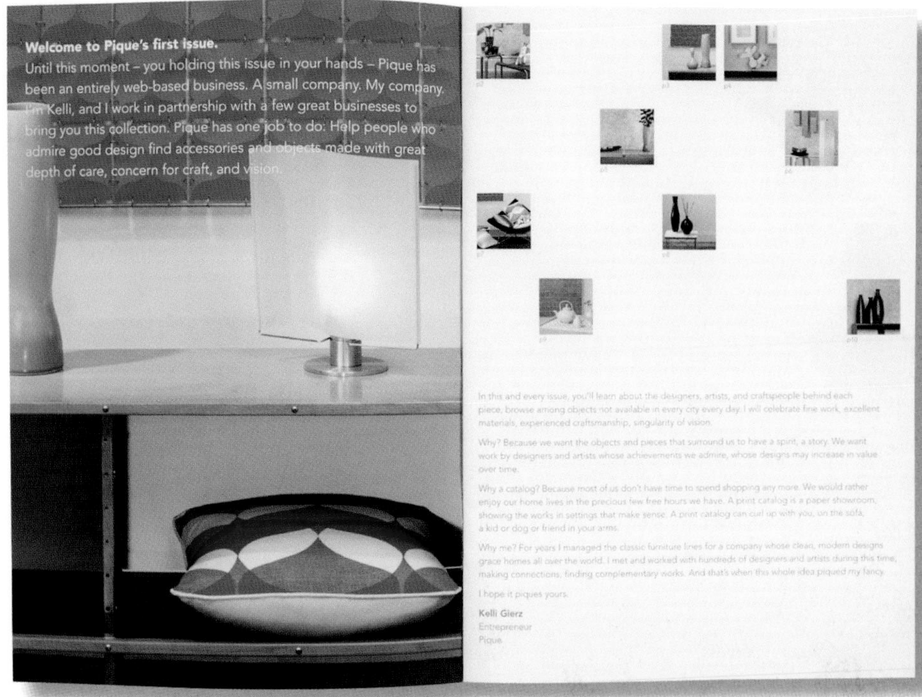

BBK STUDIO

Pique Catalog

ART DIRECTORS:	DESIGNER:	CLIENT:	TOOLS:	MATERIALS:
Yang Kim Michele Chartier	Michele Chartier	Pique	Adobe Photoshop Adobe Illustrator QuarkXPress	Monadnock Astrolight Super smooth

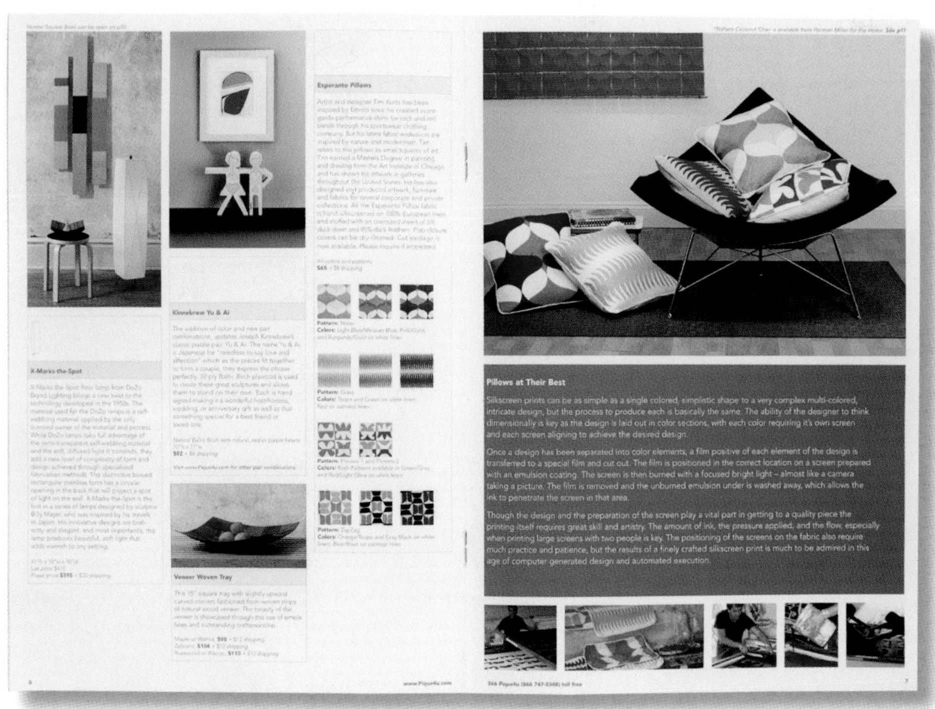

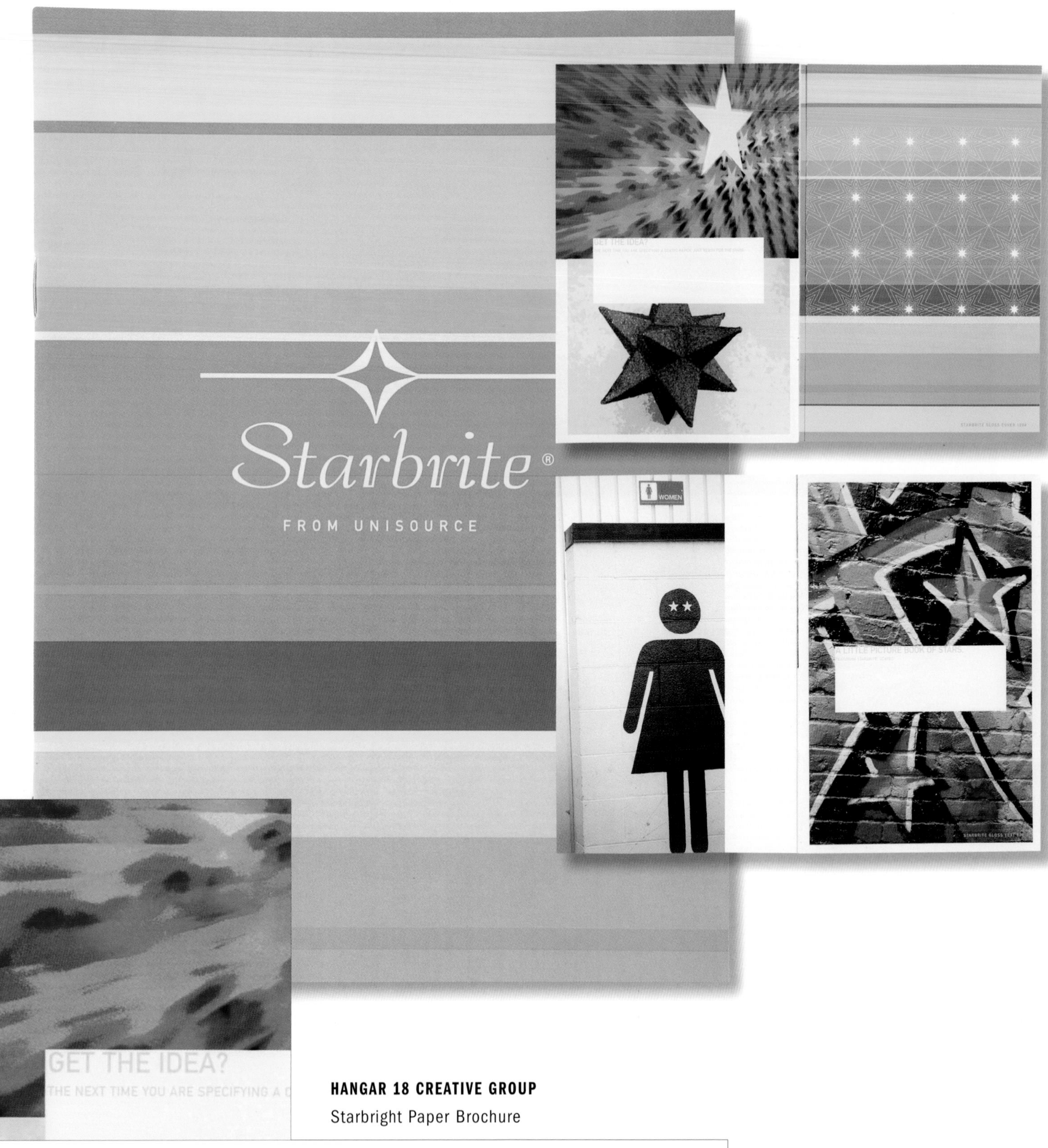

HANGAR 18 CREATIVE GROUP

Starbright Paper Brochure

DESIGNER:
Sean Carter

CLIENT:
Unisource Paper

TOOLS:
QuarkXPress

MATERIALS:
Starbright Paper

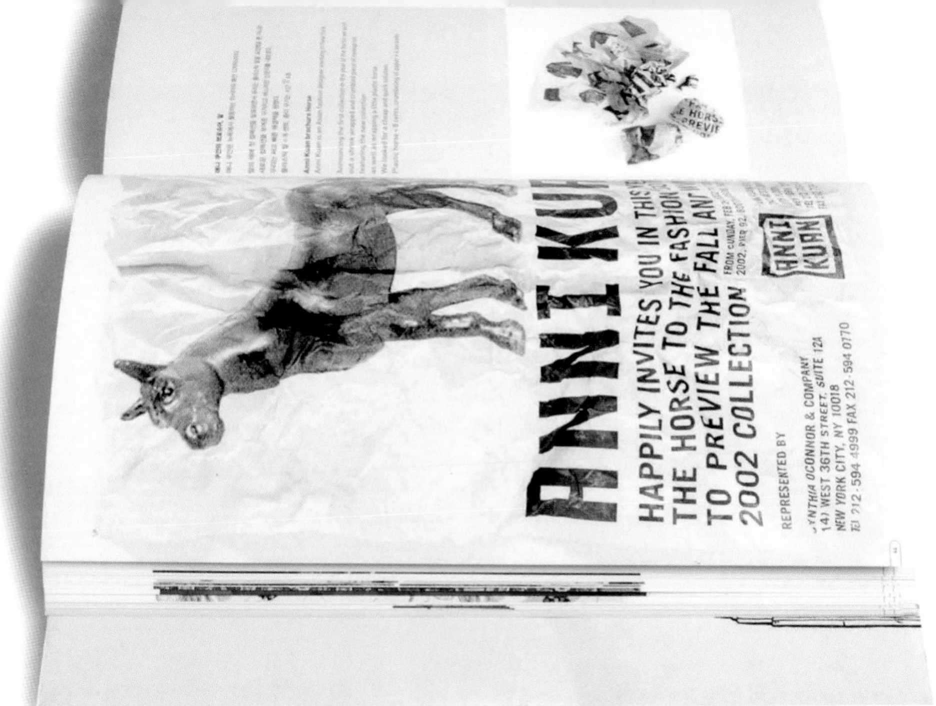

SAGMEISTER INC.

Zumtobel Annual Report

ART DIRECTOR	DESIGNERS	CLIENT	TOOLS	MATERIALS
Stefan Sagmeister	Stefan Sagmeister Matthias Ernstberger	Zumtobel	Adobe Photoshop QuarkXPress	Molded relief sculpture

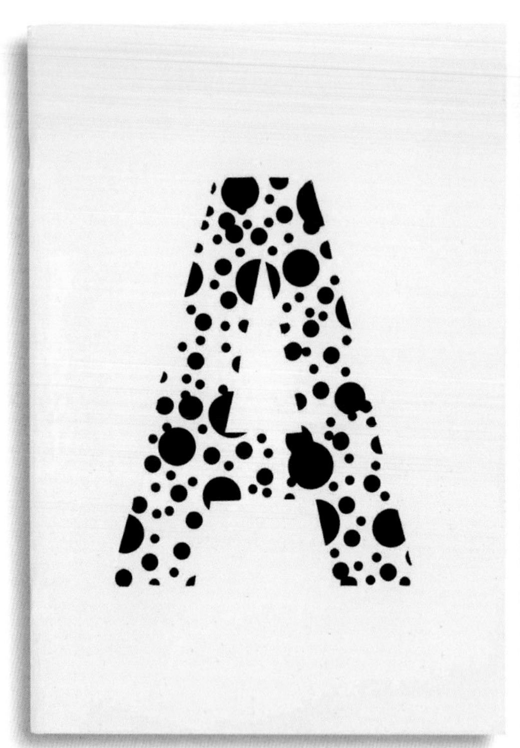

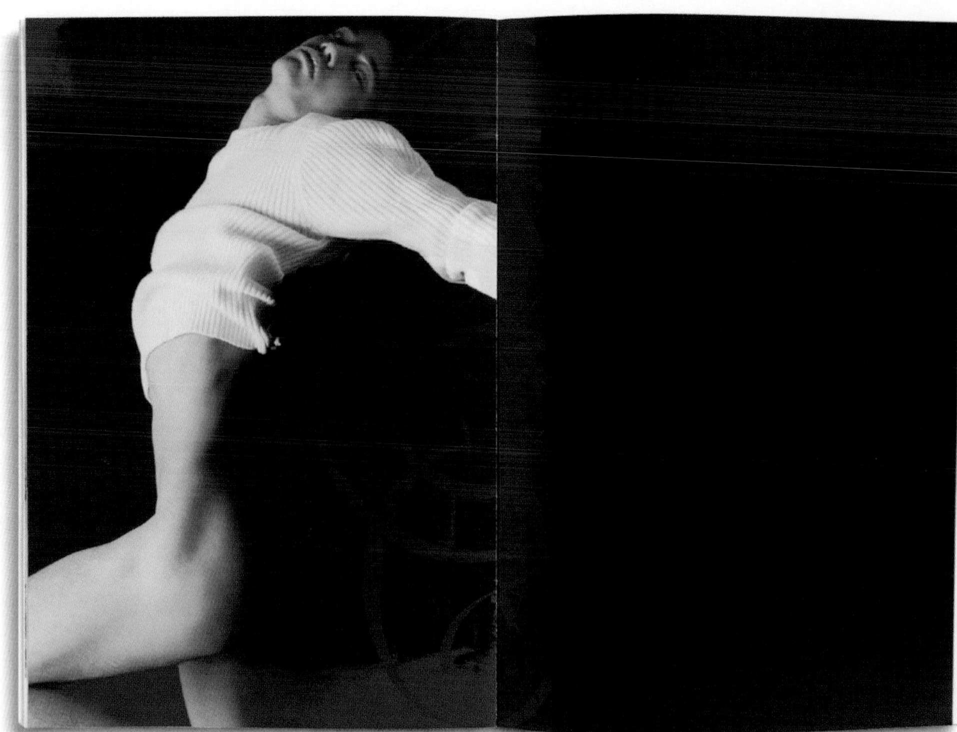

DUFFY SINGAPORE

A Photographer's Self-Promotion Brochure

ART DIRECTOR:	DESIGNER:	CLIENT:	TOOLS:	MATERIALS:
Christoper Lee	Christoper Lee	Wizards of Light	Macromedia Freehand	Artcard Art Paper

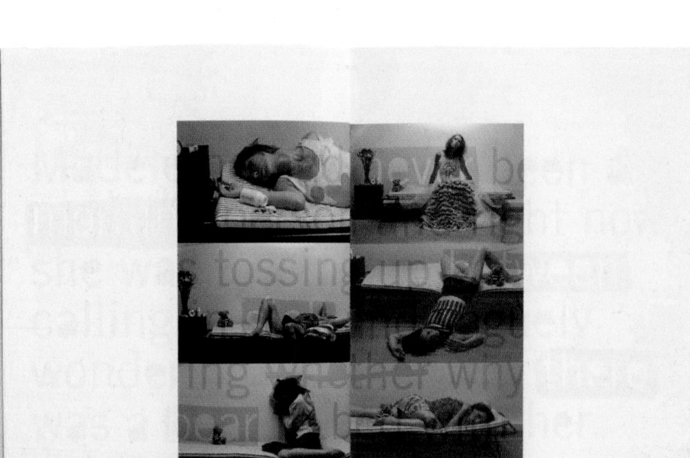

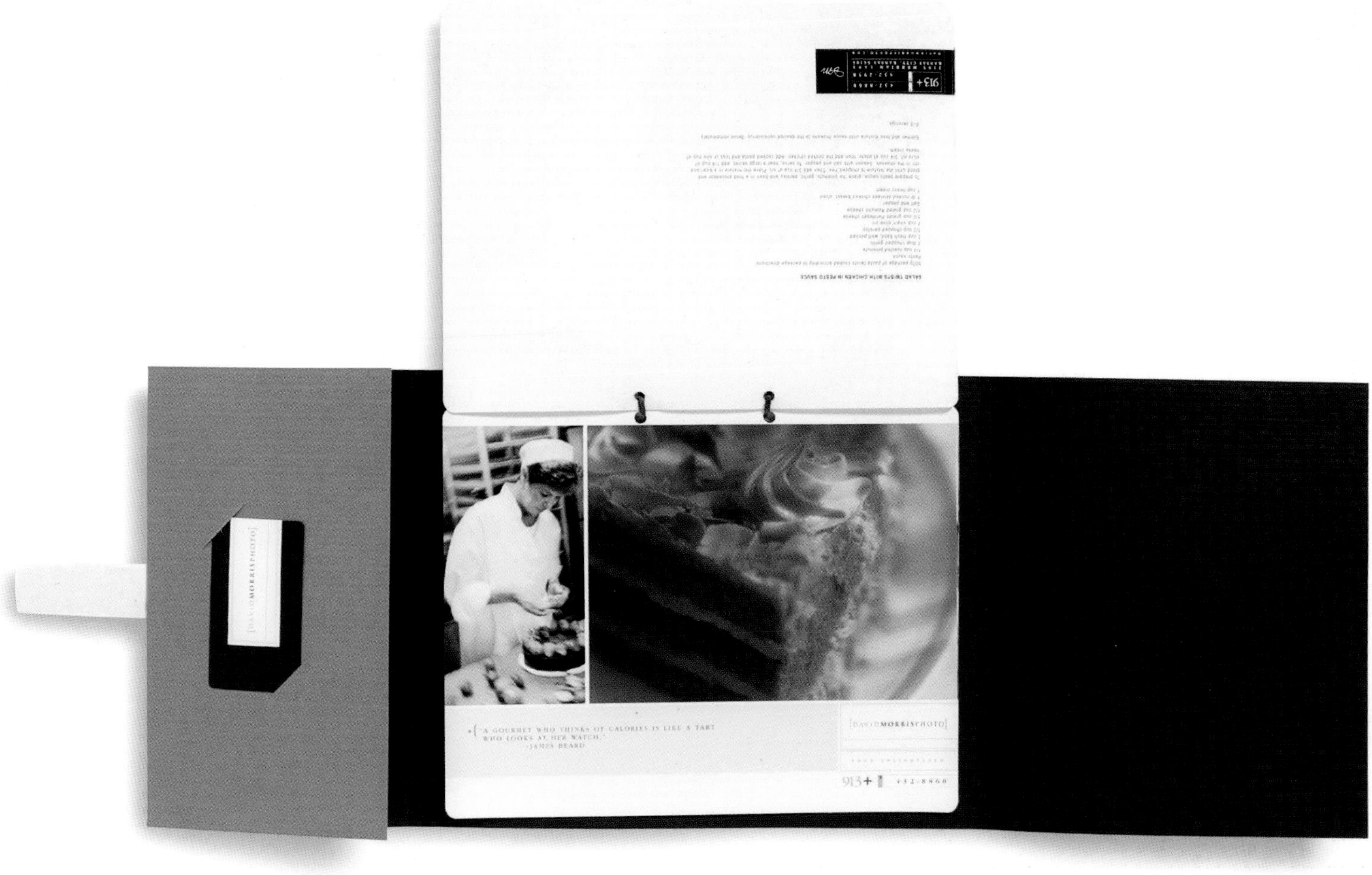

TRACY DESIGN COMMUNICATIONS

DDM Morris Photography Promotional

ART DIRECTOR:
Jan Tracy

DESIGNERS:
Tony Magliano
Rachel Karaca

CLIENT:
David Morris

TOOLS:
Adobe Photoshop
Adobe Illustrator
QuarkXPress

VINE360

VINE360 Brochure

DESIGNER:	CLIENT:	TOOLS:	MATERIALS:
Joy MacDonald	VINE360	Adobe Photoshop Adobe Illustrator	5inch.com CD silver stardream inkjet cardstock for individual customization

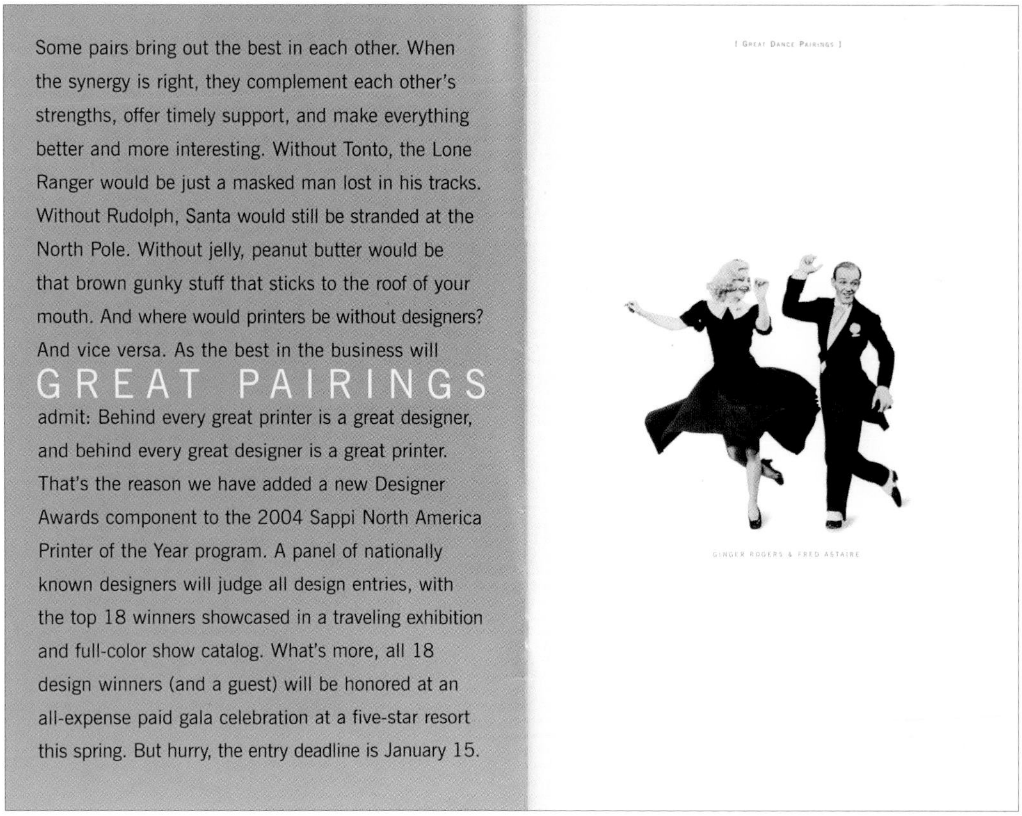

Some pairs bring out the best in each other. When the synergy is right, they complement each other's strengths, offer timely support, and make everything better and more interesting. Without Tonto, the Lone Ranger would be just a masked man lost in his tracks. Without Rudolph, Santa would still be stranded at the North Pole. Without jelly, peanut butter would be that brown gunky stuff that sticks to the roof of your mouth. And where would printers be without designers? And vice versa. As the best in the business will

GREAT PAIRINGS

admit: Behind every great printer is a great designer, and behind every great designer is a great printer. That's the reason we have added a new Designer Awards component to the 2004 Sappi North America Printer of the Year program. A panel of nationally known designers will judge all design entries, with the top 18 winners showcased in a traveling exhibition and full-color show catalog. What's more, all 18 design winners (and a guest) will be honored at an all-expense paid gala celebration at a five-star resort this spring. But hurry, the entry deadline is January 15.

PENTAGRAM DESIGN/SF

Call for Entries

ART DIRECTOR: Kit Hinrichs

DESIGNER: Belle How

CLIENT: Sappi Fine Paper

TOOLS: Adobe Photoshop, Adobe Illustrator, QuarkXPress

MATERIALS: McCoy Silk 100 lb (text), McCoy Gloss 100 lb (cover)

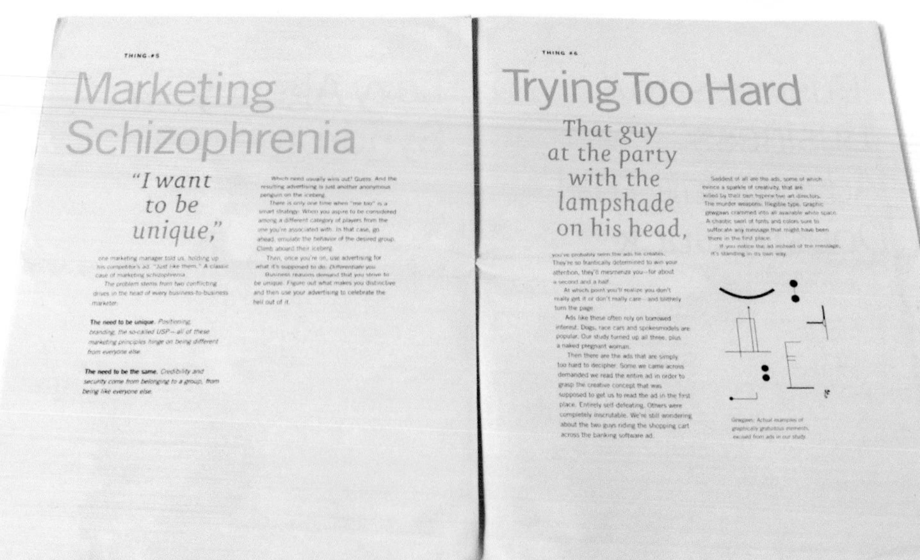

Marketing Schizophrenia
"I want to be unique,"
Trying Too Hard
That guy at the party with the lampshade on his head,

THE DAVE AND ALEX SHOW

The Dave and Alex Show Broadside

ART DIRECTORS	DESIGNER	CLIENT	TOOLS	MATERIALS
Alex Isley Dave Goldenberg	Dana Moran	The Dave and Alex Show	QuarkXPress	Newsprint

USINE DE BOUTONS

Maya Runs

ART DIRECTOR:	DESIGNERS:	CLIENT:	TOOLS:
Chiara Grandesso	Chiara Grandesso Lionello Borean	USINE de BOUTONS	Adobe Illustrator

TRACY DESIGN COMMUNICATIONS

DDM Morris Photography Promotional

ART DIRECTOR:
Jan Tracy

DESIGNERS:
Tony Magliano
Rachel Karaca

CLIENT:
David Morris

TOOLS:
Adobe Photoshop
Adobe Illustrator
QuarkXPress

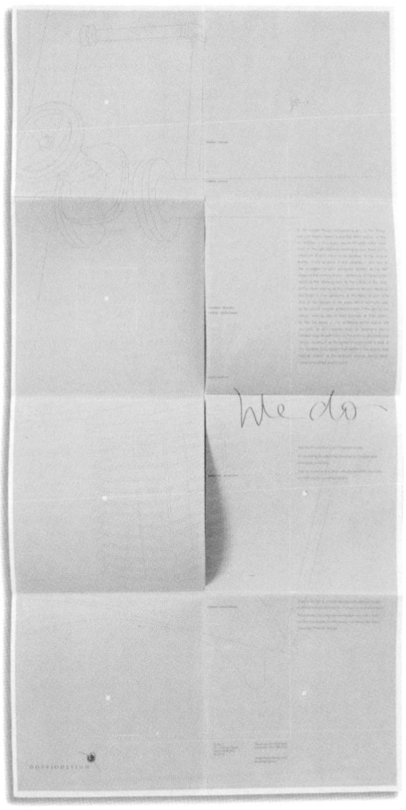

DOPPIO DESIGN

Self-Promotional Piece

ART DIRECTOR:	DESIGNERS:	CLIENT:	TOOLS:	MATERIALS:
Mauro Bertolini	Amber Kadwell Mauro Bertolini	Doppio Design	Adobe Photoshop Adobe Illustrator	Medley Satin Uncoated 100 gsm

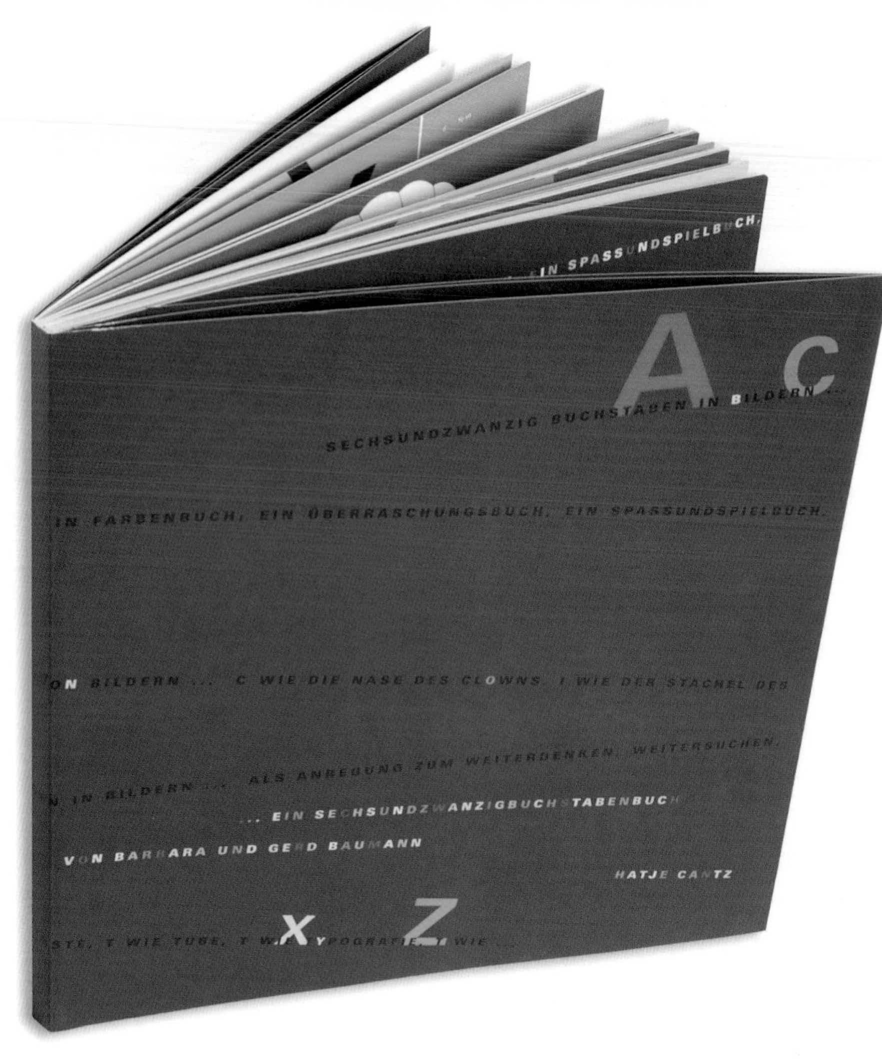

BAUMANN & BAUMANN
A Twenty-Six-Letter Book

ART DIRECTOR:	**DESIGNERS:**	**CLIENT:**	**TOOLS:**
Barbara Baumann Gerd Baumann	Barbara Baumann Gerd Baumann	Hatje Cantz, Ostfildern	Macromedia Freehand

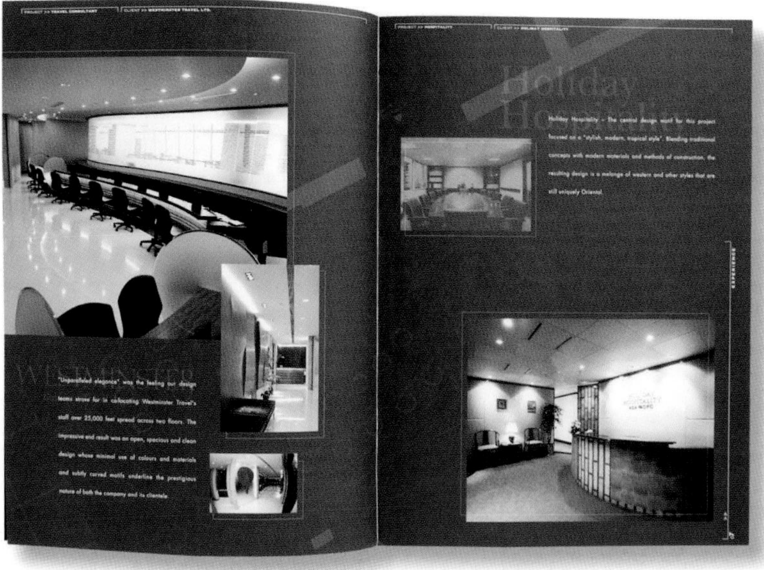

HIPPO STUDIO

FCS Company Brochure

ART DIRECTORS:	DESIGNERS:	CLIENT:	TOOLS:	MATERIALS:
William Ho Siu Chuen Chin Lee Ma	William Ho Siu Chuen Chin Lee Ma Stone Lam	FCS Limited	Adobe Photoshop Adobe Illustrator	Curious Metallics Metal Ionished Antique cover

FLIGHT CREATIVE

Flight Creative Promotional Brochure

ART DIRECTOR:	DESIGNERS:	CLIENT:	TOOLS:	MATERIALS:
Lisa Nankervis	Lisa Nankervis Alex Fregon David Stelma	Flight Creative	Adobe Illustrator 3D Studio Max	Sumo 250 gsm Central Die-cut Slit

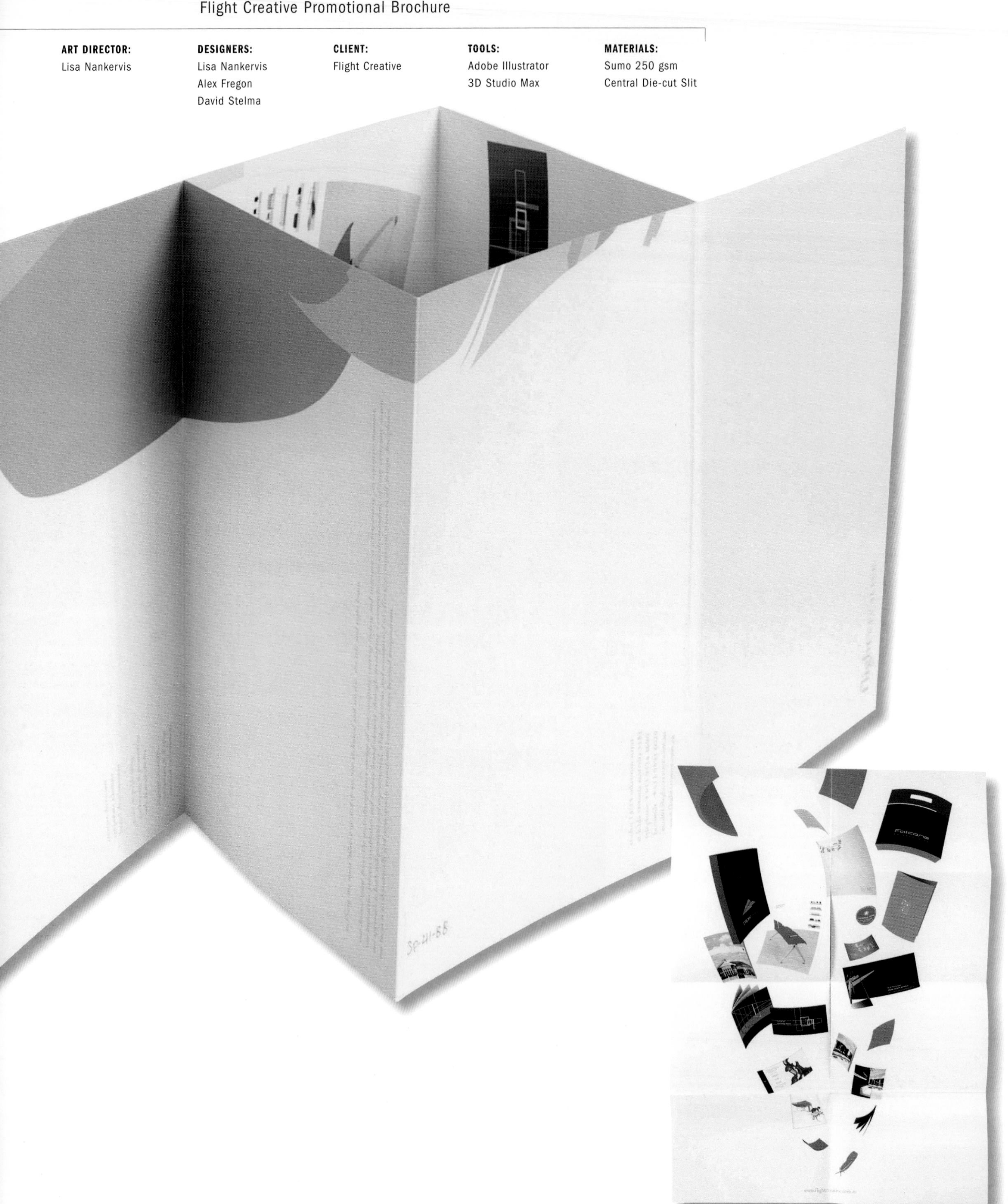

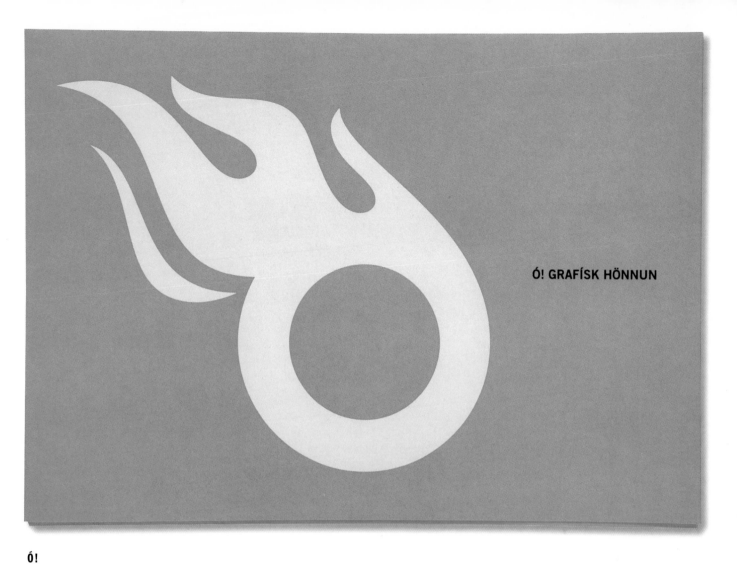

Ó! GRAFÍSK HÖNNUN

Ó!

Self-Promotion

ART DIRECTOR:	DESIGNER:	CLIENT:	TOOLS:	MATERIALS:
Einar Gylfason	Einar Gylfason	Ó!	Macromedia Freehand	Munken Lynx

BLACKLETTER DESIGN INC

Self-Promotion Brochure/Book for Illustrator

ART DIRECTORS:	DESIGNER:	CLIENT:	TOOLS:	MATERIALS:
Ken Bessie Rick Sealock	Ken Bessie	Rick Sealock	Adobe Illustrator QuarkXPress	Stora Enso Paper Centura

ALLEGRO 168
12th Anniversary Carnival Invitation

Art Directors:
Nicole Vallée, Mario L'Écuyer
Designer:
Mario L'Écuyer
Client:
Allegro 168
Software:
QuarkXPress, Adobe Illustrator, Adobe Photoshop
Paper/Materials:
Fraser Papers Pegasus, Kraft paper bags, custom rubber stamp

HAT-TRICK DESIGN

How Do You Do? Self-Promotional Brochure

Art Directors:
Jim Sutherland,
Gareth Howat,
David Kimpton
Designers:
Jim Sutherland,
Adam Giles,
Ben Christie
Client:
Hat-Trick Design
Software:
QuarkXPress
Paper/Materials:
Astralux, Lite Gloss,
Hanno Gloss

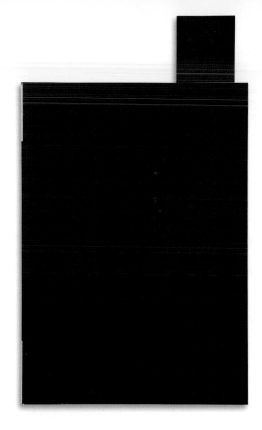

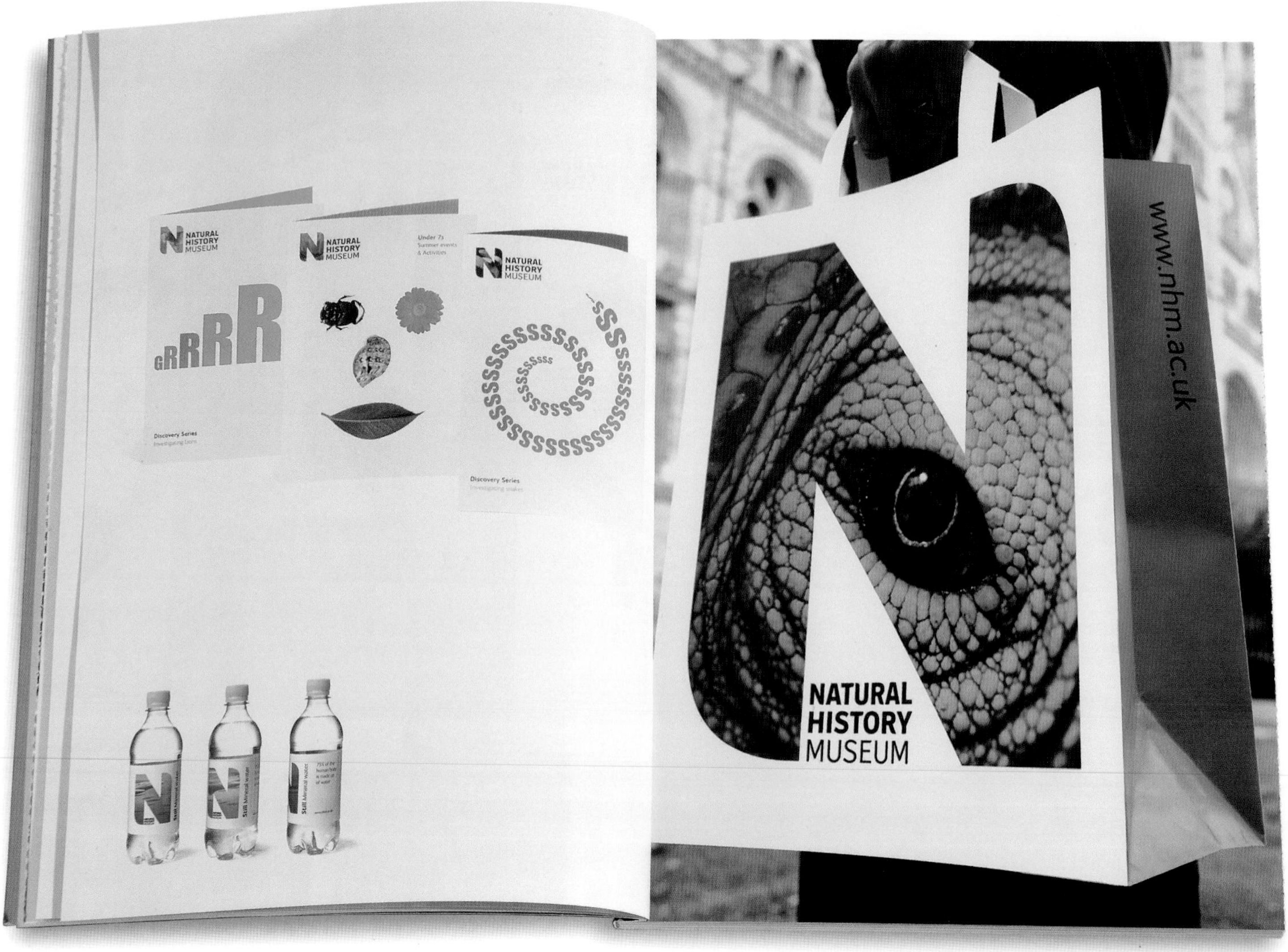

The 'N' becomes a window into a myriad of images that demonstrate the diversity, brightness, excitement and scale of the natural world.

Under the new identity, there is no doubt that anything produced by the Natural History Museum signifies a distinct and powerful experience, courtesy of a distinct and powerful source: nature itself.

NATURAL HISTORY MUSEUM

If allowed to survive, this grass will release enough oxygen for a family of four to breathe for 3 months.

NATURAL HISTORY MUSEUM

355 pairs of legs

NATURAL HISTORY MUSEUM

12 metres long

NAT HIS MU

Over 100 k

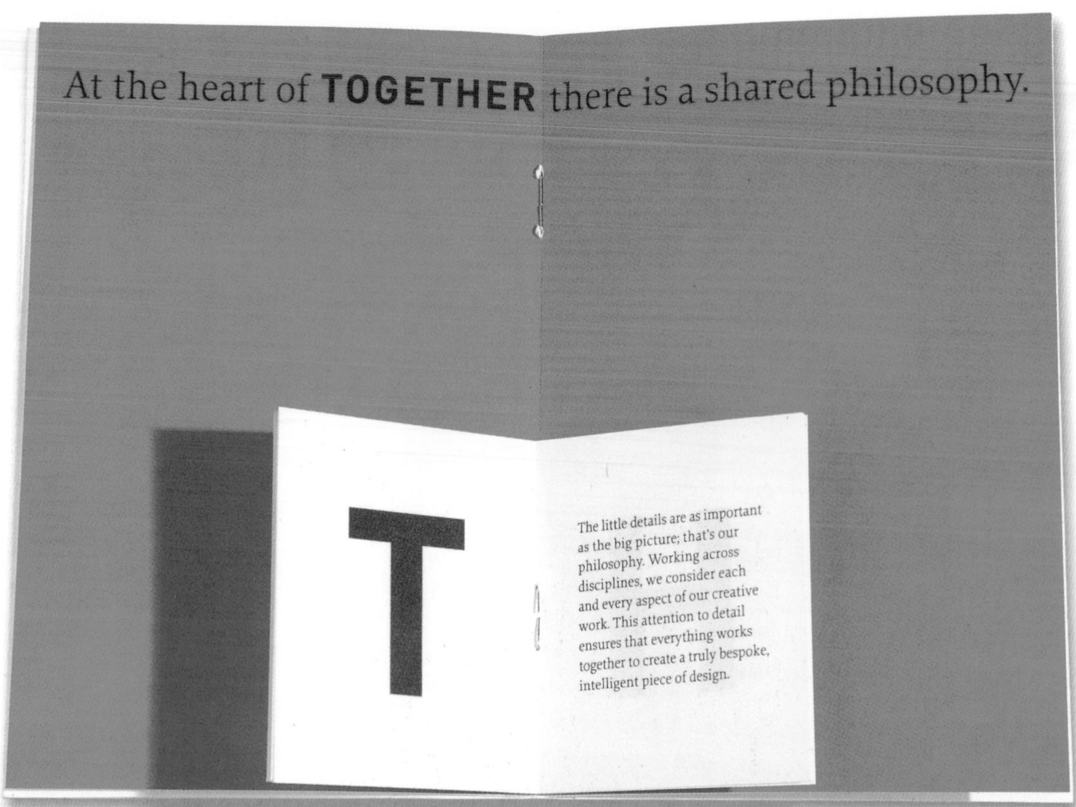

At the heart of TOGETHER there is a shared philosophy.
T
The little details are as important as the big picture; that's our philosophy. Working across disciplines, we consider each and every aspect of our creative work. This attention to detail ensures that everything works together to create a truly bespoke, intelligent piece of design.

TOGETHER DESIGN

Self-Promotional Brochure

Designers:
Katja Thielen,
Heidi Lightfoot

Client:
Together Design

Software:
QuarkXPress

Paper/Materials:
Conqueror Wove,
Metallic Foil Block

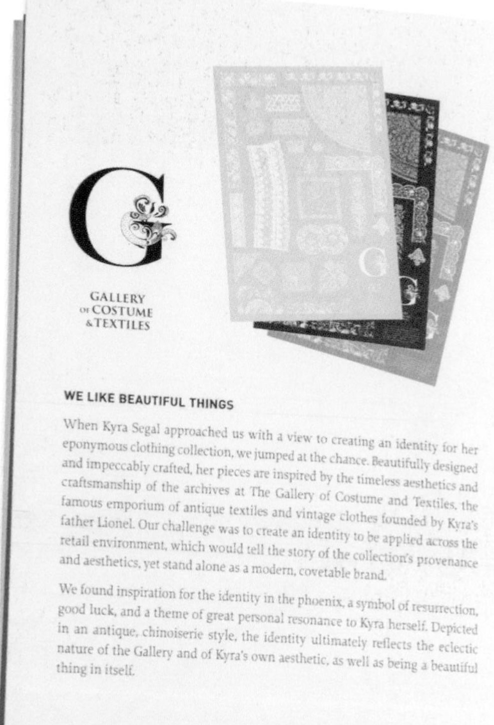

GALLERY OF COSTUME & TEXTILES
WE LIKE BEAUTIFUL THINGS
When Kyra Segal approached us with a view to creating an identity for her eponymous clothing collection, we jumped at the chance. Beautifully designed and impeccably crafted, her pieces are inspired by the timeless aesthetics and craftsmanship of the archives at The Gallery of Costume and Textiles, the famous emporium of antique textiles and vintage clothes founded by Kyra's father Lionel. Our challenge was to create an identity to be applied across the retail environment, which would tell the story of the collection's provenance and aesthetics, yet stand alone as a modern, covetable brand.
We found inspiration for the identity in the phoenix, a symbol of resurrection, good luck, and a theme of great personal resonance to Kyra herself. Depicted in an antique, chinoiserie style, the identity ultimately reflects the eclectic nature of the Gallery and of Kyra's own aesthetic, as well as being a beautiful thing in itself.

WE LIKE FINDING REASONS TO CELEBRATE
Which is why we were only too keen to work on a project which would set the corks a-popping on a regular basis. Katja from Together comes from a wine-making family in the Mosel valley, and the time was right to introduce their wines to the UK market. With no retail presence and a largely word-of-mouth approach to marketing, they needed a website to support their all-important ordering system, as well as a redesigned logo for bottle labels, tags, postcards and wine corks.
We developed a new logo and commissioned illustrations which became the backbone of the website. Taking the form of a conversation, the site features both real and fictitious characters taking the visitor on a tour of the Thielen wine cellar, and engagingly holding forth about the wines, and the history, philosophy and techniques behind them. The creative work has a look, feel and tone which is refreshingly different and unique, which may reflect the fact that most of the contributors were paid in wine, a good deal of it in advance, for inspiration's sake. www.thielenwine.com

ARTS,
ENTERTAINMENT,
AND EVENT
BROCHURES

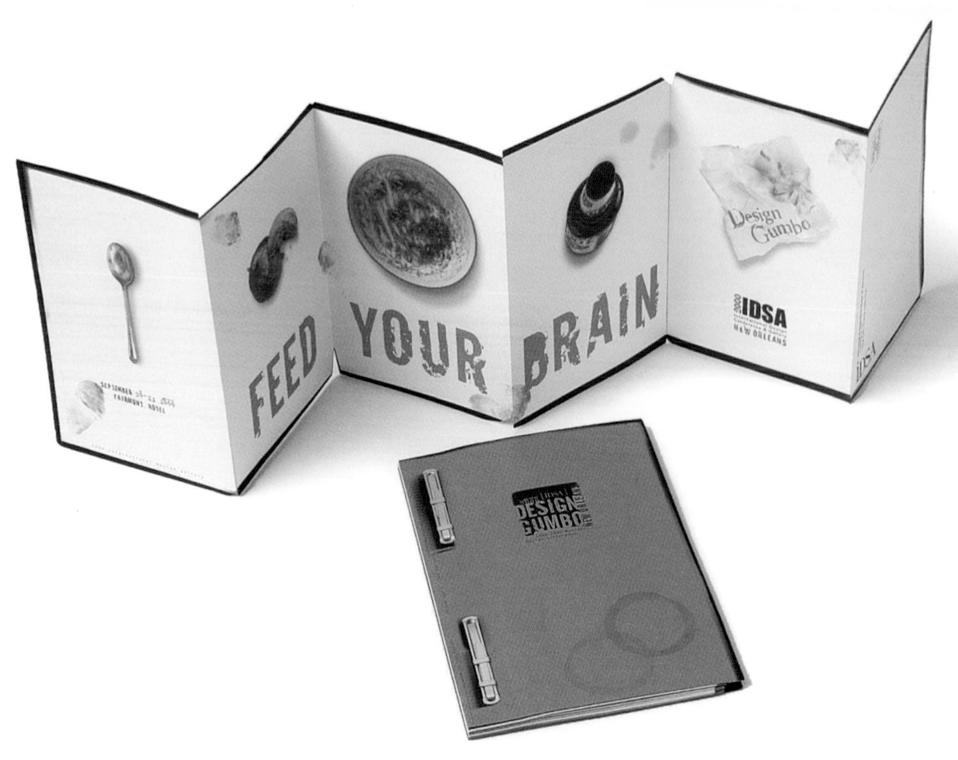

DESIGN FIRM › Bolt
ART DIRECTORS › Jamey Boiter, Mark Thwaites, Deanna Mancuso
DESIGNERS › Jamey Boiter, Mark Thwaites, Deanna Mancuso
ILLUSTRATOR/PHOTOGRAPHER › Stephanie Chesson
COPYWRITERS › IDSA & Bolt
CLIENT › IDSA
TOOLS (SOFTWARE/PLATFORM) › Photoshop, Illustrator, QuarkXPress
PRINTING PROCESS › 4-color, spot metallic

DESIGN FIRM › Trickett & Webb Ltd.
DESIGNERS › Lynn Trickett, Brian Webb, Katja Thielen
PHOTOGRAPHER › Adam Mitchinson
CLIENT › The London Institute
TOOLS (SOFTWARE/PLATFORM) › QuarkXPress
PAPER STOCK › Munken Lynx and Parilux
PRINTING PROCESS › Four-color lithography

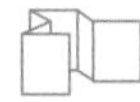

DESIGN FIRM > Sayles Graphic Design
ART DIRECTOR > John Sayles
DESIGNER > John Sayles
ILLUSTRATOR > John Sayles
CLIENT > Pattee Enterprises
TOOLS (SOFTWARE/PLATFORM) > QuarkXPress, Macintosh
PRINTING PROCESS > Offset

DESIGN FIRM › Lowercase, Inc.
ART DIRECTOR › Tim Bruce
DESIGNER › Tim Bruce
ILLUSTRATOR/PHOTOGRAPHER › Tim Bruce
CLIENT › Writers' Theatre Chicago
TOOLS (SOFTWARE/PLATFORM) › QuarkXPress, Macintosh
PAPER STOCK › Cougar

DESIGN FIRM › INOX Design, Milan
ART DIRECTORS › Claudio Gavazzi, Sabrina Elena
DESIGNERS › Claudio Gavazzi, Sabrina Elena
COPYWRITER › Michela Sartorio
CLIENT › MTV Networks
TOOLS (SOFTWARE/PLATFORM) › QuarkXPress, Photoshop
PAPER STOCK/PRINTING PROCESS › Opaque coated paper
PRINTING PROCESS › Four-color offset, gloss varnish

DESIGN FIRM › LA Weekly
ART DIRECTOR › Sheryl Scott
DESIGNER › Sheryl Scott
CLIENT › LA Weekly Music Awards
TOOLS (SOFTWARE/PLATFORM) › QuarkXPress, Photoshop

BISQIT DESIGN
WORLD SNOOKER MARKETING PACK

DESIGNER:
DAPHNE DIAMANT
PATRICK DEVLIN

PHOTOGRAPHER:
RANKIN

CLIENT:
WORLD SNOOKER

SOFTWARE AND HARDWARE:
ILLUSTRATOR
PHOTOSHOP
QUARKXPRESS
MAC

MATERIALS:
MEDLEY AND PVC PACK

PRINTING:
MIDAS

UK

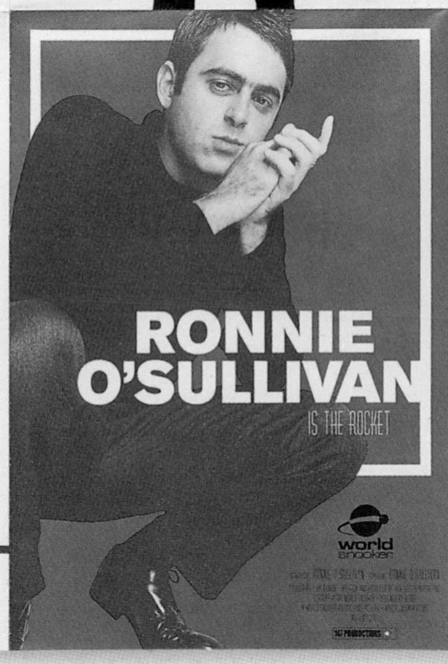

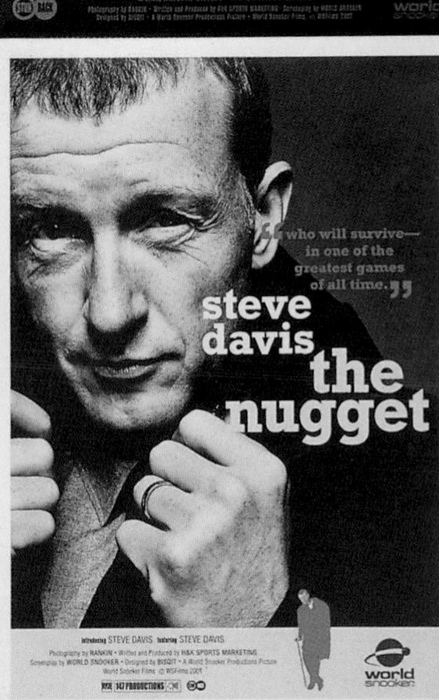

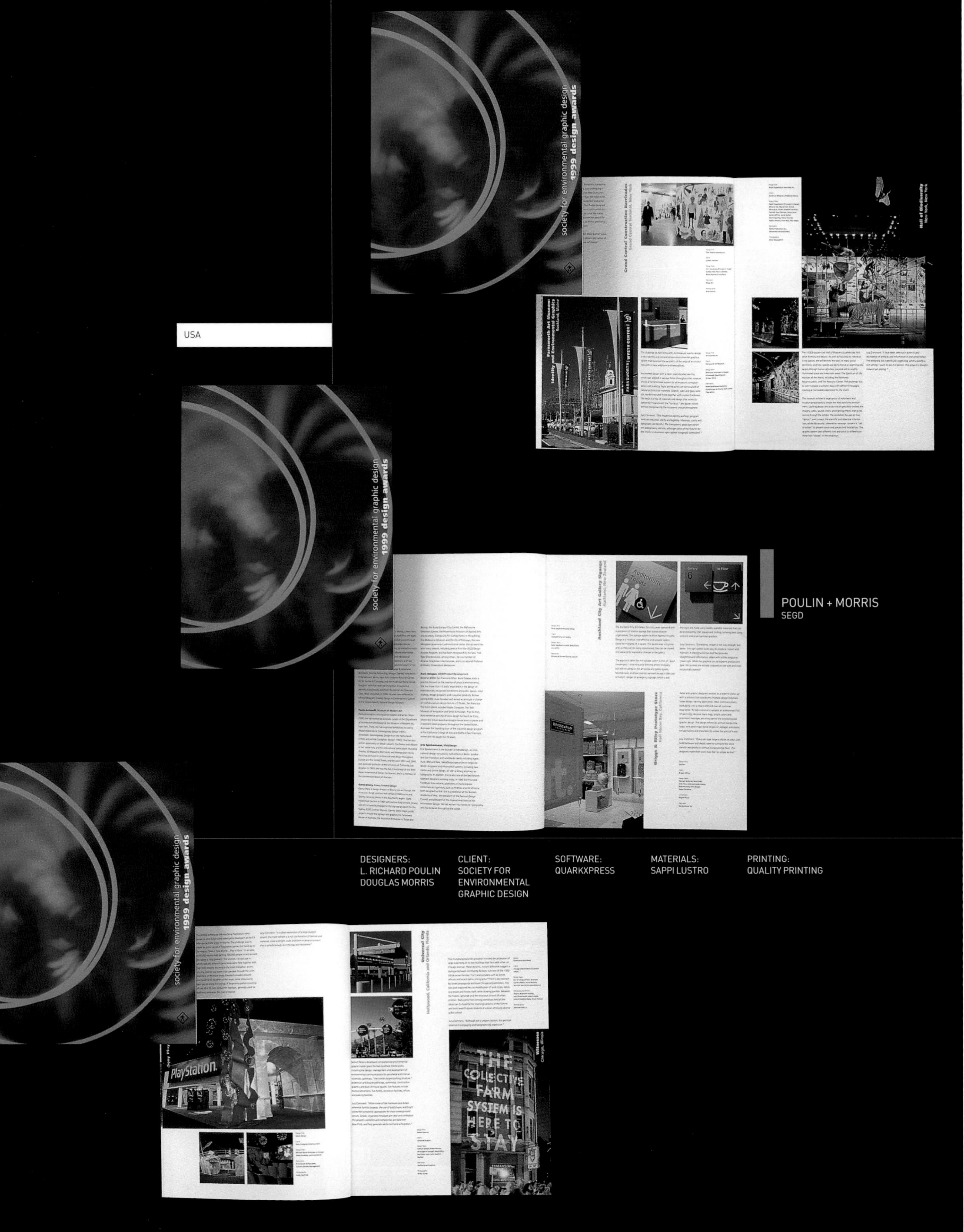

USA

POULIN + MORRIS
SEGD

DESIGNERS:
L. RICHARD POULIN
DOUGLAS MORRIS

CLIENT:
SOCIETY FOR ENVIRONMENTAL GRAPHIC DESIGN

SOFTWARE:
QUARKXPRESS

MATERIALS:
SAPPI LUSTRO

PRINTING:
QUALITY PRINTING

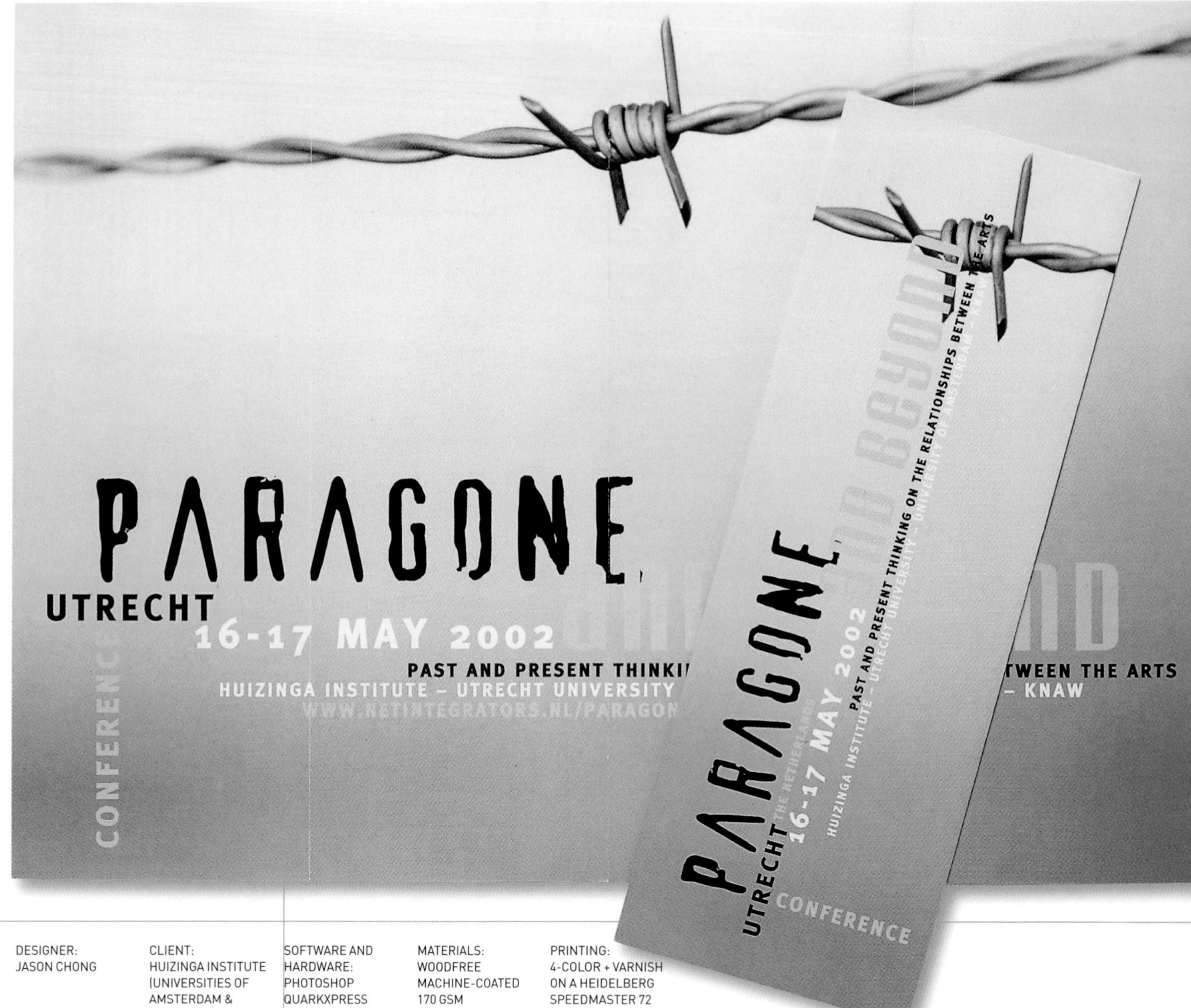

ART DIRECTOR:
JASON CHONG

DESIGNER:
JASON CHONG

CLIENT:
HUIZINGA INSTITUTE (UNIVERSITIES OF AMSTERDAM & UTRECHT)

SOFTWARE AND HARDWARE:
PHOTOSHOP
QUARKXPRESS
APPLE CUBE
PC

MATERIALS:
WOODFREE MACHINE-COATED 170 GSM

PRINTING:
4-COLOR + VARNISH ON A HEIDELBERG SPEEDMASTER 72 PRESS

NET INTEGRATORS – NET DESIGN
CONFERENCE POSTER/FLYER/PROGRAM (PRO BONO)

RT DIRECTOR: NNIE LACHAPELLE

DESIGNER: ANNIE LACHAPELLE

CLIENT: CINÉMATHÈQUE QUÉBÉCOISE

SOFTWARE: ILLUSTRATOR PHOTOSHOP QUARKXPRESS

CANADA

KO CREATION
LA REVUE

FABIO ONGARATO DESIGN

LINEAGE: THE ARCHITECTURE OF DANIEL LIBESKIND

AUSTRALIA

ART DIRECTOR: FABIO ONGARATO

DESIGNER: JAMES LIN

CLIENT: JEWISH MUSEUM OF AUSTRALIA

MATERIALS: NORDSET

PRINTING: GUNN & TAYLOR

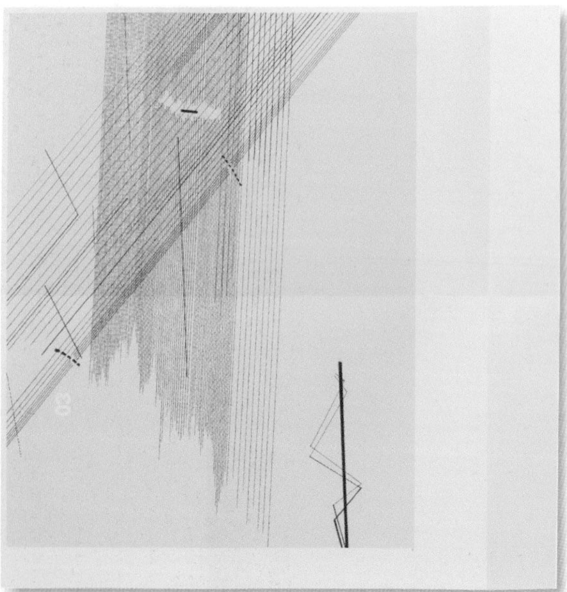

ART DIRECTOR:
DANIEL BASTIAN

DESIGNERS:
DANIEL BASTIAN
MAYA DA SILVA
JUTTA HOFFMANN

PHOTOGRAPHER:
TOM KLEINER

CLIENT:
DESIGN ZENTRUM
BREMEN

SOFTWARE:
PHOTOSHOP
QUARKXPRESS

MATERIALS:
ZANDERS MEGA
MATT 135 OFFSET

PRINTING:
FRANKE DRUCK

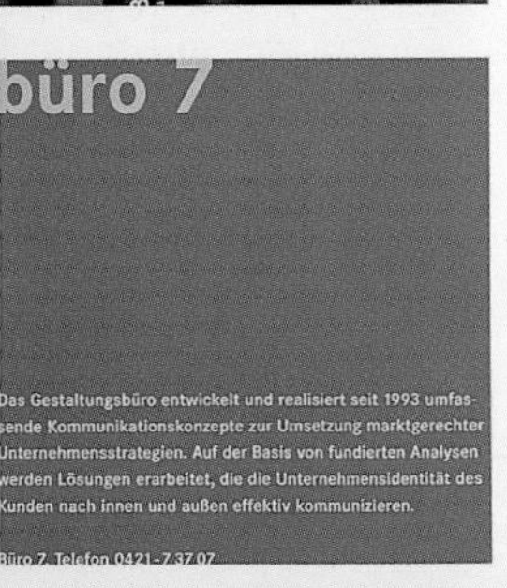

büro 7
Das Gestaltungsbüro entwickelt und realisiert seit 1993 umfassende Kommunikationskonzepte zur Umsetzung marktgerechter Unternehmensstrategien. Auf der Basis von fundierten Analysen werden Lösungen erarbeitet, die die Unternehmensidentität des Kunden nach innen und außen effektiv kommunizieren.
Büro 7, Telefon 0421 - 7 37 07

gruppe für gestaltung
14 Gestalter unterschiedlicher Fachrichtungen arbeiten in den Bereichen Werbung, Grafik, Interieurdesign und Möbelgestaltung. Diese Zusammenarbeit unterschiedlicher Disziplinen führt zu ganzheitlichen Gestaltungslösungen.
Gruppe für Gestaltung, Telefon 0421 - 33 86 80

GERMANY

bremer gestalten

Eine Ausstellung im Design Zentrum Bremen

Achtzehn x Bremer Design

josef hattig

Mein Haus versteht Designförderung immer als Wirtschaftsförderung und auch als Hilfe zur Selbsthilfe. Sie soll sowohl die Innovationskraft von Unternehmen stärken als auch das im Bundesland Bremen vorhandene kreative Potential sichtbar machen und mehren.

Das Design Zentrum Bremen hat daher eine Ausstellungsserie begonnen, in der die Vielfalt kreativer Dienstleistungen im Designbereich am Beispiel vorwiegend kleinerer und jüngerer Designbüros gezeigt wird.

Wir hoffen, daß bereits die erste Ausstellung dieser Reihe vielen mittelständischen Unternehmen, aber auch Existenzgründern den Anstoß gibt, Design in ihre Unternehmensstrategie einzubeziehen.

Der Ausstellung, die im Rahmen von „Advantage: Design" der Design-Initiative der deutschen Wirtschaft stattfindet, wünsche ich einen großen Erfolg, zahlreiche Kontakte zwischen Unternehmern und Designern und viel öffentliche Resonanz.

Josef Hattig
Senator für Wirtschaft, Mittelstand, Technologie
und Europaangelegenheiten

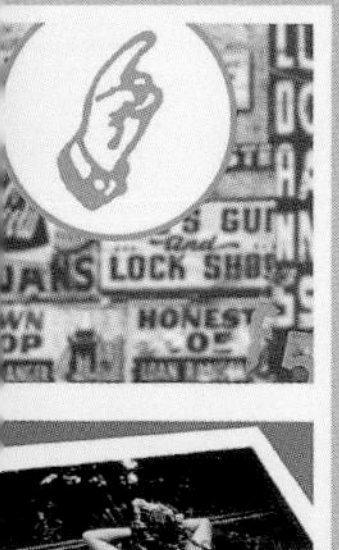

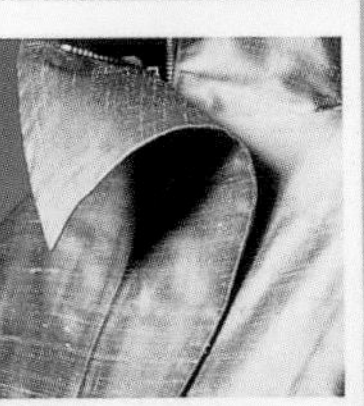

FORM5 + BÜRO7
BREMERGESTALTEN

renate wedepohl

Schmuck zum Gernetragen. Egal ob zum Alltagskleid oder zum kleinen Schwarzen, die Kollektionen der Schmuckdesignerin verleihen jedem Outfit den letzten Schliff. Ausgewogene Proportionen und klassische Materialien bestimmen das charakteristische Erscheinungsbild ihrer Werke. Schlichtes Silber, üppiges Gold und kühles Platin stehen sich oft komplementär gegenüber und erzeugen einen spannungsreichen Kontrast zwischen strenger Geometrie und verspielten Ornamenten.

Renate Wedepohl, Telefon 0421 - 70 39 22

lina namuth

Seit 1984 entwirft die Künstlerin in ihrer eigenen Werkstatt Damen- und Herren-Oberbekleidung aus hochwertigen und originellen Stoffen. Jedes Stück erscheint als Unikat oder im Rahmen einer Kleinserie, was dem Kunden große Individualität garantiert. „Mein Ziel ist es, Kleidung zu entwickeln, die das Leben angenehm macht, die Patina ansetzen darf wie ein gutes Möbelstück, in der man alles tun kann." Die Mode von Lina Namuth ist schlicht, bequem, elegant und einfach zu tragen.

Lina Namuth, Telefon 0421 - 32 63 66

USINE DE BOUTONS

MALOFANCON PRESS BROCHURE

ITALY

ART DIRECTORS:
LIONELLO BOREAN
CHIARA GRANDESSO

DESIGNERS:
LIONELLO BOREAN
CHIARA GRANDESSO

CLIENT:
MALOFANCON
FURNITURE

PRINTING:
CMYK + 1 PANTONE

5453

SOME TRAINS IN AMERICA

ART DIRECTOR:
VINCE FROST

DESIGNER:
VINCE FROST

PHOTOGRAPHER:
ANDREW CROSS

CLIENT:
CHRIST BOOT/
PRESTEL

MATERIALS:
EURO ART SILK
170GSM

PRINTING:
EBS, ITALY

UK

FROST DESIGN
SOME TRAINS IN AMERICA

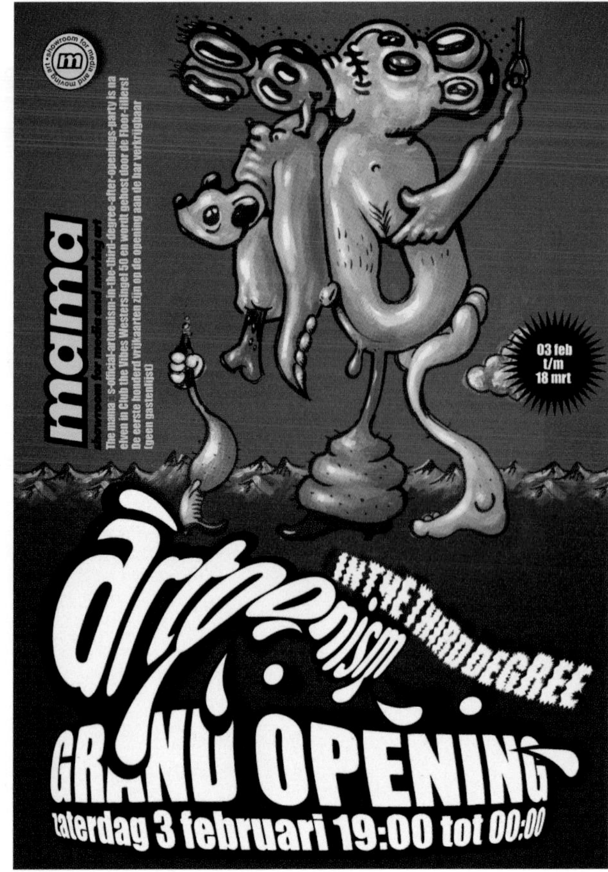

àrtoonism
IN THE THIRD DEGREE
LUUK BODE
CIRQUE DE PEPIN
HANS VAN BENTEM
DJ CHANTELLE
UN CADAVRE EXQUISE
mama
3 feb.
18 mrt.
2001
Artoonisten United

Onder de titel 'Artoonism in the third degree' presenteert showroom MAMA het werk van Luuk Bode, Cirque de Pepin, Hans van Bentem & DJ Chantelle. De derde tentoonstelling alweer in de serie 'Dutch Artoonists'. De Artoonisten bouwen hun kunstwerken op uit elementen, ontleend aan underground strips, Japanse manga en massamedia.'

àrtoonism
IN THE THIRD DEGREE

LUUK BODE, CIRQUE DE PEPIN (PEPIJN VAN DEN NIEUWENDIJK), HANS VAN BENTEM & DJ CHANTELLE

De 4 Artoonisten hebben de showroom van MAMA tot hun eigen hardpop-tempel omgebouwd. Tekeningen in flikkerend Neon, referenties aan ornamenten uit de tempels van Cambodja, maar ook de laatste technologische ontwikkelingen; voor sommigen de nieuwe religie, voor anderen het gouden kalf.

Het werk van de Artoonisten is vaak doorspekt met satire. De zoete zeepbel van de reclame wordt vaak met humor en confronterende beeldtaal doorgeprikt. Klassieke evergreens maar daarom niet minder geliefde thema's zijn Seks en Religie; maar ook actuele onderwerpen zoals gen-manipulatie en kunstmatige intelligentie passeren de revue. Zoals een portret van een groen figuur op gigantische Nike-schoenen. De maker, Luuk Bode, beeldde deze muisachtige hulk af met aureool en afgetraind lichaam. De optelsom van Marvel- en Disney-genen op Nike's lijkt een onoverwinnelijke, nieuwe heilige voort te brengen.

De Artoonist ontleent de bouwstenen voor zijn composities aan massamedia, verpakkingen, reclame en natuurlijk cartoons; of dit nu Marvel, Disney of obscure Manga betreft. Hieraan worden fantastische elementen toegevoegd, die hun oorsprong hebben in sciencefiction en de (hedendaagse) mythologie. "Mensen zitten meer tijd voor hun pc, videospelcomputers of tv dan ze op straat lopen. De media zijn dus net zo belangrijk als de wereld om ons heen. Mario Bros is even wezenlijk als de groentenboer op de hoek." aldus de Artoonisten.

Toen MAMA de vier artiesten uitnodigde om gezamenlijk te exposeren, stonden ze erop om voor de expositie werk te maken waarbij ze met zijn vieren in en door elkaar zouden werken. In navolging van de vroege surrealisten vouwden zij het tekenvel in vieren en tekenden ieder een deel. De eerste artiest tekende een kop, de tweede het bovenlichaam, de volgende het onderlichaam. Nadat de laatste artoonist de voeten toe had gevoegd, werd de tekening werd onthuld en zagen de artoonisten wat de anderen hadden gemaakt. Zo ontstaat het zogenaamde 'Cadavre Exquise'. Een gouden recept voor een serie zeer bizarre tekeningen. Do try this at home!

ART DIRECTOR:	DESIGNER:	ILLUSTRATOR:	CLIENT:	SOFTWARE:	MATERIALS:	PRINTING:
PING-PONG DESIGN	PING-PONG DESIGN	PING-PONG DESIGN LUUK BODE CIRQUE DE PEPIN HANS VAN BENTEM DJ CHANTELLE	MAM SHOWROOM FOR MEDIA AND MOVING ART	ILLUSTRATOR PHOTOSHOP QUARKXPRESS	REVIVA OFFSET POLAR SUPER GESATINEERD	OFFSET

PING-PONG DESIGN
ARTOONISM

AUSTRALIA

T DIRECTOR:	DESIGNER:	CLIENT:	MATERIALS:	PRINTING:
BIO ONGARATO	JAMES LIN	KAREN WALKER	SILK GLOSS	ENERGI

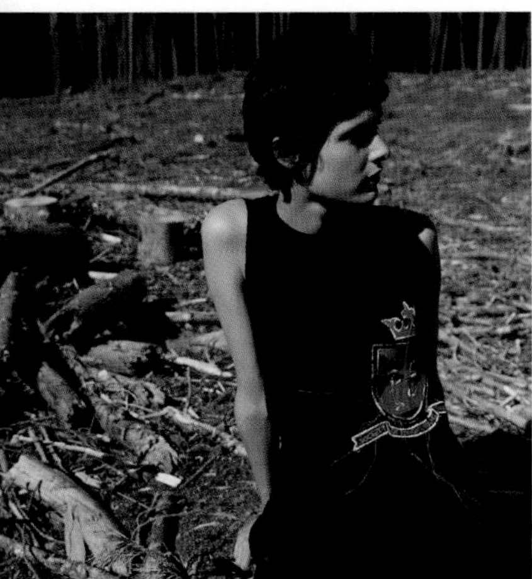

KAREN WALKER
WOMAN STOCKISTS

UK
LONDON
GOLD KIOSK
SANDERSON STORE
50 BERNERS ST
LONDON
PH: 1 212 582 4437

GOLD KIOSK
ST MARTIN'S LANE STORE
48 ST MARTIN'S LANE
LONDON
PH: 1 212 582 4437

USA
NEW YORK
HEDRA PRUE
281 MOTT ST
NEW YORK
PH: 1 212 343 9205

TG-170
170 LUDLOW ST
NEW YORK
PH: 1 212 995 8660

NEW JERSEY
ZOE
10 HULLFISH ST
PRINCETON
PH: 1 609 497 0704

WELLSELEY
GRETTA LUXE INC
94 CENTRAL ST
WELLSELEY MA
PH: 1 781 237 7010

BURLINGHAME
SUSAN OF BURLINGHAME
1403 BURLINGHAME AVE
BURLINGHAME
PH: 1 650 347 0452

LOS ANGELES
STACEY TODD
13025 VENTURA BLVD
STUDIO CITY
LOS ANGELES
PH: 1 310 308 6964

NOODLE STORIES
8323 WEST 3RD ST
LOS ANGELES
PH: 1 323 651 1782

MIAMI
MERCURY GIRL
920 LINCOLN RD
MIAMI
PH: 1 305 534 0211

GOLD KIOSK
DELANO STORE
1685 COLLINS AVE
MIAMI BEACH
PH: 1 212 582 4437

SEATTLE
FAST FORWARD
1918 FIRST AVENUE
SEATTLE
PH: 1 206 728 8050

SAN FRANCISCO
TAXI
1615 HAIGHT ST
SAN FRANCISCO
PH: 1 415 431 9614

SANTA MONICA
SHARON SEGAL
420 BROADWAY
SANTA MONICA
PH: 1 310 576 6062

HONG KONG
LANE CRAWFORD
70 QUEEN'S ROAD
CENTRAL HONG KONG
PH: 85 2 2118 3388

LANE CRAWFORD
PACIFIC PLACE 88
QUEENSWAY
HONG KONG
PH: 85 2 2118 3668

SISTYR MOON
SHOP 1U WINDSOR HOUSE
CAUSEWAY BAY
HONG KONG
PH: 852 2895 6336

SOUL SISTYR
GROUND FLOOR
24 WYNDHAM ST
CENTRAL HONG KONG
PH: 852 2525 0992

JAPAN
TOKYO
BARNEYS
3-18-5 SHINJUKU
SHINJUKU KU
TOKYO 160-0022
PH: 81 3 3352 1200

BARNEYS
36-1YAMASHITA-CHO
NAKA-KU
YOKOHAMA CITY
KANAGAWA 231-0023
PH: 81 45 671 1200

BEAMS
1-15-1 JINNAN
SHIBUYA-KU
TOKYO 150-0041
PH: 81 3 3780 5501

DIPTRICS
7-10-10-502
MINAMIAOYAMA
MINATO-KU
TOKYO
PH: 81 3 3409 0089

AUSTRALIA
MELBOURNE
DERNIER CRI
7 LEAKE ST
ESSENDON
MELBOURNE
PH: 61 3 9379 5122

MAGGIE POTTER
258 TOORAK RD
STH YARRA
MELBOURNE
PH: 61 3 9827 5488

SHREW
188C BARKLY ST
ST KILDA
MELBOURNE
PH: 61 3 9534 7337

ESSENCIA
510 MALVERN RD
PRAHAN EAST
MELBOURNE
PH: 61 3 9510 8220

SYDNEY
ORSON & BLAKE
83-85 QUEEN ST
WOOLAHRA
SYDNEY
PH: 61 2 9326 1155

ORSON & BLAKE
489 RILEY ST
SURRY HILLS
SYDNEY
PH: 61 2 8399 2525

ROBBY INGHAM
422-428 OXFORD ST
PADDINGTON
SYDNEY
PH: 61 2 9332 2124

MYER GRACE BROS
426 GEORGE ST
SYDNEY
PH: 61 3 9661 4495

BELINDA
MLC CENTRE SHOP 703
CNR KING & MARKET STS
SYDNEY
PH: 61 2 9233 0781

BELINDA
8 TRANSVAAL AVE
DOUBLE BAY
SYDNEY
PH: 61 2 9328 6288

FLINDER'S WAY
238 FILNDERS LANE
MELBOURNE
PH: 61 3 9654 3331

PERTH
PERISCOPE
68 KING ST
PERTH
PH: 61 8 9321 9696

CARLTON
RPM
SHOP 350
LYCON ST
CARLTON
VICTORIA
PH: 61 3 9347 4245

SORRENTO
DEB'S BOUTIQUE
24 OCEAN BEACH RD
SORRENTO
PH: 61 3 5984 1617

NEW ZEALAND
AUCKLAND
KAREN WALKER
6 BALM ST
NEWMARKET
AUCKLAND
PH: 64 9 522 4286

KAREN WALKER
15 O'CONNELL ST
CENTRAL AUCKLAND
PH: 64 9 309 6299

WELLINGTON
KAREN WALKER
126 WAKEFIELD ST
CENTRAL WELLINGTON
PH: 64 4 499 3558

CHRISTCHURCH
PLUME
83 CASHEL ST
CHRISTCHURCH
PH: 64 3 366 1663

DUNEDIN
PLUME
310 GEORGE ST
DUNEDIN
PH: 64 3 477 9358

QUEENSTOWN
ANGEL DIVINE
SHOP 12 THE MALL
QUEENSTOWN
PH: 64 3 442 8988

INVERCARGILL
LIZ THOMAS
PROVINCIAL CHAMBERS
32 KELVIN ST
INVERCARGILL
PH: 64 3 214 1139

KAREN WALKER
MENSWEAR STOCKISTS

NEW ZEALAND
AUCKLAND
CRANE BROTHERS
2-4 HIGH ST
DEBRETTS HOTEL
CENTRAL AUCKLAND
PH: 64 9 377 5333

WELLINGTON
AREA 51
CORNER CUBA MALL
& DIXON STREETS
CENTRAL WELLINGTON
PH: 64 4 385 6590

AUSTRALIA
SYDNEY
ORSON & BLAKE
489 RILEY ST
SURRY HILLS
SYDNEY
PH: 61 2 8399 2525

TRADE ENQUIRIES
WHOLESALE

USA ASIA & EUROPE
THE NEWS
KYOKO KAGEYAMA
495 BROADWAY
LEVEL 5
NEW YORK
NY 10012
PH: 1 212 925 9700 EXT 104
FAX: 1 212 925 1550
EMAIL:
kkageyama@495news.com

AUSTRALIA
PAUL MALONEY FASHION
AGENCY
PAUL MALONEY
PO BOX 3148
TAMARAMA
SYDNEY 2026
AUSTRALIA
PH: 61 2 9130 3403
FAX: 61 2 9300 8979
EMAIL:
big-m@zipworld.com.au

NEW ZEALAND
KAREN WALKER
MURRAY BEVAN
PO BOX 6694
WELLESLEY ST
AUCKLAND 1036
NEW ZEALAND
PH: 64 9 358 0864
FAX: 64 9 358 0865
EMAIL:
murray@karenwalker.com

EDITORIAL

USA ASIA & EUROPE
THE NEWS
TAHLIA MCLEOD
495 BROADWAY
LEVEL 5
NEW YORK
NY 10012
PH: 1 212 925 9700 EXT121
FAX: 1 212 925 1550
EMAIL:
tmcleod@495news.com

AUSTRALIA
SPIN COMMUNICATIONS
ALISON HAINSWORTH
99 STANLEY ST (CNR
STANLEY & PALMER STS)
DARLINGHURST
NSW 2010
AUSTRALIA
PH: 61 2 9361 4655
FAX: 61 2 9361 4547
EMAIL:
a.hainsworth@spin.com.au

NEW ZEALAND
KAREN WALKER
MURRAY BEVAN
PO BOX 6694
WELLESLEY ST
AUCKLAND 1036
NEW ZEALAND
PH: 64 9 358 0864
FAX: 64 9 358 0865
EMAIL:
murray@karenwalker.com

PRESS

USA ASIA & EUROPE
THE NEWS
TAHLIA MCLEOD
495 BROADWAY
LEVEL 5
NEW YORK
NY 10012
PH: 1 212 925 9700 EXT121
FAX: 1 212 925 1550
EMAIL:
tmcleod@495news.com

AUSTRALIA / NEW ZEALAND
KAREN WALKER
MURRAY BEVAN
PO BOX 6694
WELLESLEY ST
AUCKLAND 1036
NEW ZEALAND
PH: 64 9 358 0864
FAX: 64 9 358 0865
EMAIL:
murray@karenwalker.com

KAREN WALKER
MENSWEAR
ALL ENQUIRIES
MURRAY BEVAN
PH: 64 9 358 0864
EMAIL:
murray@karenwalker.com

ART DIREC
AND DESIG
FABIO ONG
DESIGN
PHOTOGRA
DEREK HEN
ASSISTANT
TANIA VELL
FILM PROC
PIX PHOTO
MODELS
HANAH CO
62 MODELS
NICK AUST
HOIPOLLOI

WITH GENE
SUPPORT F
CPI PAPERS
PRE PRESS
COLOUR SC
PRINTING
ENERGI PO

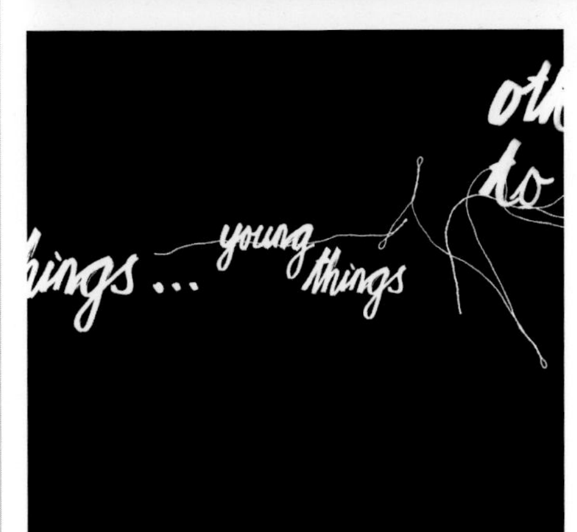

FABIO ONGARATO DESIGN
KAREN WALKER WINTER 2001

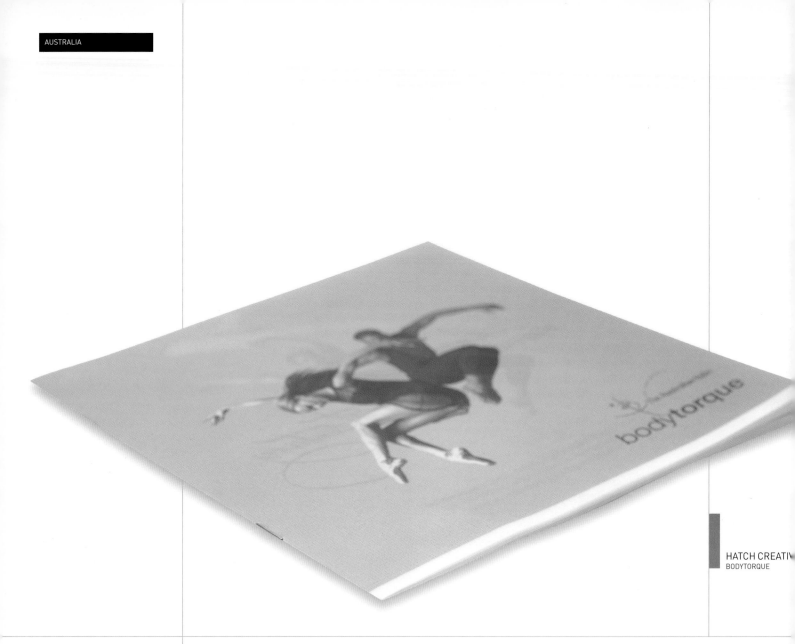

HATCH CREATIV
BODYTORQUE

ART DIRECTOR: SASKIA ERICSON

DESIGNER: SASKIA ERICSON

PHOTOGRAPHER: LOIS GREENFIELD

CLIENT: THE AUSTRALIAN BALLET

SOFTWARE: ILLUSTRATOR, PHOTOSHOP, STREAMLINE

MATERIALS: GILCLEAR OXFORD GILBERT PAPER

PRINTING: 4-COLOR PROCESS BAMBRA PRESS

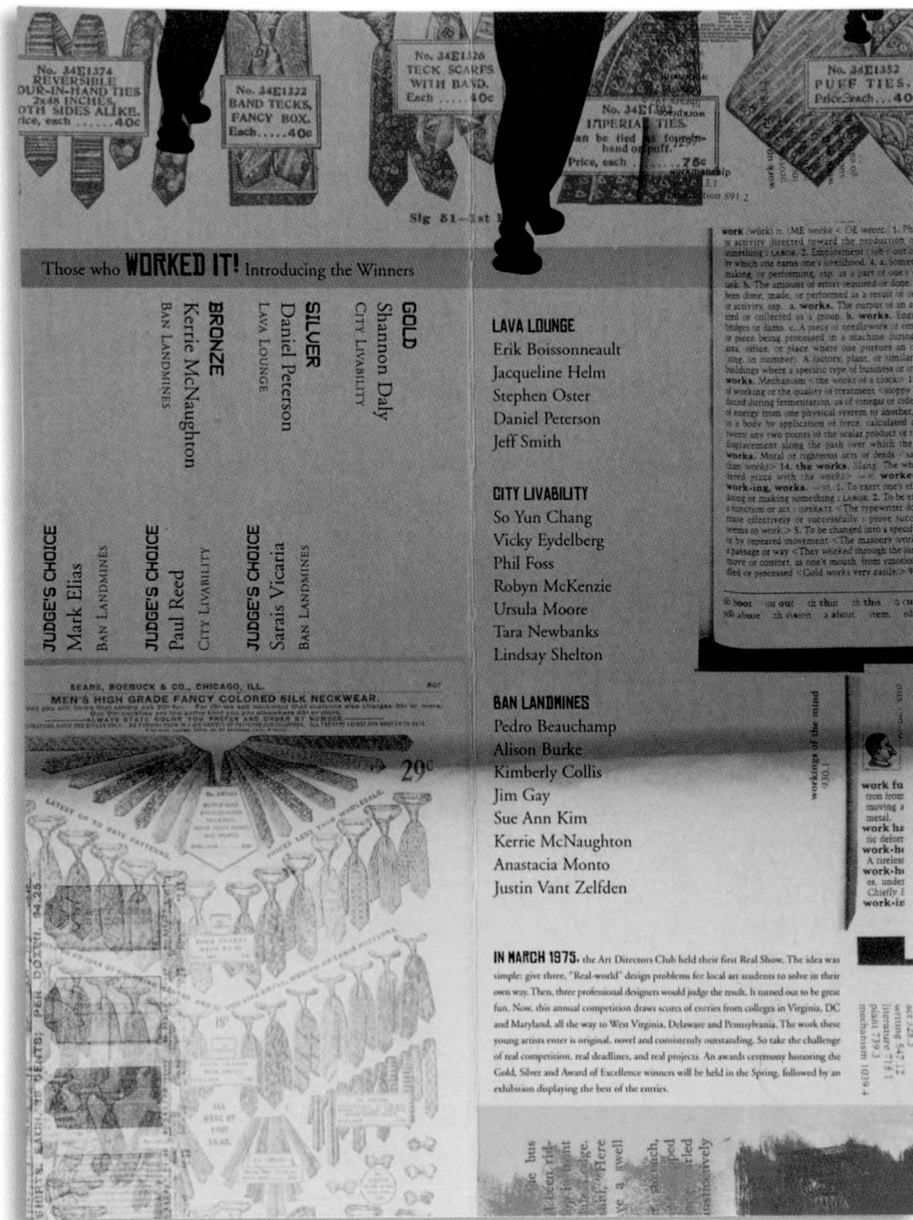

FUSZION COLLABORATIVE

Real Show Reception

ART DIRECTOR:	DESIGNER:	CLIENT:	TOOLS:	MATERIALS:
John Foster	John Foster	ADCMW	Adobe Photoshop Adobe Illustrator QuarkXPress	Domtar Titanium

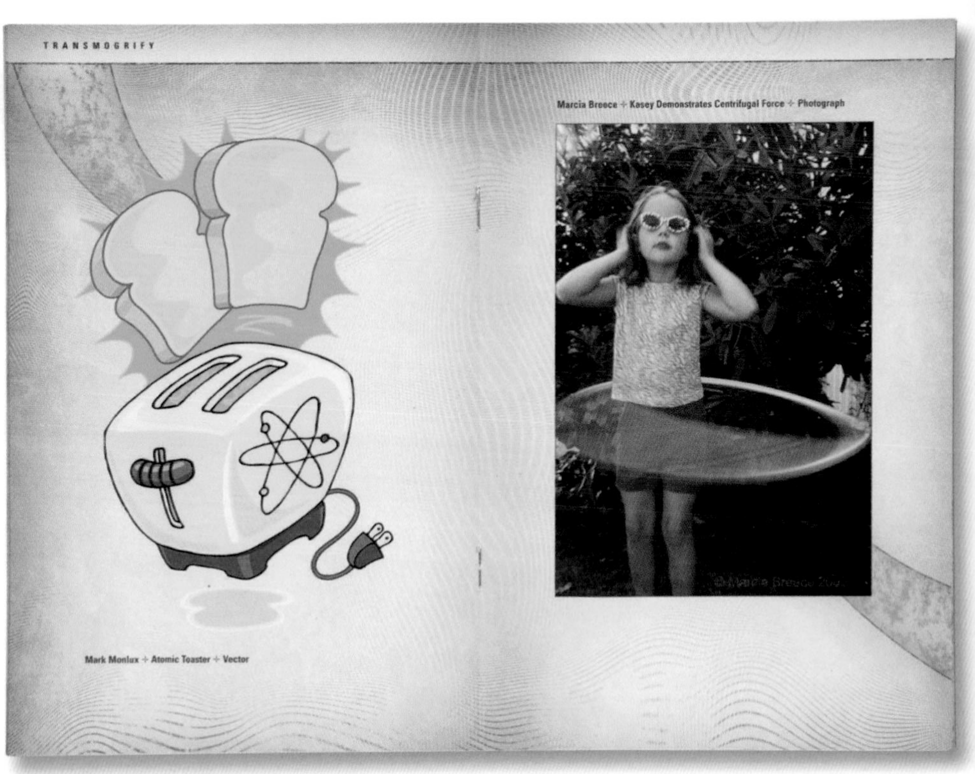

TRANSMOGRIFY
Marcia Breece + Kasey Demonstrates Centrifugal Force + Photograph
Mark Monlux + Atomic Toaster + Vector

GREENZWEIG DESIGN

Art Jam 6—Buyers Invitation

ART DIRECTOR:
Tim Greenzweig

DESIGNER:
Tim Greenzweig

CLIENT:
Graphic Artists Guild
Seattle

TOOLS:
Adobe Photoshop
QuarkXPress

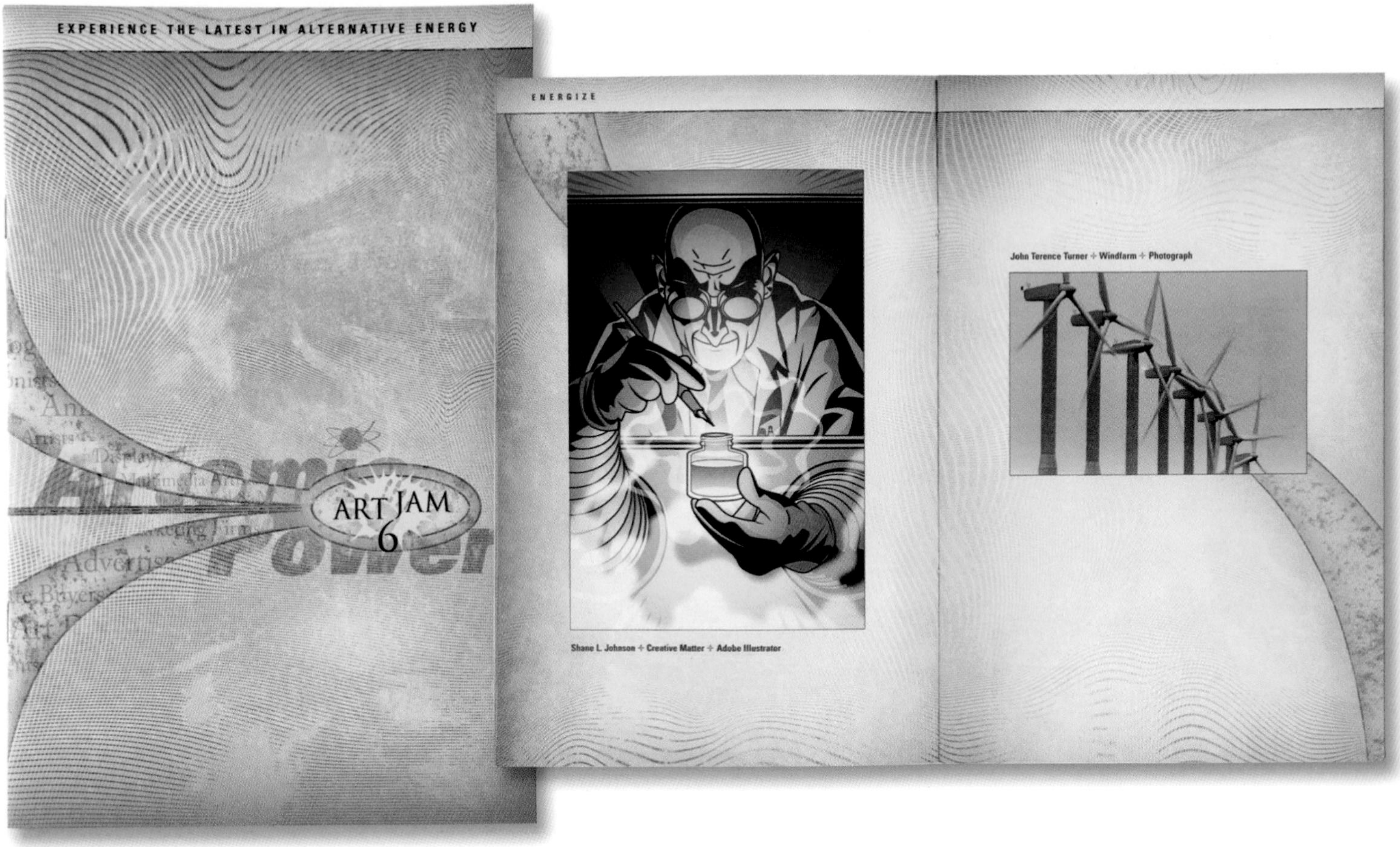

ELFEN

Craft Catalogue

ART DIRECTOR:	DESIGNER:	CLIENT:	TOOLS:	MATERIALS:
Guto Evans	Matthew James	Wales Arts International	Macromedia Freehand QuarkXPress	Curtis Echo Artik matt

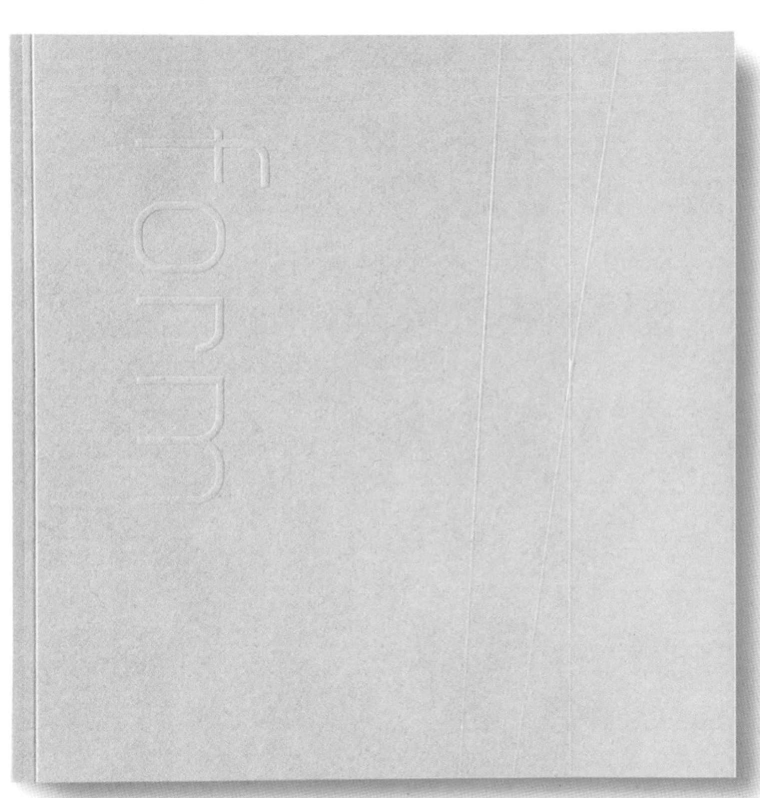

fig. 2
Commemorating the Great Naval Battle of the Japan Sea (detail), late Meiji era, canceled 1906

THE RUSSO-JAPANESE WAR

During the Russo-Japanese War (1904–5), more than one million Japanese soldiers fought Russian troops for control of Korea and Manchuria. Postcards—which from the beginning had been used for documentation, memorialization, and propaganda—were particularly relevant in wartime and became the preferred way for families to maintain contact with the armed forces and follow the progress of the war. The Japanese government issued five sets of postcards with scenes of battles, courageous soldiers, and victory celebrations. The demand for these was so great that between 400,000 and 700,000 individual cards were issued. In addition, approximately one thousand sets of privately printed postcards (forty-five hundred different designs) fed the frenzy, and by the time the war was over, an estimated four thousand postcard outlets existed in Tokyo alone.

Among the privately printed postcards is an image, extending across three cards, with a sinking Russian ship juxtaposed against a stylized map of Japan (fig. 2). The inscription along the bottom edge notes that the cards were designed for a competition, presumably in commemoration of Japan's victory.

On June 1, 1906, the government issued its last set of postcards, celebrating the Japanese victory. This set included a photographic image documenting thousands of people waiting in line to buy these postcards (see page 15, fig. 12). At top and lower right of the card are lithographs showing customers completing their purchases and an official providing commemorative stamps. One observer noted: "When unsuccessful buyers were given a notice that all cards had gone, they stoned the office and smashed window panes."

5

fig. 9
Takahashi Haruka (dates unknown), New Year's Card: Goat, Shōwa era, 1931
Atsuo (dates unknown), New Year's Card: Women in Au Courant Fashion with Cityscape, Taishō–early Shōwa eras
fig. 10

NEW YEAR'S POSTCARDS

The exchange of greetings at New Year's—traditionally in the form of personal visits—has been a revered custom in Japan since ancient times. When the mail system was established, however, the increasingly popular postcard became the favorite way to send good wishes to friends and relatives. It has been estimated that in 1905, for example, more than one hundred million postcards were sent to commemorate the New Year.

Many New Year's cards feature the twelve animals of the East Asian zodiac, which originated in China but has been known in Japan for almost two thousand years. The animals are placed in a traditional order to count the years. The years of the goat (fig. 9), for example, are 1907, 1919, 1931, and so on, up to 2003.

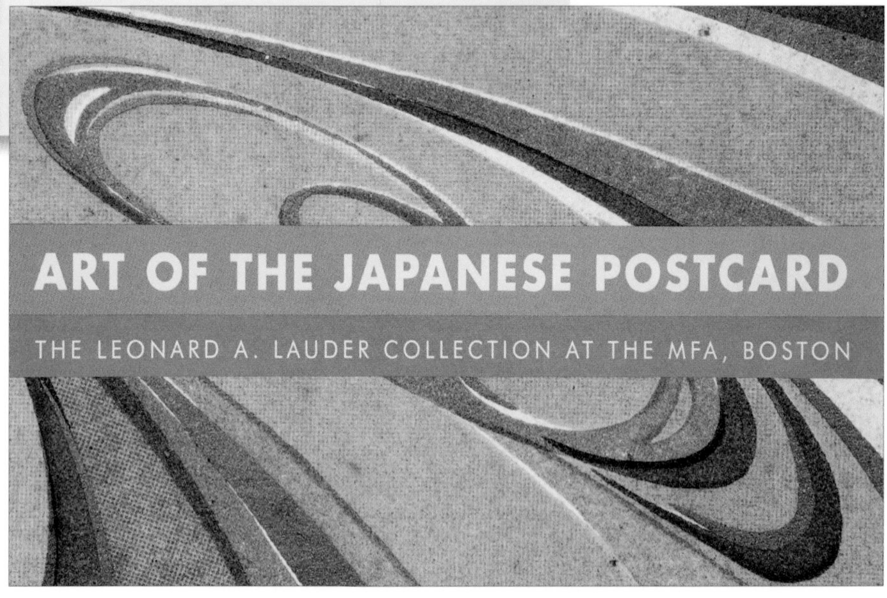

ART OF THE JAPANESE POSTCARD
THE LEONARD A. LAUDER COLLECTION AT THE MFA, BOSTON

MUSEUM OF FINE ARTS, BOSTON

Japanese Postcard Exhibit Brochure

ART DIRECTOR:	**DESIGNER:**	**CLIENT:**	**TOOLS:**	**MATERIALS:**
Janet O'Donoghue	Melissa Wehrman	Museum of Fine Arts Boston	Adobe Photoshop QuarkXPress	Monadnock Astrolite Silk Text 100 lb

fig. 7
Commemorating the Ninth Tournament of Far Eastern Athletes, early Shōwa era, 1930

POSTCARDS AS ADVERTISEMENTS

Early Japanese advertising postcards primarily featured photographs, but designers soon enriched these photographs with lively, swirling borders influenced by Art Nouveau. After 1914, advertising design entered a new era in which many styles of modern art were employed by artists who decided to become graphic designers rather than painters (fig. 7). Due to mechanical forms of reproduction and an increasing valuation of technology, graphic design—which created multiples for mass consumption rather than unique objects for the individual—became a field in its own right.

Sugiura Hisui was a central figure in gaining recognition for graphic design as a legitimate artistic pursuit. Working in an eclectic, East/West style, Hisui produced posters, brochures, magazine illustrations, and postcards for a number of companies, including the department store Mitsukoshi (fig. 8).

Founded as a dry-goods store in central Edo, Mitsukoshi (still operating today) flourished with Japan's economy and soon had branches throughout the country and elsewhere in Asia, hiring consultants who had studied American department-store management. Mitsukoshi introduced glass display cases and show windows and installed the country's first escalator in the main store. Mitsukoshi ultimately hired women as salesclerks, a job previously held only by men in Japan. In another radical departure from tradition, the store no longer required shoppers to leave their shoes at the entrance of the store.

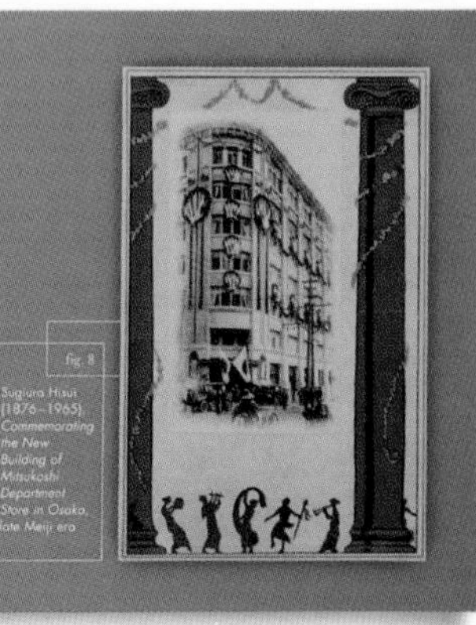

fig. 8
Sugiura Hisui (1876–1965), Commemorating the New Building of Mitsukoshi Department Store in Osaka, late Meiji era

ROSE

The Flower Cabinet Exhibition Catalog

Art Director:
Simon Elliott
Designer:
Terry Stephens
Client:
Barbara and Zafer Baran
Software:
QuarkXPress, Adobe Photoshop
Paper/Materials:
Consort Royal Satin 250 gsm, Fenner Redeem 70 gsm

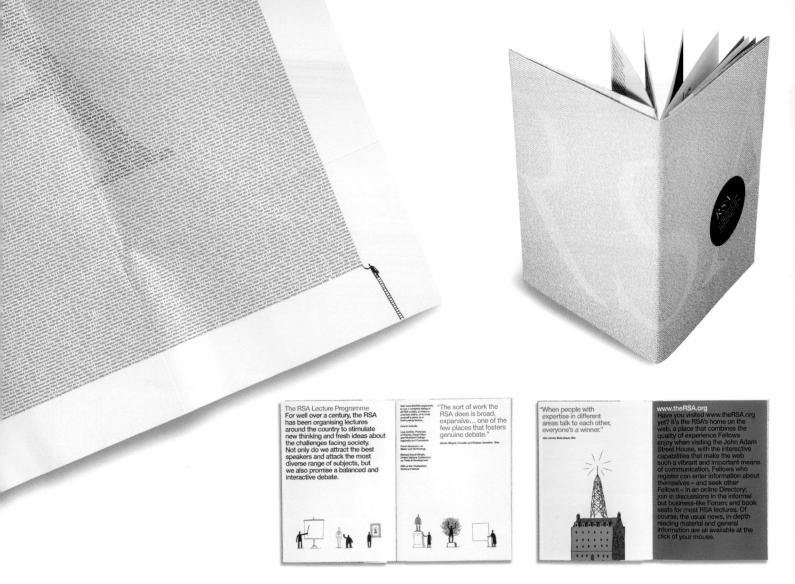

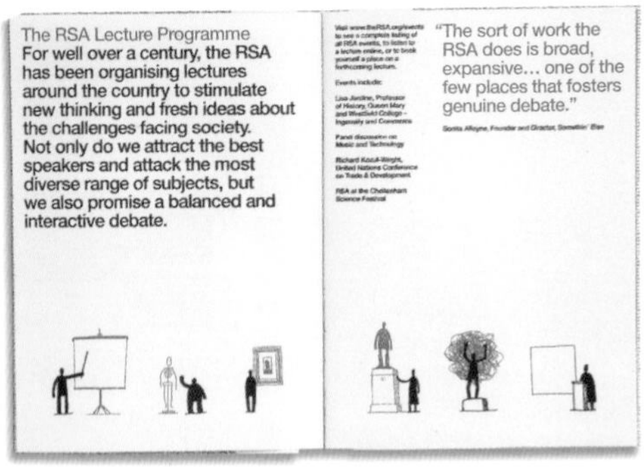

The RSA Lecture Programme
For well over a century, the RSA has been organising lectures around the country to stimulate new thinking and fresh ideas about the challenges facing society. Not only do we attract the best speakers and attack the most diverse range of subjects, but we also promise a balanced and interactive debate.

Visit www.theRSA.org/events to see a complete listing of all RSA events, to listen to a lecture online, or to book yourself a place on a forthcoming lecture.

Events include:

Lisa Jardine, Professor of History, Queen Mary and Westfield College – Ingenuity and Commerce

Panel discussion on Music and Technology

Richard Kozul-Wright, United Nations Conference on Trade & Development

RSA at the Cheltenham Science Festival

"The sort of work the RSA does is broad, expansive... one of the few places that fosters genuine debate."

Sonita Alleyne, Founder and Director, Somethin' Else

"When people with expertise in different areas talk to each other, everyone's a winner."

Alex James, Bass player, Blur

www.theRSA.org
Have you visited www.theRSA.org yet? It's the RSA's home on the web, a place that combines the quality of experience Fellows enjoy when visiting the John Adam Street House, with the interactive capabilities that make the web such a vibrant and important means of communication. Fellows who register can enter information about themselves – and seek other Fellows – in an online Directory; join in discussions in the informal but business-like Forum; and book seats for most RSA lectures. Of course, the usual news, in-depth reading material and general information are all available at the click of your mouse.

RSA Projects
The RSA delivers its mission through a portfolio of interdisciplinary projects, whose current aim is the advancement of a society keen on creativity and its principled exploitation. In particular the Programme aims to encourage innovation and invention; to help both the technology and the arts-based industries, to improve the national competence (knowledge, skills and behaviours); and to improve and extend professional standards.

The Society supports this activity by obtaining sponsorship from a diverse range of sources. Important among these is the expertise, effort and financial contribution of its Fellows. For more information, visit www.theRSA.org/projects

Project 1
Can the professions survive? – professional values for the 21st century
There is a widespread perception that the professions are under threat. No longer able to claim special privileges as disinterested, altruistic occupational groups acting detachedly in the public interest, professions are finding their traditional values and loyalties eroded.

In this climate, can – and should – the professions survive?

We are establishing a new project that seeks to consider some of these issues. The overall aim of the project is to re-invigorate the concept of a 'profession', to enlarge its application and to encourage the professions in the UK to become a more significant, trusted, and creative force for economic and social good.

The Comino Foundation has contributed towards the costs of this project.

Project 2
Science, Citizenship and the Market
This project is a major element of the RSA's move to strengthen its interventions in manufactures and commerce. All industry depends on a continuing flow of new science to maintain its product and process base but, as the recent GM controversy made clear, science-based industries ignore public opinion and perception at their peril. The failure to anticipate public reactions to a new technology can be expensive and damaging both for companies and for society.

We have made a significant investment to establish a project that will investigate the ways in which companies can benefit from incorporating socially sensitive antennae into their decision-making framework. One of the strengths of the project will lie in the collaboration between the RSA and a leading university: the project is being developed by the Science and Technology Studies Department of University College, London.

Project 3
The Economy of the Imagination
'The Economy of the Imagination' project, inspired by the New Statesman Lecture given by Lord Evans of the same title, aims to "find the line where high culture and commerce can meet to mutual advantage," as he put it. By examining each arts-based industry in turn, we will identify risk-takers who shun the easy temptation to produce formulaic, market-oriented products and support more innovative works. It is this risk-taking that we want to encourage.

www.theRSA.org/projects

NB:STUDIO
RSA New Members Handbook

Art Directors:
Nick Finney, Ben Stott, Alan Dye
Designers:
Nick Vincent, Tom Gauld
Client:
RSA

LIPPA PEARCE

Circular 12, Issue 12

Art Director: Domenic Lippa
Designer: Domenic Lippa
Client: The Typographic Circle

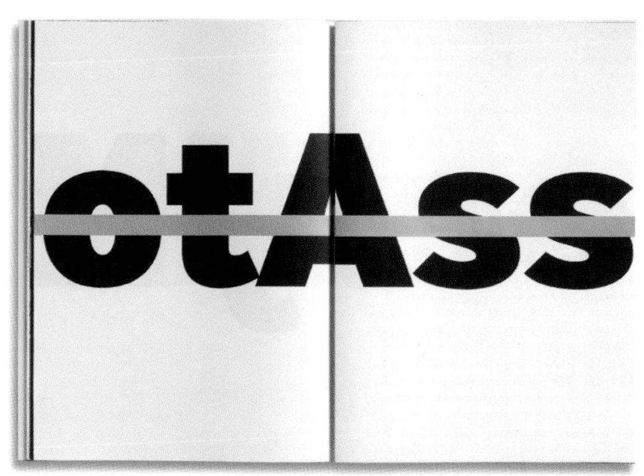

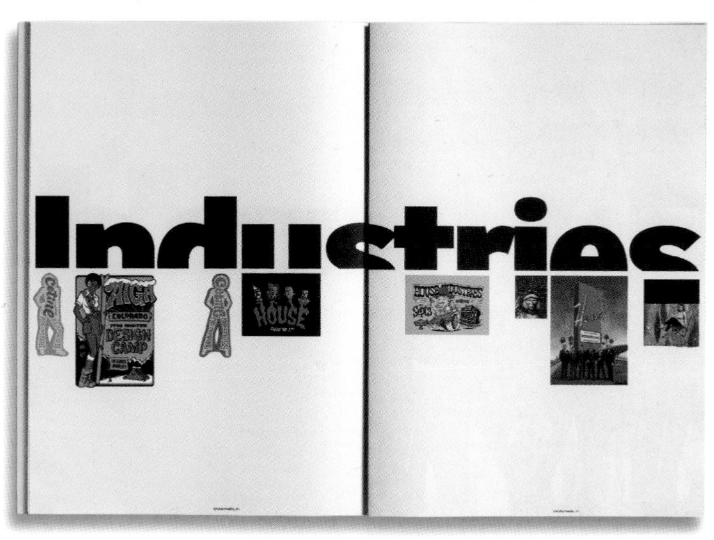

SAGMEISTER INC.

The Guggenheim, Douglas Gordon

Art Director:
Stefan Sagmeister
Designer:
Matthias Ernstberger
Typography:
Marian Bantjes
Production:
Lara Fieldbinder,
Melissa Secundino
Writer:
Nancy Spector
Client:
The Guggenheim Museum, Berlin
Software:
Adobe CS
Paper/Materials:
Postcards

AIGA

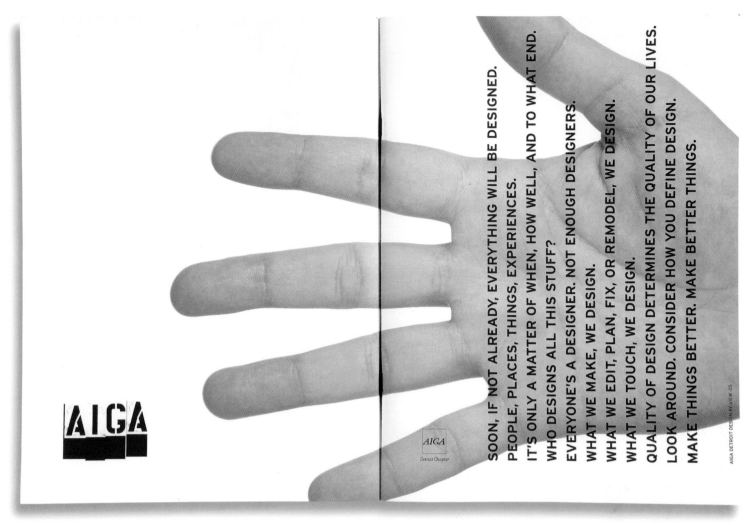

SOON, IF NOT ALREADY, EVERYTHING WILL BE DESIGNED.
PEOPLE, PLACES, THINGS, EXPERIENCES.
IT'S ONLY A MATTER OF WHEN, HOW WELL, AND TO WHAT END.
WHO DESIGNS ALL THIS STUFF?
EVERYONE'S A DESIGNER. NOT ENOUGH DESIGNERS.
WHAT WE MAKE, WE DESIGN.
WHAT WE EDIT, PLAN, FIX, OR REMODEL, WE DESIGN.
WHAT WE TOUCH, WE DESIGN.
QUALITY OF DESIGN DETERMINES THE QUALITY OF OUR LIVES.
LOOK AROUND. CONSIDER HOW YOU DEFINE DESIGN.
MAKE THINGS BETTER. MAKE BETTER THINGS.

AIGA
Detroit Chapter

AIGA DETROIT DESIGN REVIEW :05

BBK STUDIO
AIGA Detroit Design Re:View '05 Awards Book

Art Director:
Kevin Budelmann
Designers:
Brian Hauch,
Jason Murray
Client:
AIGA Detroit
Software:
Adobe Illustrator,
Adobe Photoshop,
QuarkXPress

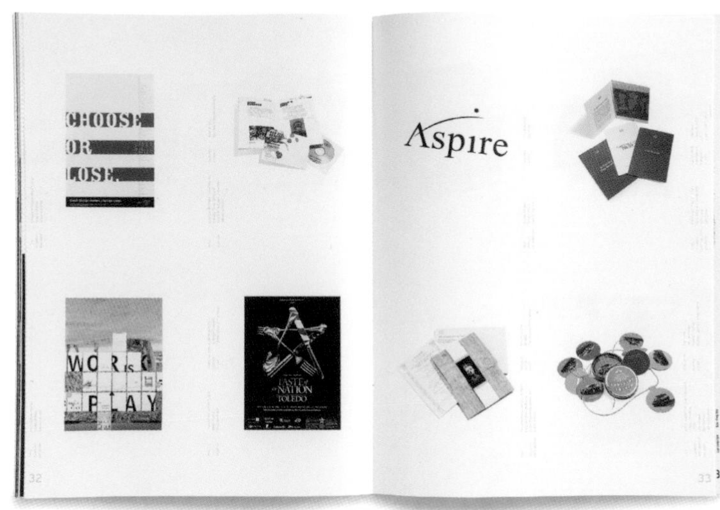

BILLY BLUE CREATIVE, PRECINCT
AGDA Awards Invite to Sydney

Art Directors:
Justin Smith,
Geordie McKenzie
Designers:
Justin Smith,
Geordie McKenzie
Client:
AGDA
Software:
Adobe Illustrator,
Adobe Photoshop,
QuarkXPress

Imagine this installation is a setting for a story about a journey. Write your story down on the other side of this card
FILL A SPACE
WHAT WAS MONIKA THINKING ABOUT
?
Serpentine Gallery
Monika Sosnowska
5 December 2004 - 16 January 2005
MONIKA SOSNOWSKA ART PACK
(Things to do in the exhibition and at home)
5 December 2004 - 16 January 2005

BC, MH
JAMES LAMBERT
Monika Sosnowska Art Pack

Designers:
Ben Chatfield,
Mark Hopkins,
James Lambert
Client:
Serpentine Gallery
Software:
Adobe Illustrator,
QuarkXPress
Paper/Materials:
Beer Mat Board

VIVA DOLAN
COMMUNICATIONS
& DESIGN INC.

Prospectus Brochure

Art Director:
Frank Viva
Designer:
Todd Temporate
Client:
The Interior
Design Show
Software:
QuarkXPress
Paper/Materials:
Knightkote Matte
80 lb text cover

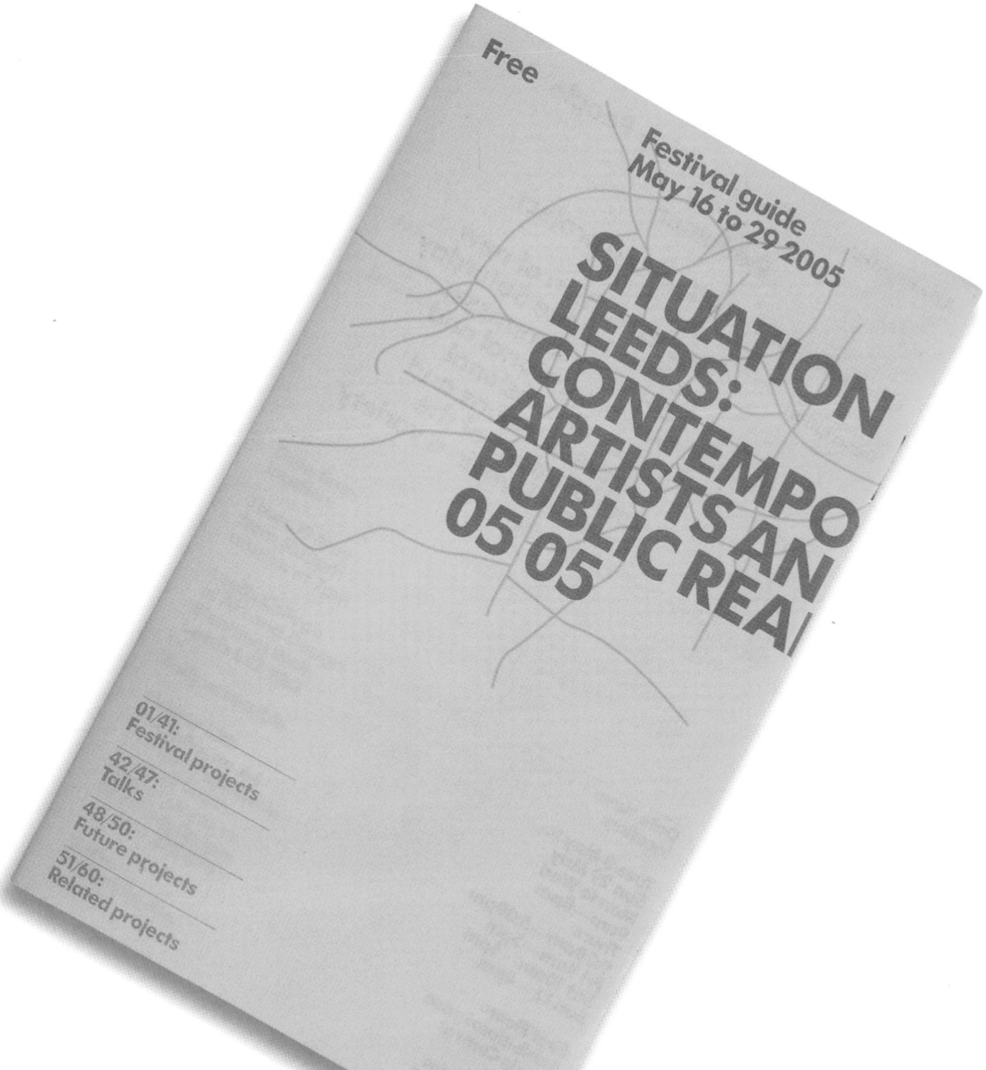

Free

Festival guide
May 16 to 29 2005

SITUATION
LEEDS:
CONTEMPO
ARTISTS AN
PUBLIC REA
05 05

01/41:
Festival projects
42/47:
Talks
48/50:
Future projects
51/60:
Related projects

DESIGN PROJECT
Situation Leeds
Festival Guide

Art Directors:
Andy Probert,
James Littlewood
Designers:
Andy Probert,
James Littlewood
Client:
Situation Leeds
Software:
QuarkXPress,
Freehand
Paper/Materials:
Kaskad Flamingo
Pink, Raflatac
Glossprint (Robert
Horne)

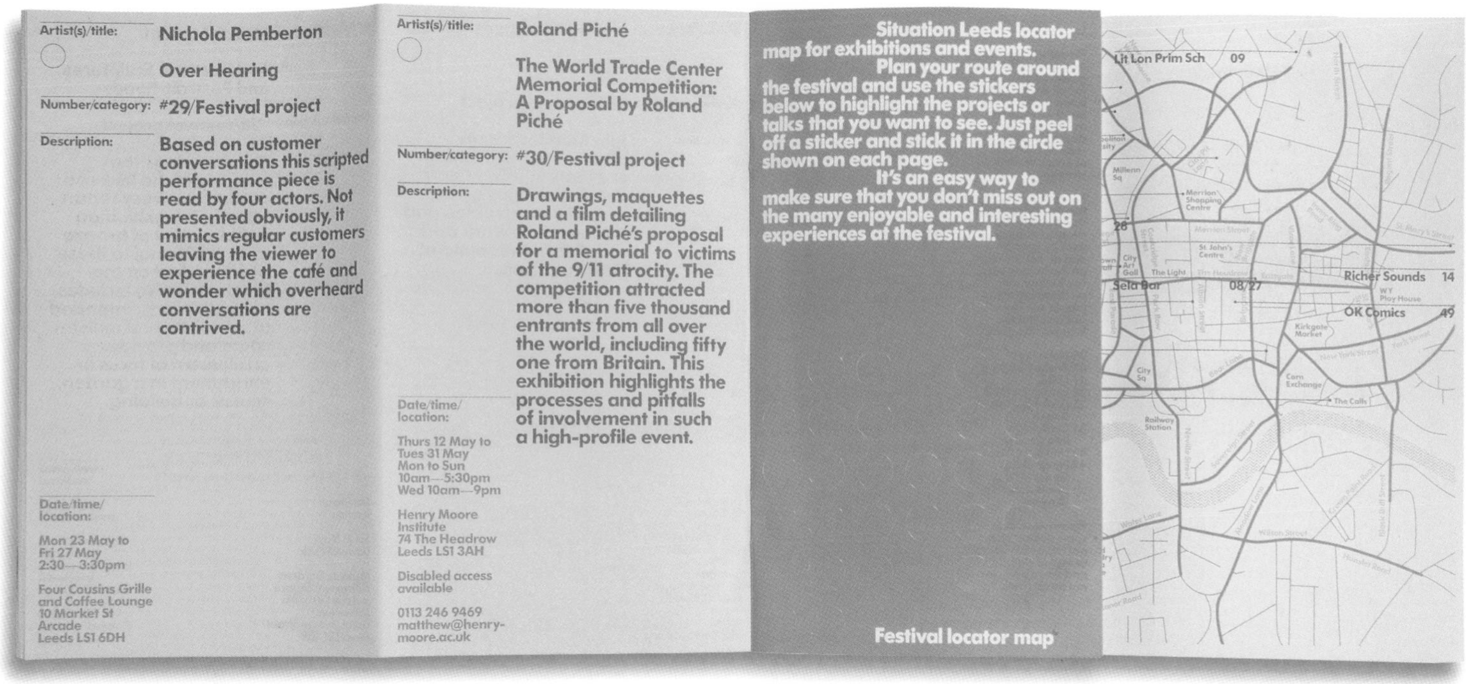

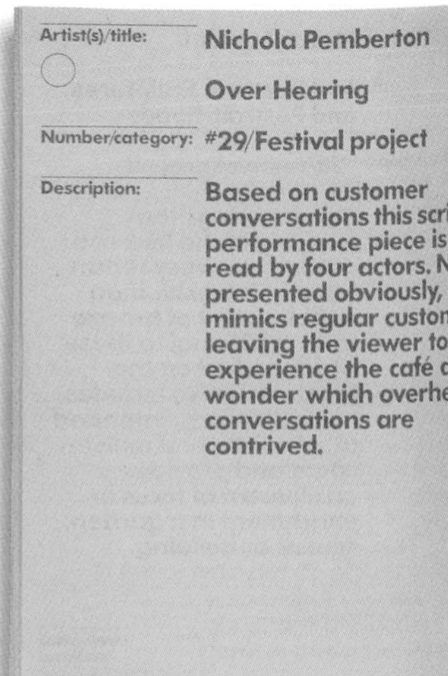

Artist(s)/title:
Nichola Pemberton
Over Hearing
Number/category:
#29/Festival project
Description:
Based on customer conversations this scripted performance piece is read by four actors. Not presented obviously, it mimics regular customers leaving the viewer to experience the café and wonder which overheard conversations are contrived.
Date/time/location:
Mon 23 May to Fri 27 May 2:30—3:30pm
Four Cousins Grille and Coffee Lounge 10 Market St Arcade Leeds LS1 6DH

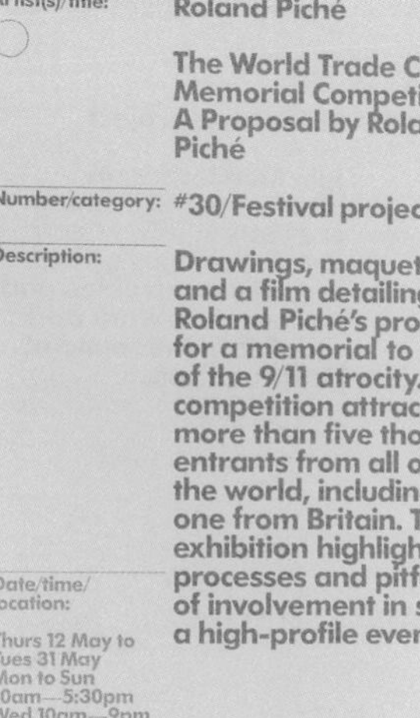

Artist(s)/title:
Roland Piché
The World Trade Center Memorial Competition: A Proposal by Roland Piché
Number/category:
#30/Festival project
Description:
Drawings, maquettes and a film detailing Roland Piché's proposal for a memorial to victims of the 9/11 atrocity. The competition attracted more than five thousand entrants from all over the world, including fifty one from Britain. This exhibition highlights the processes and pitfalls of involvement in such a high-profile event.
Date/time/location:
Thurs 12 May to Tues 31 May Mon to Sun 10am—5:30pm Wed 10am—9pm
Henry Moore Institute 74 The Headrow Leeds LS1 3AH
Disabled access available
0113 246 9469 matthew@henry-moore.ac.uk

Situation Leeds locator map for exhibitions and events. Plan your route around the festival and use the stickers below to highlight the projects or talks that you want to see. Just peel off a sticker and stick it in the circle shown on each page. It's an easy way to make sure that you don't miss out on the many enjoyable and interesting experiences at the festival.

Festival locator map

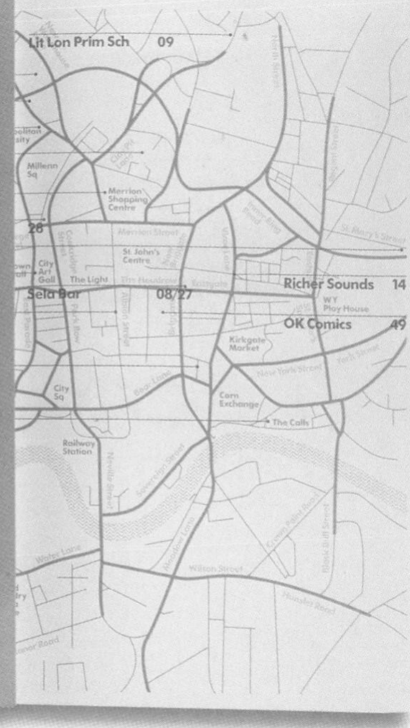

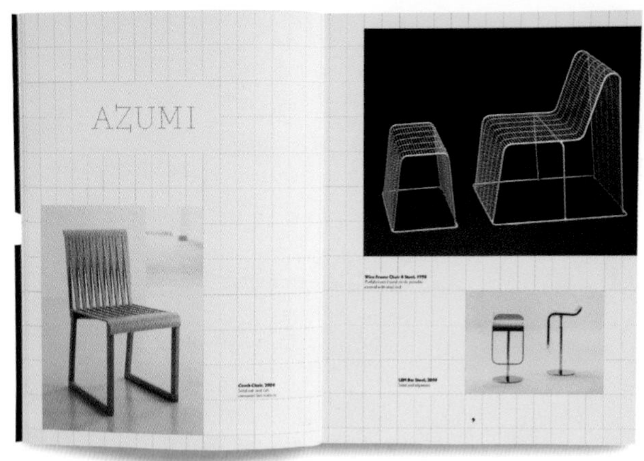

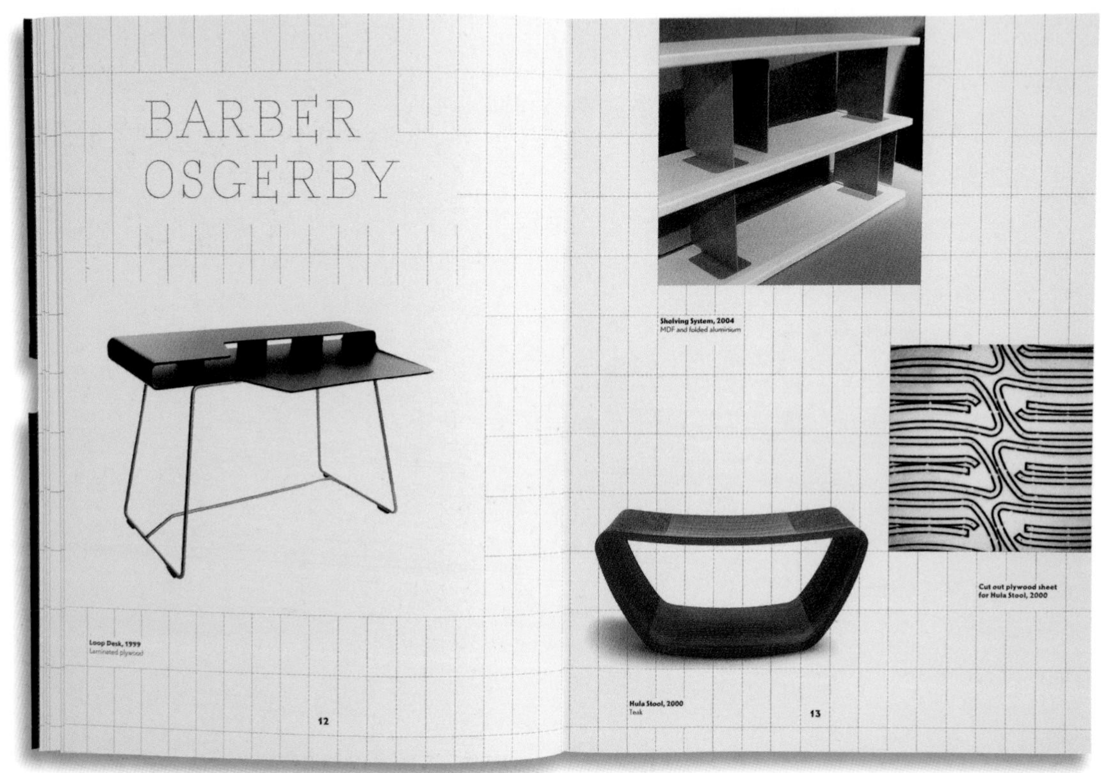

KERR/NOBLE

Jerwood Furniture Prize Catalog

Art Director:
Kerr/Noble
Designer:
Kerr/Noble
Client:
Crafts Council

GOLLINGS
& PIDGEON
The Plot Thickens Catalog

Art Director:
David Pidgeon
Designer:
Marianna Berek-Lewis
Client:
Heide Museum of Modern Art
Software:
QuarkXPress
Paper/Materials:
Freelife Vellum White, Encore Super Gloss Recycled

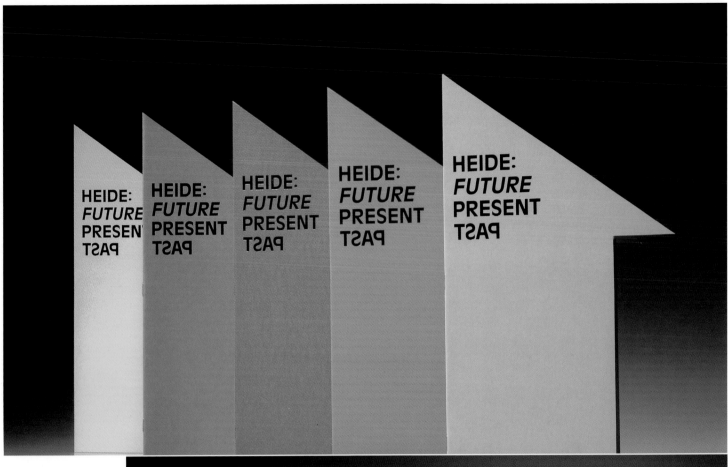

GOLLINGS
& PIDGEON
**Future Present
Past Catalog**

Art Director:
David Pidgeon
Designer:
Tina Chen
Client:
Heide Museum of
Modern Art
Software:
Adobe InDesign
Paper/Materials:
Optix: Inga Turquoise,
Suni Yellow, Janz
Orange, Reva Green,
Raza Red, Monza
Satin Recycled

SAS DESIGN

Awards Catalog

Art Directors:
Christine Fent,
Hanja Hellpap,
Gilmar Wendt

Designers:
Christine Fent,
Hanja Hellpap,
Gilmar Wendt

Client:
STD

Software:
QuarkXPress

Paper/Materials:
Hanno Art Matt

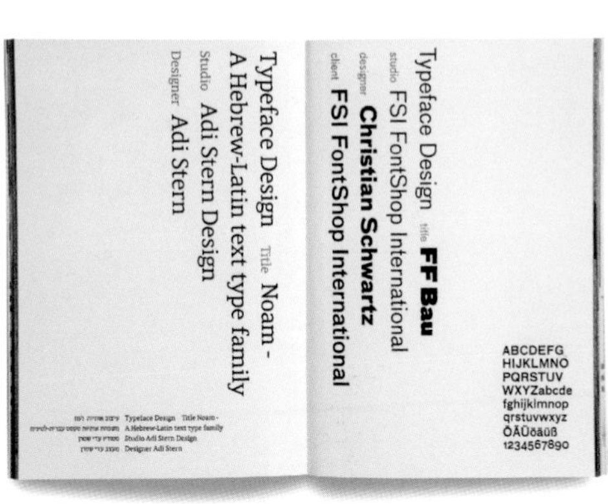

SAS DESIGN
BT Connected Worlds Arts Project Madrid

Art Director:
Gilmar Wendt
Designer:
Rosanna Vitiello
Client:
BT
Software:
QuarkXPress
Paper/Materials:
Colorplan Plain Finish Pristine White (cover), Munken Print Extra Vol 18 Parilux Gloss (text)

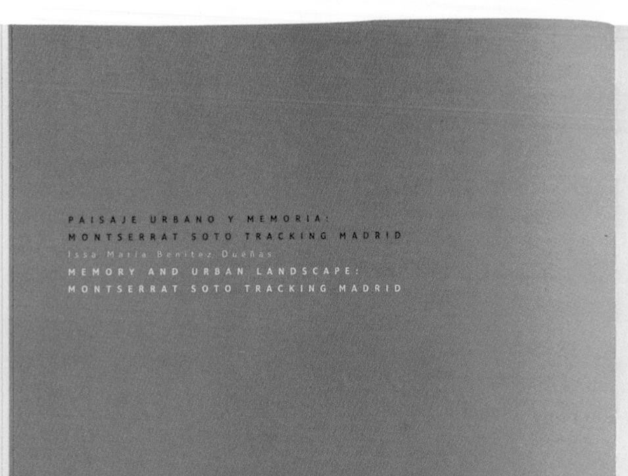

PAISAJE URBANO Y MEMORIA:
MONTSERRAT SOTO TRACKING MADRID
Issa María Benítez Dueñas
MEMORY AND URBAN LANDSCAPE:
MONTSERRAT SOTO TRACKING MADRID
¿Para qué necesitamos el arte en las ciudades? Un recorrido histórico permite decir que las artes, y en general los recursos estéticos, son necesarios no sólo por razones ornamentales sino en otros sentidos más decisivos. Encuentro al menos cuatro fines con los cuales el arte, la literatura y los medios masivos han intervenido e intervienen en espacios urbanos: para fundarlos y refundarlos, para celebrar, para espectacularizar y para nombrar u ocultar su pérdida. Néstor García Canclini
Why do we need art in cities? If we look at history we can see that the arts, and aesthetic resources in general, are necessary not just for ornamental purposes but also for more important reasons. I can identify at least four motivating factors which underlie the continuing intervention of art, literature and the mass media in urban spaces: to create and recreate these spaces, to celebrate them, to make them more spectacular, and to pinpoint or conceal their loss. Néstor García Canclini

PENTAGRAM DESIGN, SAN FRANCISCO

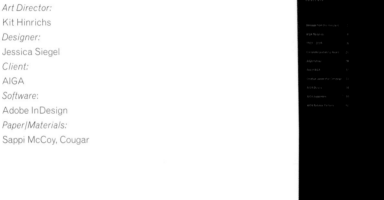

AIGA Design Legends Gala Program

Art Director:
Kit Hinrichs

Designer:
Jessica Siegel

Client:
AIGA

Software:
Adobe InDesign

Paper/Materials:
Sappi McCoy, Cougar

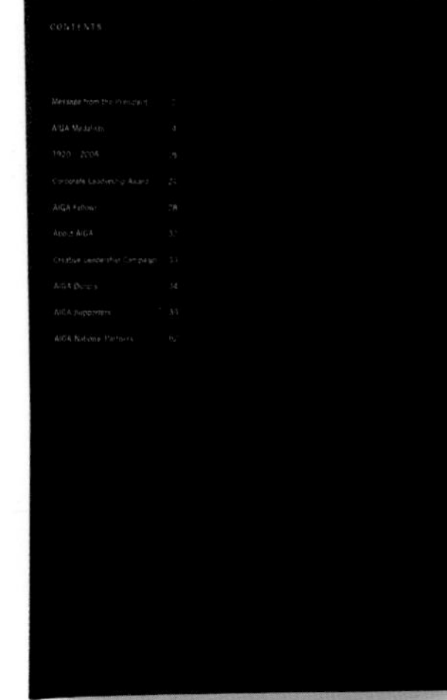

The Design Legends Gala is a nascent tradition, in only its second year, and already a celebratory occasion for all who respect the importance of the great design legacy. The gala is an opportunity for the community of designers to gather and honor those who have come before and whose creativity, inspiration, innovation and brilliant execution have defined the profession and every young designer's ambitions. This is an event where old friendships are renewed, new friendships are created and everyone is in awe of the sheer talent of the design profession.
AIGA

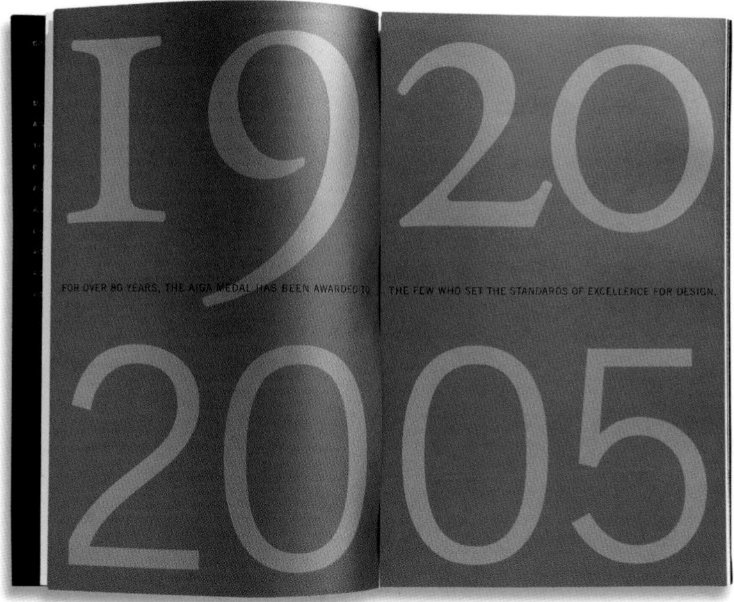

1920
2005
FOR OVER 80 YEARS, THE AIGA MEDAL HAS BEEN AWARDED TO THE FEW WHO SET THE STANDARDS OF EXCELLENCE FOR DESIGN.

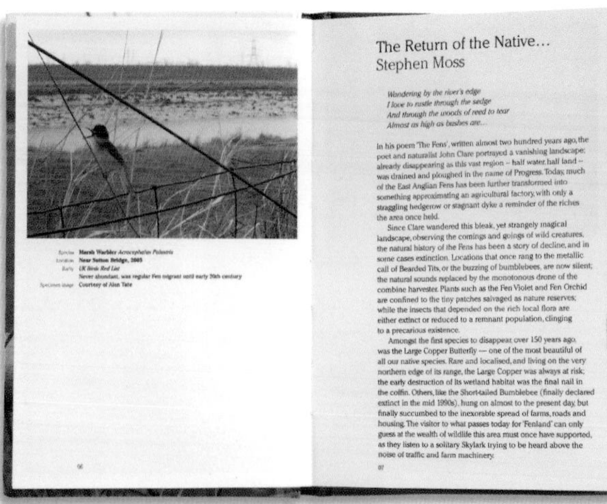

RB-M

Suky Best/
Artist's Publication

Designer:
Richard Bonner-Morgan

Client:
Film & Video Umbrella

Software:
QuarkXPress

Paper/Materials:
Neptune Unique, Fenner Paper

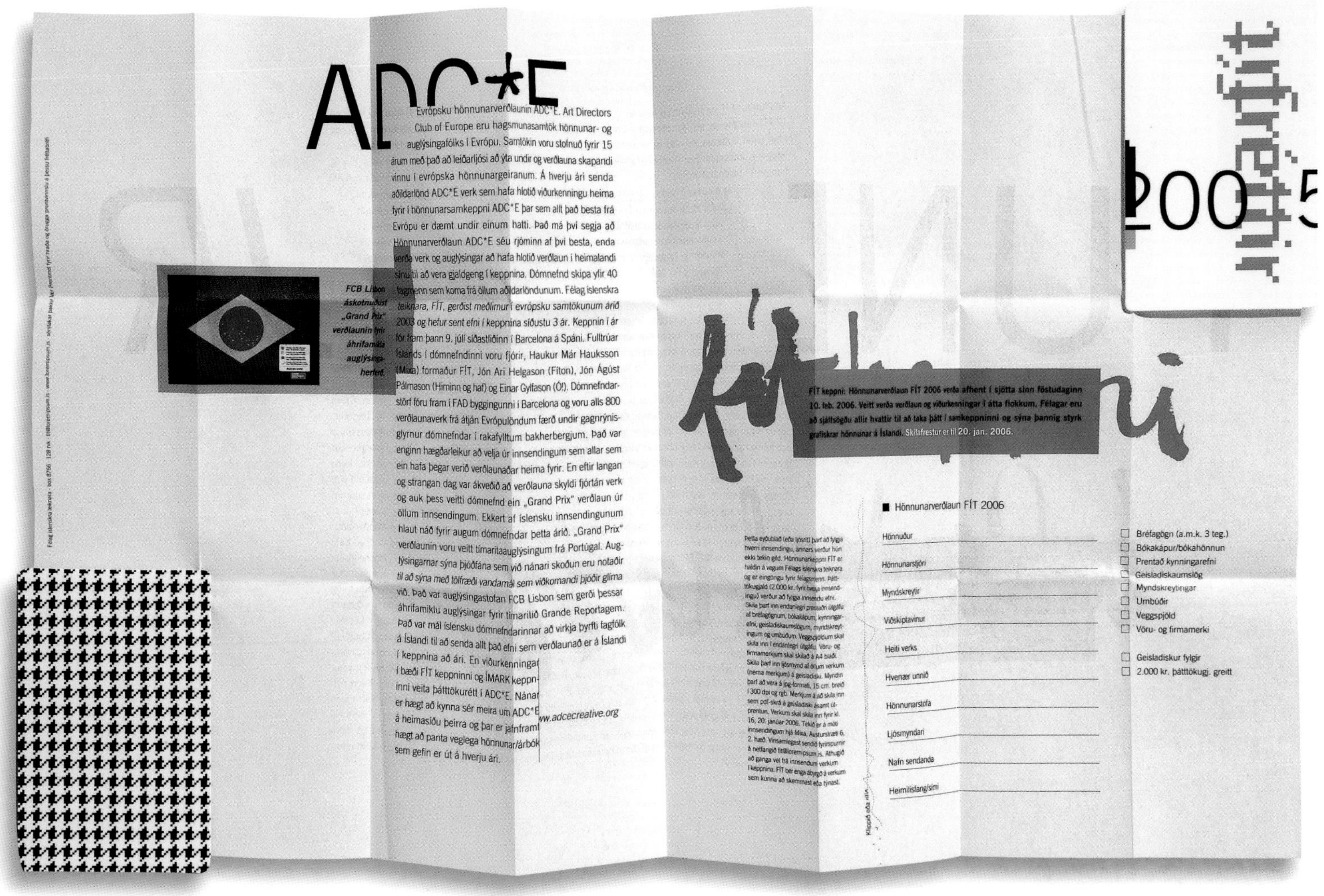

ADC*E

Evrópsku hönnunarverðlaunin ADC*E. Art Directors Club of Europe eru hagsmunasamtök hönnunar- og auglýsingafólks í Evrópu. Samtökin voru stofnuð fyrir 15 árum með það að leiðarljósi að ýta undir og verðlauna skapandi vinnu í evrópska hönnunargeiranum. Á hverju ári senda aðildarlönd ADC*E verk sem hafa hlotið viðurkenningu heima fyrir í hönnunarsamkeppni ADC*E þar sem allt það besta frá Evrópu er dæmt undir einum hatti. Það má því segja að Hönnunarverðlaun ADC*E séu rjóminn af því besta, enda verða verk og auglýsingar að hafa hlotið verðlaun í heimalandi sínu til að vera gjaldgeng í keppnina. Dómnefnd skipa yfir 40 fagmenn sem koma frá öllum aðildarlöndunum. Félag íslenskra teiknara, FÍT, gerðist meðlimur í evrópsku samtökunum árið 2003 og hefur sent efni í keppnina síðustu 3 ár. Keppnin í ár fór fram þann 9. júlí síðastliðinn í Barcelona á Spáni. Fulltrúar Íslands í dómnefndinni voru fjórir, Haukur Már Hauksson (Mixa) formaður FÍT, Jón Ari Helgason (Fíton), Jón Ágúst Pálmason (Himinn og haf) og Einar Gylfason (Ó!). Dómnefndarstörf fóru fram í FAD byggingunni í Barcelona og voru alls 800 verðlaunaverk frá átján Evrópulöndum færð undir gagnrýnisglyrnur dómnefndar í rakafylltum bakherbergjum. Það var enginn hægðarleikur að velja úr innsendingum sem allar sem ein hafa þegar verið verðlaunaðar heima fyrir. En eftir langan og strangan dag var ákveðið að verðlauna skyldi fjórtán verk og auk þess veitti dómnefnd ein „Grand Prix" verðlaun úr öllum innsendingum. Ekkert af íslensku innsendingunum hlaut náð fyrir augum dómnefndar þetta árið. „Grand Prix" verðlaunin voru veitt tímaritaauglýsingum frá Portúgal. Auglýsingarnar sýna þjóðfána sem við nánari skoðun eru notaðir til að sýna með tölfræði vandamál sem viðkomandi þjóðir glíma við. Það var auglýsingastofan FCB Lisbon sem gerði þessar áhrifamiklu auglýsingar fyrir tímaritið Grande Reportagem. Það var mál íslensku dómnefndarinnar að virkja þyrfti fagfólk á Íslandi til að senda allt það efni sem verðlaunað er á Íslandi í keppnina að ári. En viðurkenningar í bæði FÍT keppninni og ÍMARK keppninni veita þátttökurétt í ADC*E. Nánar er hægt að kynna sér meira um ADC*E á heimasíðu þeirra og þar er jafnframt hægt að panta veglega hönnunar/árbók sem gefin er út á hverju ári.

ww.adcecreative.org

FCB Lisbon áskotnuðust „Grand Prix" verðlaunin fyrir áhrifamikla auglýsingaherferð.

FÍT keppni: Hönnunarverðlaun FÍT 2006 verða afhent í sjötta sinn föstudaginn 10. feb. 2006. Veitt verða verðlaun og viðurkenningar í átta flokkum. Félagar eru að sjálfsögðu allir hvattir til að taka þátt í samkeppninni og sýna þannig styrk grafískrar hönnunar á Íslandi. Skilafrestur er til 20. jan. 2006.

■ Hönnunarverðlaun FÍT 2006

Hönnuður

Hönnunarstjóri

Myndskreytir

Viðskiptavinur

Heiti verks

Hvenær unnið

Hönnunarstofa

Ljósmyndari

Nafn sendanda

Heimilisfang/sími

☐ Bréfagögn (a.m.k. 3 teg.)
☐ Bókakápur/bókahönnun
☐ Prentað kynningarefni
☐ Geisladiskaumslög
☐ Myndskreytingar
☐ Umbúðir
☐ Veggspjöld
☐ Vöru- og firmamerki

☐ Geisladiskur fylgir
☐ 2.000 kr. þátttökugj. greitt

Klippið eða rífið

2005

Ó!

Newsletter for FIT

Art Director:
Einar Gylfason
Designer:
Einar Gylfason
Client:
FIT, Association of Icelandic Graphic Designers
Software:
Freehand
Paper/Materials:
California duo 400 gr, Z-opaque W type R 50 gr

Time

and

U wordt van harte uitgenodigd voor de opening van

Who if not we should at least try to imagine the future of all this?

7 Episodes on (ex)changing Europe

Het beeldende kunstprogramma *Who if not we...?* bestaat uit zeven tentoonstellingen en aanvullende projecten in Europa en is speciaal ontwikkeld voor het kunst- en cultuurprogramma *Thinking Forward*, dat plaatsvindt in het kader van het Nederlands voorzitterschap van de Europese Unie.

Thinking Forward bestaat uit diverse culturele activiteiten in Nederland en in de tien nieuwe lidstaten van de EU, en is een initiatief van het Ministerie van Buitenlandse Zaken en het Ministerie van Onderwijs, Cultuur en Wetenschap.
Het programma is ontwikkeld in opdracht van het Fonds voor Amateurkunst en Podiumkunsten, en de Mondriaan Stichting.

In het Stedelijk Museum CS in Amsterdam opent het programma met de tentoonstelling

Who if not we...? episode 2
Time and Again

op vrijdag 22 oktober 2004, van 17.00-19.30 uur.

Deelnemende kunstenaars:

Little Warsaw
Ján Mančuška
Deimantas Narkevičius
Paulina Olowska
Roman Ondák
Tadej Pogačar
Wilhelm Sasnal

De door Artimo uitgegeven publicatie *Who if not we...?* presenteert belangrijke artistieke en filosofische posities die ingaan op de culturele dimensies van de huidige politieke realiteit in (voornamelijk) Europa.

Tijdens de opening vindt om 18.30 uur de presentatie van het boek plaats.

Stedelijk Museum CS

Oosterdokskade 5
1011 AD Amsterdam

Dagelijks open:
10.00-18.00 uur
donderdag tot 21.00 uur
www.stedelijk.nl

Op vertoon van deze uitnodiging toegang voor twee personen.

Garderobe op de 2e verdieping

Wij wijzen u erop dat bij het Post CS-gebouw geen parkeergelegenheid is.

* thinkingforward

EU 2004

Ontwerp uitnodiging
Experimental Jetset 2004
Drukwerk robstolk (r)

EXPERIMENTAL JETSET

Time and Again

Art Director:
Experimental Jetset
Designer:
Experimental Jetset
Client:
Stedelijk Museum

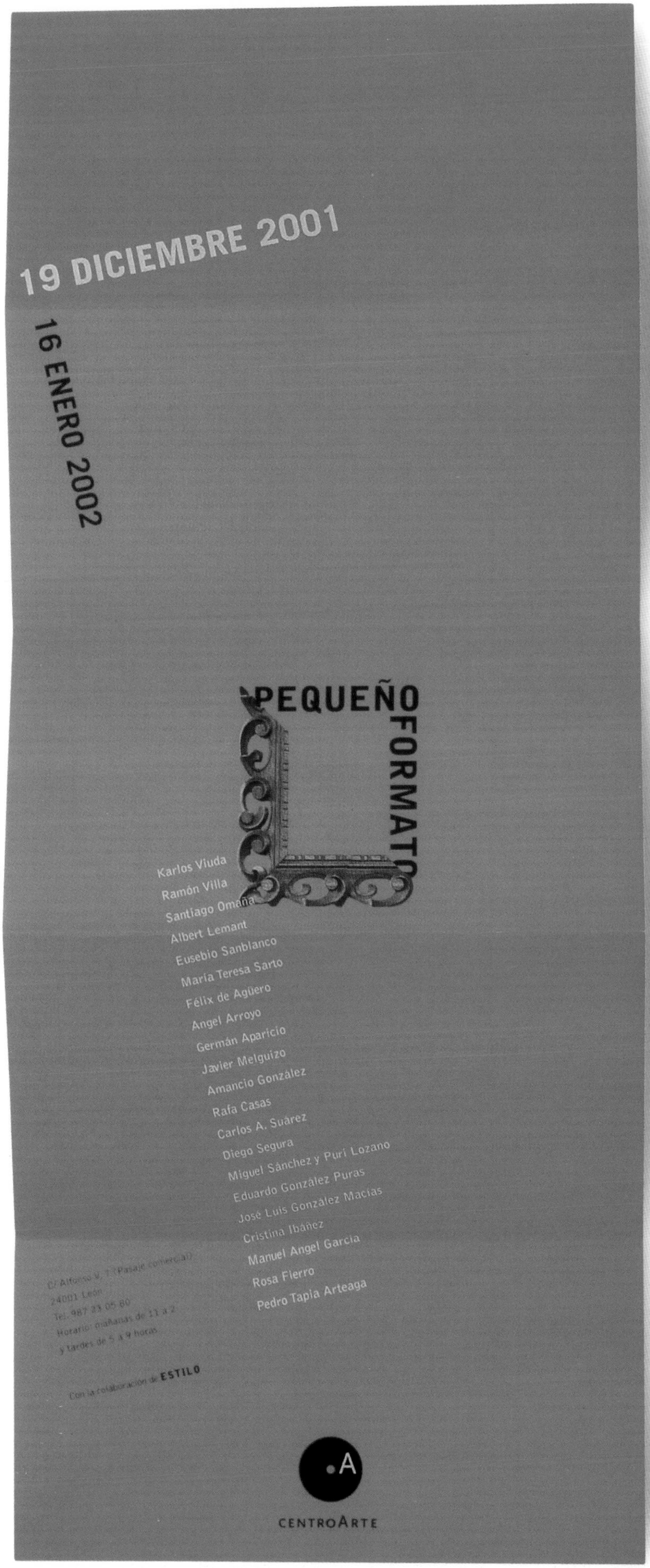

19 DICIEMBRE 2001

16 ENERO 2002

PEQUEÑO FORMATO

Karlos Viuda
Ramón Villa
Santiago Omaña
Albert Lemant
Eusebio Sanblanco
María Teresa Sarto
Félix de Agüero
Angel Arroyo
Germán Aparicio
Javier Melguizo
Amancio González
Rafa Casas
Carlos A. Suárez
Diego Segura
Miguel Sánchez y Puri Lozano
Eduardo González Puras
José Luis González Macías
Cristina Ibáñez
Manuel Angel García
Rosa Fierro
Pedro Tapia Arteaga

C/ Alfonso V, 1 (Pasaje comercial)
24001 León
Tel. 987 23 05 80
Horario: mañanas de 11 a 2
y tardes de 5 a 9 horas

Con la colaboración de ESTILO

•A
CENTROARTE

LSD
Promotional Pamphlets for an Art Gallery

Art Directors: Sonia Díaz, Gabriel Martínez
Designers: Sonia Díaz, Gabriel Martínez
Client: Centroarte
Software: Adobe Photoshop, Freehand
Paper/Materials: Offset on different papers

¿Cómo puede ocurrir que lo que subyuga nuestra imaginación, disguste a nuestros ojos? DIDEROT

La primera vez que abordé la obra de EB -ahora hace un año- realicé algunas consideraciones sobre el ascetismo de su mirada, que limitaba los materiales y reducía los elementos puestos en juego en su trabajo pictórico.

Me llamó la atención su texto explicativo "Apuntes sobre pespuntes", en el que mostraba la capacidad de reflexionar sobre su propia obra y en el que aludía a un cierto grado cero barthesiano de su trabajo, como un proceso abierto y en revisión. Frente a la tentación creciente del exceso expresivo y de la acumulación de significados, me llamó poderosamente la atención ese ejercicio de contención que emparenta con la sentencia de Mies van der Rohe "Less is more". Navegar hoy, además, en aguas de la abstracción geométrica en tiempos presididos por otros rumbos neofigurativos o por otras rumbos sin norte alguno, era, tal vez, un síntoma de osadía marinera o un propósito descabellado, que no restaban rigor y misterio a un proceso en formación y a un trabajo enraizado en las experiencias de los Neoplasticistas holandeses y en los Suprematistas soviéticos de la segunda década del siglo.

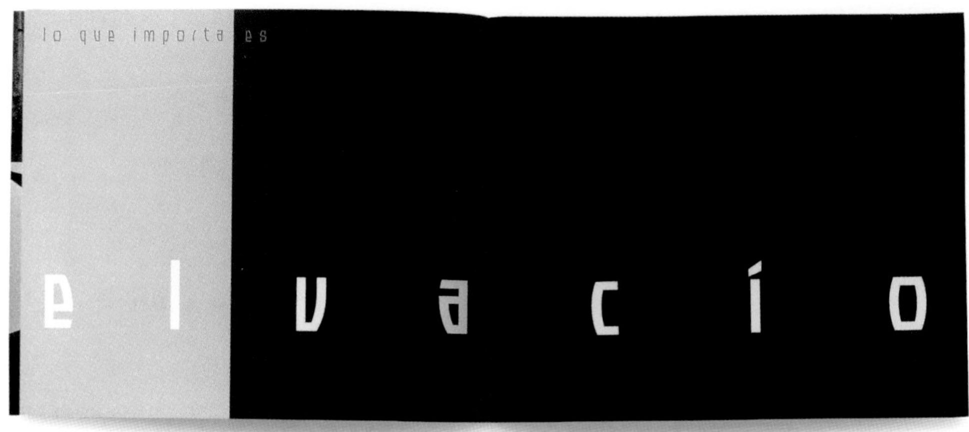
lo que importa es
el vacío

LSD
Artist's Promotional Brochure

Art Directors:
Sonia Díaz,
Gabriel Martínez
Designers:
Sonia Díaz,
Gabriel Martínez
Client:
Eduardo Barco
Software:
Adobe Photoshop,
Freehand
Paper/Materials:
Offset

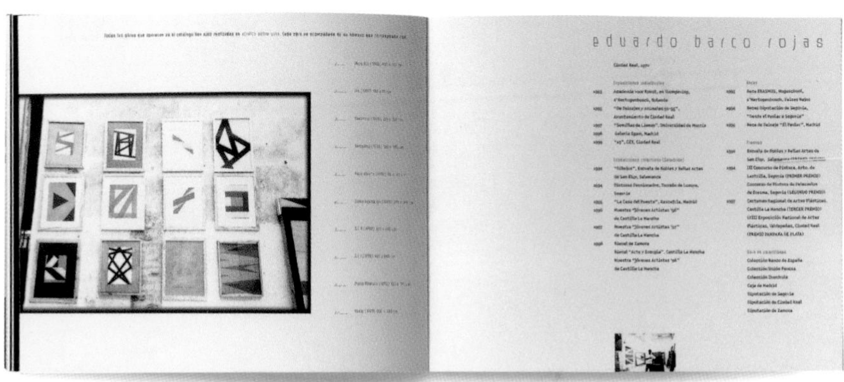
eduardo barco rojas

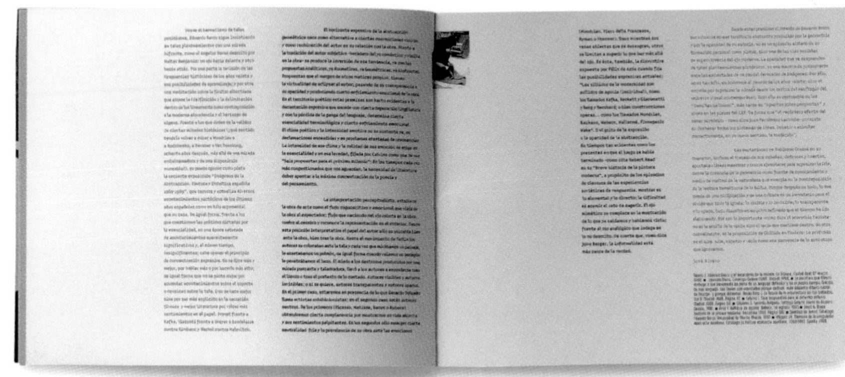

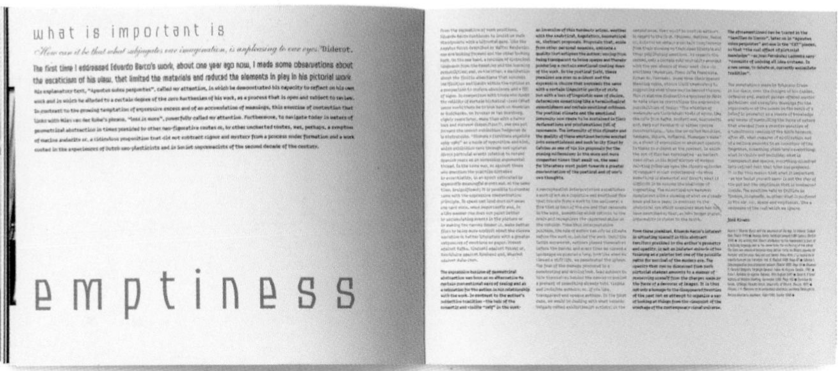
what is important is
emptiness

LSD

Brochure for a Country Hotel

Art Director:
Gabriel Martínez
Designer:
Gabriel Martínez
Client:
El Milano Real
Software:
Freehand
Paper/Materials:
Offset

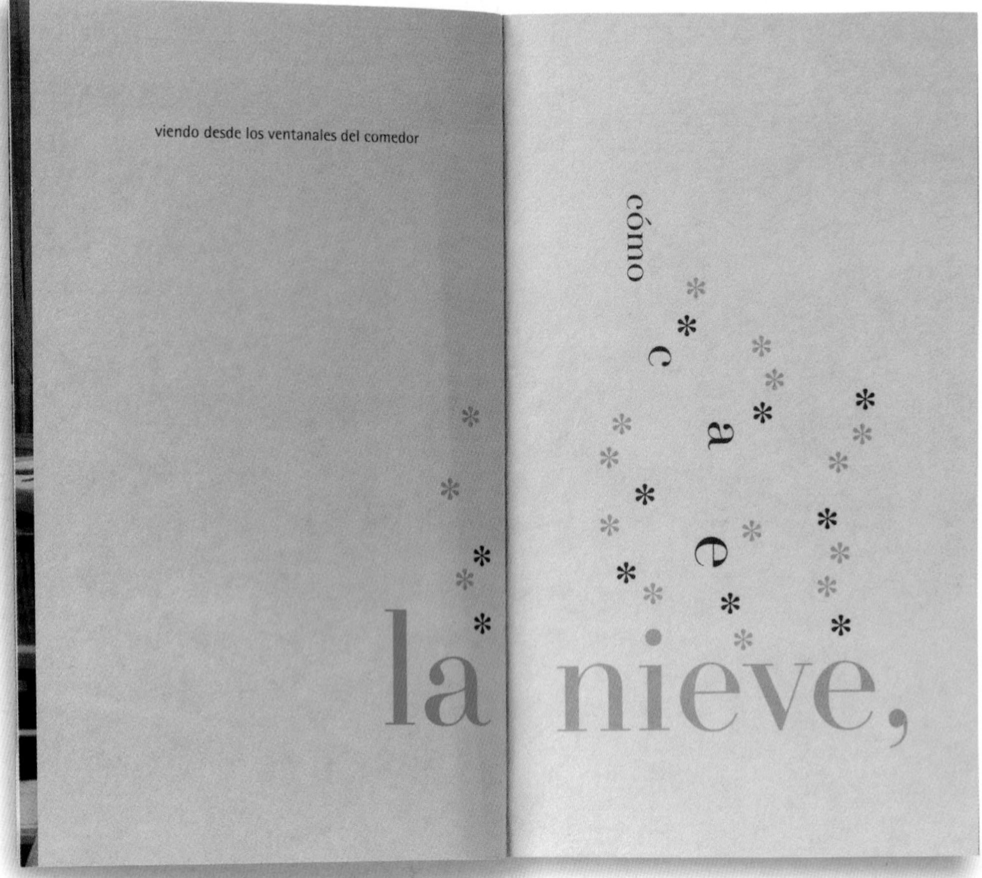

FIREBELLY DESIGN

Artist/Nonprofit Brochure

Art Director:
Dawn Hancock
Designers:
Dawn Hancock, Brent Maynard
Client:
Anchor Graphics/JET
Software:
Adobe Photoshop, Adobe Illustrator, Adobe InDesign
Paper/Materials:
Sappi McCoy Velvet

ANCHOR GRAPHICS

Anchor Graphics

Anchor Graphics works in the areas of visual arts and arts education for youth, adult, and professional artists. We are a community-based nonprofit printshop and gallery that brings together, under professional guidance, a diverse community of youth, emerging and established artists, and the public to advance the fine art of printmaking by integrating education with the creation of prints. For over fourteen years, Anchor Graphics has offered educational programs, exhibitions, and artist services revolving around the history and practice of printmaking. Anchor Graphics is a printshop, which functions as both a classroom and an atelier, fulfilling the need for affordable access to a properly equipped shop, while maintaining a focus on education within a professional artistic environment. As a non-profit organization, our ethos is three-fold. First, Anchor Graphics maintains an environment in which artists of all experience and age levels are welcome, encouraged to explore and be innovative with the printmaking medium, and supported in realizing their own creative visions. We offer open studio time that allows artists of various skill levels to work under the guidance of master printers, and an Artist-in-Residency program that brings experienced artist/printmakers from across the country to Chicago to share their knowledge and work. Second, Anchor Graphics mentors Chicagoland area youth. By introducing them to printmaking and educating them in the discipline through Press-On-Wheels workshops and high school classes, we are equipping them with fundamental life tools. Through the creation of original images and the running of professional hand presses we are teaching young people the value of cooperation and sequential planning. All of our high school classes and workshops are free to the students. We also hire interns from various colleges every year and train them in all aspects of running a nonprofit printshop and gallery. Finally, we are committed to educating the community at large about printmaking. Through exhibitions, lectures, demonstrations, and adult classes we are making this art form accessible to anyone who wishes to learn about printmaking's process and history.

04 + 05 / 48

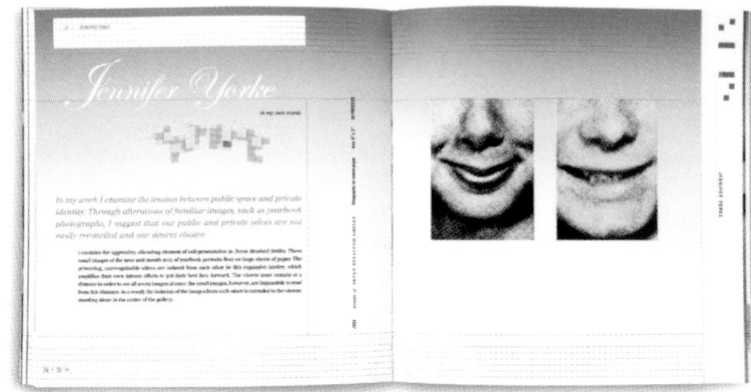

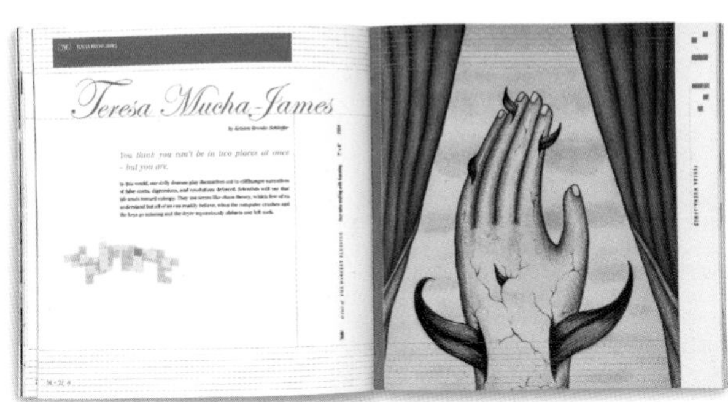

RUSSELL
WARREN-FISHER
21 Years of Complicite

Designer:
Russell Warren-Fisher
Client:
Complicite
Software:
QuarkXPress,
Adobe Photoshop

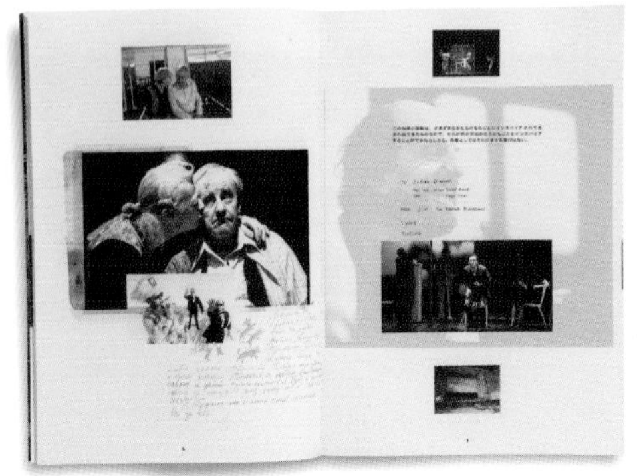

NB:STUDIO

What Is Craft?

Art Directors:
Nick Finney, Ben Stott,
Alan Dye
Designer:
Jodie Whiteman
Client:
The Hub

hub
WHAT IS CRAFT ?
Maker
Mary Butcher
Name of Nominator
Geraldine Rudge, Editor, Crafts
Title
Willow Line
Date
2003
Materials
Willow
26
Your choice?
Mary Butcher's 'Willow Line' gives traditional materials a contemporary form.The rhythmic patterns of basketwork have been abstracted into something fresh, eye-catching but at the same time pleasingly familiar.
What is Craft?
Craft is simply skill. It plays a role in every visual art from painting to product design. There was a time when craft was seen only as handwork and restricted to the making of functional objects. In the new millennium it is resuming its older role, flowing happily over boundaries between fine and applied arts.

NB:STUDIO
Schweppes Photographic Portrait Prize

Art Directors:
Nick Finney, Ben Stott, Alan Dye
Designer:
Ian Pierce
Client:
National Portrait Gallery

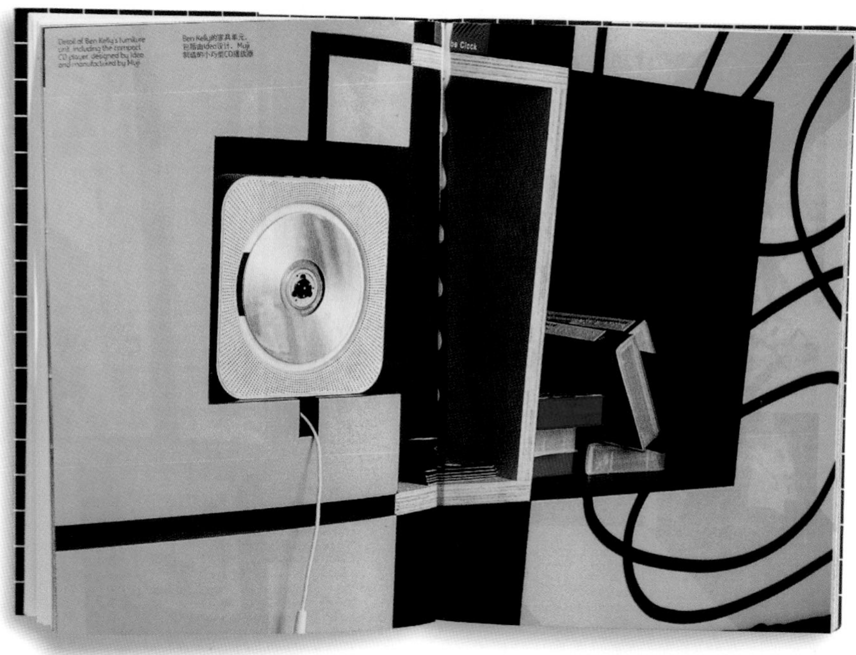

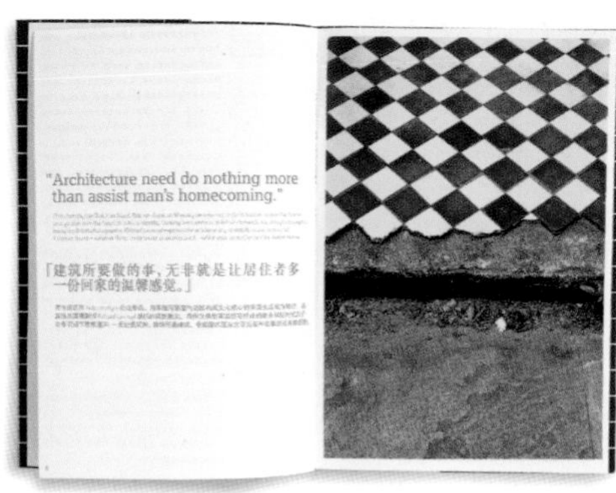

STUDIO MYERSCOUGH
Hometime

Art Director:
Morag Myerscough
Designer:
Morag Myerscough
Photographer:
Richard Learoyd
Client:
British Council

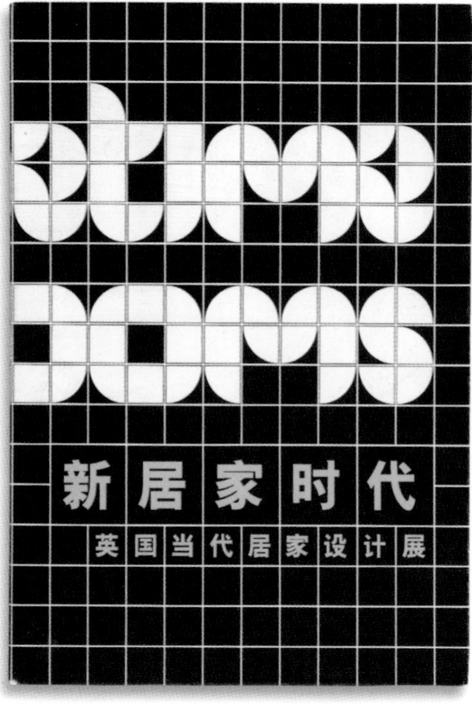

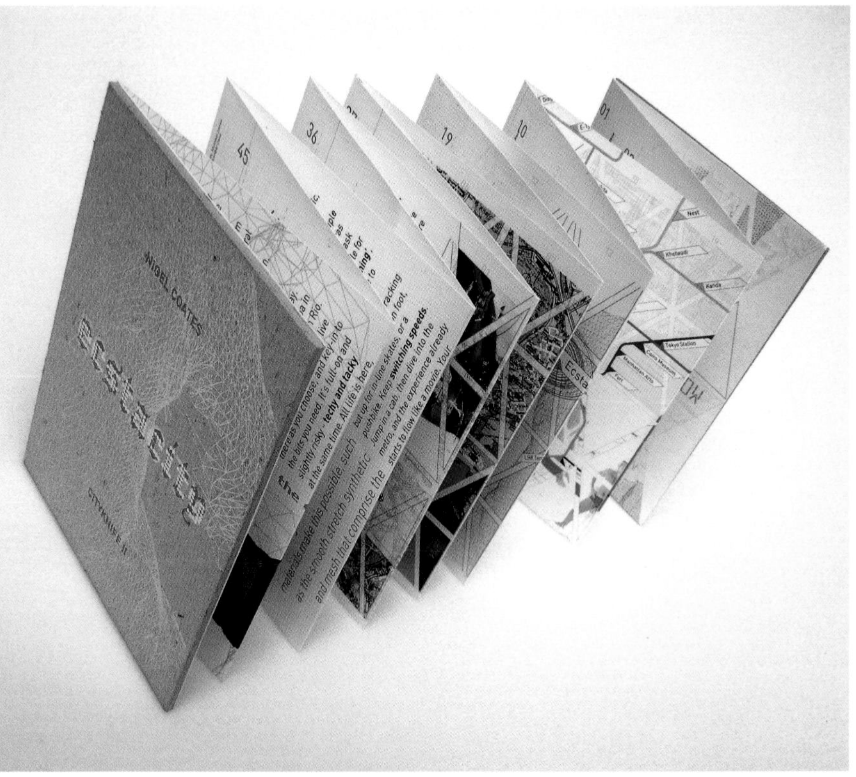

THE NIKE
CITYKNIFE II
THE
PERFECT
SHOE TO
WEAR IN

WHY NOT ASSOCIATES
Nike City Knife

Client:
Nike UK
Software:
Freehand MX

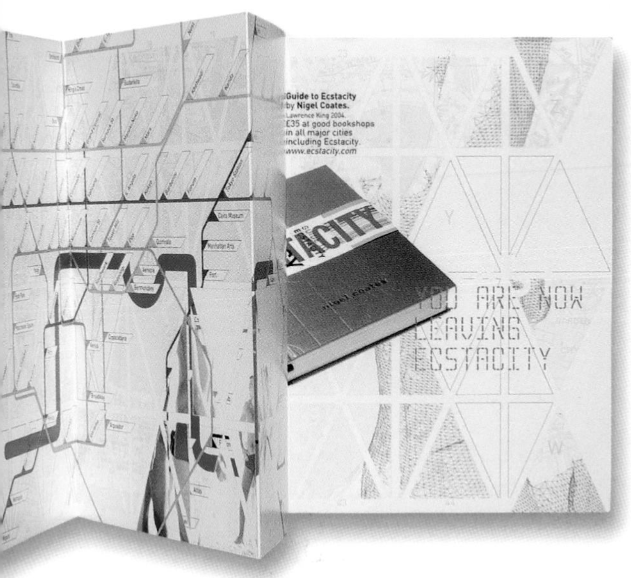

PENTAGRAM
DESIGN, BERLIN
Mozarthaus Vienna Program

Art Director:
Justus Oehler
Designers:
Justus Oehler,
Josephine Rank
Client:
Mozarthaus Vienna
Software:
QuarkXPress
Paper/Materials:
Munken Lynx

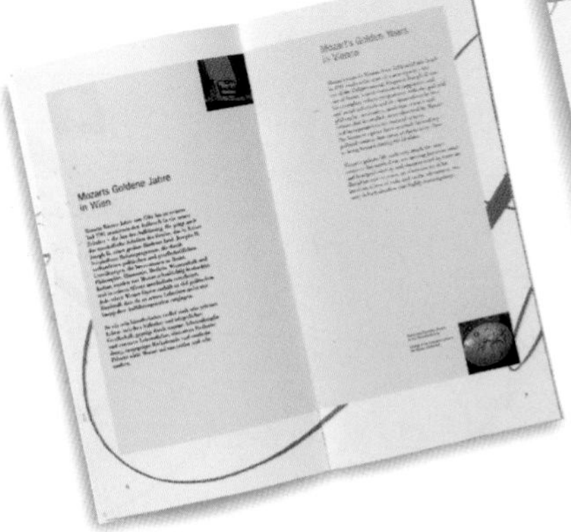

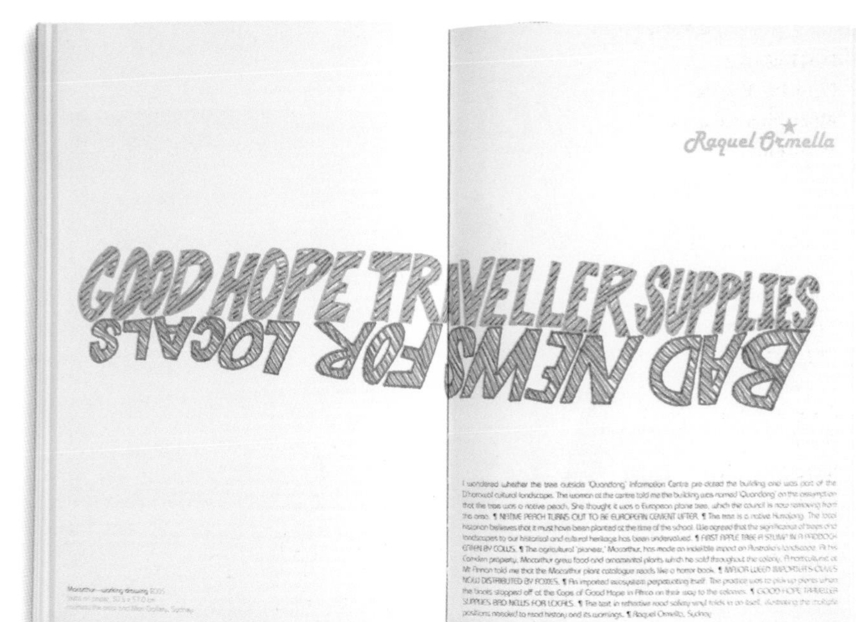

BOCCALATTE
C Town Bling Catalog

Art Director: Suzanne Boccalatte
Client: Campbelltown Arts Centre
Software: Adobe Creative Suite
Paper/Materials: Monza Foil Stamp

mattress is a threshold to sleep upon / a strange quilted force / of softening matters / and everlasting springs / a cushion for the body's travels through the times of night / at whichever hour / off the ground / off the floor / a place for yonder life / an island for refuge and panic and trauma and fatigue / a site of unimagined grief and imagined love / a thing / an artful object for flesh and blood and thought to spread like animals / adrift / falling from nowhere in divine-particular / just here / this moment / falling into rage or calm / eyes closed and seeing / infinite operas / wondrous vistas / delicate gifts subtle dangers embracing voids / dying for hours / or maybe not / instead / wide-awake / nerve ends razor-sharp / feverish / the ill or joyful creature gushes leaks seeps moults rubs squeezes / leaving itself like a ghost on the surface and more ghostly still below the surface / on the mythical heart of the thing's patience / its exact presence / weight depth length width / the body descends willingly / becomes threshold too / abandoning its own heart-dream / each laboured mattress made of earth substances pulled to light / for unprecedented passioned and dispassioned touches / the mattress-cosmos awaits something-to-come / and it does / birth / death / and every minute betwixt state / even now at this late hour / an image of it / refuge as refuse / excessive in its worn broken luxuriance / a desert / deserted / recorded / presented / simply saying 'I am'

VOICE
Photographic Exhibition Catalog

Art Director:
Scott Carslake
Designer:
Scott Carslake
Client:
Toby Richardson
Software:
Adobe InDesign, Photoshop
Paper/Materials:
Paper by Daltons, Process Color, Saddle Stitch

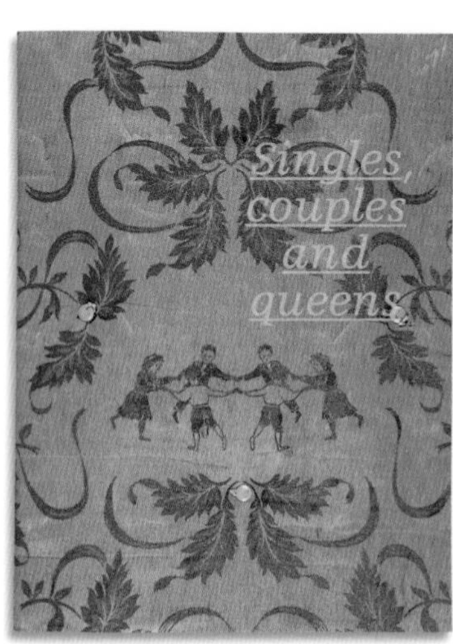

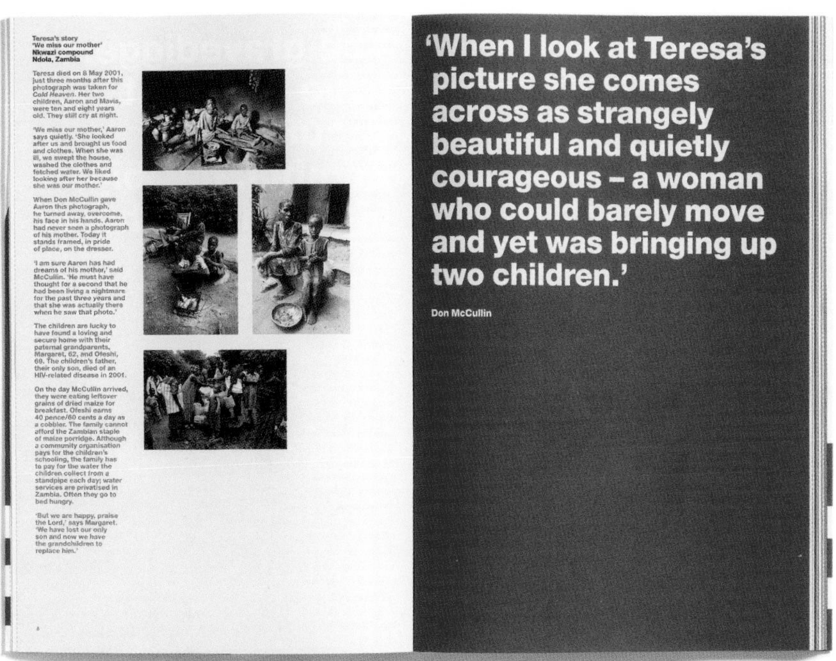

Teresa's story
'We miss our mother'
Nkwazi compound
Ndola, Zambia

Teresa died on 8 May 2001, just three months after this photograph was taken for *Cold Heaven*. Her two children, Aaron and Mavis, were ten and eight years old. They still cry at night.

'We miss our mother,' Aaron says quietly. 'She looked after us and brought us food and clothes. When she was ill, we swept the house, washed the clothes and fetched water. We liked looking after her because she was our mother.'

When Don McCullin gave Aaron this photograph, he turned away, overcome, his face in his hands. Aaron had never seen a photograph of his mother. Today it stands framed, in pride of place, on the dresser.

'I am sure Aaron has had dreams of his mother,' said McCullin. 'He must have thought for a second that he had been living a nightmare for the past three years and that she was actually there when he saw that photo.'

The children are lucky to have found a loving and secure home with their paternal grandparents, Margaret, 62, and Ofeshi, 69. The children's father, their only son, died of an HIV-related disease in 2001.

On the day McCullin arrived, they were eating leftover grains of dried maize for breakfast. Ofeshi earns 40 pence/60 cents a day as a cobbler. The family cannot afford the Zambian staple of maize porridge. Although a community organisation pays for the children's schooling, the family has to pay for the water the children collect from a standpipe each day; water services are privatised in Zambia. Often they go to bed hungry.

'But we are happy, praise the Lord,' says Margaret. 'We have lost our only son and now we have the grandchildren to replace him.'

'When I look at Teresa's picture she comes across as strangely beautiful and quietly courageous – a woman who could barely move and yet was bringing up two children.'

Don McCullin

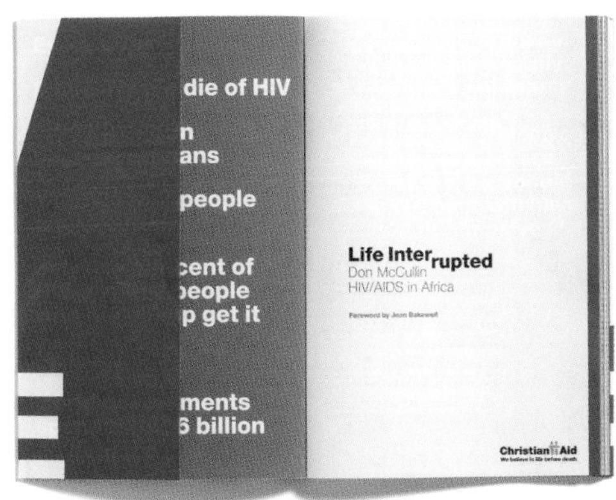

LIPPA PEARCE

"Life Interrupted" Catalog for Don McCulin Exhibition

Art Director:
Harry Pearce
Designer:
Harry Pearce
Client:
Christian Aid

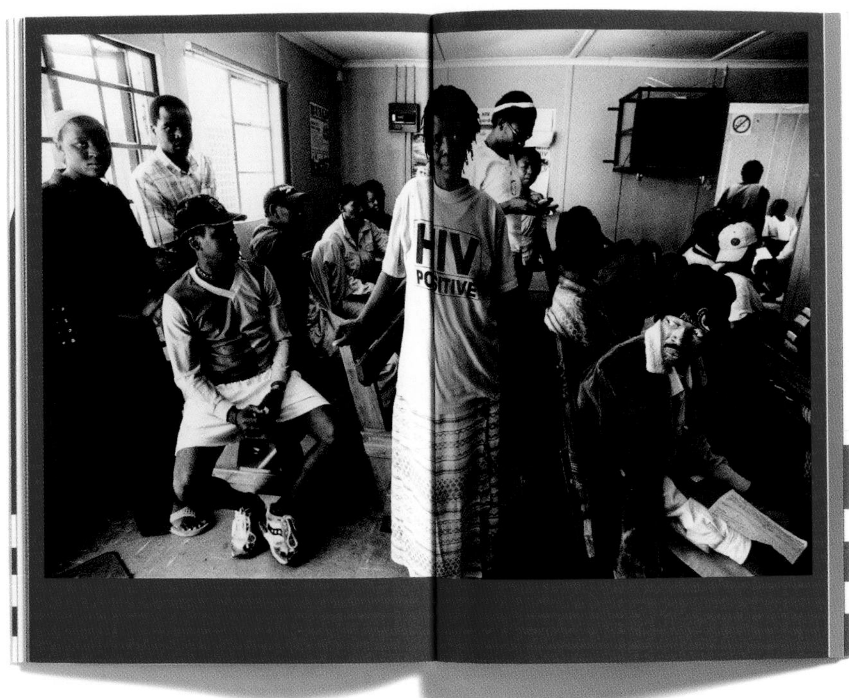

PENTAGRAM DESIGN, LONDON

Ballpoint

Art Director: Angus Hyland

Client: Parker Pens

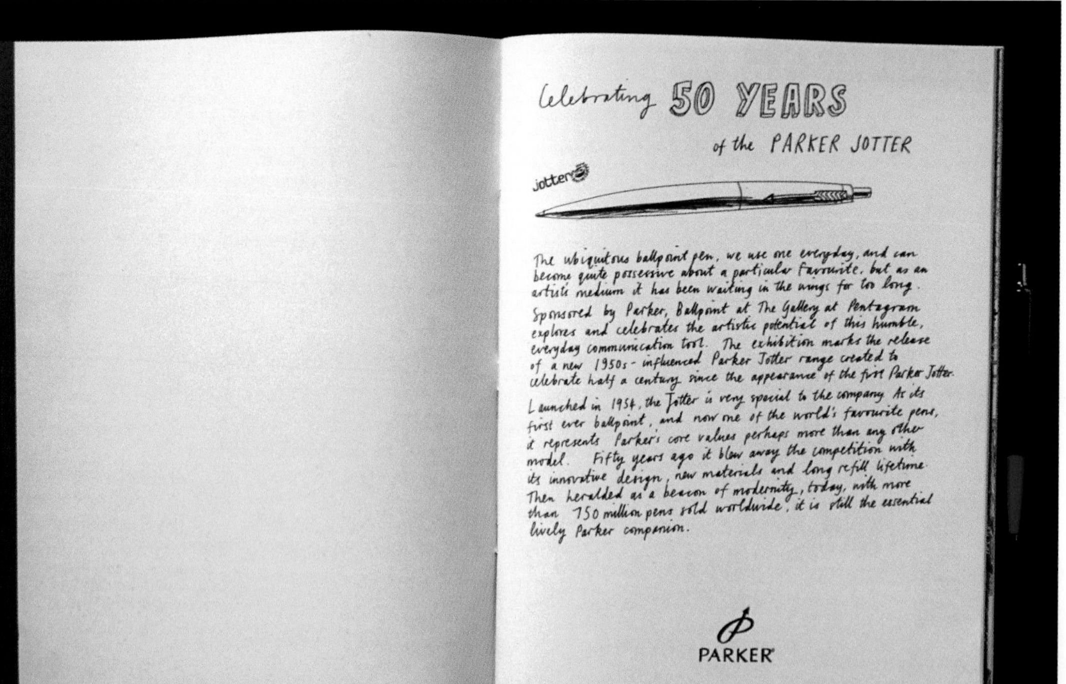

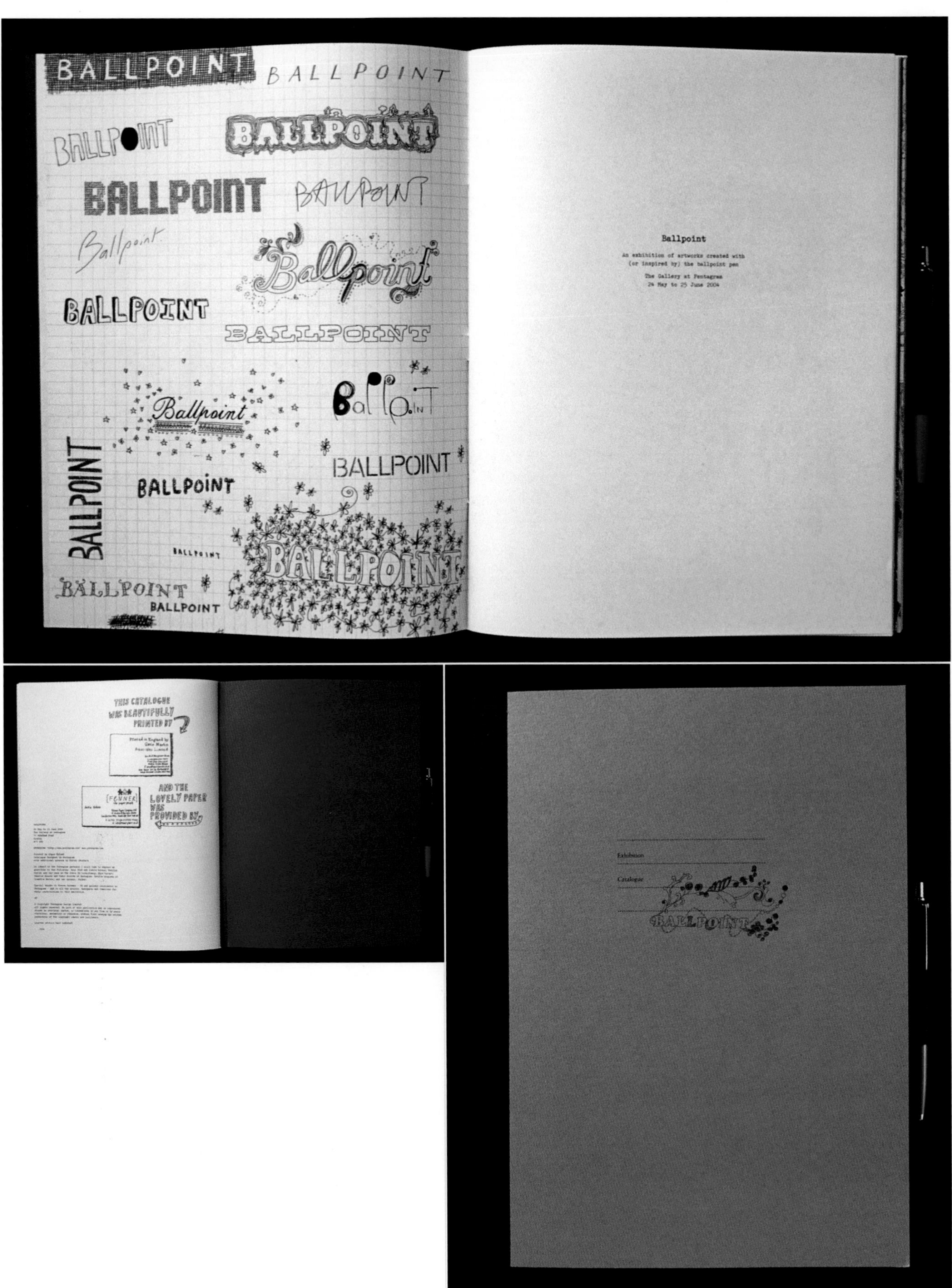
BALLPOINT
Ballpoint
An exhibition of artworks created with
(or inspired by) the ballpoint pen
The Gallery at Pentagram
24 May to 25 June 2004
THIS CATALOGUE WAS BEAUTIFULLY PRINTED BY
AND THE LOVELY PAPER WAS PROVIDED BY
Exhibition
Catalogue
BALLPOINT

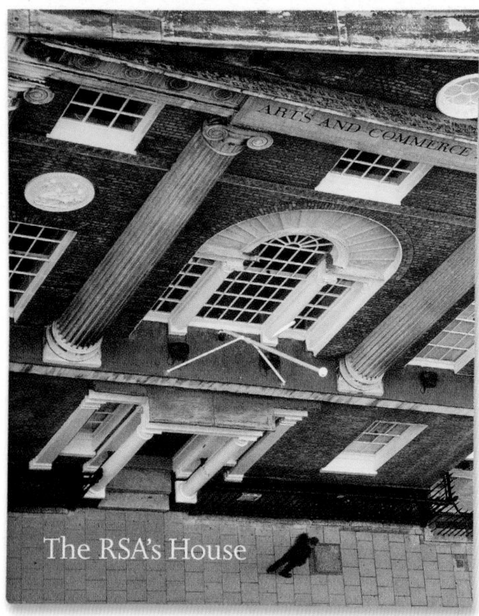

ATELIER WORKS

RSA House Guide

Art Director:
Ian Chilvers
Designer:
Ian Chilvers
Client:
Royal Society of Arts
Software:
QuarkXPress

directory of contributors

2D3D
Mauritskade 1
Den Haag 2514 HC, The Netherlands

300 Million
1 Rosoman Place
London EC1R OJY, UK

After Hours Creative
5444 E. Washington, Suite 3
Phoenix, AZ 85034

Ajans Ultra
Aslan Yatagis.Feza ap.33/1/12, 80060 Cihangir
Istanbul 80060, Turkey

Allegro 168
150 Cathcart Street
Ottawa, Ontario K1N 5B8, Canada

Allemann Almquist & Jones
301 Cherry Street, 3rd floor
Philadelphia, PA 19106

Aloof Design
5 Fisher Street
Lewes, East Sussex, BN7 2DG, UK

Alterpop
1001 Mariposa Street #204
San Francisco, CA 94107

And Partners
158 West 27th Street Floor 7
New York, NY 10001

Antfarm Inc.

Arias Associates
502 Waverley Street
Palo Alto, CA 94301

Aspen Interactive
7036 Park Drive
New Port Richey, FL 34652

Atelier Works
The Old Piano Factory, 5 Charlton Kings Road
London NW5 2SB, UK

Bakken Creative Co.
801 Clay Street
Oakland, CA 94607

Bandujo Donker & Brothers
22 West 19th Street, 9th floor
New York, NY 10011

BBK Studio
648 Monroe NW, Suite 212
Grand Rapids, MI 49503

BC, MH James Lambert
32 Sunbury Workshops, Swanfield St
London E2 7LF, UK

Billy Blue Creative, Precinct
PO Box 728 North Sydney
NSW 2059, Australia

Bisqit Design
5 Theobalds Road
London WC1X 8SH, UK

Blackletter Design Inc.
Wigan Road, Ashton-in-Marketfield
Wigan, WN4 9SU Manchester, UK

Bloch + Coulter Design Group
2440 S. Sedelveda Blvd. #152
Los Angeles, CA 90064

Blok Design
822 Richmond Street West, Suite 301
Toronto, ON M6J 1C9, Canada

Boccalatte
Studio 43.61 Marlborough Street
Surrey Hills, Sydney, NSW 2010, Australia

Bolt
1415 South Church Street
Charlotte, NC 28227

Brunazzi & Associati
22 Via Andorno
Torino, 10153 Italy

Buro 7
Humboldstrasse 64
Bremen 28203, Germany

Cacao Design

Cahan & Associates
171 Second Street, 5th floor
San Francisco, CA 94105

Cartlidge Levene
238 St Johns Street
EC1V 4PH London, UK

Cem Erutku Tasarim Studyosu
Tarilk Zafer Tunayasok
3/6 Gunussuyu, Istanbol, Turkey

CF Napa

Cheng Design
University of Washington, box 353440, art building room 102
Seattle, WA 98195

Clarity Coverdale Fury
120 South 6th Street, Suite 1300
Minneapolis, MN 55402

Clark Creative Group
251 Rhode Island Street #204
San Francisco, CA 94103

Country Companies Design Services
1711 GE Road
Blooming, IL 61701

Cox Design
5196 Hummingbird Road
Pleasanton, CA 94566

Creative Conspiracy, Inc.
862 Main Avenue, Suite 850
Durango, CO 81301

Cross Colours Ink
8 Eastwood Road
Dunkeld West 2196 Johannesburg, South Africa

CSAA Creative Services
100 Van Ness Avenue
San Francisco, CA 94102

Design Asylum PTE LTD
46B Club Street
Singapore 069423

Design Project
Round Foundry Media Centre, Unit G15, Foundry St
Leeds LS11 5QP, UK

Dinnick & Howells
2943 Markham Street
Toronto, Ontario M6J 296, Canada

Doppio Design
25 Rosemary Avenue, Oranjezicht
Cape Town 8001 South Africa

Dowling Design & Art Direction
Navigation House, 48 Millgate
Newark, NG24 4TS, UK

Edelman Public Relations Worldwide
636 Broadway Suite 707
New York, NY 10012

Elfen
Ty Meandros, 54A Bute Street
Cardiff Bay CF10 5A5, UK

Emerson, Wajdowicz Studios
1123 Broadway, Suite 1106
New York, NY 10010

Emery Vincent Design
15 Foster Street, level 1, Surrey Hills
Sydney NSW 2010, Australia

Erbe Design
1500 Oxley Street
South Pacadena, CA 91030

Experimental JetSet
Jan Hanzenstraat 37, 1st floor
1053 SK Amsterdam, The Netherlands

Fabio Ongarato Design
569 Church Street
Richmond, Victoria 3121, Australia

Fauxpas
Hardturmstrasse.261
Zurich CH 8005, Switzerland

Firebelly Design
2701 W Thomas, 2nd floor
Chicago, IL 60622

Fitch
10350 Olentangy River Road
Worthington, OH 43085

Flight Creative
117.5 S. Union Street
Traverse City, MI 49684

Flore Van Ryn
7 Rue de la Seconde Reine
1180 Bruxelles, Belgium

Foco Media gmbh & cte
Spitzwegstr 6
Munich 81373 Germany

Fork Unstable Media GMBH
Juliusstrasse 25
Hamburg 22769, Germany

Form
47 Tabernacle Street
London EC2A 4AA, UK

Fossil
2280 N. Greenville Avenue
Richardson, TX 750082

Frost Design
The Gymnasium, Kings Way Place
Sans Walk, London EC1R 0LU, UK

Fuszion Collaborative
901 Prince Street
Alexandria, VA 22314

Gee + Chung Design
38 Bryant Street, Suite 100
San Francisco, CA 94105

Giorgio Rocco Communications
Via Domenichino 27
Milano 20149 Italy

Gollings & Pidgeon
147 Chapel Street
St. Kilda, Victoria, Australia

Graif Design
165 E. Highway CC
Nixa, MO 65714

Graphiculture
322 1st Avenue North, Suite 500
Minneapolis, MN 55401

Greenzweig Design
600 First Avenue, Suite 330
Seattle, WA 98104

Greteman Group
142 North Mosley
Wichita, KS 67202

Hallmark Loyalty
2501 Mcgee Street, Drop 19
Kansas City, MO 64108

Hand Made Group
Sartori, 16
52017 Stia, Italy

Hangar 18 Creative Group
220-137 West 3rd Avenue
Vancouver, BC, V6J 1K7, Canada

Hartford Design, Inc
954 W. Washington, 4th floor
Chicago, IL 60607

Hatch Creative
Suite 1, 147 Chapel Street, St Kilda
Melbourne, Victoria 3182, Australia

Hat-Trick Design
Studio 11, Clink Street Studios
1 Clink Street, London SE1, UK

Hebe.Werbung & Design
Magstadterstrasse 12
Leonberg 71229, Germany

HGV
2-6 Northburgh Street
London EC1V 0AY, UK

Hippo Studio
58 Queen's Road East
Wanchai, Hong Kong

Hornall Anderson Design Works, Inc.
1008 Western Avenue, Suite 600
Seattle, WA 98104

Howry Design Associates
354 Pine Street, #600
San Francisco, CA 94104

Huddleston Malone Design
56 Exchange Place
Salt Lake City, UT 84111

IAAH
727 Duffosat Street
New Orleans, LA 70115

ICO Design Consultancy
75-77 Great Portland Street
London W1W 7CR, UK

IE Design
1600 Rosecrans Avenue, Building 6B
Manhatten Beach, CA 90266

Imelda Agency
Poljanska cesta 25
SI-1000 Ljubljana, Slovenija

Inaria
270 Lafayette Street, Suite 906
New York, NY 10012

INOX Design
Via Terraggio II
Milan, Italy

Iridium
43 Eccles Street, 2nd floor
Ottawa, ON K1R 653, Canada

Kamper Brands
510 Washington Avenue, South
Minneapolis, MN 55415

Kan & Lau Design Consultants
28/F Great Smart Tower,
230 Wanchai Road, Hong Kong

Kerr/Noble
Studio 53, Pennybank Chambers
33-35 St. John's Square, London EC1M 4DS

Kesselskramer
Lauriegracht 39
Amsterdam 1016 RG, The Netherlands

Kinetic Singapore
2 Leng Kee Road Thye, Hong Centre
#04-03A Singapore 159086, Singapore

KO Creation
6300 Park Avenue, Suite 420
Montreal, QC H2V 2H8,Canada

Kolegram
37 St. Joseph Boulevard
Gatineau Quebec J8Y 3V8, Canada

LA Weekly
6715 Sunset Boulevard
Los Angeles, CA 90028

Lava Graphic Designers
Van Diemenstraat 366
1013CR Amsterdam, The Netherlands

Lead Dog Digital
245 E 25th Street 3J
New York, NY 10012

Lee Reedy Creative
1542 Williams Street
Denver, CO 80218

Lippa Pearce
358A Richmond Road
Twickenham TW1 2DU, UK

Liska & Associates, Inc
515 North State Street, 23rd floor
Chicago, IL 60610

Lloyds Graphic Design LTD
17 West 107th Street, apt 5W
New York, NY 10025

Lorenz Advertising
9320 Chesapeake Drive, #214
San Diego, CA 92123

Louey/Rubino Design Group Inc.
2525 Main Street, Suite 204
Santa Monica, CA 90405

Lowercase, Inc.
213 W. Institute Place, Suite 311
Chicago, IL 60610

LSD
San Andres, 36 2o P6
Madrid 28004, Spain

Made Thought
181 Cannon St Rd, 2nd floor
London E1 2LX, UK

Marius Fahrner Design
Suttnerstrasse 8
Hamburg 22767, Germany

Melissa Passehl Design
1275 Lincoln Avenue, Suite 7
San Jose, CA 95125

Metal
1210 West Clay Suite 17
Houston, TX 77019

Michael Courtney Design
121 East Boston
Seattle, WA 98102

Michael Patrick Partners
532 Emerson Street
Palo Alto, CA 94301

Michal Granit Design Studio
P.O. Box 303
Sdeh Varburg, 44935, Israel

Mike Lackersteen Design
35 Rochester Square
London NW1 9RZ, UK

Miriello Grafico Inc.
419 West 6 Street
San Diego, CA 92101, UK

Mirko Ilic Corp.
207 East 32nd Street
New York, NY 10016

Monster Design
3022 Commerce Street
Dallas, TX 75226

Musuem of Fine Arts, Boston
465 Huntington Avenue
Boston, MA 02215

Mutabor Design
Barnerstrasse 63/HOF
Hamburg 22765, Germany

Mytton Williams
15 St. James's Parade
Bath BA1 1UL, UK

NB: Studio
24 Store Street
London WC1E 7BA, UK

Nesnadny & Schwartz
10803 Magnolia Drive
Cleveland, OH 44106

Net Integrators - Net Design
Post Box 59016
Amsterdam 1040 KA, The Netherlands

Nina David KommunikationsDesign
Nierderkassler Kirchweg 56
Duesseldorf 40547, Germany

No.Parking

O!
Armuli 11
Reykjavik 108, Iceland

Oden Marketing and Design
22 N. Street, Suite 300
Memphis, TN 38103

Oh Boy, A Design Company
49 Geary Street, Suite 530
San Francisco, CA 94108

Palmquist Creative
P.O. Box 325
Bozeman, MT 59771

Paula Kelly Design
164 Fifth Avenue
New York, NY 10010

Pentagram Design/ Berlin
Leibnizstrasse 60
Berlin 10629, Germany

Pentagram Design/ London
11 Needham Road
London W11 2RP, UK

Pentagram Design/SF
387 Tehama Street
San Francisco, CA 94103

Pepe Gimeno- Proyecto Grafico
C/Cadiers, s.n. Pol. D'Oradors
Godella, Valencia E-46110, Spain

Perks Design Partners

Ping-Pong Design
Rochussenstraat 400
3015 ZC Rotterdam, The Netherlands

Popcorn Initiative
1602 Robin Road
Orlando, FL 32803

Poulin + Morris
286 Springs Street, 6th floor
New York, NY 10013

Q
Sonnenbergerstrasse 16
Wiesbaden 65193, Germany

Radley Yeldar
326 City Road
London ECN 2SP, UK

RB-M
100 De Beauvoir Road
London N1 4EN, UK

Rose Design Associates
30 Great Guildford Street
London SE1 0HS, UK

Russell Warren-Fisher
Beech House, Bradford Road
Hawthorn, Wiltshire, UK

Ruth Huimerind

Sagenvier Design Kommunikation
Sagerstrasse 4
6850 Dornbirn, Vorarlberg, Austria

Sagmeister Inc.
222 West 14 Street
New York, NY 10011

Salterbaxter
8 Teleford Road
London W10 5SH , UK

SamataMason, Inc.
101 South First Street
Des Plaines, IL 60016

SAS Design
6 Salem Road
London W2 4BU, UK

Sayles Graphic Design
3701 Beaver Avenue
Des Moines, IA 50310

SEA
70 St John Street
London EC1M 4DT, UK

Segura Inc.
1110 North Milwaukee Avenue
Chicago, IL 60622

Shamlian Advertising
10 E. Sprout Road
Springfield, PA 19064

Sibley Peteet Design
1409 South Lemar, Suite 234
Dallas, TX 75215

Squires & Company
2913 Canton Street
Dallas, TX 75226

Stilradar
Schwabstr. 10a
70197 Stuttgart, Germany

Stoltze Design
15 Channel Center Street #603
Boston, MA 02210

Studio Myerscough
26 Drysdale Street
London N1 6LS, UK

Subplot Design Inc.
301-308 Homer Street
Vancouver, BC V6B 2V2, Canada

Taxi Studio LTD
93 Princess Victoria Street
Clifton, Bristol BS8 4DD, UK

The Bonsey Design Partnership
179 River Valley Road
Singapore 179033

The Chase
1 North Parade, Parsonage Gardens
Manchester M3 2NH, UK

The Kitchen
52-53 Margaret Street
London W1W 8SQ, UK

The Point Group

Together Design
106 Cleveland Street
London W1T 6NX, UK

Tracy Design Communications, Inc.
118 S.W. Boulevard
Kansas City, MO 64108

Trickett & Webb Ltd.
The Factory, 84 Marchmont Street
London, WCIN IAG England, UK

Tycoon Graphics
402 Villa Gloria 2-13-7 Jingumae, Shibuya-ku
Tokyo 150-0001 Japan

University of Iowa Foundation
One West Park Road
Iowa City, IA 52244-4550

Usine De Boutons
Via Guido Franco 99/B Cadoneghe
Padova 35010, Italy

Vine360
50 N 4th Ave #18B
Minneapolis, MN 55401

Vinje Design Inc
1043 Contra Costa Drive
El Cerrito, CA 94530

Viva Dolan Communications and Design
99 Crown's Lane, Suite 500
Toronto, Ontario M5R 3P4, Canada

Voice
217 Gilbert Street
Adelaide, South Australia, 5000 Australia

Weymouth Design
332 Congress St
Boston, MA 02210

Why Not Associates
22c Sheoherdess Walk
London N1 7LB, UK

Willboughby Design Group
602 Westport Road
Kansas City, MO 64111

William Homan Design
1316 West 73rd Street
Minneapolis, MN 55423

Zappata Disenadores S.C.
Lafayete 143 Apzunes 11590
Mexico City, Mexico

Zucchini Design PTE LTD
28A Mosque St
Singapore 059506

index